# Romance and Rhetoric

DISPUTATIO



Previously published volumes in this series are listed at the back of this book.

VOLUME 19

# ROMANCE AND RHETORIC

## Essays in Honour of Dhira B. Mahoney

Edited by

Georgiana Donavin and Anita Obermeier

BREPOLS

**British Library Cataloguing in Publication Data**

Romance and rhetoric : essays in honour of Dhira B. Mahoney. -- (Disputatio ; v. 19)
1. Literature, Medieval--History and criticism.
2. Rhetoric, Medieval--Europe. 3. Narration (Rhetoric)--History--To 1500. 4. Romances--History and criticism.
I. Series II. Mahoney, Dhira B. III. Donavin, Georgiana.
IV. Obermeier, Anita.
809'.02-dc22

ISBN-13: 9782503531496



D/2010/0095/77
ISBN: 978- 2-503-53149-6

Printed in the U.S.A on acid-free paper

# CONTENTS

# ACKNOWLEDGEMENTS

Thanks to the Brepols staff, the Disputatio Editorial Board, our respective institutions, and the many friends of Dhira B. Mahoney, we have enjoyed enthusiastic support in our work on this volume. Simon Forde and Richard Utz offered encouragement in the early stages of our work; Dallas G. Denery II, upon joining the Disputatio Editorial Board, and Cary J. Nederman reviewed the manuscript. We thank Westminster College and the Gore Endowment for grant monies that allowed us to collaborate in person, the English Department at the University of New Mexico for funding a graduate assistant, and Marisa Sikes for providing that assistance in the form of proofreading essays and compiling the index. A special thanks is due Dhira B. Mahoney's loyal and wonderful former students who shared their teaching and mentoring stories with us: Karen Bollerman, Christina Francis, Geoff Gust, Judith Lanzendorfer, Ryan Muckerheide, Stephanie Volf, and Audrey Walters. Thanks to Kirsten Gwin and Meghan Hekker for their help in proofreading and compiling the manuscript. Finally, we are especially grateful to the many members of the International Arthurian Society, International Courtly Literature Society, Medieval Institute at Western Michigan University, and the Medieval Association of the Pacific who showed such kind interest in this tribute.

Dhira B. Mahoney

# DHIRA B. MAHONEY: A TRIBUTE

Georgiana Donavin and Anita Obermeier

*Sometimes I think of Dhira's contribution to academe as a monument: imposing, awe-inspiring, elegant, and polished.*

— Stephanie Volf

*Rather than providing all of the answers for her students, Dhira listens, suggests, and directs.*

— Ryan Muckerheide

*Fellow students and I who have taken multiple classes with Dhira consider ourselves 'Dhira Groupies'.*

— Audrey Walters

To describe and appreciate Dhira B. Mahoney's character and academic achievements are delightful and daunting tasks. If three words could sum up Mahoney, they would be generosity, hybridity, and elegance — generosity to both students and colleagues, hybridity in interdisciplinary research and teaching, and elegance in her manner of relating to others and expressing her ideas.

As native of India with a BA and an MA from Oxford University as well as a PhD from the University of California, Santa Barbara, Mahoney bridges three continents. She received her BA from Oxford in English Language and Literature, attending Lady Margaret Hall, where she participated in her fiftieth reunion in 2007. Under the tutelage of Frank C. Gardiner, she completed her PhD at UC Santa Barbara in 1974, with a dissertation entitled 'Sir Thomas Malory's *Morte Darthur*: Romance in the Heroic Mode'. Malory would become one of her major fields of publication. With her Assistant Professorship at the University of Arizona in both Middle English literature and composition studies,

Mahoney began to fuse the fields of Medieval Studies and Rhetoric, a most fruitful combination as one hallmark of her scholarship is the elegant manner of her own writing. During her job interview at Arizona State University, she dazzled with her lyrical, mellifluous, and precise language. When asked about the secret to her impressive presentation skills, she humbly responded: 'I work at it, sentence by sentence, over and over until I am happy with it.' It is this attention to detail that makes possible not only her beautiful expression, but also her fascinating observations about the rhetorical forms and effects of medieval literary works.

At both the University of Arizona and Arizona State, as well as inside professional organizations in which Mahoney is active, her stellar gift of generosity is well known. She has given much of her time and herself in often quiet service to students, colleagues, community, and profession. She has organized and chaired many conference panels and, because of her dual expertise in Medieval Studies and Rhetoric, she is a sought-after referee for a long list of journals and presses; *Studies in Medieval and Renaissance History*, *Arthuriana*, and ACMRS have counted her as an editorial or advisory board member. Mahoney was the Secretary Treasurer of the International Courtly Literary Society, North American Branch, from 1989 to 1995 as well as Medieval Association of the Pacific Vice President in 1998–2000 and President in 2000–02. While maintaining so many professional obligations, Mahoney was an award-winning teacher, who for twenty-five years taught the gamut of English medieval language and literature and more. In breadth and in depth, she instructed more than twenty courses including composition, surveys of British literature, various medieval literature courses, Old English, Middle English, History of the Language, *Beowulf*, Chaucer, classes on medieval women, theories of medieval authorship, Arthurian Legend, and even postcolonial literature. If one can trust anecdotal evidence, Mahoney often 'hooked' new students with her impressive knowledge and gentle encouragement, opening up fruitful lines of research for which students acknowledge intellectual debt. They characterize her quiet and comforting confidence, her steady and calm support, and keen and precise readerly eye as invaluable, but also admit that she was a tough teacher. They admire and seek to emulate Mahoney for her graceful manner, understated humour, and her obvious interest in increasing student success through intellectual and stylistic advice.

The wide range of Mahoney's teaching demonstrates the rewards of mastering many divergent texts in the Old and Middle English canon. Besides proving her command over an array of primary texts, Mahoney employed interpretive methods from feminist, rhetorical, art historical and postcolonial studies in challenging her students. Her graduate seminar 'Who Painted the Lion, Tell Me, Who?' explored conflicting and contradictory images of women in the Middle Ages, including Margery Kempe, by studying primary works by male and female authors in light of their cultural contexts and generic conventions. In her course on 'Medieval Theories of Authorship' Mahoney also 'converted' students from other English subdisciplines to Medieval Studies by making ample use of texts with the prefatory materials and effectively combining the written text with the visual aids of presentation miniatures. Her course on the 'Indo-British Encounter' capitalized on her Indian roots and British education, while presented to an American audience. In the course most central to her main area of research, 'The Arthurian Legend: Transformations and Recyclings', Mahoney combined interpretive methods to offer a variety of ways of explaining the enduring strength and attraction of the Arthurian legend from its beginnings in the medieval period to contemporary literature and popular culture.

The expertise with which Mahoney has taught Arthuriana, gender, and rhetoric indicates a dialectical relationship between her pedagogy and her scholarship on these same topics. From Mahoney's earliest work in graduate school in Santa Barbara proceeded an estimable collection of articles and book chapters on Malory, as well as an edited anthology on the Grail cycle. Three of her essays on Malory ('Malory's Tale of Sir Tristram: Source and Setting Reconsidered', 'Narrative Treatments of Name in Malory's *Morte Darthur*', and 'The Truest and Holiest Tale: Malory's Transformation of *La Queste del Saint Graal*') have been reprinted, showing the widespread usefulness of her work, even in a time when there is so much being published on Arthuriana.[1] During her earliest enquiries into Arthurian studies, rhetorical strategies and gender constructions already formed a part of her analysis and planted the seeds for her later work on Margery Kempe, Christine de Pizan, and the rhetoric of prologues and epilogues.

[1] Dhira B. Mahoney, 'Malory's Tale of Sir Tristram: Source and Setting Reconsidered', *Medievalia et Humanistica*, n.s., 9 (1979), 175–98 (repr. in *Tristan and Isolde: A Casebook*, ed. by Joan Tasker Grimbert (New York: Garland, 1994), pp. 223–53); 'Narrative Treatment of Names in Malory's *Morte D'Arthur*', *English Literary History* (*ELH*), 47 (1980), 646–56 (repr. in *Literature Criticism from 1400 to 1800*, LXXXVIII (Farmington Hills, MI: Thomson-Gale, 2003)); 'The Truest and Holiest Tale: Malory's Transformation of *La Queste del Saint Graal*', in *Studies in Malory*, ed. by James W. Spisak (Kalamazoo: Medieval Institute Publications, 1985), pp. 109–28 (repr. in *The Grail: A Casebook*, ed. by Dhira B. Mahoney, Arthurian Characters and Themes, 5 (New York: Garland, 2000), pp. 379–96; with subsequent citations referring to *Studies in Malory*, ed. by Spisak).

From her earliest publication, 'Malory's Tale of Sir Tristram: Source and Setting Reconsidered', Mahoney shows an interest in Malory's characters and the rhetorical strategies by which the narrator encourages identification with them. With Tristram's character, as Mahoney demonstrates, the reader's impression depends on the narrator's presentation of the love interest in Isolde. Although French tradition emphasizes the great lover in the two best knights, Lancelot and Tristan, Mahoney notes that Malory privileges their prowess and subsequently includes more tournament and combat scenes. Mahoney further illustrates how prowess for Malory is intimately bound up with identity building for aspiring knights and their 'worship'. She concludes that 'The Tale of Sir Tristram' 'displays worship in [the] action' of the central character.[2] In 'Narrative Treatment of Names' and '"Ar ye a knight and ar no lovear?": The Chivalry Topos in Malory's *Book of Sir Tristram*', Mahoney continues her exploration of courtly love themes and their relationship to the level of the readers' identification with Tristram. In the former essay, Mahoney traces the epithets attached to Isolde, noting that she is most often referred to as 'La Beale Isode', especially in situations where Malory emphasizes her relationship to Sir Tristram. Rarely is she designated 'quene', unless as she accompanies King Mark. Mahoney argues that this detail about Isolde's naming, which illustrates Malory's privileging of her relationship with Tristram, provides evidence against Lumianski's contention that *The Book of Tristram* mirrors and highlights the adulterous relationship of Lancelot and Guinevere and in that way impugns its central character. In '"Ar ye a knight and ar no lovear?"' Mahoney examines 'the chivalric equation' in which '[l]ove inspires prowess and prowess in its turn begets love'.[3] She shows that Palomydes, stalwart but often misguided, 'becomes a kind of cracked mirror to Tristram, reflecting the latter's chivalry, but always with some flaw that mars the line'.[4] In the French sources, Palomydes is a more experienced and deserving knight, but Malory manipulates his character to reveal how Tristram, the truly honourable, deserves Isolde's love. By withholding the information that Mark eventually kills Tristram,

[2] Mahoney, 'Malory's Tale of Sir Tristram', p. 253.

[3] Dhira B. Mahoney, '"Ar ye a knight and ar no lovear?": The Chivalry Topos in Malory's *Book of Sir Tristram*', in *Conjunctures: Medieval Studies in Honor of Douglas Kelly*, ed. by Keith Busby and Norris J. Lacy (Amsterdam: Rodopi, 1994), pp. 311–24 (pp. 311–12). For a different facet of Mahoney's research and a linguistic and historical study of medieval weaponry, see 'Malory's Great Guns', *Viator*, 20 (1989), 291–310, and 'Malory's "Great Guns" Revisited', *Bibliographical Bulletin of the International Arthurian Society*, 44 (1993), 236–40.

[4] Mahoney, '"Ar ye a knight and ar no lovear"', p. 321.

Malory can conclude the *Book of Sir Tristram* with a scene depicting Tristram's reward in their happy home at Joyeuse Garde.

Beyond Tristram, Mahoney has been particularly interested in the characterization of Gareth, the hermits populating the Arthurian forest, and the hermetic impulses of Lancelot and Guinevere. As in her work on Tristram, Mahoney investigates the changes that Malory makes to his French sources in order to specify a Malorian rhetoric of characterization. In 'Narrative Treatment of Name', she points out that Malory assigns names and family affiliations, even when none exist in his French sources. Especially in tales of the Fair Unknown, like that of Gareth, Malory manipulates the revelation of the hero's name to match the moment when he has proved himself worthy of his lineage and rank. Because of questions about the Fair Unknown's lineage, Mahoney argues that *The Tale of Gareth* constitutes a 'comedy of class'.[5] Just as Malory's depiction of Gareth's class arises from both romance and realistic models, so his presentation of hermits relies on both a redaction of his sources, mainly the Vulgate *Queste*, and on his observation of the hermetic life at Guy's Cliff, a hermitage only a few miles north of Warwick, the reputed home of Malory.[6] Mahoney discusses how the conclusions to the lives of Lancelot and Guinevere are based on these hermetic ideals.

Especially in her early work on Tristram and Malory's presentation of the great Arthurian lovers, Mahoney has offered fine insights on the *Morte Darthur*'s construction of gender. In 'Symbolic Uses of Space in Malory's *Morte Darthur*', she offers a nuanced reading of masculine and feminine spaces.[7] Unlike Chaucer who develops interior and exterior scenes in detail, Malory is more interested in the symbolic association with spaces throughout the *Morte Darthur*. Mahoney compares masculine open space in need of military defence with feminine enclosed space, particularly the chamber, which may be a place of intrigue, danger, and even crime. For a contrast between masculine and feminine spaces, Mahoney recounts the episode of Morgan le Fay's entrapment of Alexander the Orphan. In order to draw him into sex inside her chambers, Morgan tricks Alexander into a vow that he will remain in La Beale Regarde's vicinity for a year and day.

[5] Dhira B. Mahoney, 'Malory's *Tale of Gareth* and the Comedy of Class', *Arthurian Yearbook*, 1 (1991), 165–93.

[6] Dhira B. Mahoney, 'Hermits in Malory's *Morte Darthur*: The Fiction and the Reality', *Arthurian Interpretations*, 2.1 (1987), 1–26.

[7] Dhira B. Mahoney, 'Symbolic Uses of Space in Malory's *Morte Darthur*', in *Re-Viewing 'Le Morte Darthur': Texts and Contexts, Characters and Themes*, ed. by K. S. Whetter and Raluca L. Radulescu (Cambridge: Brewer, 2005), pp. 95–106.

Alexander, discovering the plot, enables the raiding and burning of the castle so that he might patrol the open land after Morgan's departure. Thus, he fulfils his vow while avoiding an affair with Morgan. Continuing with feminine spaces by describing the women's apartments commonly constructed for ladies of high rank, Mahoney demonstrates Guinevere's authority over her chambers and why in 'The Knight of the Cart', Lancelot could accuse Mellyagaunt of wrongly drawing the curtain to inspect the sleeping queen. Since the apartments consist of a series of enclosed spaces, with the canopied bed as the innermost sanctum, Mellyagaunt's intrusion represents a violation akin to rape. Mahoney concludes, 'Space, then, for Malory, is important not for its visual aspect, or for its contribution to naturalism. When he bothers to indicate spatial relations or describe the characters' surroundings it is because of their symbolic value. Male or female, individual space is defined by possession, by ownership and bound up with individual honor'.[8]

In the subject matter of these first articles, she turns names, places, and spaces into signifiers and develops the rhetoric of their reiteration. The next thematic cycle to occupy Mahoney was the semiotics and rhetoric of the Grail. With 'The Truest and Holiest Tale: Malory's Transformation of *La Queste del Saint Graal*',[9] Mahoney enters the scholarly fray about how faithfully Malory translated the Vulgate *Queste* into his *Morte*. She argues that Malory does 'not so much secularize' his source 'as anglicize it'.[10] While the main trajectory of the French *Queste* is retained and chivalric standards measured against spiritual values, Malory cuts 'much of the doctrinal exegesis of the French' to arrive at a value system more in accordance to his fifteenth-century world where 'spiritual pursuits could be considered complementary rather than competitive elements of a knightly life'.[11] Most of the essay investigates whether a balance between the spiritual and competitive inheres in the characters of Lancelot and the three Grail knights, Bors, Perceval, and Galahad. Mahoney perceptively counters critics focused on Lancelot's adultery with the notion that his sin is 'idolatrous' love for Guinevere, as the French Lancelot thinks that 'the source of his valor was the Queen'; for Malory's Lancelot, 'the source of his valor is himself', but 'both Lancelots have to learn that the true source is God'.[12] Mahoney reaches the conclusion that 'the Tale of the Sankgreal does not negate the heroic-chivalric

[8] Mahoney, 'Symbolic Uses of Space in Malory's *Morte Darthur*', p. 105.

[9] Mahoney, 'Truest and Holiest Tale', pp. 109–28.

[10] Mahoney, 'Truest and Holiest Tale', p. 110.

[11] Mahoney, 'Truest and Holiest Tale', p. 110.

[12] Mahoney, 'Truest and Holiest Tale', p. 120.

values of the *Morte Darthur* as a whole. Only from the perspective of eternity is the greatest of all earthly institutions seen as fragile and finite, doomed inevitably to fall.'[13]

Mahoney's work on the Grail culminated in 2000 in *The Grail: A Casebook*, the fifth volume in Garland's popular series on Arthuriana, and her best-known publication. The volume contains twenty essays from a star-studded cast of medievalists. Twelve articles focus on topics from the commonly agreed upon medieval starting point of the Grail story — Chrétien's *Perceval* — to the fifteenth century, while the remainder deals with the Grail in the nineteenth-century medieval revival in art and literature, as well as in twentieth-century literature and film. With seven essays specifically composed for this volume and thirteen previously published ones, the Casebook strives for coverage of major works from *Perceval* to *Excalibur* in a 'near-definitive work'.[14] Mahoney's introduction to the Grail Casebook, a 115-page monograph in its own right, has been hailed as 'one of the best in the series so far [...] lucid and thorough'.[15] This magisterial introduction showcases Mahoney's great expertise in Grail literature and history as well as her superior analysis and synthesis of the material. Conversationally, Mahoney used to refer to her chosen field of study as the 'quagmire of romance'. Here, concerning Grail literature, she effortlessly drains the swamp, revealing that the existing medieval versions can be grouped into three rhetorical strains focusing on Perceval, Joseph of Arimathea, and the *Queste* (Galahad story). The three strains illustrate the competing nature of Grail narratives, since there is no such thing as 'the Grail' or one definitive story about it. Mahoney's introduction also summarizes theories of origin, talismans, and motifs of the Grail legend before branching out into subheadings dealing with the various vernacular versions of the Grail, including French, German, Welsh, and English sections. Texts that are not the major focus of the ensuing essays Mahoney treats more extensively in her introduction. Mahoney has done a great service to scholars and students alike by brilliantly condensing and visualizing in the 'Comparative Table of Medieval Texts' much of the sometimes contradictory information on the Grail.[16] This table illustrates the differences and commonalities in the key texts with the motif categories of Questers, Grail Shape, Fisher

[13] Mahoney, 'Truest and Holiest Tale', p. 124.

[14] Peter H. Goodrich, 'Review of *The Grail: A Casebook* by Dhira B. Mahoney', in *Arthuriana*, 11 (2001), 121–23 (p. 122).

[15] Goodrich, 'Review of *The Grail*', p. 121.

[16] Mahoney, 'Introduction', in *The Grail: A Casebook*, ed. by Mahoney, pp. 1–101 (p. 100).

King, Wasteland, and Question Test. Ultimately, Mahoney's analysis asserts the nationalist aspects of the Grail throughout its eight-century run and also its status as an 'enduring symbol of aspiration, of the hope of something Other in this materialistic world'.[17] The Grail Casebook has quickly become the standard against which other such endeavors are measured.

In her work on Arthuriana, as we have seen, Mahoney gives substantial energy and thought to both gender construction and the rhetoric of characterization Malory employs in creating it. In the 1990s, she turned her attention to two women authors and their forms of self-characterization. Considering the contrast between Margery Kempe and other holy women who marked themselves out as religious outsiders by entering a cloister or a cell, Mahoney develops the idea that Kempe's tears signified her religious difference and thus lent her power.[18] As Mahoney remarks, 'Continence and white clothes are effective markers, nonverbal signs, of separation, but a more striking instrument of separation for Kempe, because more dramatic and more disruptive to those around her, is her tears'.[19] Following Windeatt and Atkinson, Mahoney distinguishes Kempe's early sentimental weeping, first noted in Chapter 3, from the emotional paroxysms and outcries Kempe evinces during her first trip to Jerusalem. However, Mahoney notes that 'weeping and crying' often occurs as a phrase, bringing together the two responses. While Kempe's gift of tears can be compared to that of Marie of Oignies or Angela of Foligno, Kempe did not submit herself to bodily tortures to relieve the purgatorial pain of others, but suffers pain and social exile for her tears. This exiling at once diminishes and uplifts her social position, since it separates her as a woman of God. Mahoney compares the tears to Kempe's prayers, which often came together. Mahoney notes that while the tears and prayers operate outside the norms of ecclesiastical patriarchy, Kempe reconciles herself to the patriarchal rhetoric of church prayer in the ending orison of Book II. Mahoney concludes that as Kempe developed confidence in the power of her tears and prayers, she was able to move from third to first person and project her voice into 'a prayer which is both a model for others and a validation of itself'.[20]

[17] Mahoney, 'Introduction', p. 78.

[18] Dhira B. Mahoney, 'Margery Kempe's Tears and the Power over Language', in *Margery Kempe: A Book of Essays*, ed. by Sandra J. McEntire (New York: Garland, 1992), pp. 37–50.

[19] Mahoney, 'Margery Kempe's Tears', p. 39.

[20] Mahoney, 'Margery Kempe's Tears', p. 49.

In 'Middle English Regenderings of Christine de Pizan' Mahoney presents the ways in which the manuscript tradition for Christine de Pizan can illustrate a masculine appropriation or even erasure of Christine's feminine narrators and their womanly authority.[21] Considering this masculinized reception of Christine, Mahoney concentrates on Hoccleve's translation of her *L'Epistre au dieu d'Amours*, his *Letter to Cupid* of 1402. *L'Epistre au dieu d'Amours* is the first installment of Christine's ongoing refutation of Jean de Meun, and Mahoney's intention is to investigate whether Hoccleve's adaptations, additions, and reductions participate in the misogynist strand of the manuscript tradition or support Christine's feminist position and deliver her womanly voice. While recognizing that Hoccleve blunts the edge of Christine's feminism by, for instance, excising her impassioned defences of women and sentimentalizing the role of the Virgin Mary, Mahoney concludes that he nevertheless 'preserves Christine's war against hypocrisy and deception in male-female relationships and against the pervasiveness of literary misogyny'.[22]

Aside from making significant contributions in the areas of Arthuriana and gender studies, Mahoney focuses her third scholarly trajectory on the study of prologues and epilogues, the locus of many an authorial rhetorical stance. Two essays on English prologues and a forthcoming book form a compelling body of work. In her groundbreaking work on the iconography of book-presentation in medieval manuscripts, 'Courtly Presentation and Authorial Self-Fashioning: Frontispiece Miniatures in Late Medieval French and English Manuscripts',[23] Mahoney juxtaposes the authorial self-presentations in discourse and image of French writers Jean Wavrin and Christine de Pizan to that of English authors Hoccleve and Lydgate. Wavrin's self-image as a modest author but duty-bound historian supports Edward IV's claim to power. Christine derives her authority from the fact of gendered difference. Hoccleve and Lydgate weave issues of war, peace, and moral government into their prologues to function as a kind of *Fürstenspiegel* to their patrons. Mahoney's sizeable study concludes that these presentation situations may be 'symbolic and performative',[24] staging preferred

[21] Dhira B. Mahoney, 'Middle English Regenderings of Christine de Pizan', in *The Medieval 'Opus': Imitation, Rewriting and Transmission in the French Tradition, Proceedings of the Symposium Held at the Institute for Research*, ed. by Douglas Kelly (Amsterdam: Rodopi, 1996), pp. 405–27.

[22] Mahoney, 'Middle English Regenderings in Christine de Pizan', p. 421.

[23] Dhira B. Mahoney, 'Courtly Presentation and Authorial Self-Fashioning: Frontispiece Miniatures in Late Medieval French and English Manuscripts', *Mediaevalia*, 21 (1996), 97–160.

[24] Mahoney, 'Courtly Presentation', p. 127.

interaction scenarios with patrons. The text and image work synergistically to put the authors in the best light; even though the text of the presentation miniature is dominated by the conventions of the humility topos, including self-deprecation and garnering of audience goodwill, the authors convey strength and self-importance. After all, the presentation scenario displays reciprocity: '[T]he patron confers authority and dignity on the writer, while the writer, on his knees, offers advice to the great.'[25] Mahoney's work places English presentation miniatures in the same league with their much more numerous French counterparts.

Mahoney carries on her exploration of modesty topoi with her next essay, 'Gower's Two Prologues to *Confessio Amantis*'.[26] Armed with the theories of the *Auftragstopos* (commissioning topos) and liminality, Mahoney delves into the thicket of the two versions of the prologue (and epilogue) to Gower's *Confessio Amantis* to shed new light on the political background informing these revisions. Gower had initially prefaced his *Confessio* with the charming story of King Richard II inviting the author onto his barge on the Thames and asking him to write something new about love. As Gower became more disillusioned with the King, he revised prologue and epilogue, the liminal frame of a literary work, as Mahoney calls it, cutting out Richard and substituting Henry of Derby, the later Lancastrian king, Henry IV. Mahoney, however, successfully questions the privileging of this Lancastrian liminal frame by editors and translators who relegate the Ricardian version to the status of a variant. Mahoney argues that the Ricardian liminal frame was more suitable to the literary intent of the *Confessio*, while the Lancastrian version emphasized sociopolitics. Ultimately, Mahoney answers the question why *Confessio Amantis* manuscripts with the Ricardian frame were still produced after Richard's deposition and death with an insight from her essay on the presentation miniature: that the commissioning on the barge could have been merely a careful topos by Gower and perhaps not a reality; hence its political value was not essential to fifteenth-century readers. These two articles on prologues form the basis of Mahoney's forthcoming book, *Medieval Liminal Rhetoric: The Self-Authorizing Frame*, in which she explores how the medieval *ars dictaminis* informed prologue and epilogue conventions in historiography, vernacular poetics, translation, and early printing.

We, too, have elected to weave the thread of medieval rhetoric through the essays presented in this volume. As a reflection of Mahoney's current central interest, we open with a section entitled 'Prologues and Pictures' that enquires

[25] Mahoney, 'Courtly Presentation', p. 127.

[26] Dhira B. Mahoney, 'Gower's Two Prologues to *Confessio Amantis*', in *Re-Visioning Gower*, ed. by R. F. Yeager (Asheville, NC: Pegasus, 1998), pp. 17–37.

into the rhetoric of both discursive and pictorial introductions to medieval texts. The first essay, Ann Dobyns's 'Exemplars of Chivalry: Rhetoric and Ethics in Middle English Romance', guides us in thinking about the use of classical rhetoric in the structure and characterization of three Middle English romances. Dobyns illustrates the ethical imperative of tales from the Thornton Manuscript — *The Romance of Sir Isumbras*, *Sir Degrevant*, and *Sir Eglamour* — and shows convincingly that the prologue to each romance exhorts the audience to imitate exemplary, heroic conduct. Moving to the German world chronicles in our second essay, 'Jans der Enikel's Prologue as a Guide to Textual Multiplicity', Maria Dobozy examines Jans's own *Weltchronik* (1275) and traces its reception through the different prologues that were attached to and mingled with this text throughout the late Middle Ages. Dobozy demonstrates a growing preference among late medieval readers of German world chronicles for comprehensive coverage, standardization of the author's voice, and theological framing. In the final essay of this section, Corine Schleif's 'Gifts and Givers that Keep on Giving: Pictured Presentations in Early Medieval Manuscripts', we see the introduction to a medieval book from an interdisciplinary perspective combining art and textual history. Schleif studies a number of early medieval donation images to enquire into both the historical specifics and theoretical consequences of medieval book dedications. Because presentation miniatures depict an eternal present, Schleif remarks, contemporary readers and observers of these illuminations are involved in the gift of the medieval book. All the authors in this section share a concern with readership — with teaching, involving the audience, or responding to new expectations — and the prologue rhetoric that accomplishes these goals.

Prologues and dedication miniatures are often vehicles for self-fashioning, as they present the authorial persona or describe motivations for reading, writing, or giving the text at hand. Also interested in the concept of authorial self-fashioning, the essays in the second section of this anthology enquire into the authority that famous late medieval authors claimed for their works. 'Women and Rhetoric' treats both feminine forms of authority appropriated by male authors and the masculine forms of discourse deployed by female writers. All of the authors explored here — John Lydgate, Margery Kempe, and Christine de Pizan — employ autobiographical narratives to explain the inspiration for and the validation of their writings. According to Georgiana Donavin in 'The Light of the Virgin Muse in John Lydgate's *Life of Our Lady*', Lydgate's narrator describes how the Virgin Mary sparks his invention, provides his matter, and guides his eloquence. Through brilliant light imagery, Lydgate characterizes the Mother's methods of enlightenment and spotlights scenarios from her life for meditation. With a climactic presentation of the Candlemas tapers, *The Life of*

*Our Lady* culminates in the Feast of the Presentation: not a truncated ending to the life of the Virgin but an appropriate image of Lydgate's illumination through Mary's inspiration. While Lydgate's narrator speaks through and for the Virgin, Margery Kempe, as both Rosalynn Voaden and Elizabeth Archibald note, is happy to speak for herself. Employing a close analysis of *The Book of Margery Kempe*, Elizabeth Archibald concentrates on Kempe's self-referential remarks and how they compare to those made by Christine de Pizan in *Christine's Vision*, *A Path of Long Study*, *The Book of the City of Ladies* and other works. In '"Sisters under the Skin": Margery Kempe and Christine de Pizan', Archibald notes that while many differences pertaining to class and education divide these authors, they are similar in the ways in which they defied the strictures of the men around them in attempts to establish their own authority. Unusual in their prolixity and publication, both women reverted to narratives of their own lives as a way of explaining their relevance and authorial purposes. The rhetoric of self-fashioning, which is central to Mahoney's scholarship on prologues and on Margery Kempe, is a strategy crucial to these two women authors. In contrast to Kempe's intimate references to her personal life and visions, she masked her identity as a preacher, according to Voaden. In 'Wolf in Sheep's Clothing: Margery Kempe as Underground Preacher', Voaden argues that Kempe consciously undertook a preaching tour during her travels in England but disguised her preaching in the same way that she disguised her lay status in white clothing. Since preaching by women was forbidden and especially suspect during the persecution of Lollards, Kempe always avoided the pulpit and denied that her public speaking constituted sermons. Nevertheless, according to Voaden, Kempe delivered simple homilies in the tradition of the *Devotio Moderna* and Continental saints whom she admired. Margery Kempe forged a preacher's identity that eluded the strictures of male clerics, such as the Archbishop of York.

All forms of rhetoric reach out to an audience, whether in the self-fashioning of late medieval writers who claim authority through gendered positions or in the appeals of prologues and dedication miniatures that seek the goodwill of the readers or recipients. The texts analysed in the third section of this anthology 'Lyric, Song, and Audience' especially emphasize 'audience' in that they are performances, connected to song, set in music or meant to be performed in front of a throng of playgoers. In the first essay of this section, Phyllis R. Brown analyses a *ballade* by the well-known poet and composer, Guillaume de Machaut. 'Rhetoric and Reception: Guillaume de Machaut's "Je maudi"' looks closely at the literary history of cursing and Machaut's employment of it in response to Petrarch's 'Blessed be the Day'. Brown's careful reading of 'Je Maudi' reveals a poem that paradoxically questions human greatness at the same time that it participates in an international literary competition for the position of greatest poet. In the next essay, Christina Francis moves from lyrics to singing with '"Maken Melodye": The Quality of Song in Chaucer's *Canterbury Tales*'. Francis evaluates Chaucer's characterizations of singing — the Prioress's nasal tones, the Squire's nighttime warbling, Absolon's airy feminine voice and others — that encourage the reader to make judgements. Because Boethian music theory and Guidonian methods of practice were based on rational categories and processes, Francis finds that Chaucer launches criticisms at characters that approach music irrationally or impiously. Often in *The Canterbury Tales*, she remarks, Chaucer associates negative character attributes with birdsong. With John Damon's 'Enacting Liturgy: *Estote fortes* in the Croxton *Play of the Sacrament*', the topic of church music, which both Francis and Brown touch upon, comes to the fore. While Francis evaluates the vocal resonance in the religious song of certain Canterbury pilgrims and Brown shows a history of cursing in the Psalms, Damon deals directly with the antiphon *Estote fortes*, its various contexts in liturgy and sermon, and its position in the Croxton play. Damon argues that the *Estote fortes* is an aid to *The Play of the Sacrament*'s propaganda against Lollards and presentation of the Otherness of Muslims and Jews.

The fourth and final section resonates with and responds to the area of scholarship Mahoney is best known for: the Grail and Malory. Both Anita Obermeier and Kevin J. Harty explore the Grail but from different perspectives, Obermeier investigating the history of Grail narratives and Harty concentrating on twentieth-century film. Obermeier's 'The Rhetoric of Symbolism: The Grail of Fertility and Sterility' regroups Mahoney's three medieval Grail strains — the Perceval strain, the Joseph of Arimathea strain, and the *Queste* strain.[27] Examining medieval Grail narratives for fertility and sterility topoi, Obermeier posits a French Perceval strain, the German Perceval strain, and the Vulgate Cycle strain. Since the Vulgate Cycle version privileging sterility is the one that Malory anglicizes and popularizes in his *Morte Darthur*,[28] Galahad's story becomes the de facto metanarrative of the Grail. Moving from text to film, Kevin Harty discovers a hitherto unidentified Grail episode in a pre–World War II German film. In his 'Arnold Fanck's 1926 Film *Der Heilige Berg* and the Nazi Quest for the Holy Grail', Harty situates this movie into a larger history of Grail films and

[27] Mahoney, 'Introduction', p. 2.

[28] See Dhira B. Mahoney, 'Truest and Holiest Tale' pp. 379–96.

into the specific phenomenon of German filmmaking during the Third Reich. But Fanck's *Der Heilige Berg* clearly shows that German cinema had, through the genre of the mountain film, readily embraced Nazi ideology before Hitler totally solidified his position by becoming chancellor, and that part of that embrace was the appropriation of what many would argue was among Christianity's most sacred icons and relics, the Holy Grail from which Christ supposedly drank at the Last Supper.

Judith Lanzendorfer and Alan Lupack round out the volume with their essays on Malorian intratexts. Lanzendorfer follows Mahoney's work on Gareth both in dealing with the Fair Unknown tales and in extrapolating rhetorical principles from them. By classifying and noting Malory's use of folkloric motifs in the *Morte Darthur*, Lanzendorfer illustrates the coherence and connectedness of all eight books, challenging Vinaver's eight-book theory. Two helpful tables to her essay demonstrate how in his first use of a folkloric text Malory spends a great deal of energy and time introducing related characters, scenes, and actions, but then relies on these introductions when the motif recurs later in the *Morte*. Likewise, Lupack examines how Malory uses rhetorical devices — such as oral prophecies, interpretations, and proverbs as well as letters and inscriptions (on tombs, swords, etc.) — for structural linking, revelation of theme, and definition of character. Not surprisingly, the written intratexts confer authority in the *Morte*, but the same might be said of the spoken word when it appears in forms that bespeak authority. Whether the general truth of a proverb, the foreknowledge of a prophecy, the accuracy of an interpretation of a prediction, a dream, or a vision, the fidelity to events of an inscription, or a deathbed statement inscribed in a letter, Malory utilizes them to lend authority to parts of his tale, to help him depict his characters, reveal his themes, and unite his story.

As we humbly present this volume to Dhira B. Mahoney — colleague, mentor, and friend — and hope that she will accept it as a token of the affection and esteem in which she is held by so many in the worldwide community of medieval scholars, we return one more time to admire the generosity, hybridity, and elegance that mark her professional life. We wholeheartedly agree with Christina Francis, one of Dhira's doctoral students: 'There are a million little things that add up to one tremendously accomplished teacher, mentor, and woman.' We also acknowledge that we can only faintly attempt to achieve her standard of rhetorical elegance, as Dhira truly is 'la miglior fabbra'.

# Prologues and Pictures

# Exemplars of Chivalry: Rhetoric and Ethics in Middle English Romance[*]

Ann Dobyns

Early in the fifteenth century a Yorkshire country gentleman named Robert Thornton compiled a manuscript of English texts, presumably for his family's entertainment and edification. This manuscript, commonly referred to simply as the Thornton Manuscript, included histories, romances, religious and medical works.[1] Owen J. Daly has argued convincingly that the collection coheres in the way the parts, at least the romances and saints' lives, 'resolved for their audience certain historically conditioned spiritual and social

[*] In 1981, when I was beginning research for my dissertation, the article that most influenced my thinking about Sir Thomas Malory's rhetoric of character was Dhira Mahoney's 'Narrative Treatment of Name in Malory's *Morte D'Arthur*', *English Literary History* (*ELH*), 47 (1980), 646–56. Her demonstration of the ways in which Malory chose titles for characters that fit the roles they are playing at any particular moment in the narrative helped me think about the way dialogue also reflects role. Perhaps more importantly, her general approach has deeply influenced my thinking about the rhetorical and ethical nature of medieval narrative. In the very first sentence of that article, Professor Mahoney states what appears in retrospect a most obvious observation. She notes that '[t]he nature of any form of prose fiction is dictated by the author's attitude towards his readers or audience, and, as a corollary, towards his fictional material — his characters and the events which involve them' (p. 646).

[1] For a facsimile, see *The Thornton Manuscript (Lincoln Cathedral MS. 91)*, ed. by D. S. Brewer and A. E. B. Owen (London: Scolar, 1975). For a list of the items collected, see *The Thornton Romances: The Early English Metrical Romances of Perceval, Isumbras, Eglamour, and Degrevant: Selected from Manuscripts at Lincoln and Cambridge*, ed. by James Orchard Halliwell (London: Camden Society, 1844), pp. xxvi–xxxvi.

conflict'.[2] That the romances had such a rhetorical appeal is also supported by comments such Ian Johnson's that we find in romances a similar concern that we find in the lyrics, religious works, and saints' lives, and that is a concern with exemplary conduct.[3] While the overlap among texts that address ethical issues certainly can be accounted for if we acknowledge the religious sensibility of the late Middle Ages, or what Daly calls 'the problem of the relationship between religious and secular values',[4] we may also find evidence of their place within a tradition of classical education, the education in the liberal arts that informed the literary ancestors of these late Middle English works.

Medieval romance has generally been seen, as William Calin indicates, as 'a narrative that recounts the fortunes of a simple, noble, active hero. It tells his deeds of love and prowess, a story of adventure located in a supernatural setting or with supernatural elements. The hero's career mirrors a pattern of test and ordeal and of initiation and establishment in the world of the court.'[5] This definition represents a fairly typical and, I think, accurate characterization of what was the most dominant genre, if we may still use that contested term, in the Middle Ages. What such a definition suggests, as critics have often noticed, is the ethical dimension of the genre — to portray exemplary action is to provide an ethical model. And yet, to say that these works present exemplary characters does not fully acknowledge the implications of this observation. I should like to suggest that Middle English verse romances enjoyed great popularity precisely because they continued a tradition associated with the origin of their French forbearers and that is their concern with the values and models of ethical behaviour they embody, a tradition directly connected to the education in the liberal arts. Indeed, I hope to demonstrate the ways these works directly address ethical dilemmas, in

[2] Owen James Daly, 'This World and the Next: Social and Religious Ideologies in the Romance of the Thornton Manuscript' (unpublished doctoral dissertation, University of Oregon, 1977), p. 9. Although one of Daly's central arguments is that Thornton, as a member of the minor gentry, was drawn to works that defined the role of his class, his discussion of the ethical dimensions of these works in many ways is consonant with a reading of these romances as exhibiting remnants of their original connections to concerns expressed in the liberal arts curriculum.

[3] Ian Johnson, 'Language and Literary Expression', in *An Illustrated History of Late Medieval England*, ed. by Chris Given-Wilson (Manchester: Manchester University Press, 1996), pp. 127–51 (p. 131).

[4] Daly, 'This World and the Next', p. 8.

[5] William Calin, *The French Tradition and the Literature of Medieval England* (Toronto: University of Toronto Press, 1994), p. 432.

what J. Allan Mitchell has called, in his study of exemplary narrative in Chaucer and Gower, 'a rhetoric of exemplarity'[6]. More specifically I intend to show how the opening lines of romances may provide signals of the values at issue in the exemplary narratives that follow.

## *Romance and the Liberal Arts Tradition*

The courtly romance, C. Stephen Jaeger argues, developed as a part of the ethical education of the secular court.[7] The exemplary figure of the twelfth century appeared in the literary works as a response to 'clerical concerns to civilize the lay nobility'.[8] And, he points out, these lessons in manners had their origin in the liberal arts curriculum that 'dominated the cathedral schools from the late tenth to the early twelfth centuries'.[9] As Jaeger explains,

> [T]he literature of the courts after ca. 1155 appears like a literature of pure fantasy and high-flung fairy-tale ideals when read in isolation. But when read against the background of *cultus virtutum*, it appears as the bearer of a long-established code of refined manners.[10]

Jaeger's observation that courtly literature was from the outset concerned with refined manners and, I would add, the ethical implications of such manners, provides a way to talk about romance and its appeal throughout the Middle Ages, particularly in the late Middle English period when the world often seemed *unsyker*, as Malory's characters often say. This need for stable values led to an interest in texts that explored virtuous behaviour.

The liberal arts curriculum was, of course, one that educated the person in the implications of virtuous ideals for human behaviour. This Ciceronian view of eloquence dominated the twelfth-century texts. In addition to studying and writing commentary on classical texts, writers of contemporary works addressed their writing to issues of right conduct. For example, although the *artes poetriae*

[6] J. Allan Mitchell, *Ethics and Exemplary Narrative in Chaucer and Gower* (Cambridge: Brewer, 2004), particularly Chapter 1, 'Reading for the Moral: Controversies and Trajectories', and Chapter 2, 'Rhetorical Reason: Cases, Conscience, and Circumstances'.

[7] C. Stephen Jaeger, *The Envy of Angels: Cathedral Schools and Social Ideals in Medieval Europe, 950–1200* (Philadelphia: University of Pennsylvania Press, 1994), p. 306. Also see Chapter 12, 'Court Society'.

[8] Jaeger, *Envy of Angels*, p. 310.

[9] Jaeger, *Envy of Angels*, p. 326.

[10] Jaeger, *Envy of Angels*, p. 328.

seem to focus primarily on grammar, the *trivium*, as John of Garland explains in the introduction to his *Parisiana poetria*, links together the three fields of knowledge as interdependent. His book, he says, belongs to the three: 'Grammar, since it teaches how to speak properly; Rhetoric, since it teaches how to speak elegantly; and Ethics, since it teaches or instills a sense of what is right, and from this according to Cicero every virtue springs.'[11]

Reading poetry was, of course, a part of the liberal arts curriculum, explicitly as a part of grammatical training. Literary analysis as well as the linguistic study of Latin texts was a part of grammar.[12] But in addition to its practical application, the study of poetry included an ethical dimension. Suzanne Reynolds, in her study of medieval reading, quotes from Alexander Nequam's *Sacerdos ad altare accessurus*, written at the end of the twelfth century, and provides his reasons for having a young boy read satirists and historiographers: 'From here, let him read the satirists and the historiographers, so that at a young age he might learn that vices too are to be avoided and he might desire to imitate the noble deeds of heroes.'[13] Although Alexander Nequam goes on to warn against the reading of classical love poetry at an early age, he does demonstrate the extent to which reading historical works was an education in moral edification. And the genre of romance, which flowered in the twelfth century also, like the histories and satires, provided models of the vices and virtues.

The Middle English verse romances were, for the most part, translations of French romances, and even those for which scholars have found no French antecedent were part of the tradition that traces back to the twelfth-century courtly literary tradition. As Calin tells us, 'The French presence [...] is pervasive and total throughout the corpus.'[14] As such, these works maintain their link to the ethical tradition out of which their ancestors grew. Despite changes in the form and some subject matter of these English works, they still focus on the exploits and challenges of a hero and the ideals implicit in the ways in which he

[11] 'Gramatice, quia docet congrue loqui; Rethorice, quia docet ornante dicere; Ethice, quia docet siue persuadet ad honestum, quod est genus omnium uirtutum secundum Tullium': *The Parisiana poetria of John of Garland*, ed. and trans. by Traugott Lawler (New Haven: Yale University Press, 1974), pp. 2–3.

[12] For a discussion of the grammatical and rhetorical glosses of Latin literary texts, see Suzanne Reynolds, *Medieval Reading: Grammar, Rhetoric and the Classical Text* (Cambridge: Cambridge University Press, 1996).

[13] Reynolds, *Medieval Reading*, p. 7.

[14] Calin, *French Tradition*, p. 429.

accepts and responds to those challenges. As such, they provide models of ethical behaviour.

One way romances show evidence of this ethical dimension is in their place within a schema established in classical rhetorical texts. D. H. Green has argued, in a study of the beginnings of medieval Romance, that

> Isidore of Seville transmitted a classical rhetorical model to the three types of narrative, *genera narrationis*. According to his theory one of these types, *historia*, was a true record of events that had actually taken place, but at some distance in time from present memory. By contrast, *fabula* recounted fictitious events that neither had taken place nor could have conceivably done so [...]. Logically situated between these two extremes was the *argumentum*, dealing with events that had not happened, but could have.[15]

We see evidence of this schema in John of Garland's work when he points out that 'narration rooted in plot is of three species, namely Fable, History, and Realistic Fiction'.[16]

Green argues convincingly that the fictional romance exists in the realm of *argumentum* and *fabula*. The otherworldly contexts of the romances would seem to meet the characteristics of *fabula*. And yet, these works with their recounting of old stories that might have happened also function within the realm of *argumentum*. And so while the genre developed to provide entertainment, its very nature seemed to bring together the concerns of *fabula* and *argumentum*. Indeed, such fictional narratives often explored issues in the realm of moral virtues, but in a way quite different from medieval treatises. As Zeeman points out, medieval poetry differs from what she calls 'hypothetically truer discourses of history, natural science, philosophy, and ethics' but the difference, she argues, is not 'oppositional'.[17] Rather, poetry shares concerns with these other discourses but presents its argument in more subtle ways that include being 'exemplary rather than prescriptive'.[18]

Support for the argument that the romances might have been viewed as texts written for moral edification is found in Judson Allen's studies of the ethical dimension of medieval poetry. Allen has argued that medieval critics placed poetry

[15] D. H. Green, *The Beginnings of Medieval Romance: Fact and Fiction, 1150–1220* (Cambridge: Cambridge University Press, 2002), pp. 3–4.

[16] *Parisiana poetria*, ed. by Lawler, pp. 101–02.

[17] Nicolette Zeeman, 'The Schools Give a License to Poets', in *Criticism and Dissent in the Middle Ages*, ed. by Rita Copeland (Cambridge: Cambridge University Press, 1996), pp. 151–80 (p. 155).

[18] Zeeman, 'Schools Give Licence to Poets', p. 156.

within the general field of ethics, that in their commentary on Ovid, for example, medieval critics saw the *Metamorphosis* as delighting in order to instruct in appropriate behaviour and 'to exemplify the range of possibilities of moral action'. Allen thus sees the authors of medieval poems both delighting and instructing as a way to explore ethical conduct, providing the reader with models so that he might 'inform his own life by the experience of the text'.[19] Further, he points out, these commentators make clear the role of the reader in enacting the moral action implied in the *Metamorphosis*. The text exemplifies the 'range of possibilities of moral actions' and the reader was 'to inform his own life by the experience of the book'.[20]

Like more explicitly didactic texts that persuade the reader to right action, poems engage readers or listeners by asking them to consider models of right behaviour. So, although they may do so through the fictitious in subject matter and context, they consider human decisions and actions that transcend the fictitious into the world of real human conduct. Like Allen, Suzanne Reynolds also comments on the fact that 'a central demand made upon classical, and indeed all literary texts in this period [is] that they be classifiable under the ethical branch of philosophy'.[21] Likewise, Nicolette Zeeman argues that '[i]n the Middle Ages poetry is justified on grounds of aesthetics and ethics: it is pleasurable, affective, persuasive, or exemplary'.[22] And so, we might say, in its setting forth exemplars of virtuous action in their heroes, and on occasion heroines, the romance genre is concerned with ethics.

The romance's concern with old stories not only brings it within the literary types of *fabula* and *argumentum* but also links it explicitly with *historia*, the true record of events that had actually taken place, but at some distance in time from present memory. The connection to *historia* is, however, through *argumentum* in that the narrative events of romance are a constructed rather than realistic account. Nonetheless, the stories provide matter for listeners to store in their memories and recall when called upon to act virtuously. We might see them as not unlike the medieval anthologies or compilations of short sections of writings so pervasive in the Middle Ages. These collections, or *florilegia* were, as Mary

[19] Judson Allen, *The Ethical Poetic of the Later Middle Ages: A Decorum of Convenient Distinction* (Toronto: University of Toronto Press, 1982), pp. 9, 17, 18.

[20] Judson Boyce Allen and Theresa Anne Moritz, *A Distinction of Stories: The Medieval Unity of Chaucer's Fair Chain of Narratives for Canterbury* (Columbus: Ohio State University Press, 1981), pp. 16–18.

[21] Reynolds, *Medieval Reading*, pp. 14–15.

[22] Zeeman, 'Schools Give a License to Poets', p. 153.

Carruthers explains, the 'compilation of extracts and maxims from great writers of the past', what she calls a kind of 'study guide' that 'brings together ethical topics, vices and virtues and socially useful habits, such as those for study or for civic behaviour'.[23] Like these study guides to civic behaviour, romance collections, or manuscript collections that included romances, with their enactment of the chivalric actions of an exemplary model, may be seen as providing commonplaces necessary for evaluating and then choosing ethical conduct. As Gregory the Great said of reading, 'We ought to transform what we read into our very selves, so that when our mind is stirred by what it hears, our life may concur by practicing what has been heard.'[24]

## *The Thornton Romances and Ethical Action*

The manuscript, Lincoln Cathedral Library MS 91, has been seen as a kind of miscellany of texts of interest and concern to a gentry family of the fifteenth century. Among the works collected in this manuscript is a group of romances including *Alliterative Morte Arthure*, *The Romance of Octovyane*, *The Romance of Sir Isumbras*, *The Romance of Dyoclicyane*, *Sir Degrevant*, *Sir Eglamour*, and *The Awentyrs of Arthure at the Terne Wathelyne*. Of these, six are in tail-rhyme form, four of which were presented in a Camden Society publication, edited by James Orchard Halliwell in 1884. Three of the romances found in the manuscript, although addressing somewhat different ethical issues, have openings similar enough to provide a convenient, representative group to explore the appeal of the romance genre into the fifteenth century, particularly to a late medieval English gentry family.[25] These three are *The Romance of Sir Isumbras*, *Sir Degrevant*, and *Sir Eglamour*.[26]

[23] Mary Carruthers, *The Book of Memory: A Study of Memory in Medieval Culture* (Cambridge: Cambridge University Press, 1990), pp. 174–75.

[24] Carruthers, *Book of Memory*, p. 164.

[25] For an extended discussion of the appeal of the romance to fifteenth-century gentry see Daly, 'This World and the Next', Chapter 9, 'The Question of Audience'.

[26] *The Romance of Sir Isumbras*, ed. by F. S. Ellis after the edn printed by J. O. Halliwell from the MS in the Library of Lincoln Cathedral, with a few corrections (Hammersmith: Kelmscott, 1997); *The Romance of Sir Degrevant: A Parallel-text Edition from MSS. Lincoln Cathedral A.5.2 and Cambridge University Ff.I.6*, ed. by L. F. Casson, Early English Text Society (EETS), o.s., 221 (London: Oxford University Press, 1949); *Sir Eglamour of Artois*, ed. by Frances E. Richardson, EETS, o.s., 256 (London: Oxford University Press, 1965).

The ethical dimension of these fictional works informs the shape the romances take. Each romance begins with a static ideal portrait that indicates the values the hero represents then sets the hero into motion as he encounters some difficulty — a controversy or a problem to be solved. The knight's conduct during the ensuing adventures figures forth his values. The romance ends with an historical perspective explaining the reason it ought to be set in the memory of the listener and recalled when making choices that determine ethical behaviour. The shape then seems to be as follows:

> Introduction: a static portrait in which the values to be exemplified, tested, or redefined provide the details of the portrait
>
> Adventure: the values set into action: the adventures and the knight's responses to the challenges exemplifying, testing, or redefining the values set out in the introductory lines
>
> Conclusion: the final setting in place of the exemplary values and the long view of history

Perhaps no more prominent a place than in the opening lines of Middle English Romance can we see the focus on the exemplary nature of these works and the emphasis on ethical behaviour. Judson Allen's discussion of the prologues to treatises provides a perspective on rhetorical effect of romances openings as well. The role of prologues, Allen says, was 'partly logical and partly rhetorical — logical in that prologues introduce or summarize, often, what the subsequent treatise discusses at length; and rhetorical in that prologues are supposed to get readers, or hearer, in a mood to be persuaded by what follows'[27] Allen sees a similar function in the prologues found in *The Canterbury Tales*.

As with a treatise, the opening of a romance puts the reader or listener in a particular frame of mind by establishing the ethical dimension of the work. It introduces the romance's ethical problem, a problem the action of the hero will address, and identifies the character who will provide the model of virtuous behaviour, judged according to the code of chivalry. These introductory lines then highlight the extent to which the central character qualifies as an exemplar of the romance's code of ethics, through his lineage, his valour, his beauty, his fame, and his honour. The three tail-rhyme romances of *Sir Isumbras*, *Sir Degrevant*, and *Sir Eglamour*, although differing in the kind of exemplary character, illustrate this ethical form.

[27] Allen and Moritz, *A Distinction of Stories*, p. 47.

Each romance begins, as I have observed, with a narrator who directly addresses his listeners and places the adventures of the hero within some larger context. Looking at the three romances in the order they are compiled in the manuscript, we find first, directly following the *Alliterative Morte Arthure* and the *Romance off Octovyane, The Romance of Sir Isumbras. Sir Degrevant* follows a *romance of Dyoclicyane the emperour and the erle Berade of Tholous, and of the emprice Beaulilione* and the *Vita Sancti Christofori. Sir Eglamour of Artasse* follows directly after *Degrevant.* After three tales and the *Awnetyrs of Arthuer at the Terne-Wathelyne*, we find *The Romance off Sir Percyvelle of Gales*, which is the last romance included in the manuscript. The three I will be considering here are then the third, the sixth, and the seventh in the grouping.

The three romances begin with what we might call prologues, in which all three include invocations to Christ: The narrator of *Isumbras* begins by asking Christ's blessing for a collective 'us', presumably himself and listeners or readers, and for heaven as a reward; the narrator of *Degrevant* begins by asking Christ to grant those who love game and adventure a sight of heaven; the narrator of *Eglamour* begins by asking both Christ's blessing for a collective 'us' and joy for others who might hear his tale.

*Sir Isumbras*:

Jhesu Crist, Lorde of hevene kynge,
Graunte us alle his dere blyssynge,
And hevene unto oure mede!
(ll. 1–3)

*Sir Degrevant*:

Jhesu, Lorde in Trynite,
Graunte tham heuen for to see
That luffes gamen and glee
And gestis to fede
(ll. 1–4)

*Sir Eglamour*:

Ihesu, that es heuens Kyng,
Gyff vs alle his blyssyng
And beyld vs in his boure;
(ll. 1–3)

These invocations function rhetorically in a manner like that which Allen attributes to the prologues to treatises. They signal to readers that they are being asked to participate in a fictional world where actions have ethical consequences.

When the narrator moves from prologue to introduction, he establishes further the didactic nature of the narratives by then turning his attention more explicitly to his audience. The narrator of *Isumbras* addresses his work to what must be a community of gentlepersons, 'hende in haule' (l. 4), and directs their attention to the historical significance of his narrative. He will tell 'Of elders that by-fore us were, | That lyffede in arethede' (ll. 5–6). The narrator of *Degrevant* and *Eglamour* likewise remind the readers that they are entering the historical realm: *Degrevant* will tell 'Whate folks sittis in fere, | Thare solde men herken and here | Of beryns that by-fore were | That lyffed in arethede' (ll. 5–8); *Eglamour* those 'that will here | Of elders that byfore vs were, | That lyued in grete honoure' (ll. 4–6). It is interesting that the Cambridge Manuscript Ff. ii. 38 version of *Degrevant* has 'off gode that before hem were' where the Thornton Manuscript reads 'Of beryns that by-fore were'.[28] The Cambridge Manuscript's emphasis on the goodness of the barons seems to indicate the exemplary nature of these heroes whose characteristic provides the model of behaviour. The turn from an address to Christ to an address to the reader then directs attention to the particular nature of the narrative at hand. Each passage points to the historical account to be set in the memory of readers who sit in the proverbial hall of the narrator's fiction.

Each narrator then identifies and introduces the exemplar of the ideals of his poem:

*Sir Isumbras*:

I wille yow telle of a knyghte,
That bothe was stalworthe and wyghte,
[And worth]ily undir wede:
His name was hattene syr Ysambrace,
Swilke a knyghte als he was
Now lyffes nowrewhare in lede
(ll. 7–12)

*Sir Degrevant*:

I will you telle of a knyghte:
Sir Degreuante fo-sothe he highte,
He was hardy and wyghte
And doghty in dede;
(ll. 9–12)

[28] See *The Thornton Romances*, ed. by Halliwell, p. 177.

*Sir Eglamour*:

I will you telle of a knyghte
That was both hardy and wyghte,
And stythe in ilk a stoure:
(ll. 7–9)

This shift from direct address to the reader to a particular introduction of the hero is evident in all three passages above. The narrator calls for the audience's attention and places the story within the realm of ethical concern — that is the readers' concern with the connections between actions and the state of their souls — and then moves to an account which will provide an imitable model from long ago. The descriptions that follow this initial identification of the exemplary model emphasize the characteristics the hero will draw upon in his adventures as he either exhibits virtuous behaviour or gradually learns appropriate and exemplary action.

Although all three heroes are *wyghte*, they can be seen as providing a continuum of exemplars. Sir Isumbras, though stalwart, valiant, and worthy, will lose all his earthly fortune. His adventures will provide an education in patience and virtuous action performed for its own sake. Sir Degrevant, also hardy, valiant, and doughty, likewise must learn the subtleties of chivalric behaviour as he learns to temper his justifiable outrage and retribution with diplomacy. Finally, in the purest model of exemplary behaviour, Sir Eglamour, who is also hardy and valiant, will have the strength of his body as well as of his character tested as he earns the hand of his beloved. The difference in the ethical concerns of each romance is demonstrated in the extended descriptions the poets provide.

*The Romance of Sir Isumbras* explores the virtuous behaviour that provides the antidote to worldly pride. The description of Isumbras stresses his strength; he is broad-shouldered, tall, and comely. He is also generous of spirit, giving rich gifts to his companions who love him. He has a beautiful wife and three handsome sons. He is also noble or courteous. One might expect from this description that he fits the ideal portrait of a chivalric knight, and yet the portrait enumerates his worldly goods, his possessions. What he lacks is a concern for *Goddis werkes.* The poet's extended description vividly illustrates the contrast between worldly goods and Christian virtue:

II

He was mekille mane and lange,
With schuldirs brode and armes strange,
That semly were to see;

So was he bothe faire and heghe,
Alle hym loffede that hym seghe,
        So hende a mane was hee!
He luffede glewmene wele in haulle,
He gafe thame robis riche of palle,
        Bothe golde and also fee;
Of curtasye was he kynge,
Of mete and drynke no nythynge,
        One lyfe was non so fre.

III

Als fayre a lady to wyefe had he
Als any erthly mane thurte see,
        With tunge als I yow nevene;
Knave childire had thay thre,
Thay were the faireste that myghte be
        Undir the kynge of hevene!
Bot in his hert a pride was broghte,
Of Goddis werkes gafe he noghte,
        His mercys for to nevene;
So longe he reyngned in his pride,
That Got wolde no lenger habyde,
        To hym he sent a stevene
(ll. 13–36)

Instead of displaying a love of God and his works and mercy, Sir Isumbras is characterized by his pride, which leads to the loss of all his earthly possessions: first his horse, hawks, and hounds, then his buildings so that his people and land are left poor, and then the clothes on his wife's and children's backs. Finally, his sons are taken by wild beasts and his wife by a Sarazin. At this point, the poet seems to draw upon the more positive elements seen in the description of Sir Isumbras found in the introduction. The courteous quality he possesses seems to provide the strength of character that allows him to transform himself through his ordeal. He is given a second chance and shows that he has learned from his ordeal and thus may transform himself and his condition. Through valiant fighting in holy wars against the Sarazins and his acts of self-degradation as he takes up the disguise of a beggar, then his understanding that his sins must be absolved and his wounds healed, he has the opportunity to win back his wife and restore the Sarazan lands to Christendom. The romance ends with the poet reassuring the audience that Isumbras and his wife lived and died with good intent and earned a place in heaven. And so, the romancer asks again for the blessing of heaven's king.

The extended description of Degrevant, like the shorter one of Isumbras, presents a somewhat mixed portrait of the knight, but this time the weight of the positive virtues shines through. His characteristics include not only his comeliness and reputation for valour, his knightly deeds, but also his expertise in music and hunting. Unlike that of Sir Isumbras, Sir Degrevant's portrait includes his piety. Before going to the hunt '[t]o here messe or he went | Trewely in gud entent' (ll. 53–54). He also possesses great lands and property, and is generous to poor folk and minstrels:

> He louede almous-dede,
> Poure folke for to fede
> With menske and with manhede;
>   Of mete he was fre;
> Gestis redy for to calle
> To here mynstralls in haulle,
> He gaf tham robis of palle,
>   Both golde and fee;
> (ll. 76–83)

His one flaw is his lack of a female partner:

> Certis, wife wolde he nane,
> Wenche ne no lemman,
> Bot als an ankyre in a stane
>   He lyvued here trewe
> (ll. 71–74)

And so his adventures include not only a test of his knightly valour but also an education in what we might call the civilizing effect of the female sensibility.[29] In order to establish the exemplary characteristics of his hero, the poet of this romance contrasts him with a foil in the figure of a neighbouring earl, who destroys Sir Degrevant's lands while the knight is on crusade. Sir Degrevant initially responds with justifiable anger and vows to avenge his loss. However, his

[29] For an extended discussion of the 'civilizing effect' of the women on Sir Degrevant's language and action in the romance, see Daly, 'This World and the Next', Chapter 3, 'Sir Degrevant'.

anger is tempered when he falls in love with his enemy's daughter. The change in his situation results in his learning that though he must seek retribution for the loss of his property, he now must do so in a way softened by what appear to be more virtuous chivalric rules of conduct. His first response when he learns that the earl has destroyed his lands is to engage his enemy in combat where the knight is victorious. However, after this initial conflict, he falls in love with Melidor. And from this point on, although Degrevant is strong, valiant, and victorious, it is through the intervention of the women that peace is finally achieved.[30]

Like Sir Degrevant, Sir Eglamour has at its heart a view of the chivalric world tempered by the female principle. Sir Eglamour is the suitor of Cristabelle, the daughter of an earl. The two pledge their love for each other and consummate that love. The earl, however, disapproves of his daughter's suitor and requires the knight to earn her hand by performing several difficult feats: defeating a giant, a boar and his owner, and a dragon. Eglamour is successful but severely injured by the third task.

While he is recovering in a foreign country, Cristabelle bears Sir Eglamour's son, which enrages her father and causes him to banish her from his kingdom. Cast out on a ship alone with only her son, Cristabelle also suffers great loss as she watches a griffin steal her child. But the exile of Cristabelle and the loss of the child lead to the conflict that will address the tensions in the romance and effect its resolution. The child is dropped in Israel, where he is found and adopted by the King of Israel, who names him Sir Degrabelle. Meanwhile, Cristabelle's ship is driven by winds to Egypt, where she is discovered by the King of Egypt, who turns out to be her uncle and thus becomes her protector. After recovering from his wounds, Eglamour return to Artois only to discover that his wife and son have been cast out and therefore must have died.

After mourning her death and giving away his lands, the knight with a retinue, departs for the Holy Land, where he lives and fights for fifteen years. In these fifteen years, Sir Degrabelle has grown into a young man while Cristabelle's fame has spread throughout the region. The King of Israel encourages his adopted son to seek the hand of the beautiful and good niece of the King of Egypt. Cristabelle agreed to the marriage on the condition that the young knight win her in combat, which he does. After the marriage, Cristabelle recognizes her son, who asks for further combat so that another knight might win her from him. Sir Eglamour, who happened to be in that country, fights his own son and wins the hand of

[30] Again, I am indebted to Daly's discussion of the importance of the female principle in the romance in 'This World and the Next', Chapter 3, 'Sir Degrevant'.

Cristabelle; the two are reunited and formally wed; then Sir Degrabelle is wed to the daughter of the Emperor of Rome, who had fallen in love with Eglamour when he was recovering from his fight with the dragon. And again the romance ends with the poet invoking Christ.

The description of Eglamour that follows his brief introduction and sets up the action just described is brief. The poet prepares the reader for a hero who is truly exemplary without perceptive flaws as he draws attention to the knight's valour, strength, and successes. Rather than an explicit description of the knight or a statement concerning his fame, the poet demonstrates his hero's well-deserved reputation by recounting the earl's recognition of his deeds of arms and also by telling of his relationship with Cristabelle, 'A fayrere lady of flesche ne bana | Was nane in Cristyante' (ll. 29–30), who loves Sir Eglamour above all early things. This description differs from the ones found in Isumbras and Degrevant in that it weaves the description of Cristabelle into that of the knight. Further, as the poet moves to the action of the poem, wherein the knight's chivalry will be tested, he reminds the reader that the relationship with Cristabelle is directly linked to his exemplary nature: 'The knyghte es hardy and bold in stele: | Thare-fore the lady loued hym wele' (ll. 37–38). And so, unlike in the other two romances, this poet plunges the readers rapidly into the action so that they might see Eglamour repeatedly perform his chivalric deeds and thus exemplify the appropriate behaviour of an exemplary knight.

## *Conclusion*

Although found in a collection compiled for a gentry rather than an aristocratic family, these romances must have provided both entertainment in their exciting deeds of arms and satisfaction in their affirmation of a moral code appealing to the late Middle Ages. As the brief explorations of the relationship between the introductions and action of these three romances demonstrates, their central concerns are with the exemplary nature of the heroes and the lessons they provide. Essentially chivalric, each work, like the extracts of longer works found in the *florilegia*, considers ethical topics, vices and virtues, and socially useful habits, such as those for study or for civic behaviour. As such they embody the concerns of their literary ancestors. Like the twelfth-century chivalric works, these late English romances portray chivalric behaviour as an enactment of virtue. Sir Isumbras, Sir Degrevant, and Sir Eglamour either are or become valiant, strong, and loyal. Their actions establish order in their realms, and their stories are worthy of storing in the memories of their listeners so that they might learn, as Alexander Nequam hoped the young readers of satires and histories would learn, 'that vices too are to be avoided and he might desire to imitate the noble deed of heroes'.

*University of Denver*

# Jans der Enikel's Prologue as a Guide to Textual Multiplicity

Maria Dobozy

In recent years literary scholars have been giving ever more attention to world chronicles as a group or genre because they were extremely popular in German-speaking areas from the mid-thirteenth to the mid-fifteenth century.[1] This fact alone makes them worthy of examination. Such popularity inevitably produced over one hundred and fifty manuscripts and with them a plethora of textual recombinations. Yet these riches have indeed caused methodological embarrassment. The problem is how to categorize and analyse a large number of texts where each text is a different mixture of two or more of the same sources. What happens when two or more independent narratives are spliced together, when each one originally had its own organization, style, and perspective? Which is 'the' text and how are we to read it? I follow the changes in the German universal or world chronicle tradition beginning with Jans der Enikel's own *Weltchronik* by

[1] Renewed interest began with Ursula Peters, 'Von der Sozialgeschichte zur Familienhistorie', *Paul und Braunes Beiträge*, 112 (1990), 404–36, and the chronicle conferences organized by Erik Kooper and the volumes he edited. See Gabrielle M. Spiegel, 'Theory into Practice: Reading Medieval Chronicles', in *The Medieval Chronicle*, ed. by Erik Kooper (Amsterdam: Rodopi, 1999), pp. 1–12. And more recently, Harald Tersch, *Unruhe im Weltbild: Darstellung und Deutung des zeitgenössischen Lebens in deutschsprachigen Weltchroniken des Mittelalters* (Vienna: Böhlau, 1996). Most recently, careful study of illuminated manuscript groups has been published by Gerhard Wolf, *Von der Chronik zum Weltbuch: Sinn und Anspruch südwestdeutscher Hauschroniken am Ausgang des Mittelalters* (Berlin: de Gruyter, 2003); *In the Beginning Was the Word: The Power and Glory of Illuminated Bibles*, ed. by Andreas Fingernagel and Christian Gastgeber (London: Taschen, 2003); and Maria Dobozy, 'Vernacular Chronicles', in *A Companion to Middle High German Literature to the 14th Century*, ed. by Francis G. Gentry (Leiden: Brill, 2002), pp. 379–96.

comparing his opening prologue to the introductory passages in three separate manuscript recombinations. I will argue that each recombination must be treated as a separate text with its own purpose and perspective. When we then compare manuscripts, we find shifts in perspective, driven not by authorial direction but rather by the reception process. Three trends are clearly discernable: the addition of more detail achieves encyclopedic breadth, the deletion or exchange of prologues erases the identity and even the impression of a single author to produce an impersonal yet universally valid text, and finally the emphasis shifts to a theological frame while retaining the lively account of secular historical events in a familiar courtly context.

German world chronicles first became popular in the mid-thirteenth century but originated in the twelfth. They recounted chronologically the history of the world combining secular and sacred history following the biblical account and also a history of the Holy Roman Empire. Our earliest world chronicle is the Vorau codex (V 276, Stift Vorau, *c.* 1147–60), a monastic production in Latin and German that combines several biblical and secular historical texts and appears to have been intended as a single book encompassing all of history. A second, and more immediate, model for the thirteenth-century chronicles is Peter Comestor's *Historia scholastica* (*c.* 1169–73), a readily accessible Latin retelling of the Bible. Peter organized the material according to the framework of the *sex aetates mundi*. Because it was appropriate for both a literate and non-literate audience, it was quickly translated into several vernaculars. In Germany this text became the most important single source for the thirteenth-century chronicles in part because Peter, like the creators of the Vorau manuscript, incorporated profane contemporary events into the biblical story.

The first chronicle in the development examined below is Rudolf von Ems's *Weltchronik* (*c.* 1250), commissioned by King Conrad IV of Germany. Rudolf is the only chronicle writer who is also an excellent, educated poet known for his courtly narratives. He explains in the prologue his intention to organize his history according to the *sex aetates mundi* framework but narrates only as far as Solomon. The second, the anonymous *Christherre Chronik* (*c.* 1250–88), commissioned by Heinrich der Erlauchte of Thuringia († 1288), was probably written by a monk because it focuses on theological issues and especially stresses salvation history in its prologue. It too remained incomplete, covering only Judges in the Old Testament. The third was written by Jans der Enikel (*c.* 1275), a member of the Viennese patriciate and possibly city notary. This narrative is complete; it begins with Creation and the Old Testament; then continues chronologically with the New Testament and Roman emperors almost up to the author's present

(1250).[2] All three chronicles rely extensively on Peter Comestor's *Historia scholastica*. Both Rudolf and Jans use the frame of the six ages, but Jans does not consistently apply it as an organizing principle. These two writers also draw on Peter Comestor for their extensive information concerning the natural world, including accurate geographic information, description of countries, and some aspects of their political history. Each of these three world chronicle texts continues to exist in its own independent textual transmission, running from the thirteenth through the end of the fifteenth century, as Ralf Plate has demonstrated.[3]

Within the first eighty years of reception, these three individual, unmixed chronicle texts were cut and pasted together to compose what I call chimeras. In the process of reproduction and recomposition, Jans der Enikel's *Weltchronik* was added to, overwritten, and adapted in numerous ways. A great many such chimeric compilations, often called multi-texts, were produced between *c.* 1380 and 1500. Of course, medieval authors and scribes in general were not constrained by the concept of authorship, plagiarism, or even adherence to the idea of a fixed text. My starting point is the intertwining of Jans der Enikel's text with the *Christherre* to produce a new composition. This textual multiplicity raises questions concerning our approach to an entire manuscript tradition as being attributable to a specific author, having a standard text, or even adhering to a particular genre. In order to understand how these texts were produced and received in their own time, I wish to examine the transmission and reception of Jans der Enikel's text by means of the prologues that have been substituted for his original.

The multi-text phenomenon poses problems in classifying manuscripts. To which author or textual tradition do we classify a text that contains most of the text of two or three sources in an intricate, chimeric mixture? For example, in the

[2] Jans has been called Jans Enikel since the eighteenth century as if Enikel were a last name. Fritz Peter Knapp in his erudite encyclopedic volumes on Austrian literature has suggested Jans von Wien. To be sure, Jans was a Viennese burger, but without the appellation Enikel, we do not recognize him. According to R. Graeme Dunphy's suggestion, the form Jans der Enikel allows us to recognize this Jans and conforms to the medieval usage and meaning of *enikel*, the 'grandson'. I follow Dunphy. See Fritz Peter Knapp, *Geschichte der Literatur in Österreich von den Anfängen bis zur Gegenwart*, II: *Die Literatur des Spätmittelalters* (Graz: Akademische Druck- und Verlagsanstalt, 1999), pt I, 237, and R. Graeme Dunphy, 'Jans der Enikel oder Jans von Wien?' *Perspecuitas*, 2003, <http://www.uni-due.de/perspicuitas/miszellen.shtml>.

[3] Ralf Plate categorized the manuscripts in order to determine which belong to the *Christherre* chronicle tradition. See his *Die Überlieferung der 'Christherre-Chronik* (Wiesbaden: Reichert, 2005), pp. 11–16.

introduction to his edition of Jans's chronicle, Philipp Strauch attributed thirty-eight manuscripts and fragments to Jans der Enikel or listed them as containing his text.[4] Yet only four of these manuscripts contain Jans's unmixed text. The remaining texts are chimeras produced by cutting and pasting together sections of Jans's work and *Christherre* and others, although in a great many cases all or almost all of Jans's text is contained in the mixture. Where Jans is secular and anecdotal, the *Christherre* attempts to present a consistent theology. Manuscripts containing the Jans-*Christherre* mixture represent a chimeric stage that combines the secular and the sacred. The compilers did not simply add one text to another in sequence, but rather, took segments on a particular topic, such as the creation of Adam and Eve or the story of Noah, from one source and spliced it into the second account. This stage is called the 'expanded' *Christherre* text, although Jans's text forms its foundation.[5] By this method more and more detail could be added to each story allowing the chimeric texts to achieve encyclopedic breadth.

At the next stage in this development from individual texts to chimeras, we find inserted into the Jans-*Christherre* chimera segments from Rudolf von Ems and other sources that have not all been identified. Texts exhibiting this more complex mixture are called Heinrich von München (HvM), an authorial name given in some manuscripts. Since we have no evidence that Heinrich von München ever existed, the name does not designate a verifiable author or compiler. Instead, it is now considered to have been used as a means to lend authorial prestige and truth-value to these huge compilations of around one hundred thousand lines that were actually produced in workshops in a collaborative effort. We can safely say that authorial attribution did not become a convention for world chronicles. However, the issue of authorial names is important. Rudolf and Jans proudly announced their identity and authorial status in their texts whereas the *Christherre* author suppressed his name. As a result when Jans's prologue is replaced with the one from *Christherre*, evidence of authorship and the authority of a single individual is also erased. Thus world chronicles in the form of most chimeric manuscripts become common property and reflect the reception process.

[4] See *Jansen Enikels Werke*, ed. by Philipp Strauch, Monumenta Germaniae Historica, Deutsche Chroniken, 3 vols (Leipzig: Hahn, 1900), III, pp. iii–xxxix.

[5] Ralf Plate, 'Wie fängt die Bibel an? Zu den Vorstufen der *Weltchronik* Heinrichs von München am Beispiel der Schöpfungsgeschichte', in *Metamorphosen der Bibel: Beiträge zur Tagung 'Wirkungsgeschichte der Bibel im deutschsprachigen Mittelalter'*, ed. by Ralf Plate and Andrea Rapp (Frankfurt: Lang, 2004), pp. 229–46 (p. 235).

Until recently the lengthy, chimeric world chronicles were assumed to be an extensive phenomenon that supplanted the three individual unmixed chronicle texts. Now we know they are primarily limited to the rather large Bavarian-Austrian dialect regions and occur from about 1380 to 1500. The manuscript transmission also reveals that unmixed texts and both stages of complex mixtures were concurrently produced throughout this period. To summarize, Ralf Plate counts three stages in the transmission of world chronicle manuscripts: the first is the one in which Jans der Enikel's *Weltchronik* and *Christherre* each exist as a separate text, the second is the intertwined Jans-*Christherre* chimera, and the third is the Heinrich von München stage.[6] Nevertheless even within each stage, each individual manuscript contains a similar but different text. Below I compare prologues with a manuscript chosen from each of the three stages just described.

Given the heterogeneity in the manuscripts, I suggest that each chimeric text be treated as a separate artefact of the medieval past because almost each one contains a unique world chronicle text. Therefore, we may not refer to them as 'variants' because that term implies a standard text from which others diverge.[7] Manuscripts also need to be examined independently of each other to the extent that we should not simply categorize them within a stemma. Although a stemma is invaluable for enabling us to group texts and outline possible directions and stages in textual transmission, it reveals little about the thematic organization or perspective of each individual chimeric text.[8] Hence a reference to a particular manuscript almost always denotes a unique chimeric text. The sheer number of texts gives us an example of history writing in process. Therefore, it is important to look for patterns of change and to discover how the overall organization of

[6] In *Die Überlieferung*, Ralf Plate's extensive study of all the *Christherre* and HvM manuscripts comparing them to Rudolf von Ems and Jans der Enikel and their sources has allowed him to group the manuscripts. The groundwork for my study is on pp. 90–124.

[7] Dorothea Klein and Johannes Rettelbach, who are instrumental in studying multi-text production, agree with my assessment and speak of 'variable text' (*offener Text*). Yet they still refer to the individual texts as 'variants'. Dorothea Klein, *Studien zur 'Weltchronik' Heinrichs von München*, III: *Text-und überlieferungsgeschichtliche Untersuchungen zur Redaktion ß* (Wiesbaden: Reichert, 1998), pt I, p. xi; Johannes Rettelbach, *Studien zur 'Weltchronik' Heinrichs von München*, II: *Von der 'Erweiterten Christherre-Chronik' zur Redaktion á* (Wiesbaden: Reichert, 1998), pt I, p. xi.

[8] Dorothea Klein is aware of the difficulty in establishing a stemma and its implications, stating that the textual changes are not static and do not permit a textual typology but must be seen instead as a process (*Studien zur 'Weltchronik' Heinrichs von München*, III, pt I, p. xiii).

chronicles changes in the process of producing chimeric texts. A comparison of the prologue in select manuscripts points to some of the discernable trends.

We have four manuscripts containing Jans's chronicle by itself, allowing us to establish the integrity of his efforts. Strauch based his edition on the two lead manuscripts, Munich and Regensburg (both late fourteenth century), of which Regensburg has the only complete text. Leipzig and Berlin (both fifteenth century) are incomplete but show changes and corrections that might well have originated with Jans himself.[9] Although none of the four was written close to Jans's lifetime, we can safely call them Jans der Enikel's *Weltchronik*. To Jans's prologue I compare three manuscripts that still contain the greater part of Jans's text but are chimeras and represent the second and third stages defined above. These are Linz 472 (late fourteenth century), Vienna 2921 (1397–98), and Vienna 2782 (1439). The manuscripts chosen for comparison are closely related in several ways. All three were produced in the same Bavarian-Austrian dialect areas as the Regensburg manuscript so that they represent the writing practices and reception of world chronicles for the period. Vienna 2921 is very closely related to the Regensburg. Not only does it contain all of Jans's *Weltchronik* text but also shares with the Regensburg a common picture cycle where most of the illustrations are placed in the same place in the text.[10]

The chosen texts then represent all three stages allowing me to follow the changes from Jans's prologue through two levels of chimeric multi-text developments. Manuscript Linz 472 is included because it contains the Jans-*Christherre* mixture and is the earliest representative of stage two, while the two Vienna manuscripts represent stage three, the HvM multi-text. It is thus possible to follow reception in a small portion of text, specifically the changes from Jans's prologue through the two types of chimeric mixture. The significant change in the chosen manuscripts is a new introductory section that has been substituted for Jans's prologue. In each case Jans's own chronicle account follows immediately. By examining the recombinations I hope to demonstrate that these texts are books in process, and by that I mean they are not the product of one author or compiler but of a reception process.

[9] See R. Graeme Dunphy, 'Introduction', in *History as Literature: German World Chronicles of the Thirteenth Century in Verse*, trans. by R. Graeme Dunphy (Kalamazoo: Medieval Institute Publications, 2003), pp. 1–27 (p. 17).

[10] Where Regensburg has 256 pictures, Vienna 2921 contains 242 pictures, of which 23 are new (*Jansen Enikels Werke*, ed. by Strauch, p. xxiii).

Other portions of text, for example the story of Job and the creation of Adam and Eve, have already been compared across manuscripts to discover the mixing technique and shifts in perspective.[11] The purpose here is to establish the shift in conceptual framework created by a new prologue and the extent to which the remainder of the text might clash with it. The Linz manuscript represents stage two and opens with the prologue from the *Christherre* chronicle. Vienna 2782 contains almost the exact same introductory lines. Although the prologues are the same in both manuscripts, Vienna 2782 is a collection of completely separate texts: a land law, Jans der Enikel's *Fürstenbuch* (a history of the Babenberg and Hapsburg dynasties), and a HvM *Weltchronik*. However, this HvM chronicle does not include Jans's complete text because the manuscript itself ends with the emperors of Rome.

Once the vernacular world chronicle as a genre became popular and the expanded chimeric texts came into high demand, these codices were produced in workshops where the scribes and illustrators worked in tandem. They had access to several sources and were thus able to produce a variety of rather expensive, plentifully illustrated codices. In a well-organized workshop, the same scribe would produce world chronicles with variable texts and would not merely copy the same text over and over. For example, the same hand in the same workshop worked on three different illustrated manuscripts: Jans der Enikel (Regensburg), a Jans-*Christherre* mixture (Munich, Bayrische Staatsbibliothek, M cgm 5, *c.* 1390), and a HvM manuscript (New York, Morgan Library, Cod. M. 769, *c.* 1375–90). Since each manuscript represents a different stage in the chimeric development we may be certain that all sorts of chimeras were being produced at the same time. We may also conclude that the various mixtures must have been compiled according to the conception and wishes of a patron and not solely according to an individual scribe's design.

Studying prologues offers an alternative means of tracking the reception process because a prologue is a rather clearly delineated portion of text; it is easily distinguishable from other segments and fulfils a relatively clear rhetorical function. The world chronicle prologues (even those with a named author) stand

[11] Plate has compared the account of Creation week to examine the process of mixing to create a chimera: see 'Wie fängt die Bibel an?'. Dorothea Klein has done a model study of the Job stories across HvM manuscripts, 'Die Hioberzählung als philosophisches Exempel: Textgeschichte und konzeptionelle Umgestaltung', in *Studien zur 'Weltchronik' Heinrichs von München*, I: *Überlieferung, Forschungsbericht, Untersuchungen, Texte*, ed. by Horst Brunner (Wiesbaden: Reichert, 1998), pp. 330–420.

outside the rhetorical tradition and eschew the usual topoi and begin with a prayer to God instead. Nevertheless these prologues still orient the readers and listeners by explaining the content, organization, and thematic concept of what follows. Prologues are unstable; they can be easily damaged at the beginning of a manuscript but they may also be replaced intentionally. Scribes consciously substituted one prologue for another most likely because they were carrying out the instructions of a patron. Because the three manuscripts under scrutiny are illuminated, we may be certain they were produced on the instructions of a patron although, unfortunately, we have no information about such patrons. Dhira B. Mahoney has pointed out the value of studying substituted prologues: 'Just as the change of a picture frame affects the painting it contains, [...] the frame subtly reshapes the reader's approach to the poem.'[12] Consequently, even without direct evidence of purpose, the resulting compositional change in the prologue material expresses a new tone, perspective, and a corresponding attempt to redirect readers' and listeners' expectations. In both Vienna 2921 and Vienna 2782, Jans's prologue has been deliberately replaced by other introductory sections with the result that the new prologue material creates a new set of expectations. As we shall see, the new introductory sections guide the reader in a more theologically reflective direction.

Jans der Enikel's own 138-line prologue states his goals and justifies his project in clear and personal terms. The primary theme expresses his literary aspirations, implying that the account is intended to entertain and edify his audience. He first invokes God's help to give him mastery (*meisterschaft*) in the sense of poetic eloquence so that he may praise God and his infinite mercy. This request leads him to express the literal impossibility of describing completely the vastness of God's creation: 'because I know fully the truth of what I will tell, that all the grains of sand and all the leaves and whatever flies or runs, if they all had tongues they could not in a thousand years completely express all the wonders, each and every one, that God created in his omnipotence everywhere'.[13] But behind this vivid nature imagery is the expectation that he wants to give an account of the entire world, God's entire creation with all its marvels. Since language and human ability cannot encompass it all, he must content himself with describing a part of

[12] Dhira B. Mahoney, 'Gower's Two Prologues to *Confessio Amantis*', in *Re-Visioning Gower*, ed. by R. F. Yeager (Asheville, NC: Pegasus, 1998), pp. 17–37 (p. 20).

[13] '[W]an ich weiz von der wârheit wol, dâ von ich ez sagen sol, daz aller griez und alliu loup und swaz ie geflouc oder stoup, wærn daz allez zungen gar, die möhten niht in tûsent jâr gar gesagen diu wunder, diu got alliu besunder mit sîner kraft beschaffen hât an einer ieslîchen stat' (ll. 13–22).

the whole. Although human inadequacy (*tumber man*) is a constantly reiterated humility topos typical of all prologues and is the stance expected of the narrator as Mahoney has shown, the marvellous content of world chronicles lends this topos literal meaning.[14] Jans also admits this project is quite new for him and must rely on God's bounteous grace for this immense undertaking and I, like Ursula Liebertz-Grün, take him at his word.[15] He lists the contents of the chronicle text proper as beginning with Creation, the Old Testament kings, then continuing to the Roman emperors and to his own time in chronological sequence. Jans's prologue and narrative lack a clear historical framework beyond the sense of chronological sequence and form given by the biblical story and the ages indicated in the Old Testament.[16]

Next Jans introduces himself proudly as a Viennese nobleman and informs the reader/listener he is about to undertake an especially difficult project of composing the book (*buoch slihten*) because this work is his own conception and not written for any patron: 'With God's aid I shall take upon myself the writing of a book and compose it according to my own conception, for the sake of God's grace that can never be completely encompassed in words.'[17] Jans thus places himself outside the rhetorical tradition. At the same time, Jans's choice of rhymed couplets for this history classifies his text as a poetic composition (*tichten*). Yet he also gives permission to anyone who is dissatisfied to improve on his text in any way; he will accept it without anger.[18] With this statement Jans identifies his book with the genre of informational texts by recognizing a scribe's freedom to change a text. He may well have anticipated that his book would indeed be changed and adapted by later scribes. Chronicles, like law books and handbooks, were considered a

[14] Dhira B. Mahoney, 'Courtly Presentation and Authorial Self-Fashioning: Frontispiece Miniatures in Late Medieval French and English Manuscripts', *Mediaevalia*, 21 (1996), 97–160. On the topos of the author's self-deprecatory remarks, see p. 100.

[15] Ursula Liebertz-Grün, *Das andere Mittelalter: Erzählte Geschichte und Geschichtserkenntnis um 1300; Studien zu Ottokar von Steiermark, Jans Enikel, Seifried Helbling* (Munich: Fink, 1984), p. 77.

[16] R. Graeme Dunphy suggests that Jans used the traditional organization according to emperors because it fit nicely with the fourth age of the *aetates* concept. See *Daz was ein michel wunder: The Presentation of Old Testament Material in Jans Enikel's 'Weltchronik'* (Göppingen: Kümmerle, 1998), p. 60.

[17] 'Wil mir nû got bî gestân, sô wil ich mich nemen an, daz ich daz buoch wil slihten, nâch mînem sinne rihten ûf die genâd der gotheit, dâ nimmer ze end wirt von geseit' (ll. 39–43).

[18] '[S]î ieman, dem ez missehag, der mach ein bezzer sag, daz wil ich lâzen âne zorn' (ll. 89–91).

genre that could and would be added to. The placement of a world chronicle next to a law book in the Vienna 2782 codex confirms this.[19]

Jans's personal investment in his text becomes evident when he expresses genuine poetic aspirations as a secular writer by wishing to learn about poetic composition (*tichten*) from those who are more accomplished than he. Playing on Walther von der Vogelweide's well-known phrase claiming travel experience from the Elbe to the Rhine and back towards Hungary, Jans draws on the authority of broad experience, travel, and eyewitness knowledge to assure the audience of his sincere poetic intentions when he writes, 'wherever poets are recognized from the sea to the Rhine, may they allow me to be their apprentice'.[20] Thus he conceives of himself as an apprentice to secular poets from whom he expects to learn the decorum (*gefuog*) or good form of poetic composition. Humility here may be a result of his status as city notary from whom poetic eloquence is not expected. Although one might doubt his sincerity, I suggest that he aligns himself with courtly poets because he models the body of his narrative after romances.[21] In this sense the prologue is a personal and intimate statement of the author's desires and goals and probably reflects the milieu for which he is writing. With this chronicle then, Jans is avowedly honing his poetic skills.

Thus far Jans has been seeking God's aid, the good will of poets, and the attention of his audience. What follows next is a break, a shocking change of direction for which the reader and listener have not been prepared. He shifts abruptly to devote eighteen lines cursing anyone who would mock or denigrate him for writing his book. He unleashes a rather long, vehement curse as he wishes multiple disabilities and unhappiness on people. He begins by casting that person into hell — then lists what should happen to him personally:

> Whoever derides me for having composed this book, I call the devil's chaplain. He must be the product of hell. May his eyes be blinded, hands and feet paralyzed and also his arms and legs. If he owns a cherished possession, may a thief steal it. May people think him

[19] Law books and other collections of information, whether for reference or teaching, are defined by the nature of their subject matter, namely that the content needs to be correct and updated. To the extent that Jans is relating historical and biblical information, he knows he is unlike romance authors who claim they are telling the true version in contrast to predecessors, and because they tell 'the' true story, they imply that no one may change it.

[20] '[S]wâ die tihter sîn bekant von dem mer hinz an den Rîn, die lâzen mich irn diener sîn' (ll. 102–04).

[21] Ursula Liebertz-Grün has commented on the way he gives his stories a courtly cast and turns characters of all periods into knights wearing courtly attire (*Das andere Mittelalter*, p. 92).

> odious and his relations find him repulsive. May the gentle Christ who rules heaven and earth help me in this.[22]

The curse expresses drastic measures in a desire for revenge instead of justice, so that when he calls on the 'gentle Christ' to enforce it, the curse becomes incongruous. The author's expectation that others may attack the book is a very real danger and familiar from other chronicles.[23] Yet, because the violent outburst in Jans's language is unmotivated, the curse appears gratuitous. As Phyllis Brown has shown erudite poets are capable of a great many subtle applications of the curse, and when they invoke God, they give a justification.[24] Jans's own language, however, is not rhetorically elegant or clever enough to impress. At the same time such abusive language also has its more sophisticated poetic models in the German *Sangspruchdichter* who assert their authority based on their panegyric and gnomic poetry that allows them to vent ruthless and harsh criticisms on those they consider ignoble and stingy. Most important for our purposes is that this unexpected, drastic shift in tone and language is typical of Jans's style and gives a foretaste of the dramatic, often volatile dialogues found throughout his narrative.

Then just as suddenly, Jans shifts topic again to say the book is about to begin. But before it does, he offers another prayer to God the Comforter. This second prayer appears somewhat out of place here because it reiterates the content of the first prayer and obliges Jans to repeat that the Bible is about to begin. The shift in terms signifies that the entire book is to be understood as a retelling of the Bible rather than any specialized history and thus sets up the expectation that the

[22] '[S]î ieman der nû spotte mîn, daz ich daz buoch getihtet hân, der sî des tievels kappelân und müez sîn der helle kint. an den ougen werd er blint. an handen, [an] füezen werd er lam, an armen, [an] beinen alsam. hab er iht, daz im sî liep, daz müez im steln ein diep. den liuten werd er widerzæm und sînen mâgen ungenæm. des helfe mir der süeze Krist, der himel und erd gewaltic ist' (ll. 110–22).

[23] From comments in a lesser-known biblical retelling produced in the fourteenth century by an Austrian layman, a contemporary of Jans, we have certain knowledge that the author was severely attacked for his work and had to defend himself repeatedly before he could complete his text, according to Gisela Kornrumpf, '*Nova et vetera*: Zum Bibelwerk des österreichischen Laien der ersten Hälfte des 14. Jahrhunderts', in *Metamorphosen der Bibel*, ed. by Ralf Plate and Andrea Rapp (Frankfurt: Lang, 2004), pp. 103–22 (p. 104). A similar concern but without the ill will towards others is expressed in the *Saxon Mirror*, IV. 84: 'This book shall make many an enemy, for all those who strive against God and Law will be enraged because it pains them to see that the law is always revealed'. Cited according to my translation, *The Saxon Mirror: A Sachsenspiegel of the Fourteenth Century* (Philadelphia: University of Pennsylvania Press, 1999), p. 178.

[24] See Phyllis R. Brown's contribution to the present volume: 'Rhetoric and Reception: Guillaume de Machaut's "Je Maudi"'.

chronicle proper will adhere to the biblical text. Jans, however, is not concerned with theology unless he can cast it as a story. Typically he takes great liberties with his tale and does not follow the biblical stories closely. But this laxity apparently did not disturb patrons who commissioned these manuscripts. In terms of style however, Jans's original prologue exhibits the same stylistic strategies as the body of the chronicle. His entire text including the prologue exhibits the same episodic structure, paratactic syntax, and sudden shifts in theme and tone that override or lose track of an initial plan.

The most important characteristics of Jans's prologue are his chatty and personal manner of formulation. He does not deal overtly with abstract theological questions or explanations. Instead he makes good use of familiar, yet memorable images and experiences. His style is intimate, his tone humble and open to correction. These characteristics are also consistent with the body of his chronicle. The language is not eloquent, nor smooth as Rudolf von Ems's rhetorically more complex narrative. Jans is primarily a storyteller, and a good one. He maintains close contact with his listeners and readers by means of direct address. (He addresses his audience three times and God twice.) And when he reassures the audience that he will maintain a brisk narrative pace, promising not to bore them, he acknowledges that the entertainment value of his account is important to them. His chronicle proper follows immediately with the creation of the angels and Lucifer's fall and is found in all the manuscripts in this study.

In contrast, Linz 472 contains a two-part introductory passage (ll. 1–582) taken from the original *Christherre* composition. The Linz prologue proper (ll. 1–303) orients the reader as to content and organization of the chronicle. In style it is not any smoother or more expressive than Jans's text. In fact, it is clumsier. Syntax is quite repetitive and the rhymes are just as easily anticipated as in Jans. Where Jans is concrete, the Linz manuscript is abstract and theologically more sophisticated and instructional. Yet the Linz narrator also has difficulty defining terms perhaps because he fails to use clear imagery. The opening frame of a lengthy prayer to God contains the humility and insufficiency topos and a long, repetitive discussion of God's existence as a trinity: 'Because of your power you are the inextinguishable sunshine that lives eternally til the end of time. Light of God alone gives off bright rays, the one and yet three, the unblemished and steadfast and of the holy trinity that is one with three names and is triune with three names.'[25] Eventually, sixty-eight lines later, the text gives the attributes of the

[25] '[D]u pist in dem gewalt dein der unerloschen sunnen schein dew immer lebent an endez zeit. liecht allein liecht schein geit got ainiger und doch dreir unuercherter wandels freir und der

three persons, namely omnipotence, wisdom, and goodness. Next are mentioned Geoffrey of Viterbo, Peter Comestor's *Historia scholastica*, the books of the Old Testament, the prophets, and the Church Fathers as authoritative sources.

Most significant for our discussion is the fact that the second section (ll. 304–582) develops the salvation theme to claim that the events in Christ's act of sacrifice were conceived before Creation. The salvation theme is presented in a theological discussion of God's master plan. It begins with God's existence before Creation as a master carpenter (*deus artifex*) who plans his project in detail before beginning the actual production. God already knows what he will produce, in which sequence, and what its attributes will be: 'God examined his creation for himself the way a carpenter reflects in his heart and considers a plan as to which elements he wants to build his house with and imagines it this way and that until he completes it.'[26] The process of creation thus contains three stages: the will, the plan, and its execution. The description of the execution then turns into a rather lengthy and tedious reiteration of the role of each person in the Trinity, culminating in a portrayal of the triune God in his sublime perfection as creator. God's will to create, his planning, and his foreknowledge of Lucifer's and man's fall, and his plan for Christ's sacrifice together define the nature of the Trinity and the reasoning behind the salvation plan. It follows that, if God's salvation strategy originated in the design for Creation, then this introductory material also confirms the typological link between the Old and New Testaments and implies that all events are guided by God's plan for the unfolding of world history. In Linz 472 this section is immediately followed by Jans's text telling of Lucifer's fall.

The Linz prologue and master carpenter section are derived from the *Christherre* and are identical to Vienna 2782, although an occasional single line is missing in one or the other manuscript. Vienna 2921 omits the 303-line *Christherre* prologue found in the other two manuscripts and begins instead with the master carpenter section, which corresponds almost exactly to Vienna 2782. Right after this section, both Vienna 2921 and 2782 contain an additional segment that

heiligen trinitat die ainig drei namen hat und driualtig in drein namen ist' (Linz, Universitätsbibliothek, Cod. 472, ll. 7–15).

[26] '[G]ot sach die geschaft ye pey ym an als noch ein weyser zimmerman in seinem herzen trachet und mit fürgedanken achtet mit als welichen sachen er sein haus wil machen und inmageniert das sunst und so und ye pas und pas uncz daz er es volpringt' (ll. 21–29). In order to highlight the way source texts are cut and pasted in these chimera manuscripts, I am citing here from Vienna, Nationalbibliothek, Cod. 2921, which is almost identical to the carpenter section of Linz 472, ll. 24–32, and Vienna 2782.

characterizes them as belonging to the third or HvM stage of chimeras. This narrative section is the 'Council of Virtues' that presents a second theological foundation for the redemption and is found in the earliest HvM compilation.[27] The following table offers a comparison of Jans's text with the content of the three manuscripts. Jans's prologue has been deleted, but his section on the Fall of Lucifer follows immediately in all manuscripts. The presence of the Council of Virtues in the two Vienna manuscripts indicates the HvM tradition.

**Comparison of Jans der Enikel's *Weltchronik* to the introductory sections (A, B, and C) as found in the three manuscripts.**

| | Jans | Linz 472 | V 2921 | V 2782 |
|---|---|---|---|---|
| Jan's Prologue | x | 0 | 0 | 0 |
| A. *Christherre* Prologue | 0 | x | 0 | x |
| B. Deus artifex | 0 | x | x | x |
| C. Council of Virtues | 0 | 0 | x | x |
| Jan's Fall of Lucifer | x | x | x | x |

Often called the 'Four daughters of God', this much cited theological story exists in several variants in Latin but also in German from the mid-twelfth century on.[28] The advisory council in both Vienna 2921 and 2782 is essentially a type scene like the ones in heroic poetry in which the ruler holds council with his barons. Since this occurs before Creation, God's self-reflective process is described as a dividing of himself while he speaks to himself: 'God in his majesty sat in council with the trinity.'[29] This phrasing may reflect the earlier tradition of an innertrinitarian dialogue deciding on the procedure for Creation.[30] Our version

[27] The council of virtues section in Vienna 9470 (an HvM prototype manuscript) is almost identical to the two manuscripts I discuss here. See Rettelbach, *Studien zur 'Weltchronik' Heinrichs von München*, II, pt I, 114–15, and for text, II, pt II, 88–93.

[28] For the many German versions see *Die deutsche Literatur des Mittelalters: Verfasserlexikon* (Berlin: de Gruyter, 1978–95), IX, cols 396–402.

[29] '[G]ot in seiner maygestat des mit der gothait ward czerat' (Vienna 2921, ll. 296–97).

[30] On the tradition in Germany where in the 'St. Trudperter Hohelied' (Song of Songs) originally the persons of the trinity (omnipotence, wisdom, and goodness) debated among themselves, see Friedrich Ohly, 'Die Trinität berät über die Erschaffung des Menschen und über seine Erlösung', *Beiträge zur Geschichte der deutschen Literatur*, 116 (1994), 242–84 (p. 243).

goes beyond the Trinity, as God divides himself into a council of peers consisting of fourteen virtues he embodies: justice, love, mercy, goodness, chastity, humility, constancy, loyalty, generosity, good will, obedience, moderation, discipline, and modesty.[31]

The council's manner of proceeding follows the typical pattern for any royal council. God outlines for the assembly what will happen, namely that Lucifer and the angels will revolt (l. 328) and man will disobey his commands (ll. 331–32). After some discussion God asks for a judgement. In their extremely polite deliberation the virtues focus on mankind only. Justice opts for punishment, saying, 'and should he be disobedient, your grievance is justified. But mercy was truly sorry to hear this judgement. She spoke, good lord, have mercy. Justice is resolute in her thinking, is quick with a decision. Lord please mitigate it and look how your human is by nature frail; none of it is wickedness.'[32] In the end mercy and love prevail. God determines that man will be redeemed through the cleansing blood of Christ as he says: 'before I let mankind be lost forever because of my anger, I will give my [son] a human life'.[33] Having initially posed the question of the two 'falls' together, God implies that Lucifer as the first of God's creations to fall prefigures Adam's fall.

What follows next in both Vienna 2921 and 2782 is the chronicle proper with Jans's account of the creation of the angels and the complete Lucifer story with its burlesque dialogue and the three-day rain of devils tumbling into hell. From this point on, Vienna 2921 contains Jans's text exclusively to the extent that it corresponds very closely to the Regensburg text. In essence then, Vienna 2921 reproduces Jans's chronicle except for the master carpenter and council of virtues sections that together are used in place of a prologue. Thus Vienna 2921 avoids the *Christherre* prologue, which is more abstractly theological in its discussion of the Trinity and more scholarly in listing sources.

The construction of dialogue is the most obvious difference among authors. In the council of virtues, the virtues discuss calmly, are never aggressive, and are far more polite and agreeable than any interaction in Jans, who is always more

[31] '[W]ann got ist mit den tugenden vol' (Vienna 2921, l. 315).

[32] '[U]nd wirt [er] dir ungehorsam du pist ym vol von schulde gram. aber die parmherczichait was die red ain rechtes lait. sy sprach genad herr gut die gerechtichait hat vesten mut ir red ist gar swind. herre got die lind[ere] und sich wie dein mentsch ist perait von der natur plödichait es ist alles nicht ain achust' (ll. 338–48).

[33] '[E]e daz durch mein czorn der mentsch ymmer werd verlorn ee wil ich meinen [sun] geben ain sich mentschleiches leben' (ll. 396–99).

down to earth and whose characters are more volatile. In almost every dialogue Jans includes an undercurrent of emotional confrontation or aggression that forces certain words or decisions. The use of dialogue in the story of Lucifer's fall will demonstrate how each prologue relates to the body of Jans's text. This section is typical of Jans's lively dialogues that take on a life of their own, where one character's speech and the immediate response of another drives the action, often without motivation.[34] Thus the interaction between God and Lucifer is beholden to its own rhetorical-narrative frame or logic. When God praises Lucifer as the most wondrous of his angels, he awakens Lucifer's pride so that he chooses to rule as God's equal. When Jans's own prologue precedes the Lucifer section, God's foreknowledge or omniscience does not come into play. As a result, it appears that by praising Lucifer so highly, God has inadvertently caused his angel to revolt. The reader or listener cannot anticipate Lucifer's actions because they develop out of the specific dialogue that kindles Lucifer's pride.

The newly substituted sections lack Jans's personal tone and involvement with the material and with the audience. The authoritative narrators of the *Christherre* prologue and the other introductory segments present themselves as objective transmitters of theological information gleaned from the most important and reputable sources. The new theological material establishes clear expectations and offers typology as a means for understanding the events that follow. The master carpenter section and the advisory council of virtues provide a context and a rationale to the Lucifer story. In fact, it is the structural juxtaposition of the introductory matter and the Lucifer dialogue that sets the typological frame. The council segment confirms God's unified design for salvation because it states that after Lucifer's expulsion God wants to save mankind in order to repopulate heaven with loyal servants (*knechte*). At one level, since God has already conceived his plans, any praise and admiration of Lucifer is superfluous because God's foreknowledge relieves him of causal responsibility in the revolt of the angels. But taken at another level, one might read this scene as an act of God that causes Lucifer's revolt in order to guarantee the salvation events to follow. Such a reading would signify that Lucifer's fall is the prefiguration of Adam's *felix culpa*. This juxtaposition demonstrates yet again that God's omnipotence and guidance is behind all human and natural events. If we take this introductory material seriously as a guide to the chronicle proper, it clearly creates the expecta-

[34] See my article, 'Historical Narrative and Dialogue: The Serious and the Burlesque in Jans der Enikel', in *Narrative Strategies in Medieval German Literature (Kalamazoo Papers 2000–2006)*, ed. by Sibylle Jefferis (Göppingen: Kümmerle, 2008), pp. 151–68.

tion that the chronicle text itself is also to be understood as one unified plan, at least symbolically.

Consequently in these three manuscripts, Jans's secular approach to history writing and personal involvement in his narrative was discarded for a more abstract and theological introduction to the story of God's plan for the world. The differences in the texts compared suggest two potential uses or goals. Jans der Enikel preferred the chatty, homespun narrative style that entertained while he encompassed world history from God's act of creation to his own age. He seems to have tailored his narrative to specific audience interests, particularly because his account reads well aloud. In contrast, manuscripts Linz 472, Vienna 2921, and Vienna 2782 reflect a different set of users who evidently wanted a simple, yet theologically authoritative and informative text with a definite devotional component. The prologue and introductory material in Linz 472 and Vienna 2782 explain the Trinity, produce the theological foundation for world history, and confirm the typological framework for understanding biblical figures and salvation history. Instead of continuing in this vein, however, the theological introduction is interwoven with a biblical retelling from *Christherre* and with a historical account from Jans that is mostly an entertainingly anecdotal and thus memorable sequence of stories about biblical and historical figures. So it seems that a theologically pious prologue is desirable, but then the remainder of the chronicle need not follow the Bible with any great accuracy. A well-told story is more important for many patrons. We have long known that Jans's narrative was very popular in its own right, but now it has been shown that his text was even more influential because it forms the basis of *Christherre* mixtures like Linz 472 and is also the primary text in Vienna 2921.

Even though a great many correspondences exist among manuscripts, this short survey shows that the stitching together of several texts as in these chimeras reveals at least two different sets of expectations and needs. Vienna 2921 lacks the *Christherre* prologue and contains only the master carpenter and the council of virtues. Although both of these sections demonstrate God's master plan, they do so by concrete analogy and dramatic dialogue that presents the devotional message far more vividly to readers and listeners. The new introductory material frames a desire for entertainment as a pious exercise, thus combining the best aspects of the straight biblical *Christherre* with secular storytelling. Vienna codex 2782 certainly fits this description of what patrons wanted, but its world chronicle text also needs to be examined as part of a larger composition within its manuscript. Thus all three manuscripts actually need to be viewed as distinct texts created for individualized use.

Since the chimeric texts reflect commissions filled in workshops, we may note that the trend in the fourteenth century in the Bavarian-Austrian region is to create encyclopedic books containing biblical and secular historical information while also transmitting the unmixed *Christherre* and Jans der Enikel texts. This practice lasted about one hundred years. My comparison nevertheless shows direction, namely that Jans's prologue was less successful than the *Christherre*. Jan's prologue is intimate and less theologically authoritative in tone. Yet in terms of audience and patron reception, Jans's storytelling narrative was definitely popular. Patrons apparently accepted a break in perspective when an authoritative salvation story preceded an entertaining and at times ribald retelling of the biblical and subsequent historical events. In such cases the goal may have been to lend piety to the chronicle text itself and to turn the act of reading or listening into a pleasurable devotional exercise. In sum, the plethora of manuscript texts reflects the ease with which several sources were manipulated to create chimeras that interweave separate texts for individualized use. Each chimera documents one instance in a continuous process of creation and reception of biblical-historical material by a large lay public. Therefore, these chimeras attest to a dynamic literary production that is governed by patrons and workshops rather than by individual authors.

*University of Utah*

# Gifts and Givers that Keep on Giving: Pictured Presentations in Early Medieval Manuscripts

Corine Schleif

This essay is dedicated to Dhira B. Mahoney for two reasons: first Professor Mahoney's work is important to our understanding of prologues, epilogues, and dedication images within the context of literary works. She has examined the ways in which authors employed them to present works to patrons. I would therefore like to use this opportunity to discuss my ideas on a selection of related images in which a donor or maker presents his or her work to a recipient. The second reason is more personal. In contrast to these ostentatious manifestations of giving, Dhira herself has often quietly given of her time in reading and critiquing the work of others. I myself was often the beneficiary of this generosity, which is, I think, the most important form of gift that one scholar can give to another.

I would like to analyse a selection of early examples from the larger context of dedication images, which provide one of the matrices for the presentation miniatures that Professor Mahoney analysed together with their verbal pendents, authorial prologues. This broader category not only encompasses authors but also donors, commissioners, scribes, and illuminators who give their work to God, a saint, saints, ruler, patron, or other users of the object. Springing from roots in late antiquity, these images are among the oldest and most continuous traditions in medieval book illumination.[1] One of my aims is to apply and expand observations

[1] Kurt Weitzmann, 'Book Illustration of the 4th Century: Tradition and Innovation', *Akten des VII. Internationalen Kongresses für christliche Archäologie, Trier, 5–11 September 1965* (Vatican City: Pontifico Instituto di Archeologia Cristiana, 1969), pp. 257–81 (pp. 271–76). On

that Mahoney has made in her very focused study of late medieval authorial presentation miniatures and texts.[2] I will also take advantage of modern theory, particularly that of Marcel Mauss, and postmodern criticism of that theory to analyse these motifs from a conscious perspective of historical distance and to bring them into current discourses.[3]

For the sake of clarity, argument, and perhaps in keeping with my own level of comfort and practice as an art historian, I wish to use a simply defined concrete form of visual image as the basis of my explorations, rather than an abstract or functional category. This form, which can also take on tangible three-dimensional materiality and which can occur in any medium, shows in its most basic configuration a person in the act of giving an object; a recipient of the gift may or may not be present. Throughout the course of the entire Middle Ages and into the early modern period, givers were shown presenting a wide variety of things that they hold in their hands: buildings — especially models of churches, books — open or closed, stained-glass windows, shrines and other reliquaries (presumably) containing relics, portable altars, altar crosses, maps, and even chunks of earth from which grow miniature trees and bushes — implying that the clods with vegetation are intended synecdochically to signify land or territory. Usually these dedication images mark and adorn objects at their outer borders. Like prologues, dedication folios and presentation miniatures commonly introduce a manuscript or printed book as a frontispiece. In other cases, smaller dedication images may inhabit the lower margins of full-page miniatures that function as introductory folios. Similarly, the spaces near the edges of liturgical objects, reliquaries, or in the corners of book covers frequently harbour such representations that acknowledge the origins and the originators of the works.

Closely related to this category of givers bearing gifts are depictions of pious venerators without gifts, that are commonly used in those cases in which the gift is so evident that a representation is unnecessary. In this latter category,

the genesis of dedication images generally, see *Der Darmstädter Hitda-Codex, Bilder und Zierseiten aus der Handschrift 1640 der Hessischen Landes- und Hochschulbibliothek*, ed. by Peter Bloch and Erich Zimmermann (Frankfurt a.M.: Propyläen, 1968), p. 88.

[2] Dhira B. Mahoney, 'Courtly Presentation and Authorial Self-Fashioning: Frontispiece Miniatures in Late Medieval French and English Manuscripts', *Mediaevalia*, 21 (1996), 97–160.

[3] My citations follow Marcel Mauss, *The Gift: The Form and Reason for Exchange in Archaic Societies*, trans. by W. D. Halls, foreword by Mary Douglas (London: Routledge, 2002). The introduction to the translation by Ian Cunnison in Marcel Mauss, *The Gift: Forms and Functions of Exchange in Archaic Societies* (London: Cohen & West, 1970) is likewise helpful.

sometimes termed devotional images, figures kneel at the outer boundaries of their gifts: occupying the outer recesses of the architectural structures they have wrought, for example, the tapering spaces on the left and right of a tympanum over a portal, the wings of the shrine or predella of an altarpiece, or the lower registers of epitaphs.

In all of these cases the motif of the giver can be perceived as ancillary to any understanding of the utility of the object itself and as detached from the action in any larger sacred narrative or hieratic representation, so that the role of the giver is that of pious devoted witness and/or petitioner. On the one hand, the motif of the giver is neither a part of the created object/image it graces nor of the world of those who use/view the piece to which it is affixed; on the other hand, it belongs to both. Likewise the donor decorously and deferentially assumes a humble position, yet at the same time audaciously reminds audiences of his or her doing as *conditio sine qua non* for the object.

Of the larger category of images showing a giver, I have chosen a subset that includes a recipient and in which a book is presented. My study focuses on selected examples from the first half of the Middle Ages. The literature on these presentation miniatures has concentrated largely on cataloguing and inventorying, tracing composition and style from roots in antiquity, and categorizing various forms.[4] Stimulated by some anthropological insights, I would like to probe behind the forms and beyond the conventions, to analyse how particular examples set about accomplishing their presumed goals. We might think of this in terms of pictorial rhetoric, that is, the art of imagining and imaging, as well as in the larger context of visual rhetoric, by which I here refer to the art of the coordinated fashioning of painted pictures and inked words on the surfaces of folios of manuscripts.

[4] The excellent inventory by Joachim Prochno, *Das Schreiber- und Dedikationsbild in der deutschen Buchmalerei* (Leipzig: Teubner, 1929), is still very useful. In the introduction, he voices intentions to produce a second more analytical volume, but his early death left this task unfinished. Peter Bloch's studies linking antecedent motifs, establishing categories, and coining vocabulary has laid the basic structural groundwork. See Peter Bloch, *Das Hornbacher Sakramentar und seine Stellung innerhalb der frühen Reichenauer Buchmalerei* (Basel: Birkhäuser, 1956); Peter Bloch, 'Zum Dedikationsbild im Lob des Kreuzes des Hrabanus Maurus', in *Das erste Jahrtausend: Kultur und Kunst im Werdenden Abendland an Rhein und Ruhr*, ed. by Victor Elbern, 3 vols (Dusseldorf: Schwann, 1962), I (text), 471–94. The dissertation by Bodil Bang Ottesen, 'The Development of Dedication Images in Romanesque Manuscripts' (unpublished doctoral dissertation, University of Maryland, 1987), likewise traces the development of the dedication image and establishes formal types.

In his famous pictorial poem *De laudibus sanctae crucis*, written between 806 and 814 and revised in *c.* 830, Hrabanus Maurus incorporated what is today considered the oldest 'medieval' dedication miniature.[5] Since documentation and sources on Hrabanus abound, this work provides ample opportunity to examine particular forms within a specific historical context. The earliest surviving recensions of the poem, dating from the ninth and tenth centuries, include an image of Hrabanus approaching from the right, bowing slightly, and holding a book in his outstretched hands. Either one or two deacons watch on the left as a centrally enthroned Pope Gregory IV extends his hand or hands to receive the book. In the miniatures in the Vienna, Amiens, and Cambridge manuscripts, Gregory actually clutches the volume,[6] so that a moment is created, in which the book is in the hands of both giver and recipient.[7]

In his provocative and insightful *Essai sur le don, forme archaïque de l'échange* published in 1925, Marcel Mauss analyses not only the social importance of giving in many cultures but also the concomitant 'obligation' of receiving the gift.[8] Gift giving — material, immaterial, or imagined — relies on the acceptance of the gift, which assumes many related implications. Even semantically speaking, something can be offered, but that something only becomes a gift when it is received. Mauss bases his analyses largely on gift exchange among groups of equal status or that

[5] Prochno, *Das Schreiber- und Dedikationsbild*, pp. 11–16; Bloch, 'Zum Dedikationsbild im Lob des Kreuzes', pp. 471–94; *Liber de laudibus sanctae crucis: Vollständige Faksimile-Ausgabe im Originalformat des Codex Vindobonensis 652 der Österreichischen Nationalbibliothek*, ed. by Kurt Holter with commentary (Graz: Akademische Druck- und Verlagsanstalt, 1973); Hans Belting, 'Review of *Liber de laudibus sanctae crucis: Vollständige Faksimile-Ausgabe im Originalformat des Codex Vindobonensis 652 der Österreichischen Nationalbibliothek*', in *Zeitschrift für Kunstgeschichte*, 41 (1978), 162–65; Herrad Spilling, *Opus Magnentii Hrabani Mauri in honorem sanctae crucis conditum: Hrabans Beziehung zu seinem Werk* (Frankfurt a.M.: Knecht, 1992); Michele Camillo Ferrari, 'Hrabanica, Hrabans *De laudibus sanctae crucis* im Spiegel der Neueren Forschung', in *Kloster Fulda in der Welt der Karolinger und Ottonen*, ed. by Gangolf Schrimpf (Frankfurt a.M.: Knecht, 1996), pp. 493–526; Celia Chazelle, *The Crucified God in the Carolingian Era: Theology and Art of Christ's Passion* (Cambridge: Cambridge University Press, 2001), pp. 99–118.

[6] The images for this article may be viewed on the author's own dedicated site <http://www.public.asu.edu/~cschleif/gifts.html>. For this image, see Figure 1 on this site.

[7] Vienna, Nationalbibliothek, MS 652, fol. 2$^v$; Amiens, Bibliothèque municipale, MS 223, fol. 2$^v$; Cambridge, Trinity College Library, MS B 16.3, Dedication folio; reproduced by Prochno, *Das Schreiber- und Dedikationsbild*, pp. 12*, 14*.

[8] Mauss, *Gift*, pp. 16–18.

initiated by those who strive to achieve a relationship on par with another group.[9] Medieval dedication images, such as that of Hrabanus and Pope Gregory, force us to broaden our scope to include exchanges in which a person of lesser rank makes a *prestation* — to use the Maussian term referring to the entire act of giving — to someone whose higher rank is decidedly unattainable. Here the acceptance of the gift bears slightly different and perhaps even greater import. The giver must first dare to suggest that he or she has a gift that will be of significance for the person of higher rank in a very hierarchical society. The acceptance, real or only imagined as imaged, confers the ultimate approbation on the giver. This custom of ascribing equal representation to giving and receiving by showing the recipient actively taking the gift is continued into early modern times, but, although it was common during the early Middle Ages, it later forms the exception rather than the rule.

It is not surprising that Hrabanus would so self-consciously exhibit himself in this way. One of his greatest accomplishments as abbot at Fulda was recording the names of all the monks so that they could be individually memorialized through rituals of confraternity that involved the reading of names and exchange of lists among monasteries.[10] In the *De laudibus sanctae crucis*, Hrabanus also wove his own name into several of the word pictures that make up the small sub-poems in various shapes within the larger full-page poems, all of which comprised the *carmina figurata*. For example, in one of his geometric motifs he incorporated 'Magnentius Hrabanus Maurus made this work'.[11] Inventively he likewise included himself in his visual exercises by positioning beneath one of his crossword-puzzle-like crosses a devotional image of himself labelled with *titulus* and including, the words of his prayer as a sub-poem superimposed on his kneeling body.[12] Although Hrabanus extends his gratitude to Hatto, an artist who participated in the project, scholars debate whether Hrabanus himself may have

[9] For anthropological purposes, Raymond Firth has expanded on some of the observations by Mauss to take the relative status and rank of giver and recipient into account as well as their different levels of resources. See his remarks in the chapter 'Themes in Economic Anthropology: a General Commentary', in *Themes in Economic Anthropology*, ed. by Raymond Firth, Association of Social Anthropology Monograph, 6 (London: Routledge, Kegan & Paul, 1967), as well as Michel Panoff, 'Marcel Mauss's "The Gift" Revisited', *Man*, n.s., 5 (1970), 60–70 (p. 67).

[10] Raymund Kottje, 'Schriftlichkeit im Dienst der Klosterverwaltung und des Klösterlichen Lebens unter Hrabanus Maurus', in *Kloster Fulda*, ed. by Schrimpf, pp. 177–92.

[11] 'Magnentius Hrabanus Maurus hoc opus fecit': Vienna, Nationalbibliothek, MS 652, fol. 5r.

[12] See <http://www.public.asu.edu/~cschleif/gifts.html>, Figure 2.

painted the images in the word configurations.[13] It is worthy of note that Hatto's (self-)image is not included.

Hrabanus may have perceived a complex and comprehensive *prestation* narrative that he takes up at several places in his work. The image of the author beneath the cross, itself in combination with the accompanying verses, testifies that the work is devoted to the praise of the cross. What is more, in the two oldest rescensions, both believed to have been fashioned while Hrabanus was still at Fulda, yet a third miniature includes the author and addresses the work's origins. On the folio immediately preceding that of the miniature with Pope Gregory, an illumination shows Hrabanus recommended by Alcuin, appearing before Saint Martin of Tours.[14] Gestures and positioning play an important role: Hrabanus is depicted approaching from the left, his feet apart and left knee flexed to express the vigor of his stride. The figure of Alcuin engulfs that of Hrabanus: Alcuin's arm protectively draped over the shoulders of Hrabanus with parts of Alcuin's anatomy closer to the enthroned saint than is Hrabanus, all of which denotes Alcuin's role as mediator.[15] The saint, already in possession of several bound volumes that he holds against his upper torso, raises his hand in the sign of blessing in the direction of the large codex that Hrabanus holds in his outstretched hands. In the accompanying text, Hrabanus writes in the first person as if he were either ghost-writing his own letter of recommendation, or as if he had previously recorded the voice of Alcuin, prior to his death in 804, as Alcuin lauded the virtues of his pupil Hrabanus. In either case the text was meant for the ears of Pope Gregory. According to one theory, the three representations are the accumulated vestiges of individual no-longer-extant codices that were made at the Fulda abbey and dedicated respectively: the first copy to the cross itself, another to the monastery of St Martin at Tours where Hrabanus had studied under the tutelage of Alcuin, and a third to Pope Gregory IV by whom Hrabanus hoped to be appointed to the archbishopric of Mainz — an aspiration that was fulfilled

[13] *Liber de laudibus sanctae crucis*, ed. by Holter, commentary volume, pp. 9–11; *Rabanus Maurus in seiner Zeit, 780–1980* [exhibition catalogue] (Mainz: Mittelrheinisches Landesmuseum, 1980), p. 34.

[14] Rome, Vatican Library, MS Reg. Christ. Lat. 124, fol. 2ᵛ; Vienna, Nationalbibliothek, MS 652, fol. 1ᵛ; reproduced by Prochno, *Das Schreiber- und Dedikationsbild*, pp. 11* and 12*. See <http://www.public.asu.edu/~cschleif/gifts.html>, Figure 3.

[15] On the gesture of commendation, recommendation, or accompaniment, see Bloch, *Das Hornbacher Sakramentar*, pp. 58–59; Bloch, 'Zum Dedikationsbild im Lob des Kreuzes des Hrabanus Maurus', pp. 471–94.

much later with the aid of Emperor Lothar.[16] I would suggest, since Hrabanus himself could closely advise the production of these manuscripts, it is likely that the motifs were not collected or collated through the copying process merely as lingering inadvertent leftovers. Rather they might have been intended here to function cumulatively or even serially. The representation with Saint Martin may show a kind of presaging and spiritual commissioning of the pictorial poem; the subsequent illumination on the next folio would then signal the presentation and acceptance of the finished book, and the image of Hrabanus beneath the cross would express the ultimate goal of the work, thus affecting for Hrabanus threefold acknowledgment of his work.

The sequence must be considered a kind of pictogram or personified diagram. Although the characters are identified as real historical personalities and they are rendered with the degree of verisimilitude that was expected during the Carolingian era, they could never have come together. Imagined meetings through which Hrabanus fashioned his own doing through the approbation of an early Christian saint, an official in the court of Charlemagne who had been his mentor, and a reigning pope in the company of his entourage could take on visual form as pictorial reality, not lived or performed reality. In the miniatures, the author likewise humbly cloaks his own authorial agency in the terms of a commissioned work that he executes in the service of persons mightier than he. Of course, what by today's standards would first appear as voluntary self-effacement might have in its day been perceived as a dauntless yet decorous self-fashioning that put him personally into active relationships with personages of higher standing, some dead, some alive. At this moment in history these forms of higher approbation certainly carried more weight than would assertions of artistic innovation or creative applications of fourth-century traditions in the pictorial poem, the qualities for which his work is often praised today.

If we analyse the miniatures and look for their formal antecedents, we find that both conform to late antique images that show frontal views of rulers who assume central positions seated on a throne, as their subjects pay them homage approaching as if striding into the image from the left or the right. The best-known examples that conform to this type do not show historical persons but personifications of the provinces or the 'Barbarians' bearing tribute, for example those on consular diptychs such as the Barberini Diptych dating from *c.* 500, in the Louvre. Art historians have long demonstrated that this formal composition

[16] Prochno, *Das Schreiber- und Dedikationsbild*, pp. 11–16; *Liber de laudibus sanctae crucis*, ed. by Holter, pp. 22–31.

as well as its content survives in the famous double-folio representation of the Four Provinces Bringing Tribute to Emperor Otto III in the Gospel Book of Otto III, dating from *c.* 1000.[17] On the early ninth-century ivory cover for the Lorsch Gospel Book, the composition was employed to represent the three Magi, who, like the personifications of the provinces, approach the enthroned Virgin and Child bringing their offerings. Peter Bloch persuasively demonstrated that the first dedication images likewise adopted this compositional form, and we may observe that some of the notions of paying tribute and bringing offerings also linger here in this extended usage.[18] The early art historical literature often postulates that the images ultimately imitate court ceremonies; at the same time, however, the iconography is employed as evidence for such rituals. Dhira Mahoney has convincingly argued against the assertions of previous scholars, who held that the late medieval authorial presentations were always pictorial representations of ceremonies or re-presentations. Erik Inglis, looking more generally at late medieval presentations, has located a mere seven examples of what he characterizes as narrative accounts of rituals of presentation, two of which he believes anticipate a ceremony before it has taken place — an assertion he makes of the miniatures as well, since they have all been incorporated into the object as it was made. The five other examples he believes report an actual event after it has occurred.[19] Following Mahoney's critical approach, a more nuanced interdisciplinary look at all of the pictorial and textual sources on presentation images also from the early Middle Ages is now certainly in order if we wish to disentangle the uses of metaphor from actual enactments, the performance of ritual from the performance of memory, as well as to appreciate the ways in which various media participated in providing the religious models of and models for society — to paraphrase Clifford Geertz.[20]

[17] Fridolin Dressler, Florentine Mütterich, and Helmut Beumann, *Das Evangeliar Ottos III. (Clm 4453) der Bayerischen Staatsbibliothek München*, commentary volume to facsimile (Munich: Fischer, 1978); Wolfgang Christian Schneider, 'Imperator Augustus und Christomimetes: Das Selbstbild Ottos III. in der Buchmalerei', in *Europas Mitte um 1000*, ed. by Alfried Wieczorek and Hans-Martin Hinz, 3 vols [exhibition catalogue] (Theiss: Stuttgart, 2000), II, 798–808. See <http://www.public.asu.edu/~cschleif/gifts.html>, Figure 4.

[18] Bloch, *Das Hornbacher Sakramentar*, p. 59.

[19] Erik Inglis, 'A Book in the Hand: Some Late Medieval Accounts of Manuscript Presentations', *Journal of the Early Book Society for the Study of Manuscripts and Printing History*, 5 (2002), 57–97; I wish to thank Joyce Coleman for calling this article to my attention.

[20] Cliford Geertz, 'Religion as a Cultural System', *Anthropological Approaches to the Study of Religion*, ed. by Michael Banton (London: Tavistock, 1966), pp. 1–46.

During the Carolingian era, the import of giving a book and having it accepted must have been widely understood among book users, and the associated pictorial syntax must have enjoyed instant recognition. Remarkable are two representations, in which tiny, for the most part unidentified, figures take part in a book presentation. In both cases, the recipients, although of high standing, are not rendered as rulers positioned frontally seated on a throne, but are rather shown in profile as are the givers of the codices, thus underscoring the active engagement on both sides.[21] In a Gospel book, a small medallion embedded within the initial *L* from the *Liber generationes* of the first chapter of Matthew contains an archbishop receiving a book from a cleric.[22] In the Marmoutiers Sacramentary, a figure identified through the lettering on his throne as Abbot Raganald rises to bless a throng of clerics and lay, who approach, bowing before him, the first of whom distinguishes himself from the crowd by presenting the Abbot with an oversized book that the cleric carries open as a considerable burden resting on his back.[23] Again in these cases we witness the significance of the gift's acknowledgment and the importance of the one who acknowledges, since in both cases the receiver's office is supplied and in one case also his name. Recently Bernhard Jussen has conducted a semantic analysis of early medieval sermon and tractate texts with respect to the use of various terms for gift and giving. He notes that here too acceptance of the gift by God or a personage of high rank was semantically important.[24]

The original viewers of the miniatures, who may have included the recipients represented, would have known the identities of those important characters depicted without *tituli*. The clerics must have thought that for future generations of users it would be enough to be recognized as those individuals responsible for the making of the book in which their tiny, simply rendered figures are contained.

[21] On traditions and frontal and profile views see Meyer Shapiro's semiotic analysis *Words and Pictures: On the Literal and the Symbolic in the Illustration of a Text* (The Hague: Mouton, 1973).

[22] Wolfenbüttel, Herzog August Bibliothek, MS 16 Aug. Fol. Evangeliar, fol. 5$^{r}$; Prochno, *Das Schreiber- und Dedikationsbild*, pp. 10*–10.

[23] Autun, Bibliothèque municipale, MS 19 bis: Marmoutiers Sacramentary, fol. 173$^{v}$; Prochno, *Das Schreiber- und Dedikationsbild*, pp. 9–9*. See <http://www.public.asu.edu/~cschleif/gifts.html>, Figure 5.

[24] Berhard Jussen, 'Religious Discourses of the Gifts in the Middle Ages: Semantic Evidences (Second to Twelfth Centuries)', in *Negotiating the Gift: Pre-Modern Figurations of Exchange*, ed. by Gadi Algazi, Valentin Groebner, and Berhard Jussen (Gottingen: Vandenhoeck & Ruprecht, 2003), pp. 173–92 (p. 183).

Indeed, in his comprehensive study of images of scribes, authors, donors, and commissioners, Joachim Prochno notes that many of them are not accompanied by identifying inscriptions.[25] For these persons, it must have sufficed to be deemed one of the originators.

Dedication pages are frequently included in Ottonian manuscripts, but the sequence of folios in the late tenth-century Hornbach Sacramentary boasts the longest and largest linear visualization of a book being given and received.[26] In this series of four full-page illuminations with inscriptions festively lettered in gold on purple ground on the facing pages, the book is presented and then re-presented so that it moves from the possession of one individual through three others finally coming to rest in the hands of Christ. The series begins on folio 7$^{v}$: a tonsured monk hands the book to another tonsured figure, whose crozier identifies him as an abbot.[27] The text on folio 8$^{r}$ reads:

> Pastor Adalbert, highly conversant in heavenly teachings, abbot, worthy of reverence, preserved in great accomplishments: receive this gift graciously. It is presented to you by Eburnant, who although unworthy, is from his heart completely devoted and always the most willing servant of your wishes. Lord, so I extend to you this book, that I wrote myself, that you as a monk enliven out of it pious reverence. I beseech you therefore, that the scribe, just as you, will receive heavenly reward.[28]

Thus Eburnant identifies himself as the writer or scribe, whose work probably included not only the lavishly produced facing pages of text but also the skillfully rendered figural miniatures.[29] Abbot Adalbert, whose rule of the monastery at Hornbach in the Palatinate began no later than 972 and ended no earlier than 993, is undoubtedly the administrator who commissioned the monk Eburnant to make the manuscript for their monastery, and Eburnant thus defers to Adalbert

[25] Prochno, *Das Schreiber- und Dedikationsbild*, p. vii.

[26] Solothurn, Zentralbibliothek, Codex U 1; Prochno, *Das Schreiber- und Dedikationsbild*, pp. 30–31*. For a detailed analysis of the postures and gestures as well as transcriptions and German translations of the facing page texts, see Bloch, *Das Hornbacher Sakramentar*, pp. 23–27, 68–76, and *Ornamenta Ecclesiae: Kunst und Künstler der Romanik*, ed. by Anton Legner [exhibition catalogue] (Cologne: Schnütgen-Museum, 1985), pp. 139–42, 150.

[27] See <http://www.public.asu.edu/~cschleif/gifts.html>, Figure 6.

[28] According to the transcription in Bloch, *Das Hornbacher Sakramentar*, p. 23: 'Pastor Adalberte, summa cate caelibus arte / Qui meritis constas vitae venerabilis abbas. / Praebeo quod dulus gratanter suscipe munus / Eburnant vilis tibi tota mente fidelis / Semper ubique tui promptissimus assecla voti / Scriptor domne tibi praesens quem porrigo libri / Quo tu cum sanctum celebres christicola cultum / Tecum scriptori pia praemia posce mereri'.

[29] Bloch, *Das Hornbacher Sakramentar*, p. 17.

asking that he, as the person responsible for initiating the project, enliven the work as pious gift.[30] Mauss was among the first of the anthropologists to point out that the thing given is not inert. It is 'invested with life'.[31] These words prompt us to ponder the many ways in which the sacramentary was alive and would remain alive longer than its makers and saintly patrons, passing on into many more hands of users. For this reason, this book, like other medieval books, was a most suitable place to affix memorial images and inscriptions.

Upon turning the page, the reader sees the figure of Adalbert handing the book to an individual whose tonsured head is encircled by a gold nimbus.[32] The text on the opposite page reads:

> Pirmin, first among us, shining as a golden light on earth, brightly transfigured by God's glory and by the fervor of your faith, do not reject the gift of your servant Adalbert. May your goodness receive me myself in this gift, which I extend to you, although not as I must as your debtor. Here it shall always and eternally remain in your service, I beseech you. Should a wayward robber take it away out of this building, it shall punish the sin through the revenge of divine anger.[33]

Saint Pirmin was the founder of the monastery, and here stands for the monastery as an ongoing institution and community. This text articulates quite self-consciously many aspects of pious gifts that Mauss would later observe to be general characteristics of gift exchange in many cultures, including the notion that through a gift the giver is giving herself or himself and a portion of the self continues to reside in the gift.[34] Indeed all of the examples studied here include pictures of the giver that go on down through time with the gift. If we take the images literally, the giver never relinquishes his hold on the gift. Thus it could be expected that the giver within the gift and his wishes would continue for all time to be respected by recipients. Perhaps even more astonishing is the potential apotropaic power that the author recognizes in this object and invokes in the event that it is removed from the monastery of Hornbach. Book curses, some of

[30] For historical sources on Hornbach, see Bloch, *Das Hornbacher Sakramentar*, pp. 19–21.

[31] Mauss, *Gift*, p. 16.

[32] See <http://www.public.asu.edu/~cschleif/gifts.html>, Figure 7.

[33] According to the transcription in Bloch, *Das Hornbacher Sakramentar*, p. 25: 'Praesul Permini fulgens lux aurea mundi / Incola clare dei succensus amore fidei / Istud Adalberti munus non descipe servi / Dextra sed alma tui capiat me munere tali / Quod tibi vile fero non quantum debitor exto / Hic tibi servitio maneat rogo tempore cuncto / Aedibus ex istis ferat hoc si frivolus hostis / Ulcio divinae quod crimen vindicet irae'.

[34] Mauss, *Gift*, p. 16.

which approach the comical, are certainly not unusual in this period.[35] Yet, this curse specifically demands that the book avenge the transgression, and thus likewise expresses the implicit magical or supernatural powers, perhaps also irrational functions, that Mauss perceives as intrinsic to gifts. In contrast to the request that Adalbert enliven the book for purposes of devotion, here we read that this animated object is likewise charged with meting out punishment. Quite typically the curse is directed toward a thief who would remove it from the institution and thus separate it from the donor's intended recipients and purpose. Although on this point Mauss follows other anthropologists who collected evidence among the Maori, whose gifts were charged with destroying persons when the implicit givers' conditions were not met, even more emphatically, expectations could be attached to medieval objects, especially books since the written word facilitated such embedded colophonic messages.[36] Indeed the power of the medieval book curse lies in the fact that writers — either scribes or donors — had the temerity to attach these threats as permanent potential doom conveyed in the same medium as the sacred texts themselves. In the Hornbach Sacramentary, the sainted founder of the abbey is addressed as the witness to the destructive power with which the donor has imbued his gift.

Turning another leaf, the viewer sees the next pair of figures. Here Saint Pirmin bows his head so that his cheek touches the hand of another saint who is in the act of receiving the codex.[37] Thus the miniature shows more intimate contact between the founder and the monastery's titular saint than in all the other pairs of figures. The text reads:

> Gatekeeper, who has been entrusted with the keys to the hall of heaven, likewise shepherd of the community, Saint Peter, called the Rock, who has been given the great power to redeem sinners, with extreme feelings, Pirmin, bowing, approaches you. Here I extend to you that which the abbot entrusted to me. He wants to please you through the giving of this divine book, which is dedicated to you and devoted from his heart so that because of it the doors of heaven can be opened.[38]

[35] On clamours and curses, see Lester K. Little, *Benedictine Maledictions: Liturgical Cursing in Romanesque France* (Ithaca: Cornell University Press, 1993). See also Phyllis R. Brown's essay, 'Rhetoric and Reception: Guillaume de Machaut's "Je Maudi"', in the present volume.

[36] Mauss, *Gift*, pp. 13–16.

[37] See <http://www.public.asu.edu/~cschleif/gifts.html>, Figure 8.

[38] According to the transcription in Bloch, *Das Hornbacher Sakramentar*, p. 26: 'Janitor aethereae commissis clavibus aulae. / Pastor et ecclesiae dictus de nomine Petrae / Utque reos solvas data cui veneranda potestas / Adsum Perminius dimisso pectore pronus. / Haec tibi com-

Thus Pirmin repeats the expectation of eternal salvation as a return gift, and the author of the text has rhetorically connected it with Saint Peter's special role as the keeper of the keys to heaven, implicitly the head of the Church with its power to administer grace. By mentioning that Pirmin's gift proceeds from his heart or his soul (*mens*) the author employs a semantic constellation that Jussen has found often in medieval discourses of the gift, one that stresses the value not of the utility or luxury of the object itself but the manner in which it is given and the attitude of the giver.[39]

The final folio in the series shows Saint Peter giving the book to a figure with a crossed nimbus.[40] The accompanying text reads:

> Teacher of virtues, one who leads us to heaven, you with the divine sceptre, purchase us sinners, save those born on earth. Peter, your unworthy bearer of the keys, your charge and the object of your protection, with whom you were close and whom you saved from great dangers, extends to you what he has received, Adalbert's gift of the abbot. Give him for this earthly gift the reward of eternal life, so that he deserves to stand in the margins of the Eternal Book. In this the writer and the patron of the writer delight together.[41]

Interestingly the author goes so far as to ascribe a humility topos to Saint Peter, whom he quotes as calling himself 'unworthy'. This final text conveys a more strongly worded demand for reciprocity, in which Peter asserts that he 'deserves' to have his name in the Eternal Book — although another expression of modesty follows, in that Peter only claims a place in the 'margins'. One of Mauss's major tenets is the receiver's obligation to reciprocate with a return gift. In donation narratives like this one, the notion of making God one's debtor is not uncommon, although the pictorial gift giving always and only is represented in one direction.[42] To a degree, this somewhat surprising *do ut des* was already promoted

mendans meus ut mihi credidit abbas / Vilia divini tibi mittit xenia libri / Quem tibi sacravit ac tota mente patravit / Caeli cui cardo pateat pro munere servo'.

[39] Jussen, 'Religious Discourses', pp. 179–83.

[40] See <http://www.public.asu.edu/~cschleif/gifts.html>, Figure 9.

[41] According to the transcription in *Das Hornbacher Sakramentar*, p. 27: 'Virtutum doctor pie noster ad aethera ductor / Salvans terrigenas caeli qui ceptra gubernas / Claviger indignus sub te nutritus alumnus. / Sepius adiutus tua per munimina Petrus / Do tibi quod praefert meus abbas munus Adalbert / Cui pro terrenis da vitae praemia donis / Perpetis ut libri mereatur margine scribi /Gaudeat hinc scriptor pariter scriptoris et actor'.

[42] In the essay on sacrifice, which Mauss authored in collaboration with Henri Hubert, the two anthropologists address transcultural practices of making offerings to deities in order to compel their benefaction. See 'Essai sur la nature et la fonction du sacrifice', *Année Sociologique*,

by the Church Fathers. In the rhetoric of Tertulian, 'A good deed makes God or Christ a debtor.' Employing an even more mercantile metaphor, John Chrysostomus contended that the faithful should view good works as currency and buy their salvation cheaply as if they were at an annual fair.[43] Such crass, cold, and calculating demands were theologically problematic. In other words, a great degree of theological acrobatics was necessary to justify these ostensibly simplistic statements. Eliana Magnani S.-Christen contours the doctrinal logic using eleventh- and twelfth-century sources. Humankind could exchange ephemeral temporal goods for permanent eternal salvation because God had bestowed this facility through the sacrifice of his son. Saints, particularly the patrons of monasteries who were the beneficiaries of donors' largess, were thus obligated to testify on behalf of the donors before God.[44] Needless to say, the right of the faithful to negotiate with God was as old as the rhetoric of the Genesis story of Jacob, who wrestles with an angel in order to extract a blessing. Stepping back once more to assume historical and critical distance, we might consider the ideology of gift exchange, here particularly in forms that reflected and promoted the medieval feudal paradigm. Giving and taking evoked the patterns of loyalty, commitment, and protection that were manifest in bonds of fealty and vassalage.[45]

In her work on late medieval authorial presentations Dhira B. Mahoney carefully contrasted the texts with the images. The Hornbach Sacramentary provides a rare example in which text and image are given equal space. The images present a motif that was instantly recognizable as a set of dedication representations, they convey the notion of a chain of mediation, they express self-reflexivity through the depiction of a book — the book in which the images occur — and they show through their careful rendering of garments and facial features that the individuals, at least those at the beginning of the sequence are reasonably ordinary

2 (1899), 29–138; *Sacrifice: Its Nature and Function*, trans. by W. D. Halls, foreword by E. E. Evans-Pritchard (London: Routledge, 1964).

[43] Hermann Henrici, *Üeber Schenkungen an die Kirche* (Weimar: Böhlau, 1916), pp. 6–10; Eliana Magnani S.-Christen, 'Transforming Things and Persons: The Gift *pro anima* in the Eleventh and Twelfth Centuries', in *Negotiating the Gift*, ed. by Algazi, Groebner, and Jussen, pp. 269–84 (p. 281).

[44] S.-Christen, 'Transforming Things and Persons', pp. 280–81.

[45] S.-Christen, 'Transforming Things and Persons', p. 282; Ludolf Kuchenbuch, '*Porcus donativus*: Language Use and Gifting in Seigneurial Records between the Eighth and the Twelfth Centuries', in *Negotiating the Gift*, ed. by Algazi, Groebner, and Jussen, pp. 193–246.

persons with whom viewers could easily identify. The texts on the other hand are set apart as special, luxuriously produced inscriptions in verse, they identify all of the characters, their carefully crafted content is molded to fit these individuals, and each text is composed as a prayer, written in the first person, and expressing the person's innermost desires for salvation.

One obvious question remains: who authored these texts and pictures? If we approach the question somewhat empathically, we might imagine a dialogical origin within the Hornbach monastery, with Adalbert initiating the project of producing a sacramentary manuscript and assigning the work or at least some of it to Eburnant, who with the consent of his abbot strives to put himself at the lowest level in the chain of intercession. We will never know whether Adalbert had conceived the pictorial and textual cycle consisting of the last three images and texts and Eburnant added himself as the first gift giver, or whether Eburnant was the author of the idea for the entire sequence. A recent technical discovery about the dedication image in the nearly contemporary Codex Egberti aids us in our imaginings. A large central image of Bishop Egbert enthroned is flanked by smaller figures of two tonsured monks, Keraldus on the left and Heribertus on the right.[46] While Keraldus raises the book that he holds so that Egbert can take possession of it, Heribertus simply holds a book in his outstretched hands. Doris Oltrogge and Robert Fuchs have established that the presence of Keraldus was planned from the outset but Heribertus was added to the composition while the work was in progress.[47] It is unknown exactly what roles the two monks played; perhaps one was the scribe and the other the illuminator. It is, however, quite imaginable that either Heribertus joined the project after the miniature was roughed out or that he expressed a wish to be included in the visual 'credits' for the project only after the work was underway.

Other examples of relaying the gift from one participant to the next abound. Illuminators of the tenth through the twelfth centuries appear to have delighted in the challenge of inventing ways of conveying these chains of advocacy and intercession that provided the implicit content for the relays or repetitions in

[46] See <http://www.public.asu.edu/~cschleif/gifts.html>, Figure 10.

[47] The pigments of the cowl worn by Heribertus are of a slightly different mixture than that of Keraldus, and the figure of Heribertus is painted over the purple ground rather than anticipating the figure by leaving the space for the figure blank as was done with Keraldus. Subsequent to the addition of the figure the gold details were applied to the entire miniature. See Doris Oltrogge and Robert Fuchs, 'Mit Infrarot und Röntgenstrahl: Ergebnisse naturwissenschaftlicher und kunsttechnologischer Untersuchungen des Egbert-Codex', in *Der Egbert Codex* [exhibition catalogue] (Trier: Stadtbibliothek, 2006), pp. 189–216 (pp. 198–99).

which a book or a *prestation*, as gesture of acclamation or supplication, was suggestively passed along like a bucket of water in a bucket brigade. According to Prochno, the custom of splitting the chain into its discrete links of exchanges goes back at least as far as the Reims Sacramentary (*c.* 800), which was destroyed in an eighteenth-century fire.[48] In at least two books that survive, the passing of the gift is spread over more than one folio: the Darmstadt Pericopes dating from *c.* 970, and the even more elaborate Egbert Psalter, completed between 977 and 980, in which each participant occupies his own page.[49] Some of the chains represented on single folios are arranged horizontally, for example that in an early eleventh-century manuscript in Einsiedeln containing Saint Gregory's *Moralia of Job*, which reads from left to right or that in the *Heiligenleben* in Berlin, which follows from right to left.[50] In another chain, the book first implicitly assumes a horizontal direction moving from left to right and then a vertical one, ending with a half-length image of Christ at the top of the folio.[51] The chain of dedication in an eleventh-century Gospel book possibly from Arras now in Boulogne-sur-Mer, follows a vertical composition.[52] In each of the four last examples, the book is depicted only once and the figures are otherwise linked through their placement, their gestures, or the direction of their gazes. If we were to include here all *prestations* in which the book is not pictured our list would be substantially longer.

One of the most innovative chains of *prestation* without depicting the actual giving of the book is that in the initial *P* that introduces the first text column in Florus's commentary on the letters of Saint Paul, a manuscript produced in the years 1163–64 in and for the monastery at Corbie and today housed in the Bibliothèque nationale de France in Paris.[53] Working cleverly with his compass,

[48] Prochno, *Das Schreiber- und Dedikationsbild*, p. 29.

[49] Prochno, *Das Schreiber- und Dedikationsbild*, pp. 28–29, 32–33; *Psalterium Egberti, Facsimile del ms. CXXXVI del Museo Archeological Nazionale di Cividale del Friuli a cura di Claudio Barberi* (Venice: Ministero per I beni e le attivita culturali del Friuli-Venezia, 2000), and commentary volume.

[50] Einsiedeln, Stiftsbibliothek, Hs. 151, fol. 1ᵛ; Berlin, Staatsbibliothek, Hs. Theol. Lat. Fol. 268, fol. 234ᵛ; Prochno, *Das Schreiber- und Dedikationsbild*, pp. 24, 98.

[51] Munich, Bayerische Staatsbibliothek, Clm 6831, fol. 2ʳ; Prochno, *Das Schreiber- und Dedikationsbild*, p. 100.

[52] Boulogne Sur-Mer, Bibliothèque de la Ville, MS 9, fol. 1ʳ; Prochno, *Das Schreiber- und Dedikationsbild*, p. 71.

[53] J. J. G. Alexander, *Initials from Large Manuscripts* (New York: Braziller, 1978), no. 24; *Ornamenta Ecclesiae*, p. 239 (Roswitha Neu-Kock). See <http://www.public.asu.edu/~cschleif/gifts.html>, Figure 11.

the illuminator incorporated several round frames and mandorlas that harmonize as repetitions of the circular forms of the loop of the *P*, the crescent moon of a starry sky, and the winding tendrils of an interlace pattern. Read from bottom to top, the first circle frames a harp-playing hybrid animal. The next is inhabited by the lay illuminator, who identifies himself with the *titulus* 'Felix', and defines his contribution by showing himself seated with a board, parchment, and pots of paint. The following medallion exhibits a venerating monk identified as Richerus. According to the manuscript's colophon he commissioned the manuscript. In the mandorla at the juncture of the stem and the loop of the initial, Saint Paul, with his characteristic receding hairline is seated following the manner of late antique author portraits. A banderole connects him with the woman, whose *titulus* identifies her as 'Phoebe' in the narrative below and to his left. The text recommends her to the congregation at Rome, which is represented as men labelled 'Romani' emerging from the city to the right, marked 'Roma'. Across the loop of the *P* in another almond-shaped frame a nameless character in classical garb sits and writes on a board attached to his chair via a moveable arm. His back turned to the other figures in this historiated and inhabited initial, he faces the right column of text on the folio. In the uppermost mandorla, Christ, his hands raised in the gesture of blessing and displaying an orb, rules over all. If indeed the writer is Florus, then the scribe Johannes Monoculus who supplies his name and the date in the book's colophon is remarkably omitted from the chain of intercession, supplication, and benefaction. We do not know if the illuminator and/or commissioner made these decisions; nor are we privy to their motivations, but we note that only the necessary labels were included as *tituli* and that authors here play an important role.

Compared with all the other 'chains' of giving and receiving, the Hornbach Sacramentary is unique in that the middle participants, Adalbert, Pirmin, and Peter, all have dual roles. Each is both a giver and a receiver, and thus the changed identities that the gift effected are expressed, while the notion that the recipient is obliged to reciprocate is diagrammatically elaborated in such a way as to confound the simple notion of the counter-gift directed back toward the initiating donor.[54]

The most common forms of book *prestations* during the early Middle Ages, however, depicted one person — a donor or commissioner of a work — handing

[54] On such complexities enabled by the gift as a modelling device see especially Gadi Algazi, 'Introduction: Doing Things with Gifts', in *Negotiating the Gift*, ed. by Algazi, Groebner, and Jussen, pp. 9–27.

a book to a saintly patron. The dedication image in the well-known Hitda Codex, a Gospel book dating from the second quarter of the eleventh century and today in Darmstadt, typifies this form.[55] The miniature shows a woman labelled above in gold letters 'Hitda Abbess', who, clad in a long tunic with opulently wide sleeves and a long and luxurious white textured or ruffled veil, holds a codex with her arms outstretched. The book is received by a second woman labelled above as 'Saint Walburga', who, likewise elaborately arrayed and veiled, stands on a pedestal, holds a golden martyr's palm, and is adorned by a golden nimbus. The illuminator has skillfully shown the Abbess entering the space of the saint which is defined by an arched opening. Above, an assortment of mighty architectural elements suggestive of church towers and transept arms serve as a monumental baldachin protecting and honouring the saint. As in the Hornbach Sacramentary, the accompanying text appears in gold on a purple-stained ground on the facing page: 'Saint Walburga, Abbess Hitda [gives, donates, or presents] this book for herself and hers.'[56]

The verb appears to have been expressed in the image and thus it could be excluded from the text. In addition to asking for benefaction for herself she requests it for those who belong to her, implying her family, which would include her biological relatives as well as her monastic family. For some, the saintly recipient might have been considered a kind of legal or administrative shorthand reference to the institution, but for many the saint was viewed as the actual intimately experienced, although ahistorical, recipient.[57] Stefen Beissel, Patrick Geary, Lester Little, and others remind us that to steal from a church was to steal from its saint; saints could allow or disallow the translation or theft of their relics; offending a monastery was to risk the wrath of its patron saint.[58] Lists of the abbesses of Meschede are no longer extant, although a lengthy list bound into the

[55] Darmstadt, Universitäts- und Landesbibliothek, Hs. 1640, fols 5$^{v}$-6$^{r}$; Prochno, *Das Schreiber- und Dedikationsbild*, p. 61; *Der Darmstädter Hitda-Codex, Bilder und Zierseiten*, ed. by Bloch and Zimmermann; Gude Suckale-Redlefsen, in *Krone und Schleier: Kunst aus mittelalterlichen Frauenklöstern* [exhibition catalogue] (Munich: Hirmer, 2005), pp. 167–69. See <http://www.public.asu.edu/~cschleif/gifts.html>, Figure 12.

[56] According to the transcription in *Der Darmstädter Hitda-Codex*, ed. by Bloch and Zimmermann, p. 13: 'Hunc Librum S[an]c[ta]e Walburg[a]e HITDA ABATISS[A] pro se suisq[ue]'.

[57] Corine Schleif, *Donatio et Memoria* (Munich: Deutscher Kunstverlag, 1990), pp. 17–18.

[58] Stefan Beissel, *Die Verehrung der Heiligen und ihrer Reliquien in Deutschland* (Freiburg: Herder 1890, 1892); Patrick Geary, *Furta Sacra* (Princeton: Princeton University Press, 1978); Little, *Benedictine Maledictions*.

codex and dating somewhat later, details substantial donations attributed to the same donor. According to one hypothesis she is identical with Ida, a granddaughter of Emperor Otto II, who ruled as abbess of Sankt Maria im Kapitol in Cologne and died in 1060.[59] If this is the case, the book provides an example of an abbess from another institution seeking to form a bond with Meschede that is forged through gift giving and articulated in word and image.

Here as with most examples observed above, all of which depicted men, the devotee and the saint or ruler are not represented in differing sizes according to their rank, nor is the presenter shown kneeling. The same observations can be made for other instances in which women are involved in *prestations*, for example, the miniature in a late eleventh-century Gospel book from the monastery at Weingarten, believed to have been fashioned in Flanders, in which Duchess Judith presents her book to Christ.[60] It would thus appear that specific gender conventions meant to underscore the humility of a female donor did not obtain during the earliest centuries of presentation images. This stands in contrast to what Dhira Mahoney has demonstrated in some authorial presentations of women from later centuries that employed humility topoi that were gender specific.[61]

Indeed the intervening centuries saw certain general trends, but also great complexity and diversity. The twelfth century produced a great many examples of images and texts that included scribes, as well as illuminators, sometimes even their assistants. Beyond books, these tendencies were likewise manifest in artists' self-portraits in frescoes and stained glass, as well as busts and figures as corbels. The thirteenth century witnessed a diminished presence of the makers of books and other objects. With the fourteenth century and into the fifteenth, the devotional images of donors without objects in their hands take the lead. By the fifteenth century, the custom of showing oneself as an individual kneeling or standing before someone of higher station and offering or presenting a book in one's outstretched hands becomes the purview of authors.

[59] *Der Darmstädter Hitda-Codex: Bilder und Zierseiten*, ed. by Bloch; Gerhard Weilandt, 'Wer stiftete den Hitda-Codex?', *Annalen des historischen Vereins für den Niederrhein*, 190 (1987), 49–83; Klaus Gereon Beuckers, *Die Ezzonen und ihre Stiftungen* (Münster: Lit, 1993), pp. 168–76.

[60] Fulda, Landesbibliothek, Hs. Aa21, fol. 2$^v$; Prochno, *Das Schreiber- und Dedikationsbild*, p. 75.

[61] Mahoney, 'Courtly Presentation', pp. 107–11.

The above sketch of several early medieval presentation miniatures and their texts might serve to show that we are only at the beginning of our analysis of images of giving. Continued work can only be productive in an interdisciplinary vein. The work of Mauss and other structuralist and economic anthropologists is helpful not as an overarching model that can be applied in order to recognize some universal or essential truth, and certainly not as a teleological paradigm through which we can place medieval culture along side early twentieth-century Pacific island cultures and judge them all as occupying archaic or primitive places in a developmental scheme. In fact, Mauss wrote his little essay in order to counter the notions of Bronislaw Malinowski, who had established a scale along which he assessed gift-giving cultures, ranking their motivations by placing the 'pure gift', that which is totally disinterested or 'altruistic', on the one end, and that which is motivated by self-interested barter on the other end.[62] Rather, anthropologists can help us approach medieval material with greater distance than we do when we seek our explanations and justifications only emically as reflections of theological principles. Historians have made impressive strides in the last years in their analyses of gift giving. I am thinking particularly of the collection of essays *Negotiating the Gift: Pre-Modern Figuations of Exchange*, from which several essays have been cited above. Some of these studies analyse the semantic fields of giving, comparing the rhetoric and semantics in various kinds of documents as well as changes of vocabulary over time. A limited number of narratives from chronicles and literary sources are likewise discussed. The picture that is beginning to emerge is one of great complexity. Both the framework of hierarchical feudal structures as well as the overlay of theology, which sometimes serves to provide contradictory countercurrents at the ideological level, must be taken into consideration when analysing how the gifts were used to represent, to enact, and to negotiate relationships. Much of the work of literature and art history still remains to be done. Dhira Mahoney continues to examine authorial prologues and epilogues, many of which fashion the authored work as a gift presented and received. Large portions of the earlier material, both images and texts, still remain unexamined. It will be especially fruitful to examine more of the literary and pictorial components comparatively to observe how various aspects of the notion of giving could be fashioned through visual and verbal rhetoric and the ways that these expressions worked together or against each other.

Presentation miniatures link the past origins of a work with future audiences by placing the giving and giver into a continuous present tense. Further, through

[62] Mauss, *Gift*, p. 93.

the ideology of the voluntary gift that the pictures put forth, they tend to negate the fact that the originators often received compensation for their work, if in no other form, at least as sustenance that a monastery provided for all members of the community within its walls. It is not the images but the texts that request or demand a counter-gift, thus articulating Mary Douglas's rather pointed reformulation of Mauss's notion: 'There are no free gifts.'[63] Georges Bataille asserts that in rituals such as potlatch giving is equated with acquiring power.[64] Pursuing works of art and literature framed as gifts by their makers and users may provide new insights into medieval and early modern cultures, and an analysis of the associated rhetoric may also prove to be a gift that keeps on giving as it makes us aware of the verbal and pictorial strategies of generosity and giving, offering and ownership that inform our own culture.

*Arizona State University*

[63] Foreword to the 2002 edition of Mauss, *Gift*, pp. ix–xxiii.

[64] Georges Bataille, *The Accursed Share*, I: *Consumption* (New York: Zone Books, 1991), pp. 63–77 (originally published in French as *La Part Maudite* (Paris: Les Éditions de Minuit, 1949)).

# Women and Rhetoric

# The Light of the Virgin Muse in John Lydgate's *Life of Our Lady*

Georgiana Donavin

In her essay 'Margery Kempe's Tears and the Power over Language', Dhira B. Mahoney illustrates how Kempe masters and feminizes rhetorical strategies from the *artes orandi* to compose the prayer that concludes *The Book of Margery Kempe*.[1] In this essay, I want to concentrate on an important source for the feminization of medieval Roman Catholic meditations: the Virgin Mary. The Virgin provided a muse and stood as a Lady Rhetorica to those who would compose prayers and religious verse: especially to John Lydgate, who in writing the *Life of Our Lady*, sought the Mother's aid in perfecting his devotional poetry.[2] Throughout the *Life of Our Lady*, Lydgate meditates on the Virgin Mother in spots of light that represent rhetorical illumination.

John Lydgate (1370–1450), monk of Bury St Edmunds and poet patronized by three English kings (Henry IV, V, and VI), as well as various nobles and merchants, wrote a substantial body of Marian literature, including 'The Ballade at the Reverence of Our Lady Qwene of Mercy', and other Marian songs.[3] In the *Life of Our Lady*, relying heavily on the *Gospel of Pseudo-Matthew*, the *Legenda aurea*, and *Meditationes vitae Christi* for apocryphal detail, he narrates the

[1] Dhira B. Mahoney, 'Margery Kempe's Tears and the Power over Language', in *Margery Kempe: A Book of Essays*, ed. by Sandra J. McEntire (New York: Garland, 1992), pp. 37–50.

[2] John Lydgate, *A Critical Edition of John Lydgate's Life of Our Lady*, ed. by Joseph A. Lauritis, Ralph A. Klinefelter, and Vernon F. Gallagher (Pittsburgh: Duquesne University Press, 1961).

[3] John Lydgate, *The Minor Poems of John Lydgate*, pt I: *The Lydgate Canon*, ed. by Henry Noble MacCracken, Early English Text Society (EETS), e.s., 107 (London: Oxford University Press, 1911).

Virgin's biography from her birth to the celebration of Candlemas.[4] Lydgate's *Life of Our Lady* was popular, existing in over forty manuscripts, but unfortunately this great number has not helped in determining the date or occasion for the poem. Five of the manuscripts, through an illustration of Lydgate kneeling and presenting his poem to the future Henry V, suggest an early date (possibly 1409) and Prince Hal's patronage.[5] On the basis of this illustration and Walter Schirmer's speculations, Derek Pearsall proposes that the *Life of Our Lady* may have been a part of Henry's promotion of vernacular doctrinal writings that could rival Lollard texts.[6] The editors of Lydgate's current critical edition, however, prefer a much later date; Ralph A. Klinefelter argues that

> [t]he presentation by Jean Galopes of his French translation of the *Meditationes Vitae Christi* [to Henry V] in May, 1420, and its relationship to the *Life of Our Lady*; the matured, more religious character of Henry by 1421; his possible gratitude to Our Lady for the success in France; and the astronomical allusions point towards 1421–22.[7]

Phillipa Hardman, on the other hand, would split the poem's composition into two chronologically distant phases, the first three books on Mary's life for a Henrican celebration of the Virgin's birthday *circa* 1409 and the latter three books on nativity feasts possibly twenty years later for monastic liturgies.[8] Although it is not my purpose to establish a definitive date for the poem, I would argue that the narrative principles of cohesion outlined in this essay make it unlikely that the *Life of Our Lady* was composed in two completely separate stages. Whatever the occasion, the *Life of Our Lady* invites meditation on the

[4] *The Apocryphal New Testament*, ed. and trans. by M. R. James (Oxford: Clarendon Press, 1926); Jacobus de Voragine, *Legenda aurea*, ed. by T. Graesse, 3rd edn (Breslau: Koebner, 1890); Lydgate might have read both the *Meditationes* (*Iohannis de Caulibus Meditaciones vite Christi, olim S Bonauenturo attributae*, ed. by M. Stallings-Taney, CCCM, 153 (Turnhout: Brepols, 1997)) and Nicholas Love's Middle English adaptation, *The Mirror of the Blessed Lyf of Jesu Christ*, ed. by Michael G. Sargent (Exeter: University of Exeter Press, 2005).

[5] London, British Library, MS Cotton Augustus A IV; Oxford, Bodleian Library, MSS Digby 232 and Rawlinson C. 446; Manchester, John Rylands, MS Eng. 1; Cambridge, Trinity College, MS 0.5.2.

[6] Walter Schirmer, *John Lydgate: A Study in the Culture of the Fifteenth Century*, trans. by Ann E. Keep (Berkeley and Los Angeles: University of California Press, 1961), p. 41; Derek Pearsall, *John Lydgate, 1371–1449: A Bio-bibliography*, ELS Monograph Series, 71 (Victoria, BC: University of Victoria, 1997), p. 19.

[7] Ralph A. Klinefelter, 'Introduction', in *A Critical Edition of John Lydgate's Life of Our Lady*, ed. by Lauritis, Klinefelter, and Gallagher, pp. 1–20 (pp. 9–10).

[8] Phillipa Hardman, 'Lydgate's *Life of Our Lady*: A Text in Transition', *Medium Aevum*, 65 (1996), 248–68 (pp. 258–59).

Virgin through a series of lit tableaux that encourage the reader to concentrate upon Mary in various poses during the events of her life.

The *Life of Our Lady* begins with the Virgin's conception, youth, and marriage to Joseph, followed by the glorification of Jesus's birth, infancy, and his relationship to the Mother. The poem is structured in six books, the third effecting a transition between a strong focus on the events in young Mary's life and a treatment of Christmas feasts.[9] The liturgical calendar propels the poem's structure, since Lydgate begins the poem on a 'long winters nyght' (I. 2), makes references to the current springtime in Books II and III, wraps up the latter in December, and dates the last three books on the Circumcision, Epiphany, and Purification according to their January and February feasts. Thus, as the 'Introduction' to our edition explains, the poet returns the *Life of Our Lady* to the beginning of the liturgical year, the same calendar upon which he claims to have composed the poem.[10] In this way, the *Life* encourages its readers to meditate upon events concerning the holy family in their proper time and to see these events in the light of the Virgin's wisdom. The poem ends at the celebration of Candlemas, rather than with the Coronation of the Virgin, but as we shall see, this seemingly truncated conclusion to the Virgin's biography has a purpose within Lydgate's interconnections among Mary, spiritual knowledge, rhetoric, and light. The shining tapers of Candlemas provide a suitable climax for the number of scenes in which Mary is placed in a poetic spotlight for meditation. Throughout the entire poem, Lydgate casts an emphasis on Mary's learning and powers of speech in resplendent beams of light imagery that highlight the Virgin, creating what Pearsall calls a 'luminous rhetoric' with a 'transfiguring effect'.[11] The poet's eloquence is heightened through the grace of the Virgin's gift of speech and shines like a stained-glass window upon the Virgin's life so that the reader might be transformed through contemplation of her. Although many critics including John Norton-Smith, Judith Davidoff, and Lois Ebin have written about the great lights and their connection to rhetoric and poetics in Lydgate's corpus, no one else has yet tapped the Virgin Mary as a source of illumination.[12]

[9] Hardman, 'Lydgate's *Life of Our Lady*', p. 249.

[10] Klinefelter, 'Introduction', p. 9.

[11] Derek Pearsall, *Gower and Lydgate* (London: Longmans, Green, 1969), p. 42.

[12] John Lydgate, *John Lydgate: Poems*, ed. by John Norton-Smith (Oxford: Clarendon Press, 1966), p. 178; Judith M. Davidoff, 'The Audience Illuminated, or New Light Shed on the Dream Frame of Lydgate's *Temple of Glas*', *Studies in the Age of Chaucer*, 5 (1983), 103–25; Lois Ebin, *Illuminator, Makar, Vates: Visions of Poetry in the Fifteenth Century* (Lincoln: University of Nebraska Press, 1988), pp. 19–48.

Lydgate opens the Prologue to the *Life of Our Lady* by recounting how he awoke from a slothful slumber on a winter's night to a beckoning star. This introduction compares to the frame of Lydgate's *Temple of Glas* in which the narrator's fretful sleep in the blackness of mid-December yields a dream of bright Venus and her temple.[13] In the *Life of Our Lady,* the shining beacon is Mary the star, *Stella Maris,* who is a 'bright poole' (I. 10), and 'passethe pliades | Bothe of shynyng and of stremes clere' (I. 22–23). Following Mary's navigation, the narrator's soul will not be plunged back into the dark, as in the *Temple of Glas,* but will proceed ever higher toward the light. Whereas the narrator of *Temple of Glas* awakes with 'gret lamentacioun' over the lost vision of his beloved (1375), the penitent of the *Life of Our Lady* enjoys the hope of grace in the end as the tapers of Candlemas shine upon him (VI. 442–55). Unlike Venus in the *Temple of Glas,* who withholds her words of comfort until the lover's entire petition is made, in the *Life of Our Lady,* Mary's fair orb dries the narrator's tears from the beginning, as the sun burns away the clouds, and offers him a light by which to see his Marian material (I. 36–49).

Lydgate rejoices that the Mother lights the way of invention and pours into his heart the matter of poetry. As Mahoney has shown, such humility topoi and the deferral of authority to another source take many forms in the prologues of medieval writings.[14] In the Prologue to the *Life of Our Lady*, Lydgate entreats the Virgin:

> So late the golde dewe of thy grace fall
> Into my breste, like skales, fayre and white
> Me to enspyre of that I wolde endyte
> With thylke bame.
>
> (I. 52–55)

These lines are replete with associations informing Lydgate's Marian poetics, especially concerning the Virgin's inspiration for poetic matter, and with their Eucharistic overtones, they imply that Mary metes out the bread of each verse's life. As the narrator requires his heart to be soaked with 'golde dewe', Mary's inventional liquor produces the *Life of Our Lady*, a text akin to the Gideon's fleece

[13] Lydgate, *John Lydgate*, ed. by Norton-Smith, pp. 67–112.

[14] Dhira B. Mahoney, 'Gower's Two Prologues to *Confessio Amantis*', in *Re-Visioning Gower*, ed. by R. F. Yeager (Asheville, NC: Pegasus, 1998), pp. 17–37 (p. 17). Also see her forthcoming book *Medieval Liminal Rhetoric: The Self-Authorizing Frame* (Turnhout: Brepols).

(Judges 6. 33–40). Lydgate casts his fleece (vellum) before the Mother for a sign of proof that he has been chosen to save his people through a script for their Marian meditations. While her grace drops upon him in shining white scales, it may be compared to the pearl of price, manna from heaven or the mysterious grain that the Mother places upon the little clergeon's tongue in Chaucer's *Prioress's Tale*, also a poem dependent upon the Virgin's inspiration.[15] As a pearly droplet, the Mother's grace distills purity of spirit into Lydgate's writing that should return sagacious pearls, not to be cast before swine, but before Mary herself. As manna or the grain placed upon the little clergeon's tongue, Mary's grace enables the author's communion: Lydgate will be fed with the bread of life that Mary 'baked', and thus the poet will feed his readers. The shape of the scale that the Virgin lets fall into the heart of Lydgate's matter is like a rain, tear, or blood drop, recalling the blood of Christ, dropping from his forehead. According to Julian of Norwich, whose fame spread across East Anglia to Bury St Edmunds, the dropping of Christ's blood compares to a downpour upon the eves of a house, or fish scales.[16] Both Julian and Lydgate obtained the image of the droplet from Psalms 64. 11 and 71. 6, occurring in the Benedictine night office for Wednesday. The whiteness and scaliness of Mary's outpouring suggest bread and flesh, while the shape implies wine and blood. Lydgate shows how his sadness is washed away by Christ's sacrifice and his barren imagination is filled with the Mother's nourishment. Spiritually healed and fortified, Lydgate might 'endyte | With [the Virgin's] bame', the balm of Gilead flowing through his stylus as a salve for the mortally sinful reader (Jeremiah 8. 22).

Concluding the Prologue, Lydgate begins to feel the Virgin's powers of invention and to see the direction provided by *Stella Maris* more clearly. Whereas he had begun the Prologue in the darkness of 'distresse' (I. 1), by the end, he has moved considerably '[e]stwarde to [...] the orient full shene' where Mary and the Christ child rise up on the horizon (I. 48). He entreats Mary further:

> And the licour of thy grace shede
> Into my penne, tenlumyne this dite
> Thorough thy supporte þat I may procede

[15] Geoffrey Chaucer, *The Prioress's Tale*, in *The Riverside Chaucer*, ed. by Larry D. Benson, 3rd edn (Boston: Houghton Mifflin, 1987), pp. 209–12. The grain has been variously interpreted as a pearl, the grain of paradise, the host, or a mere prop for the plot. For an overview, see Florence Ridley's summary of scholarship in *The Riverside Chaucer*, p. 916.

[16] Julian of Norwich, *Showings*, ed. by Edmund Colledge, James Walsh, and Jean Leclercq, Classics of Western Christianity (Mahwah, NJ: Paulist, 1978), Chapter 9, 2nd Revelation.

> Sumwaht to saye in laude ande p[r]eys of the
> And first I thynke at the natiuitee.
>
> (I. 57–61)

While the focus in the previous lines (I. 52–55) is on the Virgin's grace raining into the heart, here inspiration travels from the poet's breast to his pen and lights up the matter of the Mother's birth. The *Life of Our Lady* and its narrative of Mary's birth emerge from the Mother's inspiration, just as Mary, like Minerva, sprang from 'the fadirs sapience' (I. 178).

As Ebin argues, the cluster of terms employed in the Prologue to the *Life of Our Lady*, such as *golden*, *balm*, *liquor*, and *enlumine*, are characteristic of Lydgate's efforts to theorize his poetics.[17] Choosing golden words, the poet creates a spiritual balm from the elixir of holy liquor and light. Ebin summarizes Lydgate's aesthetic purpose as follows:

> In contrast to his immediate English predecessors, who are anxious about the limits of the poet's craft and ability of language to embody truth, Lydgate defends the inherent truthfulness of poetry and the poet's intention. He envisions the poet essentially as an illuminator who uses the power of language to shed light on the poet's matter and make it more significant and effective.[18]

In the Prologue to the *Life of Our Lady*, Mary is the chief source of this illumination. In following the Mother's light and relying on her invention, Lydgate does not so much defend the inherent truthfulness of poetic language, as Ebin contends, but burnish his rusty words with the Virgin's purity. His faith in the truth communicated through the *Life of Our Lady* and in the spiritual efficacy of its delivery is linked inextricably to his faith in the Virgin. She embodies the principles of divine invention and 'translation' that allow the mortally corrupt and contingent language of poets to rise up to a spiritual stage and be worthy of such a spotlight. As the narrator of the *Life of Our Lady* admits, his speech is '[r]ude for to Rehersen' the Virgin's story (I. 869), but he puts the poem 'mekely to her correcion' (I. 880). In the Prologue, Lydgate's poetic invention is initially weighed down by 'trowble [... o]f worldely wawes' (1. 12–13), but the Virgin releases him from spiritual pain, supplies the matter and causes the words of devotion to flow.

The invocation to the Virgin in the Prologue of the *Life of Our Lady* buoys up the narrative in Book I of Mary's girlhood in the Temple and betrothal to Joseph.

[17] Ebin, *Illuminator, Makar, Vates*, pp. 19–48.

[18] Ebin, *Illuminator, Makar, Vates*, p. 19.

Like other lives of the Virgin from the late English Middle Ages such as John Gower's *Mirour de l'Omme*, the *Life of Our Lady* depicts the young Mary as a precocious novice who prefers the chaste, contemplative life. [19] Even at five years old,

> She was as sadde in conuersacion
> And also demure, sothely forto seyne
> Form all childehode and dissolucion
> In gouernance and in descrecion
> And in talking alse wise and alse sage
> As any mayde of xxx[ti] yere of age.
> (I. 240–45)

To describe young Mary's seven virtues, the poet relies on the same brilliant images that sparked his invention in the Prologue; he compares her spiritual talents to 'the chaundelabre of gold | That some tyme bare, Seven lampes schene' (I. 358–59). These seven 'lamps' are the fear of God, charity, knowledge, strength, prudence, intelligence, and wisdom (I. 365–78), and each are held underneath a bright light so that the meditating narrator and reader might pause and pray at each spot. Overwhelmingly, Mary's gifts, enabled by the chastity that focuses her life on God, endow the Virgin with the mental acuity that she makes known in her reading, praying, and other divine utterances. The Virgin's commitment to the contemplative life through which she might exercise these spiritual gifts gives way to a betrothal only at God's command. The Virgin's light guides Lydgate through both Mary's maidenly conflicts and Joseph's doubts about his age.

When, however, in Book II the poet arrives at the Annunciation, he again doubts the poetic phrases at his disposal and his ability to arrange them. He notes that if Bernard of Clairvaux struggled with a description of the Annunciation in the homily 'De Laudibus Virginis Matris', even the greatest poet might not find the words.[20] This comparison to Bernard's preaching reveals the role that Lydgate appropriates to himself as a great advocate for the Virgin Mary. It also establishes a purpose for the *Life of Our Lady* that is similar to preaching; in this case the poet persuades his readers not of a biblical interpretation, but of an 'enlightened' way of envisioning the Virgin in their meditations. In order to present an illuminated

[19] John Gower, *The Complete Works of John Gower*, ed. by G. C. Macaulay, 4 vols (Oxford: Clarendon Press, 1899–1902). Vol. I contains the French works.

[20] Bernard of Clairvaux, *Sancti Bernardi Opera*, ed. by Jean Leclercq, C. H. Talbot, and Henri Rochais, 8 vols (Rome: Cistercian, 1957–77).

Virgin at the Annunciation, the narrator begs that a counterpart to Gabriel might be sent from heaven to purify his mouth and shape his tongue for the task (II. 429–35). Lydgate's prayer that his tongue be carved out for spiritual purposes alludes to Isaiah's claim that a seraphim touched his mouth with a burning coal from the altar and purged his unclean lips for prophecy (II. 430–35; Isaiah 6. 6–7). Similarly purified, Lydgate's newly scourged tongue becomes a torch as the truth about the Annunciation is now cast in light. The poet declares that at the Annunciation the sun of life shone his beams upon the Virgin (II. 483), that this sun pierced the Virgin as it would glass, that she in turn shone as a bright gem (II. 521–22), and that Mary sacrificed her life upon a fire of holy love, burning more brightly than stars on a frosty night (II. 603–06). The reconfiguration of the narrator's tongue in order to spark this virginal light relies not only on the passage from Isaiah, but also on trends in late medieval meditative literature of the English North. While Isaiah gave to Lydgate the motif of the sanctified tongue, northern English poets such as John of Howden who, as F. J. E. Raby comments, was incredibly influential over fourteenth- and fifteenth-century English meditational writing and whose *Philomena* was translated into Middle English, connected this motif to light and to the Virgin Mary.[21]

From the time that Anselm was Archbishop of Canterbury (1089), a venerable tradition of meditations on the Virgin flourished in England and eventually found its voice in the North in poets such as John of Howden, chaplain to Queen Eleanor, wife of Henry III. Among his *Prayers and Meditations*, Anselm's third prayer to Mary establishes a trend in lauds to the Virgin by emphasizing her perfection and the inexpressibility topos. Anselm declares, 'My tongue fails me', and in the thirteenth-century John of Howden inherits this failure, but finds the remedy that Lydgate later borrows in invoking the Virgin herself as muse for her own poetic praise.[22] In his *Philomena*, an Anglo-Latin poem providing meditations on the life of Christ and Mary's participation in it, John of Howden features passages similar to Lydgate's on the shaping of the tongue and the sparks emerging from the grindstone; he begs the Virgin to 'hew [his] ignorant tongue

[21] F. J. E. Raby, 'A Middle English Paraphrase of John of Hoveden's "Philomena" and the Text of his "Viola"', *Modern Language Review*, 30 (1935), 339–43 (pp. 339–40). The Middle English translation of the *Philomena* was published by Charlotte D'Evelyn, *Meditations on the Life and Passion of Christ*, EETS, o.s., 158 (London: Oxford University Press, 1921).

[22] Anselm, *S. Anselmi Cantuariensis archiepiscopi opera omnia*, ed. by Franciscus Salesius Schmitt, 6 vols (Stuttgart: Fromann, 1946), III, 5–91; *Johannis de Hovedene, Philomena*, ed. by Clemens Blume, (Leipzig: Reisland, 1930).

into a lyre with pleasing sounds'.[23] Here, Howden entreats the Virgin Mary to fill the role of Lady Grammar, who in medieval depictions of the Seven Liberal Arts often brandished a knife for cutting away the infelicities of speech. Once he finds his purified voice, Howden contends that Mary produces 'the lights of learning [...] interwoven in the text'.[24] Depicting the *Philomena* as a virginal light show, John of Howden elaborates upon a complicated image connecting the Virgin's wisdom, bookishness, brilliance, and domesticity.

John of Howden offers Lydgate a model for connecting the Virgin not only to a feminized tongue, lights, and inspiration, but also to domestic cloth-making and its associations with the Incarnation and language. When Howden calls Mary the light of learning woven into the text, her renown for weaving is compared to the poetic syntax that conjoins bright thoughts on her worship. The Marian apocrypha often depict the Virgin's sewing or weaving when she is a girl in the Temple or a young wife, and the *Life of Our Lady* perpetuates the legend that the purple curtain of the Temple is of her own making (I. 780–819). As Gail McMurray Gibson notes, the Virgin's cloth-making — her 'clothing' of God in her womb, as well as her loom and needle work — resonated powerfully in East Anglia, where textile imports controlled the fifteenth-century economy. A member of this economy in Bury, Lydgate, like John of Howden, indulges a number of clothing metaphors in the *Life of Our Lady*, for instance, his comment that Christ 'shall yshrouded be' in Mary's flesh (I. 480).[25] Gibson points out that while depictions of Mary's girlhood in the Temple, or of Joseph expressing his doubts, often emphasized the Virgin's sewing or weaving, Annunciation art more often focused on her scriptural study as Gabriel alights in front of a nimbed Virgin reading the Book of Wisdom.[26] In John of Howden's *Philomena*, images of clothmaking, textuality, and illumination join together to explain Mary's triumphant feminization of the poet's craft: the lights of her wisdom are threaded together in a poetic chain providing music for a tongue 'castrated' by Mary herself. The hewing of the tongue in the *Philomena* is a spiritual emasculation toward a poem about the divinely feminine — sprung from Mary's invention, dedicated to Marian matters, and wrapped in Marian 'figures'.

[23] 'Virgo [...] [d]ola linguam hanc imperitiae | In sonantis lyram placentiae': *Johannis de Hovedene, Philomena*, ed. by Blume, 3. 1–3.

[24] 'Textu luces intexta literae': *Johannis de Hovedene, Philomena*, ed. by Blume, 1071.2.

[25] Gail McMurray Gibson, *The Theater of Devotion* (Chicago: University of Chicago Press, 1989), p. 156.

[26] Gibson, *Theater*, pp. 146–68.

Lydgate's content and delivery are similarly feminized, and although he is aware of his masculine forebears such as Bernard of Clairvaux and most probably John of Howden, Lydgate privileges the Virgin's authority over all of the canons of rhetoric. This submission to feminine discursive power explains the curt nod in the epilogue to Book II to Chaucer, who, like the Virgin 'made [...] to distille and rayne | The golde dewe, dropes of speche and eloquence | Into our tunge' (II. 1632–34). Just as the Virgin's inspiration is compared in the Prologue to the dew on Gideon's fleece that quenches the heart and lights the writer's way, so Chaucer's rhetoric 'enlumyne[s]' English verse (II. 1636). For human intermediaries in divine verse, Lydgate also mentions Cicero and Petrarch, but he dispatches with these compliments quickly, explaining that all of the masters are dead and that in life they offered no direct model for the *Life of Our Lady*. Abandoning the male masters, the epilogue to Book II reveals Mary to be Lydgate's only muse, his sole 'helpe, counsel and socour' (II.1665). By studying only with Mary, he switches from the masculine to the feminine foundation for inspiration. He enquires first of Cleo and Calliope, but finds them insufficient and pledges his poetic faith in the Mother of the Word (II.1659–65). As in the Prologue, in the epilogue to Book II Mary's guidance leads the poet into the light, this time into the beginning of Book III on the nativity of Christ in the spotlight of the star over Bethlehem.

With Book III the focus shifts from the Temple or Joseph's house and Mary's preparation for a life in God's honour to Bethlehem and her participation in the life of Christ. When Mary enters the stable, 'a newe soden light | Gan the place enlumen envyron [...]' (III. 168–69); there she gives birth to the Christ child who immediately 'shed his light to glad all man kynde' (III. 177). During the Virgin Birth, the sun/Son emerges from the Virgin, and the star over Bethlehem, marking the humble place, is a counterpart to the *Stella Maris* making her accommodation there. Book III is ablaze with the ascendance of the Word, the light emanating from both Mother and Child, each paradoxically the source of the other, while the reader is invited to pause and pray. The lights die down during Book IV with its focus on the Circumcision and foreshadowing of the Passion, but rise up again as the Magi follow the star in Book V and the celebration of Candlemas begins in Book VI. As the narrator reminds us in the prologue to Book VI, the entire story is dedicated to the 'blisfull quene' (VI. 2), who 'neuere brennyng of no flesshely hete' (VI. 8), nevertheless provides a bright tabernacle for the Word.

While Mary is the mistress and matter of the *Life of Our Lady*, the speech with which she inspires the narrator is much different from her own. Specifically, while the Virgin manifests her charity, knowledge, strength, prudence, intelligence, and wisdom in *brevitas*, the poet does so with *amplificatio*. When young Mary expresses herself in the Temple, Lydgate characterizes her conversation as '[p]rudent [...] of what hir lust to shewe | Large of sentens, and but of wordes fewe' (I. 412–13). Mary's brevity is a counterpart to her virginity, verbal discipline akin to physical asceticism, as closed lips indicate her inviolable body and spirit. Restricted speech and bodily integrity are not just feminine ideals for religious virgins, however. As a Benedictine monk, Lydgate would have practised Marian circumspection in his daily life at Bury St Edmunds. According to Chapter 6 of the Benedictine Rule, 'the spirit of silence ought to lead us at times to refrain even from good speech, so much the more ought the punishment of sin make us avoid evil words'. '[C]oarse words and idle jests' are absolutely prohibited that ears and heart may be open to God's missives.[27] Regardless of Lydgate's position as a disciple listening expectantly for the Lord, he, nevertheless, shrugged off brevity and reached for its rhetorical opposite when elaborating on Mary's perfection. According to Geoffrey of Vinsauf's *Poetria nova*, the poet must display the material on 'a wide path or a narrow, either a river or a brook', by either abbreviation or amplification (III. 207–09).[28] Considering epigrammatic abbreviations unsuitable to ecstatic praise, the monastic narrator of the *Life of Our Lady* expands upon the wide path and traverses the river with a glorious magnitude not open to him outside of liturgical celebrations in the halls of Bury. As it is represented in the *Life of Our Lady*, the binary rhetorical principles of amplification/abbreviation reflect not only polarized options for praise versus epigram and poetic versus monastic speech, but also the difference between the one who must elaborate on truths already constructed (Lydgate) and the one who participates in formulating the truth (Mary). Whereas the former shows his ability in additions, the latter proves her sagacity in apt expressions.

Amplification is an important principle in all of Lydgate's poetry, and it serves the special purpose of prompting meditation in the *Life of Our Lady*. Characterizing Lydgate's expansive style, Pearsall comments on the freezing effect created by embellishments upon single scenes and contrasts such set-pieces with the more active plots of other poets.[29] While Lydgate's elaborations of tableaux may seem

[27] *St. Benedict's Rule for Monasteries*, trans. by Leonard J. Doyle (Collegeville, MN: Liturgical Press, 1948; repr. 2001).

[28] Geoffrey of Vinsauf, *Poetria nova*, trans. by Margaret F. Nims (Toronto: Pontifical Institute of Mediaeval Studies, 1967), p. 23. For an expanded discussion of the classical rhetorical tradition in Lydgate, see Joseph Gerald Marotta, 'John Lydgate and the Tradition of Medieval Rhetoric' (unpublished doctoral dissertation, City University of New York, 1972), pp. 31–60.

[29] Pearsall, *Gower and Lydgate*, pp. 26–28.

more conceptual and generalized than a narrative controlled by the deeds of individuated characters, such stable, embellished depictions do serve meditation. His strategies for embellishment derive from the traditions of classroom rhetoric, particularly from Geoffrey of Vinsauf. Lydgate deploys all of the many techniques Geoffrey teaches for amplification — repetition, circumlocution, comparison, exclamation, and their subsets — in order to halt the narrative movement and establish an image for the reader's contemplation. For instance, in Book III, Lydgate repeats the fact of Jesus's birth through a variety of circumlocutions; Jesus 'was this day in simylytude, | In erthe honourede in likenesse of man' (III. 555–56). The narrator preaches that we must accept this miracle by 'faythe alone' (III. 570), and he commences a hundred-and-fifty-line comparison between the understanding of the believer and the prophets. This comparison is rounded out with a laudatory apostrophe to Mary for having made human salvation possible. She is called the 'garnet apull, of colour golden hewed' who carried the seed of Christ the 'pepyn' inside her glowing rind (III. 741, 744, 757). Through these amplifications on the Nativity, Lydgate invites the reader to stop and consider the meaning of the Incarnation, the enlightenment of diverse biblical figures, and the savour of the golden apple that surpasses the fruit of the knowledge of good and evil.

Lydgate provides an implicit cue to his purpose of offering such meditations in his abundant use of the *Meditations vitae Christi* throughout the *Life of Our Lady*. For instance, when he compares the coming of Christ to a Bridegroom (III. 539–74) or ponders the suffering at the Circumcision (IV. 29–63), Lydgate takes his narrative of the Virgin's life directly from the vignettes for contemplation in Pseudo-Bonaventure. Moreover, he marshals Bede, Jacobus de Voragine, the Vulgate, and more to create his own meditational sequences for the three Christmas feasts of the Circumcision, Epiphany, and Purification.[30] In certain cases, the narrator expatiates upon scenes such as those of the Annunciation and Nativity and bathes them in light, as has already been shown. In other cases, he expands upon theological arguments amidst events concerning the holy family. Completing his tale of the Annunciation, for instance, the narrator addresses a fictional opponent who has no faith in the Conception (II. 652–931), and during an extended argument that 'all things are possible with God' provides a number of similes for the Virgin. Theological presentation and metaphorical rendering stop the action for over three hundred lines and arrest the reader before icons

[30] See 'Sources, Books III and IV' and 'Sources, Books V and VI', in *A Critical Edition of John Lydgate's Life of Our Lady*, ed. by Lauritis, Klinefelter, and Gallagher, pp. 97–182.

of the Virgin: a tree that bears birds (II. 680–86), an unmovable rock that cures wounds (II. 701–14), a bee that makes wax and honey (II. 862– 65). Calling his readers to meditate upon these Marian signs of wondrous fruitfulness, stability, and health under the spotlight shone by her virginal majesty, the narrator calls out:

> [B]ehalde, the clennesse of this Queen
> [...]
> May in no syde, sothely dysencrees
> [Phoebus's] clere light, ne hir perfyte bryghtnesse
> Whose fayre stremes, shullen neuer cesse
> Withoutyn eclipse, to shyne in clennesse
> For of this mayde.
>
> (II. 938–43)

Comparable to Phoebus, the Virgin shines eternally over poetical images that redound to her own worship. Neither her glory nor that of the poem shall cease, inviting continual veneration of the Mother's place in providence.

The *Life of Our Lady* is not the only devotional poem in which Lydgate employs amplification to supply images for contemplation. For instance, in *A Seying of the Nightingale*, Lydgate adapts John Peckham's *Philomela*, a poem with a title and content similar to that of John of Howden's, but structured according to the hours of worship and more focused on the comparison between the Christ's sacrifice and the nightingale's dying song. In Lydgate's Middle English version, a dream-vision of birds singing in the evening and the christological interpretation of the nightingale give way to a number of images of the Cross for the reader's meditation.[31] In her consideration of the Lydgate canon, Anita Helmbold writes that his poems 'require the reader to approach the texts [...] by considering them as visual or performance art, as well as literature'.[32] In the *Life of Our Lady* the visual serves as a meditative icon and the performance consists of an acting lesson for worship that Mary teaches Lydgate's readers. Holding his Marian spotlight upon events, metaphors, and doctrines concerning the Virgin, Lydgate illuminates the image for devotion and reminds the reader that Mary became wise through such prayerful concentration.

[31] John Lydgate, *Lydgate's Two Nightingale Poems*, ed. by O. Glauning, EETS, e.s., 80 (London: University of Oxford Press, 1900).

[32] Anita Helmbold, 'Text as Performance: Toward a More Authentic Experience of the Lydgate Canon', *Florilegium*, 17 (2000), 21–43 (p. 24).

Mary is muse for her own meditations and exemplar of devout prayer from the early stages of her story in the *Life of Our Lady*. Once she enters the Temple, Lydgate notes, Mary spends her life praying and reading, contemplating and applying her understanding to the Psalms and biblical prophecies. Through her meditations upon the Book of Isaiah, she intuits the coming of the Messiah and prays that she might be present at his birth. According to Lydgate, 'Elizabethe [... in hir] avisions' (I. 435–36), probably Elizabeth of Hungary, recorded from revelations granted to her between 1152 and 1165 seven prayers of the Virgin, and Lydgate proceeds to summarize them.[33] In the fifth petition, Mary prays that she might continue to train her thoughts upon God so that eventually she might see the 'sacrede beawtee' of the Messiah's virgin mother (I. 482), hear her delightful speech, and with her own tongue, counsel patience in suffering (I. 484–88). After she understands her own position as the Virgin Mother and travels to visit her cousin Elizabeth, also miraculously pregnant, Mary composes and recites the *Magnificat*, declaring God her 'hole desire' (II. 993), and upon the birth of the Christ child, she thanks the Lord again for his 'benyngnyte', though she 'unworthe be' (III. 258–59). Mary's prayers are God-focused with no thought for self-aggrandizement; similarly, the prayers of Lydgate's readers should be centred on the Virgin under the bright lights. As Lydgate receives a vision of Mary from a vision of Elizabeth, he participates in the feminized reproduction of contemplative images and encourages his readers to continue this reproduction by following Mary's rhetorical models for prayers and meditations.

Connections among meditations, light imagery, and Mary's wisdom abound throughout the *Life of Our Lady* and surface brilliantly in Book VI, the seeming 'surprise ending' of the poem. Although the conclusion with the celebration of Candlemas (the Purification of the Blessed Virgin and Presentation of the Christ Child in the Temple) rather than with the Coronation of the Virgin in heaven may seem curious today, it is not an incomplete ending. Filling in the 'missing' events, Book V supplies a short history of Jesus's life and Mary's ascendancy to the heavenly court and opens the possibility of a conclusion for the *Life of Our Lady* based on liturgical cycles and rhetorical themes, rather than on chronology. Beginning with Mary's nativity and ending with Candlemas, the *Life of Our Lady* imitates the cycle of devotions for Monday recommended in the *Meditationes vitae Christi* and allows Lydgate to compare his writing process to the liturgical year. Along with its liturgical underpinnings, the *Life* begins, ends, and shines

[33] The Marian prayers occur in the fourth revelation. See *Patrologiae cursus completus [...], Series Latina*, ed. by Jacques-Paul Migne, 221 vols (Paris: Garnier, 1844–91), CXCV, 114–94.

throughout with the motif of light, which Candlemas brings to fruition. Book VI opens with an invocation to Mary who 'neuere brennyng of no flesshely hete' (VI. 8) is represented by the chaste taper of Candlemas. Lydgate explains how Mary chooses out of humility to perform the rite of Purification, even though she conceived in cleanliness. Her decision to sacrifice two turtles and present herself in the Temple for spiritual cleansing is consonant with her conformity to Scripture throughout the *Life of Our Lady*; she ever desires that her life and words might be rhetoric in action, a manifestation of the divine text. Her holiness is celebrated by a procession of lights at Candlemas, Lydgate recounts, because of Pope Sergius's reconstitution of the Roman lighted victory march to Februa's temple. Mary's victory, Lydgate continues, is in her successful mediation for souls. While on earth she prayed for the opportunity to advise the future mother of God, in heaven she is a divine counsellor, her eloquent speech and wisdom applied to the eternal judgement (VI. 358–71). Of the three parts of the Candlemas taper representing the Trinity as well as the body, soul, and Godhead of Jesus, Mary is the wax, claims Lydgate, for the flame that ignites his poetry (VI. 386–403). In the light of Mary's prayers and the seven lamps of her wisdom, the poet concludes the *Life of Our Lady* (VI. 440–48).

By concluding the poem at Candlemas, John Lydgate underscores the importance of light imagery to his concept of divine rhetoric and of the Virgin Mary to literary excellence. In the *Life of Our Lady*, the Virgin's beams enlighten the poet, even as they cast Lydgate's male masters Chaucer, Petrarch, and others in the shadows. As in the Virgin Birth, the poem's matter derives from Mary herself, and the images upon which she generates light offer stopping points for the reader's meditation. The *Life of Our Lady* leads the reader on '[w]ith tapres fresshe and bright torches shene | To kepe and halowe in honour of that quene' (VI. 454–55).

*Westminster College*

# SISTERS UNDER THE SKIN: MARGERY KEMPE AND CHRISTINE DE PIZAN

Elizabeth Archibald

When I told a friend who works on Christine de Pizan that I was writing an essay comparing her with Margery Kempe, she looked disbelieving and exclaimed, 'But they are completely different — what can you possibly compare?' I was disheartened at first, but then I remembered Margery's famous encounter with the Vicar of St Stephen's in Norwich. Jesus orders her to go and speak to the Vicar, but when she asks for an hour of his time, he 'lyftyng up hys handys and blyssyng hym, seyd, "Benedicite! What cowd a woman ocupyn an owyr er tweyn owyrs in þe lofe of owyr Lord? I xal nevyr ete mete tyl I wete what ȝe kan sey of owyr Lord God þe tyme of on owyr"'.[1] Of course, Margery manages to win him over and he becomes one of her champions. Christine too had to deal with patronizing and misogynistic men. She describes one such encounter in *Christine's Vision*:

> Once a man criticized my desire for knowledge by saying that it was not fitting for a woman to possess learning because there was so little of it. I replied that it was even less fitting for a man to possess ignorance because there was so much of it.[2]

[1] *The Book of Margery Kempe*, ed. by S. B. Meech and H. E. Allen, Early English Text Society, o.s., 212 (London: Oxford University Press, 1940), I. 17, p. 38, ll. 24–27. All references are to Book I of this edition, cited parenthetically in the text by chapter, followed by the page and line numbers.

[2] *Christine's Vision*, trans. by Renate Blumenfeld-Kosinski, in *Selected Writings of Christine de Pizan*, trans. by Renate Blumenfeld-Kosinski and Kevin Brownlee, Norton Critical Edition (New York: Norton, 1997), pp. 173–201 (p. 193) (cited hereafter as *Vision*); 'Si comme une fois respondis a ung homme qui reprouvoit mon desir de savoir, disant qu'il n'appertenoit point a femme avoir science, comme il en soit pou, lui dis que moins appartenoit a homme avoir

Another similarity between Christine and Margery is that in such encounters, both frequently gave as good as they got! I am not the first scholar to make this comparison. In her anthology of visionary women writers, Elizabeth Petroff links Margery Kempe with Christine de Pizan (and with Julian of Norwich and Doña Leonor López de Córdoba), pointing out that they 'have in common a driving need to write down their own life experiences and a profound awareness of their difference from other women and from the role models offered by their society [...]. Each felt a new kind of vocation.'[3] But Petroff does not investigate the parallels between Margery and Christine in any detail. I shall argue in this essay that comparisons between the two can yield insights both into their work and into the corpus of medieval women writers: each is exceptional in her own way, but there are common factors in their exceptionality, especially in regard to their enthusiasm for autobiography and their audacious and successful self-fashioning, which they describe at most unusual length.[4]

Of course, the differences between them are very striking, so let me get them out of the way first. Christine was an educated woman able to draw on both classical and medieval authors, such as Ovid, Augustine, Dante, and Boccaccio.[5] Margery was illiterate and her knowledge of the Bible and of mystical texts depended on what was read to her by friendly priests, though as Joyce Coleman has demonstrated, her illiteracy needs to be understood in the context of a society in which public reading was common practice.[6] Christine lived in Paris and had

ignorance, comme il en soit beaucoup': *Le Livre de l'advision Cristine*, ed. by Christine Reno and Liliane Dulac (Paris: Champion, 2001), III. 9, p. 109 (cited hereafter as *Advision*). All translations of Christine's work are taken from the Norton edition unless otherwise stated.

[3] *Medieval Women's Visionary Literature*, ed. by Elizabeth Petroff (Oxford: Oxford University Press, 1986), p. 299. Petroff argues that Christine shares with the religious women writers 'didactic purpose and her understanding of women's conflicts over writing'. See also Louise D'Arcens, 'Body, Politics, and Memory: Authority in the Writing of Christine de Pizan, Margery Kempe, and Heloise' (unpublished doctoral dissertation, University of Sydney, 1997). I am grateful to Stephanie Trigg and Andrew Lynch for alerting me to the existence of this thesis, though I have not been able to include it in my discussion.

[4] I am indebted to the students at Bristol who have studied medieval women writers with me and who wrote essays comparing Margery and Christine, and also to Professor Elizabeth Sears and the editors of this volume for their valuable comments on earlier drafts.

[5] A great deal has been written about Christine in the last two decades; see the bibliographies in the Norton Critical Edition (n. 2, above), and in *Christine de Pizan: A Casebook*, ed. by Barbara K. Altmann and Deborah L. McGrady (London: Routledge, 2003).

[6] A great deal has also been written about Margery in the last two decades; see the bibliography in *The Book of Margery Kempe*, ed. by Barry Windeatt (Harlow: Longman, 2000), and

strong links with the royal court through her father, a physician and astrologer, and her husband, a notary and secretary; both men were educated and respected. Margery lived in Lynn, an East Anglian port town where her father was five times mayor; it is not clear what her husband John Kempe did, but Margery evidently thought him a lesser man than her father. Christine was very happily married and mourned her husband for many years after his premature death, which left her and her family in financial difficulties. Margery tried for years to extricate herself from her marriage, and she clearly found Christ a much more satisfactory 'husband' than John Kempe (though she did express some fondness for John and did return to nurse him when he was old and sick).

Christine wrote with erudition and rhetorical elegance in various genres, in both verse and prose — lyrics, dream visions, didactic treatises — and on a wide range of themes — her own problems, French politics, chivalry, literary decorum, and the role of women in society. She was closely involved in the production process of copies of her many books, which are often illustrated with images of her as author, writing at her desk or presenting a book to a patron. Margery waited many years to recount her religious experiences and her travels in a single, rather breathless book, and had great difficulty in finding a willing scribe; only one complete manuscript is known, and it is not clear to what extent the clerical scribes may have edited her dictation.[7] As the protagonist of many of her own narratives, Christine is highly praised by allegorical authority figures — the Sibyl, Philosophy, Reason — and is singled out by them for important tasks and experiences. Margery is always praised by Christ, it is true, and by many of his vicars on

in *A Companion to 'The Book of Margery Kempe'*, ed. by John H. Arnold and Katherine J. Lewis (Cambridge: Brewer, 2004). On the importance of reading aloud in the Middle Ages, see Joyce Coleman, *Public Reading and the Reading Public in Late Medieval England and France* (Cambridge: Cambridge University Press, 1996). Coleman remarks that illiteracy was not necessarily a disadvantage for medieval women: 'A girl subjected to the standard medieval education [...] would be led to internalize many misogynistic messages, rendering her, perhaps, more docile and manageable than an illiterate woman (compare Julian of Norwich and Margery Kempe)' (p. 224 n. 2.5).

[7] For a stimulating discussion of this problem see Nicholas Watson, 'The Making of *The Book of Margery Kempe*', and the response of Felicity Riddy, 'Text and Self in *The Book of Margery Kempe*', in *Voices in Dialogue: Reading Women in the Middle Ages*, ed. by Linda Olson and Kathryn Kerby-Fulton (Notre Dame: University of Notre Dame Press, 2005), pp. 395–434 and 435–53. Between them they offer an excellent bibliography on the question of the authorship of Margery's book. Jacqueline Jenkins argues that Margery could in fact read English in 'Reading and *The Book of Margery Kempe*', in *A Companion to 'The Book of Margery Kempe'*, ed. by Arnold and Lewis, pp. 113–28.

earth (after initial difficulties), but her narrative is all in the third person, and she is humbly described throughout as 'this creatur'; it is not clear whether this is her own choice, or that of the scribe(s).

Christine corresponded with intellectuals such as Jean Gerson, Chancellor of the University of Paris, and members of the royal family were among the dedicatees of her books; she was commissioned by the Duke of Burgundy to write the life of his brother King Charles V, and was invited to England by Henry IV. Margery managed eventually to win the respect of most of the ecclesiastics with whom she conversed, but she operated at a lower social level; her reputation was ambivalent, and she was frequently accused of Lollardry and immorality.[8] In the last twenty-five years, the work of both Christine and Margery has become much more accessible; both women are now widely studied and taught. Christine is acknowledged as an important and sophisticated writer, but Margery is still regarded by some scholars as a rather eccentric 'wannabe' mystic whose main claim to fame is her authorship of the first autobiography in English — if it can indeed be regarded as her own work.[9]

Autobiographical writing is an important point of contact between these two writers. Marilynn Desmond has recently written of Christine that 'life-writing was necessary for her to establish her credentials and authority as an author';[10] the same could well be said of Margery, who gives us a far fuller picture of her life and travels than most other religious women writers of the period. Felicity Riddy stresses the autobiographical aspect of Margery's writing, and concludes: 'The telling of her life-story is part of the "creatur's" life: she is represented as a compulsive autobiographer.'[11] Riddy points out how unusual Margery is in this respect: 'A very striking feature of the *Book*'s visions, as compared with those of other holy women that were in circulation at the time — the revelations of Birgitta of Sweden and Julian of Norwich, for instance — is that in this text they are so

[8] See the comments of Rosalynn Voaden in her essay in the present volume, 'Wolf in Sheep's Clothing: Margery Kempe as Underground Preacher'.

[9] See n. 7, above, and my discussion below; on medieval women authors more generally, see Jennifer Summit, 'Women and Authorship', in *The Cambridge Companion to Medieval Women's Writing*, ed. by Carolyn Dinshaw and David Wallace (Cambridge: Cambridge University Press, 2003), pp. 91–108.

[10] Marilynn Desmond, 'Gender, Authorship and Life-Writing in the Corpus of Christine de Pizan', in *A Cambridge Companion to Medieval French Literature*, ed. by Sarah Kay and Simon Gaunt (Cambridge: Cambridge University Press, 2008), pp. 123–36. I am grateful to Professor Desmond for allowing me to read and cite this essay before publication.

[11] Riddy, 'Text and Self', p. 445.

exclusively focused on the personal.'[12] A distinctive female authorial voice does not necessarily mean that the writer discusses herself in any detail; for instance, much critical ink has been spent on the problem of the identity and circumstances of the elusive Marie de France.

The extent to which Margery's scribes are responsible for the shape and content of her work is debatable; without rehearsing the arguments, I am going to treat Margery as the author (in some sense, though not an entirely modern one) of her book. Most critics agree that we hear much of her own voice both in the episodes she chooses to relate and in the manner in which she relates them. To some extent she seems to have modelled herself on precursors such as St Birgitta of Sweden — in Chapter 58 we learn that among the books read to her by a sympathetic priest were 'Seynt Brydys boke [Birgitta], Hyltons boke [probably the *Scale of Perfection*], Bone-ventur, Stimulus Amoris [Pseudo-Bonaventure], Incendium Amoris [Richard Rolle]' — but her style is very different from that of the earlier mystics. Perhaps the most famous example is the scene-setting for the showdown with her husband about her desire to abstain from sex:

> It befel up-on a Fryday on Mydsomyr Evyn in rygth hot wedyr, as þis creatur was komyng fro-ȝorke-ward, beryng a botel wyth bere in hir hand & hir husbond a cake in hys bosom, he askyd hys wyfe þis qwestyon, 'Margery, yf her come a man wyth a swerd & wold smyte of myn hed les þan I schulde comown kendly wyth ȝow as I have do be-for, seyth me trewth of ȝowr consciens — for ȝe sey ȝe wyl not lye — wheþyr wold ȝe suffyr myn hed to be smet of er ellys suffyr me to medele wyth ȝow aȝen as I dede sum-tyme?' (chap. 11, p. 23, ll. 9–18)

The random details in this account — the weather, the beer and cake — ring true, and are most unlikely to have been supplied by a scribe. Margery is also very frank in the opening chapters about her own vices, describing her pride, envy, covetousness, and lust (Chapters 2 and 4). Lust reappears as a problem at later stages in the book, most startlingly in Chapter 59 in the strange ordeal in which the devil shows her a parade of naked men; he tells her to choose who will have her first, and adds that he knows whom she will choose. Margery is shocked that he is right; she is appalled by the situation, but also admits that she finds it 'delectabyl to hir a-geyn hir wille' (chap. 59, p. 145, l. 23). Her candour in this episode is startling.[13]

[12] Riddy, 'Text and Self', p. 446.

[13] This episode raises questions about the role of the scribe: is this really what Margery dictated, or has the scribe intervened to tone it down, or to make it more titillating and predictably misogynist? See my forthcoming essay 'The Devil and Mrs Kempe'.

Carolyn Dinshaw argues that the autobiographical aspect of Margery's *Book* is its main claim to fame:

> That alone stakes its claim to importance. It is full of the minutiae of everyday life in late medieval England, and in particular the life and self-fashioning of a woman [...]. The *Book* is unique, revealing a woman both deeply situated *in* and profoundly *out* of her time.[14]

The same surely could be said of Christine, who includes in her work many examples of both daily life and self-fashioning. When the Sibyl offers to guide her into 'another, more perfect, world' in *The Path of Long Study*, Christine describes how she dressed for the journey:

> I put on my clothes, dressing myself in a simple manner. I arranged my hair and put on a veil because the October wind is more harmful to the eyes than the summer sun. Then I quickly tied my dress with a belt so that it would not prevent me from walking easily.[15]

It might be an exaggeration to describe Christine as a compulsive autobiographer; she does not discuss her vices (or her sex life), but she does include a lot of information about herself, her education, her marriage and widowhood, and her intellectual life in the openings of her dream visions. She can also set the scene in a very realistic and everyday way: for instance, she frequently refers to reading in her study — thus fulfilling Virginia Woolf's prerequisite for female authors of a room of her own:

> One day, in order to lament alone in this fashion, joyless, I shut myself away in a little study where I often enjoy myself by reading texts recounting various adventures. I looked through one or two books, but quickly tired of this, for I found nothing of substance that could comfort me in my state of despair [...]. The date of this painful experience was October 5, 1402 [...]. I remained there until night fell, at which point I sent for a lamp to see whether by browsing in some book, I could free myself from the grief that oppressed me.[16]

[14] Carolyn Dinshaw, 'Margery Kempe', in *Cambridge Companion to Medieval Women's Writing*, ed. by Dinshaw and Wallace, pp. 222–39 (p. 222).

[15] *The Path of Long Study*, trans. by Blumenfeld-Kosinski, in *Selected Writings of Christine de Pizan*, trans. by Blumenfeld-Kosinski and Brownlee, p. 69 (cited hereafter as *Path*); 'Adont vesti mon vestement, | Si m'atournay d'un atour simple, | Touret de nes je mis et guimple, | Pour le vent qui plus grieve a l'ueil | En octobre que grant souleil. | Et ma robe tout a esture | J'escourciay d'une cainture | Afin qu'el ne me nuisist pas | A marchier de plus legier pas': *Le Livre du chemin de long estude*, ed. by Robert Püschel, 2nd edn (Berlin: Hettler, 1887; repr. Geneva: Slatkine, 1974), ll. 700–08, p. 30 (cited hereafter as *Chemin*). In dream visions it is quite usual for the Dreamer to describe the process of getting out of bed and dressing; in the opening of *The Romance of the Rose*, which Christine certainly knew, the Dreamer washes his hands, then takes a needle and sews up his sleeves before going out to hear the birds singing.

[16] *Path*, p. 63; 'Et pour moy ainsi complaindre, | Un jour de joie remise | Je m'estoie a par moy mise | En une estude petite, | Ou souvent je me delite | A regarder escriptures | De diverses

She is also reading in her study in the opening of *The Book of the City of Ladies*. She picks up a borrowed copy of the *Lamentations of Matheolus*, hoping to find some favourable comments on women:

> But I had looked at it only for a moment when my good mother called me to supper — for it was that time already — and I put the book down with the intention of looking at it the next day.[17]

Reading a book as a prelude to a dream vision is a common feature of the genre; what is striking in these examples is the realism of the extra details, sending for a lamp and being called to supper (having a mother to act as housekeeper presumably allowed her to spend so much time reading).

Many aspects of Christine's dream visions follow the conventions of the genre — the preliminary reading, the authoritative guide, flying, revelations about the state of the world; but she is unusual in including so much autobiographical information about her upbringing and education, and about her vicissitudes as an impoverished widow, just as Margery's focus on personal details is unusual in comparison with the work of other mystics. Christine discusses her own life repeatedly (in *The Path of Long Study*, *The Book of Fortune's Transformation*, and *Christine's Vision*, and to a lesser extent in *The Book of the City of Ladies*). She writes both defensively and assertively: as a result of her husband's death, she is a victim, but as a result of her thorough education, she develops a career as a writer and is chosen by her allegorical ladies to be a spokesperson and a campaigner. Just as Christ reassures Margery constantly that she is doing his work, Christine's guides also reassure her, though in rather different terms, praising her intelligence and her intellectual ambition (I shall return to this point later).

Like Margery, Christine repeatedly engages in confrontation and controversy. In the *Letter to the God of Love*, the introduction to *The City of Ladies*, and in her contributions to the *Querelle de la Rose*, she throws down the gauntlet to

aventures. | Si cerchay un livre ou deux, | Mais tost je m'anuiay d'eulx, | Car riens n'y trouvay au fort | Qui me peust donner confort | D'un desplaisir que j'avoie | [...] Le jour que j'oz cel opprobre | Fu le V$^{me}$ d'octobre | Cest an mille quatre cens | Et deux [...] Ainsi fus la enserree, | Et ja estoit nuit serree, | Si huchay de la lumiere, | Pour le deuil qui anuy m'iere | Veoir s'en fusse delivre, | En musant sus quelque livre': *Chemin*, ll. 170–81, 185–88, 195–200, pp. 8–9.

[17] *The Book of the City of Ladies*, trans. by Blumenfeld-Kosinski, in *Selected Writings of Christine de Pizan*, trans. by Blumenfeld-Kosinski and Brownlee, p. 119 (cited hereafter as *City*); 'Mais regardé ne l'oz moult lonc espace quant je fus appellee de la bonne mere qui me porta pour prendre la reffeccion du soupper dont l'eure estoit ja venue, par quoy, proposant le veoir lendemain, le laissay a celle heure': *La Cité des dames*, ed. and trans. by Patrizia Caraffi with Earl Jeffrey Richards as *La Città delle donne* (Milan: Luni, 1997), I. 1, p. 40 (cited hereafter as *Cité*).

male writers in challenging their long-established misogyny. Although Jean de Montreuil forwarded his favourable comments on the *Roman de la Rose* to her, he did not ask for her comments, and Gontier Col was shocked that she dared to criticize Montreuil.[18] In her comments on the political situation, she offers advice to the French princes. Other medieval women writers did this too, of course — Hildegard and Birgitta, for example. But as Blumenfeld-Kosinski notes, 'The most striking feature of her historical and political writing is that it is not confined to any one genre [...]. She also writes herself into her texts in multiple ways: as witness or emotional participant; as sufferer or political advisor; as a lamenting tearful voice or a joyful celebrant.'[19] Whereas the female mystics had the justification of direct instructions from God, Christine did not, though in *The Book of Fortune's Transformation* she does comment on her own name in relation to Christ's: 'Just add the letters *I N E* to the name of the most perfect man who ever lived; no other letter is necessary.'[20] Lori Walters argues that here '[b]y redefining herself as a feminized version of Christ, Christine creates a place for herself as the feminine counterpart of the king who is the representative of Christ on earth'.[21] Whereas Margery represents Christ as the perfect surrogate husband (authoritative but supportive and loving), Christine's allegorical guides are female personifications of admirable virtues; but the three ladies who direct the building of the city are the daughters of God, and in *Christine's Vision* Christine addresses Philosophy as 'God who is really you and you who are really God'.[22] The source of her comfort is fundamentally the same as Margery's, but where Margery casts

[18] See the comments of Marilynn Desmond in 'The *Querelle de la Rose* and the Ethics of Reading', in *Christine de Pizan: A Casebook*, ed. by Altmann and McGrady, pp. 167–80. For a translation of the documents associated with the *Querelle* see *The Debate of the 'Romance of the Rose'*, ed. and trans. by David Hult (Chicago: University of Chicago Press, 2010).

[19] Renate Blumenfeld-Kosinski, 'Christine de Pizan and the Political Life in Late Medieval France', in *Christine de Pizan: A Casebook*, ed. by Altmann and McGrady, pp. 9–24 (p. 20).

[20] *The Book of Fortune's Transformation*, trans. by Blumenfeld-Kosinski, in *Selected Writings of Christine de Pizan*, trans. by Blumenfeld-Kosinski and Brownlee, p. 94 (cited hereafter as *Fortune's Transformation*); 'Le nom du plus parfait homme, | Qui oncques fu, le mien nomme, | I. N. E. faut avec mettre, | Plus n'y affiert autre lettre': *Le Livre de la mutacion de Fortune*, ed. by Suzanne Solente, 4 vols, Société des anciens textes français (Paris: Picard, 1959–66), I. 5, ll. 375–78 (I. 20) (cited hereafter as *Mutacion*).

[21] Lori J. Walters, 'Christine de Pizan as Translator and Voice of the Body Politic', in *Christine de Pizan: A Casebook*, ed. by Altmann and McGrady, pp. 25–41 (p. 35).

[22] *City*, p. 123; *Cité*, I. 3, p. 52. *Vision*, p. 197; 'Dieu qui proprement est toy et toy qui proprement est lui': *Advision*, III. 14, p. 116.

herself as Christ's much loved wife and daughter, Christine plays the favourite pupil and spokesperson. She does claim divine sanction for her writing, though she channels the divine voice indirectly.

Writing about the lives of Margery Kempe and two earlier religious women, Christina of Markyate and Marie of Oignies, Elizabeth Petroff comments:

> One of the elements common to all three discourses is the audacity of the female voice. This audacity is all the more improbable because of the irregular status of all three women. Each had chosen to live out an isolated and self-defined religious role, a dangerous project for any woman; in these three lives, that unique role was the consequence of a deliberate rejection, on the one hand, of marriage and therefore of the social world and, on the other hand, of typical convent life in an enclosed community. Those were the choices the medieval world offered women, and those were the choices that these women could not and did not make.[23]

It was audacious for any medieval woman to write a book, certainly, but audacity is a term that seems particularly relevant to Christine. The role she lived out was not a religious one, but it was 'isolated and self-defined'. Dinshaw describes Margery's autobiography as recounting 'the life and self-fashioning of a woman'. The same is true of Christine, though much of the life she recounts is the life of the mind, rather than adventures out in the world. Audacity in self-fashioning seems to me to be the hallmark of both Margery's and Christine's work, which sets them apart from other women writers of the later Middle Ages, even though they share many of the same goals as others in terms of instructing their readers on the virtuous life.

Though both Margery and Christine had support from educated men, and sometimes very high-status men (for instance the Archbishop of Canterbury and Jean Gerson), these men did not determine the nature of their writing, or oversee its production. Indeed, Margery resisted the advice of the Bishop of Lincoln that she should write down 'hir felynges' (chap. 15, p. 34, ll. 2–9). Many people advised her similarly, according to the Proem, but she resisted them all, saying that Christ would tell her when the time was right:

> Summe of these worthy & worshepful clerkys tokyn it in perel of her sowle and as þei wold answer to God þat þis creatur was inspyred wyth þe Holy Gost and bodyn hyr þat sche schuld don hem wryten & makyn a booke of hyr felyngys & hir revelacyons. Sum proferyd hir to wrytyn hyr felyngys wyth her owen handys, & sche wold not consentyn in no wey, for sche was comawndyd in hir sowle þat sche schuld not wrytyn so soone. & so it was xx ȝer & mor fro þat tym þis creatur had fyrst felyngys & revelacyons, er þan sche

[23] Elizabeth Petroff, *Body and Soul: Essays on Medieval Women and Mysticism* (Oxford: Oxford University Press, 1994), p. 157.

> dede any wryten. Aftyrward, whan it plesyd ower Lord, he comawnded hyr & chargyd hir þat sche xuld don wryten hyr felyngys & revelacyons & the forme of her levyng þat hys goodnesse myth be knowyn to alle þe world. (Proem, pp. 3, l. 20–4, l. 2)

Julian of Norwich also waited many years to write down her revelations while she pondered their meaning, but Margery seems to have been amassing material rather than searching for interpretations. When the time to write did come, she had great difficulty in finding a suitable scribe; the first one (a layman, and possibly her own son) died, and the second (a priest) was reluctant, and could not at first read his predecessor's writing.

Whoever had editorial control makes it clear that Margery was in charge. The first scribe wrote 'as mech as sche wold tellyn hym for þe tym þat þei wer togydder' (Proem, p. 4, ll. 10–11). The second was deterred by her bad reputation, and then impeded by poor eyesight, though he was able to see much better after Margery had urged him to have faith in God's grace. Windeatt notes that '[t]ranscription of the works of female visionaries is often reported to be characterised by supernatural tokens'.[24] But the scribes are usually men of some standing whose identities are known: for instance, Birgitta's vernacular writings were translated into Latin by her confessors, whose names are recorded, and Jacques de Vitry wrote the life of Marie of Oignies and her circle. We do not know the names of Margery's scribes: did she suppress them to emphasize her own self-fashioning, or did a sense of humility (whether hers or theirs) determine their anonymity, in line with the use of 'this creatur' for Margery herself? She names many other supporters and helpers in the course of her book, so the silence seems surprising.[25] Christine acknowledges no major influence or helper in the writing of her books; though she gratefully recognizes her father's belief in learning and education, she acknowledges (through the voice of Philosophy) that she would never have taken up the life of study which she enjoys so much had her husband not died.[26]

It does not seem surprising that Margery encountered more difficulty in having her story written down; she was illiterate, poor, and controversial. But it also

[24] See the note on l. 148 in Windeatt's edition of *The Book of Margery Kempe*, p. 50.

[25] Dhira Mahoney comments that '[i]n Book II her spiritual independence from her male support network provides the assurance and strength that allows her finally to appropriate the male rhetoric for her own': 'Margery Kempe's Tears and the Power over Language', in *Margery Kempe: A Book of Essays*, ed. by Sandra J. McEntire (New York: Garland, 1992), pp. 37–50 (p. 49).

[26] *Vision*, p. 200; *Advision*, III. 18, p. 123.

seems typical of her that although she enjoyed winning over senior ecclesiastics to her cause, she did not want to live under their aegis. She could have entered a nunnery, or at least settled in a town where the church authorities were sympathetic to her, such as Norwich. But that would not have allowed for the frequent controversies and challenges which she clearly enjoyed and exploited. Petroff comments on the constant activity of Margery's life, pointing to travel as an important part of her self-fashioning: in order to tell her story, she invented the first autobiography in English just as in her life she invented a new religious role, a blend of personal asceticism, public apostolate, and pilgrimage.[27] Not all her travel took the form of pilgrimage; she visited many English cities, and though some of her journeys were in response to official summonses, it seems that others were motivated by a desire to test and prove herself in front of ecclesiastical authorities, for instance her journeys to Leicester (chap. 46) and York (chap. 50). Christine's journeys are literary ones in her dream visions, but they serve a similar purpose in allowing her to assert herself, though in less confrontational circumstances. Both women give the distinct impression of spoiling for a fight.

Nancy Partner argues that because 'Margery was a literal-minded woman in many ways [...] she had no talent whatever for self-promotion: she did not understand any of the subtle negotiations which were necessary to turn personal experience into an authorized source of respect, dignity, and harmony with institutions'.[28] Margery may not have been subtle, but she seems to me to have shown an extraordinary ability to promote herself, just as Christine did. In her confrontations with suspicious clergy and laity, Margery always comes off best in the end. She resisted all encouragement to turn her experiences into a book until she felt that the time and circumstances were right. Although we do not know how her work was received and how widely it was read, it is significant that the sole surviving manuscript copy was annotated in the Carthusian Priory of Mount Grace in Yorkshire. Nicholas Watson sees Margery very differently from Partner: for him the 'persecuted, maladroit, self-justifying figure' visible to medieval and modern spectators through her obsessive weeping and crying is less dominant than 'the self-assured and coherent teacher the *Book* also reveals to us', who impressed many of her more learned contemporaries.[29]

[27] *Medieval Women's Visionary Literature*, ed. by Petroff, p. 301.

[28] Nancy Partner, 'Reading the *Book of Margery Kempe*', *Exemplaria*, 3 (1991), 254–67 (p. 266).

[29] Watson, 'Making of *The Book*', pp. 396–97.

Partner remarks that Margery lacked 'the financial and social resources of a feudal widow', by which I assume she means an aristocrat;[30] so did Christine. John Kempe was a respectable man, but not a rich one — indeed, he was in debt to his wife when she negotiated their chaste marriage (see chap. 11), and on her travels she frequently describes herself as destitute and dependent on the kindness of strangers. Christine was an outsider, Italian-born, and apparently without supportive in-laws when her husband died and left her in financial straits. Rather as Margery revels in describing all that she suffered for Christ's sake, slander and abuse and poverty, so Christine repeatedly returns to the disaster of her husband's death and her subsequent troubles, presenting herself as a tragic victim.[31] Both see themselves as marginal: Margery separated from her husband and living an itinerant life of poverty, dependent on the kindness of strangers; Christine a widow and a foreigner, the breadwinner for her family, dependent on the power of her pen and the generosity of her patrons. But both are audacious, and tenacious, in their presentation of themselves as unusual and talented, encouraged and admired by higher powers, and thus qualified to give advice on virtuous behaviour.

In Margery's case, it is Christ who singles her out. He converses frequently with her over the years, addressing her as wife and daughter, and sometimes as mother too, and encouraging her to treat him as her husband. This in itself is not surprising: the trope of Christ as Bridegroom was widespread in the later Middle Ages and was used by both male and female mystics (for instance in Richard Rolle's *Incendium amoris*, which Margery knew). What is more surprising, and more audacious, is the extent to which Christ praises and flatters her. Not only does he assure her repeatedly that all her suffering is pleasing to him and will be rewarded, but he compares her favourably with well-known saints. When she sees the sacrament and chalice moving of their own accord, for instance, Christ remarks 'My dowtyr, Bryde, say me nevyr in þis wyse' (chap. 20, p. 47, ll. 26–27). When Margery worries about the fact that she is not a virgin, Christ promises her 'þe same grace þat I be-hyte Seynt Kateryne, Seynt Margarete, Seynt Barbara, & Seynt Powle', that all who believe that God loves her will have their prayers granted (chap. 22, p. 52, ll. 10–11). This is exalted company indeed. However, Margery feels she has one particular rival in the heavenly host:

[30] Partner, 'Reading the *Book*', p. 251.

[31] See the opening sections of *Path of Long Study*, pp. 61–62, *Fortune's Transformation*, pp. 104–07, and *Vision*, pp. 188–98.

> 'A, blysful Lord,' seyd sche, 'I wolde I wer as worthy to ben sekyr of thy lofe as Mary Mawdelyn was.' Þan seyd owr Lord, 'Trewly, dowtyr, I love þe as wel, & þe same pes þat I ȝaf to hir þe same pes I ȝeve to the.' (chap. 74, p. 176, ll. 16–20)

Mary Magdalene is quite frequently mentioned in the *Book*; since Margery describes herself as tainted by lustful feelings, the saint who had once been a prostitute (as the Middle Ages believed) is an appropriate role model.[32] But Margery shows clear signs of being jealous and competitive about Mary's relationship with Christ. It is a bold step to have Christ himself link them, and raise Margery to Mary's level.

Christine too sets her sights high, though among the learned rather than the blessed. In *The Path of Long Study*, when Christine expresses her anxiety about flying to the heavens in case she should fall like Icarus, the Sibyl replies:

> I certainly understand how and for what reason all things derive their qualities from their nature. It is thus right for the feminine sex always to be fearful and afraid. Thus my words and the things that I show you please you so little that only with a great effort do you believe me. You will not fall like Icarus, for you do not wear wings attached with fragile wax; do not be afraid that you will fall. It is not presumption that leads you into this exalted region, rather it is your great desire to see beautiful things that impels you. Continue your voyage confidently and without fear, for I will guide you carefully, and I will take you back to earth.
>
> Thus was I reassured by the Sibyl more than a thousand times both here and elsewhere.[33]

This could be seen as the equivalent of the mystics' anxiety about discernment of spirits (whether visions are true or false):[34] Christine has to be reassured that her intellectual ambitions are not presumptuous and endangered, but worthy and

[32] See the comments of Rosalynn Voaden in 'Beholding Men's Members: The Sexualizing of Transgression in *The Book of Margery Kempe*', in *Medieval Theology and the Natural Body*, ed. by Peter Biller and A. J. Minnis (Woodbridge: York Medieval Press, 1997), pp. 175–90 (see pp. 184–86).

[33] *Path*, p. 82; 'Certes, bien voy comment et dont | Toute riens trait a sa nature: | Femenin sexe par droiture | Craint et tousdis est paoureux, | Car tant ne te sont savereux | Mes dis ne choses que tu voies | Que fors a grant paine me croies. | Comme Ycarus ne cherras mie, | Car a cire qui tost s'esmie | Tu n'as pas eles atachees: | Si n'aies doubte que tu chees. | Ne presompcion ne te maine | A ceste region haultaine, | Aincois grant desir de veoir | Belles choses te fait avoir | La voulenté de hault monter. | Vien seurement et ne doubter, | Car sauvement te conduiray | Et au monde te remenray. | Et ainsi fus je de Sebille | Asseuree plus de mille | Fois et ailleurs et celle part [...]': *Chemin*, ll. 1734–55, pp. 75–76.

[34] See Rosalynn Voaden, *God's Words, Women's Voices: The Discernment of Spirits in the Writing of Late-Medieval Women Visionaries* (Woodbridge: York Medieval Press, 1999).

safe. She repeatedly makes her characters sing her own praises. When the Ladies Wealth, Nobility, Chivalry, and Wisdom are debating whom to send as a messenger to France, the Sibyl suggests Christine: '"If you decide to choose her, you can be certain that she will not fail you [...]". Thus the Sibyl in her goodness was pleased to speak about me, and praised me more than was necessary.'[35] When the three Ladies appear to her at the beginning of *The City of Ladies*, Reason assures her:

> For, although we are not common to many places and our knowledge does not come to all people, nevertheless you, for the great love you have for inquiring into the truth of things through long and continuous study, for which reason you are here alone and separated from the world, you have earned to be visited and consoled by us as our dear friend, in your trouble and sadness, so that you might have a clear vision into the things that contaminate and trouble your heart.[36]

In the vision narratives, Christine puts her own praises into the mouths of powerful prophetic and allegorical figures, including the Sibyl, Reason, Rectitude, and Justice.

Caroline Walker Bynum has suggested some important distinctions between male and female authors of saints' lives. Drawing on Victor Turner's theories of *liminality*, she argues that in male-authored lives of male saints, 'images of reversal and inversion are dominant, particularly at moments of transition'; this reversal may include the description of the protagonist as female during a liminal period.[37] Male writers, she continues, 'assumed that women went through sharp crises and conversions and that their liminal moments were accompanied by gender reversal (in this case, of course, elevation)'.[38] Women writers, however, follow different

[35] *Path*, p. 86; 'S'a lui vous en voulez tenir, | Croiez qu'elle n'y fauldra point [...] Ainsi Sebille qui fu la | Sienne merci de moy parla, | Et plus loenge qu'il n'affiert | En dist [...]': *Chemin*, ll. 6284–85, 6293–96, p. 266.

[36] *City*, p. 123; 'Car quoyque nous ne soyons pas communes en plusieurs lieux et que nostre congnoissance ne viengne a toutes gens, neantmoins toy, pour la grant amour que tu as a l'inquisicion de choses vrayes par lonc et continuel estude, par quoy tu te rens ycy solitaire et soubstraicte du monde, tu as desservi et dessers estre de nous, comme chere amie, visitee et consolee en ta perturbacion et tristece, et que tu soies faicte clervoyant es choses qui contaminent et troublent ton courage en obscurté de pensee': *Cité*, I. 3, pp. 52–54.

[37] Caroline Walker Bynum, 'Women's Stories, Women's Symbols: A Critique of Victor Turner's Theory of Liminality', in *Anthropology and the Study of Religion*, ed. by Robert L. Moore and Frank E. Reynolds (Chicago: Center for the Scientific Study of Religion, 1984), pp. 105–25 (pp. 109–10).

[38] Bynum, 'Women's Stories', p. 111.

conventions, according to Bynum. So in *The Book of Margery Kempe*, 'we find constant change and excitement but no complete social drama', no crisis followed by reintegration: 'This is because Margery, for all her fervor, her courage, her piety, her mystical gifts and her brilliant imagination, cannot write her own script.'[39] Bynum concludes:

> The point I am making here is an obvious one. Women could not take off all their clothes and walk away from their fathers or husbands, as did Francis. Simple social facts meant that most women's dramas were incomplete [...]. [Ramanujan has argued that] women are in general less likely to use images of gender reversal or to experience life-decisions as sharp ruptures because women, raised by women, mature into a continuous self whereas boys, also raised by women, *must* undergo one basic reversal (i.e. from wanting to 'be' their mothers to acceptance of being fathers).[40]

Margery and Christine seem to me to be exceptions to this argument. Both could and did write their own scripts.[41] Both could be said to have undergone a complete drama.

Margery did walk away from her husband, refusing to have sex with him and to stay at home and spin, not naked but in white clothes (though it is true that she returned to him at intervals, and that he sometimes travelled with her). Christine was separated from her husband unwillingly, by his sudden death. Both women thus undergo a moment of crisis followed by some sort of reintegration in the sense of finding an appropriate niche — appropriate in their own minds, at least, since both lived unusual and somewhat controversial lives. Both clearly saw a major life change or decision as a 'sharp rupture': Margery's success in persuading her husband to live chastely; Christine's need when widowed to support her extended family by writing. Margery does not use any image of gender reversal, but remains entirely feminine in her relationship with Christ, and in her anxiety about her own sexual urges, and the threat of rape. Christine, however, describes

[39] Bynum, 'Women's Stories', p. 113.

[40] Bynum, 'Women's Stories', pp. 114–15.

[41] See Mahoney's comment on the appropriateness of the apparently abrupt ending of Book II ('Margery Kempe's Tears', p. 47): '[A]lthough she has resisted through much of her life the adoption of patriarchal language, Kempe finally finds the confidence to appropriate it for herself in her prayer at the end of Book II. Though in conventional narrative terms there is indeed no climax to Book II, its ending is highly fitting, for it is an account of Kempe's own form of prayer, presented here not in the third person like the whole of the rest of the work, but in an assured first person, speaking directly to God.' In this reading, having the confidence to *choose* to use 'patriarchal language' to describe her own practice would, paradoxically, be a form of writing her own script.

in *The Book of Fortune's Transformation* how on the death of her husband she turned into a man and took charge of the ship in which she was sailing.[42] In neither case does maternal influence seem to play much part, but both women were very much influenced by their fathers. We know nothing of Margery's education (or of her mother), but she was very conscious of being the daughter of John Brunham of Lynn. Christine attributes her love of learning to her much admired father; she praises her mother for her support, but also criticizes her for restricting the young Christine's education.[43]

If either Christine or Margery can be described as having matured into a 'continuous self', it must be regarded as a work of self-fashioning. After twenty years, Margery 'develops a narrative sense of her own past', as Sandra McEntire puts it: 'While unable to read her own text, she translates herself as it were into text for the benefit of others [...]. Once translated into text, her voice cannot be silenced.'[44] Her book is presented as 'a schort tretys and a comfortabyl for synful wrecchys, wher-in þei may have gret solas and comfort to hem and undyrstondyn þe hy & unspecabyl mercy of ower sovereyn Savyowr Cryst Ihesu' towards 'a synfyl caytyf' (Proem, p. 1, ll. 1–4, 15). But it can also be read as the triumph of Margery over all odds and most male critics. Christine also literally translates herself into text, and in spite of all her anxieties, she seems to have succeeded in supporting her family, and also in establishing a reputation as a writer and intellectual pundit. In *Christine's Vision* she tells Philosophy that in the past six years she has written fifteen major books: 'I say this, God knows, not in order to boast but to tell about my good and bad fortunes in the right order.'[45] Both women hold up a moralizing mirror to society. Margery is all too ready to point out the failings of the men she encounters (more rarely those of the women); indeed, Christ tells her 'I have ordeynd the to be a merowr amongys hem' so that people can learn from her example to be sorry for their sins (chap. 78, p. 186, ll. 13–17).[46] In Christine's *Book of the City of Ladies*, Reason carries a mirror which stands for self-knowledge; in many of her works Christine criticizes men for their misogyny and violence and

[42] *Fortune's Transformation*, pp. 104–07; *Mutacion*, I. 12, ll. 1159–1416 (I. 46–53).

[43] *City*, p. 148; *Cité*, II. 36, p. 316.

[44] Sandra J. McEntire, 'The Journey into Selfhood: Margery Kempe and Feminine Spirituality', in *Margery Kempe: A Book of Essays*, ed. by McEntire, pp. 51–68 (p. 68).

[45] *Vision*, III. 10, p. 194; *Advision*, p. 110.

[46] See Ellen Ross's comments on mirrors and women's autobiographies in 'Spiritual Experience and Women's Autobiography: The Rhetoric of Selfhood in *The Book of Margery Kempe*', in *Journal of the American Academy of Religion*, 59 (1991), 527–46.

deceitfulness, and in *The Book of the Three Virtues* she gives detailed instructions to women about how to live virtuously. She and Margery demonstrate the truth of the Wife of Bath's famous prediction:

> By God, if wommen hadde writen stories
> As clerkes han withinne her oratories,
> They wolde han writen of men moore wikkednesse
> Than al the mark of Adam may redresse.[47]

Like other female authors in the Middle Ages, Christine and Margery felt a strong vocation to instruct their readers and audiences on moral issues, but unlike other female authors (and like the Wife of Bath), they also greatly enjoyed talking about themselves, and their identity as women writers is crucial to their didactic writing. In their literary mirrors, the figure of the self-fashioned autobiographer is clearly and audaciously reflected in the foreground.

*University of Bristol*

[47] Geoffrey Chaucer, 'The Wife of Bath's Prologue', *Canterbury Tales*, III. 693–96, in *The Riverside Chaucer*, gen. ed. Larry Benson, 3rd edn (Oxford: Oxford University Press, 1987), p. 114.

# Wolf in Sheep's Clothing: Margery Kempe as Underground Preacher

Rosalynn Voaden

When Margery Kempe was in the Minster at York, she was accosted by one of the priests. 'Þu wolf,' he said to her, seizing her by the collar of her gown, 'what is þis cloth þat þu hast on?' We can be pretty sure that he was not interested in the thread count or dry-cleaning instructions for her clothing, and, indeed, this supposition is borne out, both by the way he addressed her — 'Þu wolf' — and by the answer to his question, which was supplied by some children from the monastery school who were passing: 'Ser, it is wulle'.[1] Margery was wearing a robe of white wool, and it is clear that the priest was accusing her of being a wolf in, quite literally, sheep's clothing of white wool.

Margery Kempe was a woman of the merchant class, born in Lynn around 1373. She married, had fourteen children, and claimed to have revelations wherein Christ, the Virgin Mary, and various saints appeared to her. She travelled on pilgrimage to Rome, Compostela, and the Holy Land, as well as throughout England and Northern Europe. The story of her life constitutes the first known autobiography written in English; it is extant in a unique mid-fifteenth-century manuscript, which was discovered in 1934 and has since provided academics with much food for thought and speculation about spiritual and secular life at the end of the fourteenth century.

[1] *The Book of Margery Kempe*, ed. by S. B. Meech and H. E. Allen, Early English Text Society (EETS), o.s., 212 (London: Oxford University Press, 1940), I. 50, p. 120, ll. 19–22. References to this text are given parenthetically by book and chapter number (for those using other editions), then page and line number in the Meech and Allen edition.

In what sense could this woman who claimed communication with the divine be accused of being a wolf in sheep's clothing? I will argue that there are two ways to interpret the priest's angry remark. One, the most obvious, is that Margery was wearing white; white clothing was a sign of virginity or of widowhood, and, at this point in her life, Margery was neither. White clothing symbolized chastity and dedication to a holy life; Margery had taken a vow of chastity, had dedicated herself to a holy life, yet she still lived in the world, lived with her husband, and moved about freely. She fought long and hard for the right to wear white clothes, arguing that Christ had enjoined this upon her. However, for many people, both lay and clergy, the white clothing fed their suspicions of her. Some thought that she was simply a phony, seeking attention; others suspected her of belonging to a heretical sect — on the Continent, some heretical sects dressed in white.[2]

Her assumption of white clothing is the first sense in which Margery could be seen as a wolf in sheep's clothing; however, it is not unrelated to the second sense, the sense that informs the principal argument of my essay. There is considerable evidence in the *Book* that when Margery travelled in England she was, consciously, deliberately, undertaking a preaching tour, a preaching tour that she believed to be divinely commanded. Although she always dissembled on this issue in public, her behaviour, and the climate of the time, was enough to alert ecclesiastical and secular authorities to her covert preaching, and it is this that is behind the Minster priest's accusation. He knows, and is letting her know that he knows, just what she is doing. She is preaching, in public, to both men and women, something expressly forbidden to women by the Church.

Thus far, scholars have given little concerted attention to Margery's extensive travels in England. The tendency has been for the most part to consider them in the light of Margery's continual quest for ecclesiastical affirmation of her visions and of her spiritual praxis. Although this was undoubtedly one aspect of her journeys, to acknowledge that Margery deliberately undertook a preaching tour argues for a greater purpose to what have heretofore been seen as rather purposeless rambles and opportunistic pious homilies. Margery as underground preacher adds a further layer of complexity to this fascinating woman and her text. This essay will cover three principal areas: first, the textual evidence that Margery was on a preaching tour; second, the forces acting upon her reception as preacher

[2] For a full discussion of the implications of Margery's white clothing, and responses to it, see Michael Vandussen, 'Betokening Chastity: Margery Kempe's Sartorial Crisis', *Forum for Modern Language Studies*, 41 (2005), 275–88. See also Gunnel Cleve, 'Semantic Dimensions in Margery Kempe's "Whyght Clothys"', *Mystics Quarterly*, 12 (1986), 162–70.

in early fifteenth-century England; and, third, the influences at work in her self-construction as preacher.

Margery was thoroughly embedded in an orthodox devotional life; she had various confessors, close relationships with a number of friars, monks, and priests, and met with some of the prominent theologians and churchmen of the time. However, her primary commitment was to Christ, and it was his commands that shaped her devotional praxis. Whenever there was a conflict between accepted behaviour and divine command, she, as mystics and visionaries invariably do, obeyed the higher authority. This is the case with her covert preaching tour. In 1413, when Margery was about forty, 'þis creatur was meuyd in hir sowle to go vysyten certyeyn places for gostly helth' (I. 10, p. 22, ll. 26–27). Christ, however, tells her that there is another reason that she should travel: 'My seruantys desyryn gretly to se þe' (I. 10, p. 22, l. 33). When she expresses fear of vainglory, he continues, reassuring her: 'For þei þat worshep þe þei worshep me; þei þat despysen þe þei despysen me, & I schal chastysen hem þerfor. I am in þe, and þow in me. And þei þat heryn þe þei heryn the voys of God. Dowtyr, þer is no so synful man in erth leuyng, yf he wyl forsake hys synne & don aftyr þi cownsel, swech grace as þu behestyst hym I wyl confermyn for þi lofe' (I. 10, p. 23, ll. 1–7).

Christ is telling her that she has a congregation out there, a congregation waiting to hear the voice of God. Margery is, in effect, to preach to his servants.[3] Moreover, it is the voice, not just the word, of God that they will hear, and it is worth noting that this whole passage identifies Margery with Christ in the strongest terms.[4] So, Margery did go forth, and it is evident from what occurred on her travels that this divine injunction shaped her behaviour on this and subsequent journeys in England.[5]

[3] There is a suggestion in the last part of the passage that she would have powers of absolution, in that, whatever grace she bestows upon repentant sinners, will be confirmed by God. This is clearly moving away from simple preaching into the area of sacerdotal powers, an even more contentious issue, both then and now.

[4] It is worth considering whether in this formulation, Margery (or Christ) is distinguishing between the traditional mission of the prophet/visionary to serve as a channel for the voice of God, and the role of the preacher, to explicate the word of God. See below for a discussion of what Margery probably was preaching.

[5] In her essay in the present volume, 'Sisters under the Skin: Margery Kempe and Christine de Pizan', Elizabeth Archibald remarks on Margery's desire not only to promote herself, but also to prove herself before ecclesiastical authorities.

The placement of this passage in the *Book* is also instructive.[6] It is preceded by a chapter which recounts Margery's increasing desire to live chaste, something for which she needed her husband's permission, and, obviously, his cooperation.[7] Christ promised her that if she would fast on Fridays, neither eating nor drinking, he would 'sodeynly sle' her husband (by which he means his fleshly lust). True to his word, the next time poor John approached her, he was evidently stricken with impotence, and 'he had no power to towche hir at þat tyme in þat wyse, ne neuyr aftyr wyth no fleschly knowyng' (I. 9, p. 21, ll. 12–17). Furthermore, Christ's injunction to Margery to preach is followed by the chapter describing the vow of chastity that Margery — with a little divine help and a promise to pay off his debts — finally persuaded John to undertake (I. 11, pp. 23–25).

Thus, Christ's carefully worded commandment for her to go forth to his servants is framed by two events testifying to her chastity, that is, to her fitness for a life dedicated to spreading the word of God. Margery was forty at this point; she had borne fourteen children; she may well have been menopausal; she had done the mundane business of life.[8] These events mark her movement into another phase of her life, a life of the spirit. From this point on, she spent considerable periods of time either on pilgrimage or travelling in England, visiting shrines and speaking to her 'euyn-cristyns'.

The passage I have cited is not the only occasion when Christ sent Margery forth 'to divers placys of relygyon' (I. 12, p. 25, l. 28) to give spiritual counsel and consolation. Even when she was in her sixties and there was plague around, he commanded her: 'Dowtyr, go forth to þe hows of Denney [a convent] in þe name of Ihesu, for I wole þat þu comfort hem' (II. 5, p. 202, ll. 14–15). In addition, much of the divine affirmation of Margery's preaching occurs on the spot, when Christ gives her words to answer her detractors and the strength to withstand her

[6] The arrangement of the chapters in the *Book* and their lack of chronology have long been acknowledged as problematic. However, I would argue that this particular arrangement of chapters is deliberate, either on the part of the scribe, or of Margery herself.

[7] The most comprehensive critical work on medieval chaste marriage is Dyan Elliott, *Spiritual Marriage: Sexual Abstinence in Medieval Wedlock* (Princeton: Princeton University Press, 1993). Other useful works are Elizabeth M. Makowski, 'The Conjugal Debt and Medieval Canon Law', *Journal of Medieval History*, 3 (1977), 99–114; Margaret McGlynn and Richard J. Moll, 'Chaste Marriage in the Middle Ages: *It were to hir a greet merite*', in *Handbook of Medieval Sexuality*, ed. by Vern L. Bullough and James S. Brundage (New York: Garland, 1996), pp. 103–22.

[8] For discussions of age and menopause as significant factors in the lives of medieval holy women, see *The Prime of their Lives: Wise Old Women in Pre-Industrial Europe*, ed. by Anneke B. Mulder-Bakker and Renée Nip (Leuven: Peeters, 2005).

often hostile reception. In this, he is fulfilling his promise to her, during her conversion experience, when he tells her, 'I schal ȝeue þe grace j-now to answer euery clerke in þe loue of God' (I. 5, p. 17, ll. 19–20).[9]

Up to now I have described what Margery does as preaching. The term *preaching* is problematic in many ways, and, in fact, it is this complexity that generates the tension between Margery's actions and much of her reception. Margery herself never claims to be preaching — in fact, she emphatically denies it: 'I preche not, ser, I come in no pulpytt. I vse but comownycacon & good wordys' (I. 52, p. 126, ll. 18–20).[10] She always uses the words *conuersacyon*, *comonycacon*, or *dalyawns* to describe what she is doing when she speaks to folks in public. And she does not use a pulpit, but she does speak from elevated positions — windows, doorways, stairs. In Beverly, where she is imprisoned in an upper room on suspicion of Lollardy, 'stode sche lokyng owt at a wyndown, tellyng many good talys to hem þat wolde heryn hir' (I. 53, p. 130, ll. 34–36). In York, she may have gone further, perhaps offering her 'dalyawns' in the Minster itself. She certainly has encounters with various clerics in the Minster; the priest who accuses her of being 'a wolf' is one of them. It is clear that her reputation, which may have preceded her, spread during the two weeks she spent in York, and that she had an eager audience: '& in þat tyme many good men & women preyd hir to mete & madyn hir ryth good cher & weryn ryth glad to heryn hyr dalyawns, hauyng gret merueyle of hir speche for it was fruteful' (I. 50, p. 120, ll. 12–16).

Margery's avoidance of the word *preaching* — and of a pulpit — does not reflect mere semantic hair-splitting. On the one hand, there was no theological proscription against spiritual conversation or consolation, or acts of personal holiness.[11] This is the context within which Margery presents what she is doing. On the other hand, England in the early fifteenth century saw a Lollard under every bed. Lollards, followers of a version of the teachings of John Wyclif, first

[9] For examples of Margery's ability to 'answer euery clerke', see I. 12 and 13.

[10] Genelle Gertz-Robinson identifies this strategy, usefully, as 'a rhetoric of evasion that nevertheless signals homiletic intentions'. She also argues, as I do in this essay, that for Margery, preaching is defined by location — in other words, if she is not in the pulpit, she is not preaching. See 'Stepping into the Pulpit? Women's Preaching in *The Book of Margery Kempe* and *The Examinations of Anne Askew*', in *Voices in Dialogue: Reading Women in the Middle Ages*, ed. by Kathryn Kerby-Fulton and Linda Olson (Notre Dame: University of Notre Dame Press), pp. 459–82 (p. 460).

[11] See below for a discussion of preaching *ex beneficio* as opposed to *ex ordinatio*, and how Margery draws on the former tradition.

came to general attention through the show-trial of Walter Brut (1391–93), which offered ecclesiasts and theologians the opportunity to dissect and debate Lollard teaching.[12] An unanticipated consequence of this was the spreading of knowledge of the sect on a widespread and popular level.[13] The resultant fear of Lollardy led to the enactment of strict laws to contain it, culminating in the 1401 statute *De haeretico comburendo*, which provided for the burning of those deemed to be heretics. While most of the teachings of Wyclif and the Lollards involved sophisticated matters of theology, some points achieved such general credence that the man and woman in the street believed they could, as Chaucer put it, 'smelle a Lollere in the wynd'.[14] One of these points was that Lollards not only encouraged women to read the Scriptures for themselves, but also to preach — to be *Lectrices* and *Praedicatrices*. From preaching it was but a short slide down the slippery slope to women performing the sacraments — to, God forbid (as it was believed he did), women priests, another thing of which Lollards were accused.[15]

The fact that women were, indeed, preaching is attested by a number of sources. Thomas Netter (1372–1440), Provincial of the Carmelites, recounts

[12] For the trial of Walter Brut see Alastair Minnis, '"Respondet Walterus Bryth": Walter Brut in Debate on Women Priests', in *Text and Controversy from Wyclif to Bale: Essays in Honour of Anne Hudson*, ed. by Helen Barr and Anne Hutchison, Medieval Church Studies, 4 (Turnhout: Brepols, 2005), pp. 229–50.

[13] Scholars are divided about how widespread and influential Lollardy actually was. It seems to have been concentrated in urban areas, among the merchant and tradesman classes, and tales of its evil influence may have been largely a straw dog to distract the populace from problems inherent in the new Lancastrian administration. See Paul Strohm, *England's Empty Throne: Usurpation and the Language of Legitimation, 1399–1422* (New Haven: Yale University Press, 1998).

[14] Geoffrey Chaucer, *The Epilogue to the Man of Law's Tale*, in *The Riverside Chaucer*, gen. ed. Larry Benson (Boston: Houghton Mifflin, 1987), pp. 103–04, l. 1173.

[15] There has been considerable scholarship in recent years on the topic of women preaching. See, for example, Alcuin Blamires, 'Women and Preaching in Medieval Orthodoxy, Heresy, and Saint's Lives', *Viator*, 26 (1995), 135–52; Alastair Minnis, '*De impedimento sexus*: Women's Bodies and Medieval Impediments to Female Ordination', in *Medieval Theology and the Natural Body*, ed. by Peter Biller and Alastair Minnis (York: York Medieval Press, 1997), pp. 109–39; Kathryn Kerby-Fulton, 'When Women Preached: An Introduction to Female Homiletic, Sacramental and Liturgical Roles in the Later Middle Ages', in *Voices in Dialogue*, ed. by Kerby-Fulton and Olson, pp. 31–55; and Gary Macy, *The Hidden History of the Ordination of Women: Female Clergy in the Medieval West* (New York: Oxford University Press, 2007). On Lollard women priests, see Margaret Aston, 'Lollard Women Priests?', in *Lollards and Reformers: Images and Literacy in Late Medieval Religion* (London: Hambledon, 1984), pp. 49–69.

with grave disapproval, even horror, several such incidents. One of these involved a group of women in London, elevated on stools above the congregation of men, reading and explicating the Scriptures.[16] A somewhat more sympathetic writer of a Latin homily of the period states: 'Behold, we see now so great a scattering of the gospel, that simple men *and women*, and those accounted ignorant lay men (*laici ydiote*) write and study the Gospel, and as far as they can and know how, teach and scatter the word of God.'[17] By the time Margery was embarking on her tours of England, there was good reason to make any preaching she was doing a covert activity: to be a wolf in sheep's clothing. There was considerable risk involved in doing what she did: if she were convicted as a Lollard, she would be burnt. Her own parish priest, William Sawtre, in 1401 was the first person to be burnt as a Lollard, so she knew very well that this was a real possibility. As it was, she was twice arrested as a Lollard, and townspeople several times threatened her with burning.[18]

Margery was, emphatically, not a Lollard. As she tells the Archbishop of York, 'I am non heretyke, ne ȝe xal non preue me' (I. 52, p. 124, ll. 19–20). Her preaching came from another tradition, the tradition of Continental holy women, and was also significantly influenced by popular legends of Mary Magdalene and Catherine of Alexandria. However, she was operating in a country gripped by fear of Lollardy, and therein lies the reason that she took her preaching tour underground. It is here that we can isolate the tension between her actions as Christ's divinely appointed messenger and her reception as a troublesome woman who threatened social and spiritual stability.

This tension is embodied in the conflict between two important men in Margery's life: her confessor, Alan of Lynn, and Thomas Netter of Walden. Master Alan was a Carmelite and a friend and supporter of Margery. Thomas Netter was Provincial of the Carmelites, and therefore, Alan's superior. At one point, Netter forbade Alan to meet with Margery; this was a great blow to both of them. Alan of Lynn reportedly told others that 'he had leuar a lost an hundryd

[16] Thomas Netter, *Doctrinale antiquitatum fidei catholicae ecclesiae*, ed. by F. B. Blanciotti, 3 vols (Venice: Antonio Bassano, 1757–59; repr. Farnborough: Gregg, 1967), I, 638a. I would like to thank Kathryn Kerby-Fulton for our stimulating discussion of Netter and Margery while I was writing this essay.

[17] Cambridge, Cambridge University Library, MS, Ii.iii.8, fol. 149, cited in G. R. Owst, *Preaching in Medieval England* (Cambridge: Cambridge University Press, 1926), p. 135; my emphasis. The writer goes on to suggest that this activity is intended to confound and counteract corrupt and ill-informed priests.

[18] See, for example, I. 13, p. 28, ll. 29–31: 'þow xalt be brent, fals lollare. Her is a cartful of thornys redy for þe & a tonne to bren þe wyth'.

pownd, ȝyf he had an had it, þan hir communicacyon, it was so gostly & fruteful' (I. 69, p. 168, ll. 12–15).

The issue for Netter was acceptable spiritual practice and performance by women. Netter is the author of the *Doctrinale antiquitatum fidei catholicae ecclesiae*, a work that documents Wycliffite teachings and their enactment through Lollardy, in a determined attempt to disprove and discredit them. Netter deplores teaching and preaching by women, following standard arguments that they are prohibited by virtue of their sex, their lack of wisdom, and their lack of office. He reserves particular opprobrium for 'clamourous women, seated in the doorway of their houses on stools, frivolous and noisy, full of enticement but knowing nothing at all'.[19] Netter does, however, support anchoresses, that is, women whose spiritual practice kept them both silent and hidden from the public: 'virgins, indeed, of great continence, who labour with girded loins; they profess to do this and to remain in one place perpetually, by authority of the rite'.[20] Margery clearly belonged, in his eyes, to the former group of clamourous women, seeking publicity and performing in public.

Alan of Lynn, on the other hand, seems to have been something of a champion of holy women. He read widely the works of Continental holy women and created an index of the *Revelationes* of Birgitta of Sweden,[21] which demonstrates a very positive response to the saint, a woman known to have gone on preaching tours and who publicly admonished rulers, both secular and clerical. Birgitta was one of Margery's principal models, and it is more than possible that Alan of Lynn was responsible for her extensive knowledge; he may well have told her, or read to her, of other Continental holy women. In addition, Alan evidently encouraged Margery's own study of Scripture; the accusation against him includes the claim that he 'enformyd hir in qwestyons of Scriptur whan sche wolde any askyn hym' (I. 69, p. 168, ll. 8–9). This is one of only two specific references in the *Book* to Margery being instructed in Scripture, so it can be assumed that he had a significant effect on her learning.[22]

[19] '[M]ulier (inquiens) stulta & clamosa, plenaque illecebris & nihil omnino sciens, sedet in foribus domus suae super sellam': Netter, *Doctrinale*, I, 628a.

[20] '[V]irgines enim si tantum continent, lumbi praecincti sunt opere; si hoc profiteantur perpetuo facere, lumbi praecincti sunt stabilitate membri, & officii facultate': Netter, *Doctrinale*, I, 306d–307a.

[21] Oxford, Lincoln College, MS Lat. 69.

[22] The other reference is to the priest in Lynn who read to her over a period of seven or eight years: 'many a good boke of hy contemplacyon & oþer bokys, as þe Bybyl wyth doctowrys þer-up-

Despite the difficulties and dangers attendant on preaching, Margery did not hesitate to fulfil Christ's command.[23] Her awareness of what was involved in preaching (that is, the mechanics, the technique), was shaped in part, of course, by her own extensive experience as an audience for preachers — she was an inveterate seeker of sermons and pious conversations. However, her self-construction as a woman preaching drew of necessity on other traditions. The two primary influences, as I suggested earlier, are the continental tradition of holy women and popular legends of saints' lives.

Scholars, beginning with Hope Emily Allen in the 'Prefatory Note' to her edition of the *Book* (pp. liii–lxvi), have argued that Margery's spirituality and devotional praxis owe much more to the Continental than to the Insular tradition.[24] There can be little doubt that Margery knew of the Beguines of the Low Countries; it is possible that she encountered them as she travelled through the Low Countries on her way to Jerusalem.[25] The Beguines had a tradition of study

on, Seynt Brydys boke, Hyltons boke, Bone-ventur, Stimulus Amoris, Incendium Amoris, & swech oþer' (I. 58, p. 143, ll. 25–29).

[23] It seems quite possible that Margery's spiritual community in Lynn also encouraged her travels. When she returns from a visit to London, the Dominican anchorite in Lynn welcomes her back, saying that 'it was a gret myracle hir comyng & hir goyng to & fro'. Furthermore, he states that although he has been told to have nothing more to do with her, instead he asserts that she is 'a good woman, a louere of God, & hyly inspyred wyth þe Holy Gost', and that he will not forsake her (I. 16, p. 37, ll. 21–p. 38, l. 4). For more on this possibility, see Nicholas Watson, 'The Making of the *Book of Margery Kempe*', in *Voices in Dialogue*, ed. by Kerby-Fulton and Olson, pp. 395–434 (p. 427 n. 5).

[24] This is not surprising when we consider Margery's location in Lynn (her parish church was mere yards from the edge of the quay), where new ideas and concepts of spirituality came ashore with the pilgrims and sailors returning from the Continent. The importance of this geographical accident in the formation and performance of Margery's spirituality should not be underestimated.

[25] She may also have encountered them during her later pilgrimage in Northern Europe, a pilgrimage that immediately preceded the writing of her *Book*; the experiences and insights gained on this pilgrimage could well have had a profound effect on her self-construction throughout the *Book*. See Rosalynn Voaden, 'Travels with Margery: Pilgrimage in Context', in *Eastward Bound: Travel and Travellers, 1050–1550*, ed. by Rosamund Allen (Manchester: Manchester University Press, 2004), pp. 177–95. In addition, there is evidence that three communities of women, similar to beguinages, existed in Norwich in the early fifteenth century. These are unique in England. Margery could well have been aware of them (Norman Tanner, *The Church in Late Medieval Norwich, 1370–1532* (Toronto: Pontifical Institute of Mediaeval Studies,1984), p. 58). For an excellent overview of the influence, in England and on Margery, of Continental models of female preaching see Kathryn Kerby-Fulton, *Books Under Suspicion: Censorship and Tolerance of*

and explication of the Scriptures and maintained a high degree of contact with the secular world. The Parisian theologian Peter Cantor argued, in relation to the Beguines, that preaching is a mission to be shared by all who have the faith, though he reserves formal *praedicatio* in church to ordained clergy. He wrote that preaching could be done by 'gentle admonition or *exhortatio*, and [is] an act of charity, an act for which no-one should require permission'.[26] This is the tradition of preaching *ex beneficio* — as an act of charity — as opposed to *ex ordinatio* — that is, as an ordained priest — from which Margery takes her justification.

Margery would also have been aware of the *Devotio Moderna* movement, which originated in the Low Countries and spread rapidly during her lifetime, attracting many more women than men.[27] This movement, too, encouraged women to engage in forms of public teaching and ministry. Writing around 1395, Gerhard Zerbolt, canon lawyer and apologist for the *Devotio Moderna*, argued, interpreting Aquinas, that the Sisters should offer admonitions, exhortations, informal sermons, and reflections.[28] These influences can be discerned in Margery's covert preaching and in her various defences of her activities. They are evident also in *what* Margery was preaching. Nowhere in the episodes that could be construed as preaching does she refer to her privileged communication with the divine, or adopt a prophetic role.[29] Instead, she explicates Scripture and offers homilies and *exempla*, along with admonitions and exhortations, as the Beguines and Sisters of the *Devotio Moderna* did.

While in the diocese of York, for example, she argued before the Archbishop that the Gospels gave her, a woman, leave to speak of God, that God enjoins all the faithful to speak of him and, indeed, that church teaching itself supports this:

*Revelatory Writing in Late Medieval England* (Notre Dame: University of Notre Dame Press, 2006), pp. 247–71.

[26] Cited in Walter Simons, *Cities of Ladies: Beguine Communities in the Medieval Low Countries, 1200–1565* (Philadelphia: University of Pennsylvania Press, 2001), pp. 126–27.

[27] Followers of the *Devotio Moderna* (New Devout) were also known as Sisters, or Brothers, of the Common Life. For further information on the Sisters of the Common Life, including excerpts from their writing, see Wybren Scheepsma, *Medieval Religious Women in the Low Countries: The 'Modern Devotion', the Canonesses of Windesheim, and their Writings*, trans. by David F. Johnson (Woodbridge: Boydell, 2004).

[28] Cited in Kathryn Kerby-Fulton, '*Eciam Lollardi*: Some Further Thoughts on Fiona Somerset's *Eciam Mulier*: Women in Lollardy and the Problem of Sources', in *Voices in Dialogue*, ed. by Kerby-Fulton and Olson, pp. 261–78 (pp. 261, 264).

[29] She does this only in private, for example in her conversations with confessors, or her admonitions of naughty monks.

> And also þe Gospel makyth mencyon þat, whan þe woman had herd owr Lord prechyd, sche cam be-forn hym wyth a lowde voys & seyd, 'Blessyd be þe wombe þat þe bar & þe tetys þat ȝaf þe sowkyn.' Þan owr Lord seyd a-ȝen to hir, 'Forsoþe so ar þei blissid þat heryn þe word of God and kepyn it.' And þerfor, sir, me thynkyth þat þe Gospel ȝeuyth me leue to spekyn of God. (I. 52, p. 126, ll. 6–13)

In this incident, Margery both interprets Scripture and defends her right to 'spekyn of God'. She employs the same strategy of segueing from a defence of her communication into an informal homily, on several other occasions. For example, in Canterbury, she takes the opportunity to rebut the old monk who wishes her shut up in a house of stone, and his cronies, by telling a 'tale'. The tale concerns a man who is told to perform penance by hiring others to chide and pour scorn on him for his sins. One day he finds himself in a group of people who spontaneously mock and humiliate him. When asked why he is laughing, he replies that usually he has to pay for the torment, but this day he 'may kepe my syluer in my purs'. Margery then draws the obvious parallel with herself, strongly implying the spiritual superiority of humility over the jeering of her detractors (I. 13, p. 28, ll. 1–25).

Throughout the *Book*, there are numerous examples of 'admonitions and exhortations' similar to those which Zerbolt urged on the Sisters of the Common Life. Margery does not hesitate to admonish sinners and urge their correction, even when that sinner is the Archbishop of York: 'And, ȝyf ȝe ben as wikkyd as men seyn, ȝe xal neuyr come in Heuyn les þan ȝe amende ȝow whil ȝe ben her' (I. 52, p. 125, ll. 19–21).

There are, then, a number of ways in which her knowledge of Continental holy women contributed to Margery's understanding of her mission. Grafted on to this is the influence of saints' lives such as the *Legenda aurea* and the *South English Legendary*. The *Legenda aurea* was compiled by Jacobus de Voragine, Archbishop of Genoa. It was translated into every European vernacular, and it has been said that it was the most widely read work in the late Middle Ages, barring only the Bible.[30] Although there are only two extant manuscripts of Middle English translations of the work, both dating after 1438, an argument has been made that the East Anglian friar and contemporary of Margery Kempe, Osbern Bokenham, translated the work early in the fifteenth century.[31] *The South English Legendary*

[30] *The Golden Legend*, trans. by William Granger Ryan, 2 vols (Princeton: Princeton University Press, 1993), I, p. xiii.

[31] Sister Mary Jeremy, 'The English Prose Translation of *Legenda aurea*', *Modern Language Notes*, 59 (1944), 181–83. Bokenham also later compiled the *Legendys of Hooly Wummen*, which

circulated widely, particularly in the south-west of England.[32] The approximately sixty surviving manuscripts, dating from 1300–1500, attest to its continued popularity. These two works are only the best known of the compilations of saints' lives. Many other such collections were in circulation. There can be no doubt that Margery was steeped in the lives of the saints.

Two of Margery's favourite saints were Mary Magdalene and Catherine of Alexandria, whose lives and works are detailed in these collections, as well as in virtually all compilations of saints' lives from the period. The legends always represent Mary Magdalene as preaching and converting the natives of Provence.[33] Catherine of Alexandria disputes with fifty pagan philosophers (Margery would probably have loved such an opportunity; she is nothing if not disputatious!), and makes converts by the thousand before she is eventually martyred.[34] Not incidentally, these two saints were also principal saints for the Beguines. The legends of these two women offered Margery further justification and guidance as she took on the role of preacher.[35]

If Margery as preacher was formed largely by Continental influences, her reception was distinctly Insular, a reception shaped by the strong forces at work at the very time that she undertook her mission. As is evident in the conflict between Alan of Lynn and Thomas Netter, Wycliffite teachings and fear of Lollardy informed many official responses to Margery's work. This was not a monolithic response: it seems that many highly placed churchmen such as Thomas Arundel, the Archbishop of Canterbury, and Philip Repingdon, Bishop of Lincoln, understood Margery's spirituality as something quite different from Lollardy, and enjoyed spiritual conversation with her.[36] It is also evident that many ordinary

draws on much of the same material (*Legendys of Hooly Wummen*, ed. by Mary S. Serjeantson, EETS, o.s., 206 (London: Oxford University Press, 1938)).

[32] *Middle English Legends of Women Saints*, ed. by Sherry L. Reames, TEAMS Middle English Text Series (Kalamazoo: Medieval Institute Publications, 2003), p. 7.

[33] For the influence of legends of Mary Magdalene, see Katherine L. Jansen, *The Making of the Magdalen: Preaching and Popular Devotion in the Later Middle Ages* (Princeton: Princeton University Press, 2000).

[34] Katherine Lewis offers a convincing and detailed argument for the extensive influence of legends of St Catherine on Margery. See *The Cult of St Katherine of Alexandria in Late Medieval England* (Woodbridge: Boydell, 2000), pp. 247–56.

[35] For the effect of legends of both Mary Magdalene and Catherine of Alexandria on arguments about women preaching, see Blamires, 'Women and Preaching', pp. 142–45.

[36] It should be remembered, though, that these conversations generally took place in private, and that Margery was, presumably, on her best behaviour.

men and women enjoyed hearing her, and thought her 'comownycaycon' fruitful (I. 51, p. 126, ll. 19–20). On the other hand, her public performance incited great hostility among both clergy and lay. The Archbishop of York, although he could not fault her for her beliefs, was in no doubt that he wanted her out of his diocese (I. 52, p. 128, ll. 10–24). She was clearly seen as a source of trouble, a perception borne out by the hostile reception accorded her by people in various towns. For example, in Hessle she was harassed in the street and told to 'go spynne & carde as oþer women don' (I. 53, p. 129, ll. 35–36), and in Leicester she was held by the secular authorities for three weeks with the threat of burning hanging over her head (I. 46–49, pp. 111–19).

*The Book of Margery Kempe* chronicles the experiences of a woman who sought to live the life she believed Christ willed for her, and who strove to accommodate that life to the culture and climate of the time. Her book is a series of negotiations between ecclesiastical authorities and her own spiritual convictions, backed up by Christ's injunctions and advice. However, when conflict could not be negotiated, then we see the steely determination that led her to defy the Church in order to obey Christ. This determination — and a good dose of street cunning — is evident in her underground preaching tour, in her mounting of an unofficial and invisible pulpit in towns and cities throughout England. What has previously been seen by scholars as a series of wanderings driven by spiritual anxiety and insecurity can now be seen to be a structured progress, a conscious but covert mission undertaken, in defiance of ecclesiastical doctrine and social norms, in obedience to Christ.

*Arizona State University*

Lyric, Song, and Audience

# Rhetoric and Reception: Guillaume de Machaut's 'Je Maudi'

Phyllis R. Brown

When the fourteenth-century poet-musician Guillaume de Machaut five times repeats 'je maudi' (I curse) as a unifying device in his ballade that begins with those words, he positions his poem as a curse and a love lyric during a period of considerable political, philosophical, and literary-historical upheaval, when hindsight reveals that competition had begun between vernacular French literature and vernacular Italian literature.[1] Early in the fourteenth century, the several centuries of vernacular French tradition including lyric, romance, allegory, and translations of a wide variety of texts likely contributed to a confidence in French literary ascendancy similar to that widely acknowledged for France in the eighteenth and nineteenth centuries. Thus when Dante asserted in his treatise on vernacular eloquence (1304–09) that the Tuscan dialect offered opportunities for greater eloquence than French or any other Italian dialect, some readers would at least have raised an eyebrow.[2] However, by

[1] In Pascale Casanova, *The World Republic of Letters*, trans. by M. B. DeBevoise (Cambridge, MA: Harvard University Press, 2004), Casanova dates the beginning of nationally determined competition in literature to the sixteenth century: 'International literary space was formed in the sixteenth century at the very moment when literature began to figure as a source of contention in Europe, and it has not ceased to enlarge and extend itself since. Literary authority and recognition — and, as a result, national rivalries — came into existence with the formation and development of the first European states' (p. 11). I believe it is useful to think of Machaut's poetry as an earlier example of Casanova's argument.

[2] Although Dante himself identifies French and Provençal vernacular traditions as precedents for writing in Italian and more recently, in *Dante and the 'Roman de la Rose'* (Tubingen: Niemeyer, 1981), Earl Jeffrey Richards has examined the role of *Roman de la Rose* as an influence on Dante's *Comedia*, very little scholarly attention has been paid to the intertextuality or reciprocal

the sixteenth century Florence and the Tuscan dialect had 'prevailed in the intellectual sphere', Dante, Petrarch, and Boccaccio were viewed as preeminent examples of the supremacy of the Tuscan dialect, and Petrarch's lyric sequence and a variety of literary appropriations of Petrarchism had transformed European literary sensibilities in ways that nearly destroyed appreciation of Machaut's rhetorical poetics.[3] Those sensibilities continue to shape contemporary understanding of love and love poetry.

In the years between 1356 and 1370, though, when Machaut is likely to have written 'Je maudi', Petrarch's influence on the development of vernacular Italian and on international ideas about lyric consciousness was just beginning to be possible. Petrarch reported in his speech on the occasion of being crowned Poet Laureate in 1341 that he had received coronation invitations from the Chancellor of the University of Paris and the Roman Senate on the same day.[4] Awareness of that extraordinary honour would have increased the likelihood that readers and writers interested in literary developments would be paying close attention to his writing in the vernacular as well as in Latin from the late 1350s, when Petrarch first allowed early versions of the collection of poems he referred to as 'rerum vulgarium fragmenta' to circulate. Therefore it is possible that 'Je maudi', which does not appear in the earliest Machaut manuscripts and thus may not have been written until the late 1360s or early 1370s, is a satiric response to Petrarch's sonnet 'Blessed be the day', which did circulate in at least one early collection of Petrarch's lyric sequence.[5]

influences of medieval and early modern French and Italian literature. That the competition between France and Italy pertained to much more than vernacular literary supremacy is amply attested by Petrarch's 1368 letter to Pope Urban V, Jean d'Hesdin's response, and Petrarch's 'Invective against a Detractor of Italy' (Invectiva contra eum qui maledixit Italie). See Francesco Petrarca, *Invectives*, ed. and trans. by David Marsh (Cambridge, MA: Harvard University Press, 2003), pp. 364–475.

[3] Casanova, *World Republic*, p. 10. See William J. Kennedy, *Authorizing Petrarch* (Ithaca: Cornell University Press, 1994), for a discussion of 'the authorizing of Petrarch's *Rime sparse* as a canonical lyric text for a broad fifteenth- and sixteenth-century European readership and for an equally broad assemblage of lyric poets in Italy, France, and England', pp. ix–x.

[4] Ernest Hatch Wilkins, 'Petrarch's Coronation Oration', in his *Studies in the Life and Works of Petrarch* (Cambridge, MA: Mediaeval Academy of America, 1955), p. 304. The Clerk's reference in Geoffrey Chaucer's 'The Clerk's Prologue' to 'a worthy clerk', 'Fraunceys Petrak, the lauriat poete' (ll. 27, 31), from whom he learned the story of Griselda, suggests extended interest in the event by 1374.

[5] For information on manuscript transmission, see Ernest Hatch Wilkins, *The Making of the Canzoniere and Other Petrarchan Studies* (Rome: Edizioni di storia e letterature, 1951), and

At the very least, changing the vantage point for reading Machaut's ballade to allow a broader sweep — including not only other works in Machaut's oeuvre and the manuscript context Machaut himself created for his writings, but also other developments in the European literary world — creates the possibility of rediscovering coherence and meaning otherwise not evident. Pascale Casanova writes,

> The persistent tendency of critics to isolate texts from one another prevents them from seeing in its entirety the configuration (to use Michel Foucault's term) to which all texts belong; that is, the totality of texts and literary and aesthetic debates with which a particular work of literature enters into relation and resonance, and which forms the true basis for its singularity, its real originality.[6]

Casanova goes on to argue that critics should recognize the 'international competition' every writer enters into, whether consciously or not. Awareness of the '"spiritual economy" [Paul Valéry's term] underlying the structure of the literary world' and hierarchical structures and constraints of literary history allows critics to see individual works of literature in new ways.[7] Well into the fifteenth century, Machaut's poetry ranked high in the literary economy; by the sixteenth century, his lyric poetry was dismissed as artificial and old-fashioned — a vestige of the supposedly dark ages. This essay aims to join the critics who have begun a revaluation of Machaut's lyric poetry and the late medieval rhetorical poetry associated with him by reading 'Je maudi' from a vantage point that allows a broad view of the literary history it participates in.[8]

Laurence Earp, 'The Manuscripts', *Guillaume de Machaut: A Guide to Research* (New York: Garland, 1995).

[6] Casanova, *World Republic*, p. 3.

[7] Casanova, *World Republic*, p. 10, and throughout the chapter 'Principles of a World History of Literature', pp. 9–44.

[8] Critical attention to Machaut's lyric poetry has begun to change the literary-historical views shaped by sixteenth-century thinking. Daniel Poirion's 1965 *Le Poète et le Prince: L'évolution du lyrisme courtois de Guillaume de Machaut à Charles d'Orléans* (Geneva: Slatkine, 1978) and Paul Zumthor's *Anthologie des grands rhétoriqueurs* (Paris: Union Générale d'Éditions, 1978) helped overcome critical prejudice against rhetorically self-conscious poetry and generated new interest in Machaut's lyric poetry and the poetry of the *rhétoriqueurs*. Leonard W. Johnson's *Poets as Players: Theme and Variation in Late Medieval French Poetry* (Stanford: Stanford University Press, 1990) builds on Poirion's and Zumthor's work. In addition, attention to 'rhetorical poetics' in medieval poetry by Robert O. Payne, *The Key of Remembrance: A Study of Chaucer's Poetics* (Westport, CT: Greenwood, 1963), Paul Zumthor, *Essai de poétique médiévale* (1972), trans. by Philip Bennett as *Toward a Medieval Poetics* (Minneapolis: University of Minnesota Press, 1992),

Petrarch's sonnet is frequently anthologized and translated and therefore is well known beyond specialist circles. In Robert Durling's prose translation, it reads:

> Blessed be the day and the month and the year and the season and the time and the hour and the instant and the beautiful countryside and the place where I was struck by the two lovely eyes that have bound me;
>
> and blessed be the first sweet trouble I felt on being made one with Love, and the bow and the arrows that pierced me, and the wounds that reach my heart!
>
> Blessed be the many words I have scattered calling the name of my lady, and the sighs and the tears and the desire;
>
> and blessed be all the pages where I gain fame for her, and my thoughts, which are only of her, so that no other has part in them![9]

'Blessed be the day' provides a good example of the poetic skill that makes Petrarch's collection of lyric poetry 'the foundation text of modern lyric poetry in the European languages'.[10] Literary history since the fourteenth century provides readers with clear guidelines for understanding and appreciating the sonnet, although that same literary history also obscures some of the complexity of Petrarch's verse.

Machaut's 'Je maudi' is rarely anthologized or translated. My translation is as literal as possible while retaining line divisions and stanza structure for the ballade:

> I curse the hour and the time and the day,
> the week, the place, the month, the year,
> and the two eyes by which I saw the sweetness
> of my lady who has ended my joy.
> And also I curse my heart and my thoughts,
> my loyalty, my desire and my love,

Douglas Kelly, in *Medieval Imagination: Rhetoric and the Poetry of Courtly Love* (Madison: University of Wisconsin Press, 1978), has surfaced new awareness of complexities in the ways medieval poets negotiated their relationship to tradition; see also the collection of essays honouring Payne, *The Rhetorical Poetics of the Middle Ages: Reconstructive Polyphony*, ed. by John M. Hill and Deborah M. Sinnreich-Levi (Madison: University of Wisconsin Press, 2000).

[9] *Petrarch's Lyric Poems: The 'Rime sparse' and Other Lyrics*, ed. and trans. by Robert M. Durling (Cambridge, MA: Harvard University Press, 1976), p. 138.

[10] Germaine Warkentin, 'Introduction', *Petrarch's Songbook, Rerum Vulgarium Fragmenta: A Verse Translation*, trans. by James Wyatt Cook, ed. by Gianfranco Contini (Binghamton, NY: Center for Medieval and Renaissance Studies, 1996), p. 1.

and the resistance that has made languish in weeping
*my doleful heart in a strange country.*
And also I curse greeting, charm, attire
and the glance by which love was begotten
in my heart, which keeps it in a feverish state;
and also I curse the hour when she was born,
her false seeming, her proven falseness,
her immense pride, her harshness devoid of tenderness
or pity, which keep in such languor
*my doleful heart in a strange country.*
And also I curse Fortune and her false turns,
the planet, the hour, the fate
which might view my foolish heart in such error
that I never served or loved.
But I beseech God that he defend her fame,
her well-being, her peace, bestow honour on her
and forgive her having slain with sorrow
*my doleful heart in a strange country.*[11]

It is harder to know how to read Machaut's ballade than Petrarch's sonnet. The idea of a love poem embedded in a curse — or a curse embedded in a love poem — has an uncanny quality that flies in the face of generic expectations, inviting readers to rethink the 'rules of the game' of lyric poetry by considering the 'horizon of expectation' suggested *and* transgressed by the poem.[12] For readers

[11] Nigel Wilkins presents the following text in his edition, *La Louange des Dames by Guillaume de Machaut* (New York: Barnes and Noble, 1973), pp. 77–78: 'Je maudi l'eure et le temps et le jour, | La semainne, le lieu, le mois, l'année, | Et les .ij. yex dont je vi la douçour | De ma dame qui ma joie a finée. | Et si maudi mon cuer et ma pensée, | Ma loyauté, mon desir et m'amour, | Et le dangier qui fit languir en plour | *Mon dolent cuer en estrange contrée.* | Et si maudi l'acueil, l'attrait, l'atour | Et le regart dont l'amour engendrée | Fu en mon cuer, qui le tient en ardour; | Et si maudi l'eure qu'elle fu née, | Son faus semblant, sa fauseté prouvée, | Son grant orgueil, sa durté où tenrour | N'a ne pité, qui tient en tel langour | *Mon dolent cuer en estrange contrée.* | Et si maudi Fortune et son faus tour, | La planette, l'eür, la destinée | Qui mon fol cuer mirent en tel errour | Qu'onques de moy fu servie n'amée. | Mais je pri Dieu qu'il gart sa renommée, | Son bien, sa pais, et li acroisse honnour | Et le pardoint ce qu'ocist à dolour | Mon dolent cuer en estrange contrée.'

[12] Hans Robert Jauss writes, 'for each work a preconstituted horizon of expectations must be ready at hand (this can also be understood as a relationship of "rules of the game" [Zusammenhang von Spielregeln]) to orient the reader's (public's) understanding and to enable a qualifying

since the sixteenth century, the 'horizon of expectation' for Petrarch's vernacular lyrics, the 'foundation text' against which lyric poetry is usually read, also inevitably influences any reading of Machaut's lyric. This essay investigates ways the ethos of a literary curse and ambiguities in Machaut's poem affect understanding of tone and theme. In particular, I argue that grammatical ambiguities and the turn to the allegorical figure Fortune and the idea of fame or renown in the final stanza relate to the 'horizon of expectation' for the poem and thus contribute to the poem's critical reception.

Some background biographical information will set the scene for readers who do not know Machaut's and Petrarch's work well. Although it is usual to categorize Machaut as a medieval poet-musician and Petrarch as a Renaissance writer, they were exact contemporaries, and it is likely they knew one another's work at least by reputation. Machaut, generally acknowledged to be the preeminent fourteenth-century French poet and musician, was born around 1300 and died in 1377. Petrarch, arguably the most influential intellectual of the Trecento, lived from 1304 until 1374. Before taking up residency as a canon at Reims Cathedral in the 1340s, Machaut travelled in Central and Eastern Europe and perhaps as far south as Lombardy with the court of John of Luxembourg, King of Bohemia. Petrarch supported himself after 1330 with a variety of ecclesiastical appointments, many of which seem to have been honorary. Throughout his career Petrarch was in close association with many of the most powerful leaders of Europe, including John of Luxembourg's oldest son, who became Holy Roman Emperor as Charles IV. Between about 1332 and 1349, when John of Luxembourg's daughter Bonne died, including the years when she was wife of John, Duke of Normandy (after 1350, King John II), Machaut served her. Although Machaut's relationship to John II is not well documented, two of Bonne's and John II's sons, John, Duke of Berry, and Charles V, were important patrons. Late in 1360, Galeazzo Visconti sent Petrarch to Paris to deliver an oration to John II, celebrating the Anglo-French treaty that had resulted in John II's release from captivity and return to Paris.[13] Petrarch wrote at that time of the terrible effects

reception' ('Theory of Genres and Medieval Literature', in *Toward an Aesthetic of Reception*, trans. by Timothy Bahti (Minneapolis: University of Minnesota Press, 1982), p. 79).

[13] Visconti helped France pay the first installment of the huge ransom for the release of John II in return for the marriage of his eight-year-old son to John II's eleven-year-old daughter, Isabelle. Petrarch was in Milan at the time of the wedding. Ernest Hatch Wilkins, *Life of Petrarch* (Chicago: University of Chicago Press, 1961), p. 172.

war had had on France and Paris and of contrasts to the Paris he visited in 1333: 'I recognized hardly anything, seeing a once opulent kingdom turned to ashes'.[14] While in Paris, Petrarch met frequently with Pierre Bersuire, whom he had known years earlier in Avignon and who was also a friend to Machaut. And both Machaut and Petrarch admired Philippe de Vitry (1291–1361), whom Petrarch called the only true poet among the French.[15]

Machaut and Petrarch are both significant in the development of their own vernacular literatures and with Geoffrey Chaucer form a 'triumvirate of European poets [...] attempting to shape the possibility of a subjective position for the vernacular poet outside the then-dominant mode of romance verse narrative'.[16] Machaut's and Petrarch's poetry provides evidence of shared interests in other fourteenth-century intellectual issues, such as limits on the human ability to know truth; the potential for love and love poetry to be restorative and integrative as well as spiritually destructive; the reality and nature of Fortune; and 'literary reflexivity' — the idea of 'taking the very act of writing as the object of writing'.[17]

[14] Cited in Wilkins, *Life of Petrarch*, p. 174.

[15] Margaret Bent and Andrew Wathey, 'Philippe de Vitry', *Grove Music Online*, ed. by L. Macy, <http://www.grovemusic.com> [accessed 29 August 2007]. Wimsatt's discussion in *Chaucer and his French Contemporaries: Natural Music in the Fourteenth Century* (Toronto: University of Toronto Press, 1993) of the exchange of poems between Vitry, Jean Campion, and Jean de le Mote, in which Vitry and Campion ridicule le Mote's poetry, especially his uses of literary allusion, may shed light on Petrarch's attitudes toward French poetry. Wimsatt writes, 'The influence of Vitry's friend Petrarch perhaps may be discerned in their attitude towards le Mote's classical reference, which is very like the attitude of later Humanists towards medieval writers' (p. 71). Although little of Vitry's poetry survives, he is cited frequently after 1340 as a leading intellectual. Wimsatt writes, 'there is no doubt that Machaut was the most important poet of the Middle French period' (p. 76).

[16] Warkentin, 'Introduction', p. 8. Armando Petrucci writes that in the thirteenth and fourteenth centuries libraries in Italy began to preserve texts in vernacular languages, 'at minimum French and Provençal in addition to Italian, because aristocratic education, at least at the highest levels, provided for learning and understanding the languages of "courtly" European literature through reading and usage' (*Writers and Readers in Medieval Italy: Studies in the History of Written Culture*, ed. and trans. by Charles M. Radding (New Haven: Yale University Press, 1995), p. 218).

[17] Jacqueline Cerquiglini-Toulet, *The Color of Melancholy: The Uses of Books in the Fourteenth Century*, trans. by Lydia G. Cochrane (Baltimore: Johns Hopkins University Press, 1997), p. 53. Both Petrarch and Machaut devoted years to the writing, arranging, rewriting, and rearranging their vernacular lyric output. The most authoritative Machaut manuscript, probably copied under his personal supervision, includes a heading that reads, 'Vesci l'ordenance que G. de Machau wet qu'il ait en son livre' (Here is the order that G. de Machaut wants his book to have).

Both Machaut and Petrarch evince a seemingly 'modern' concern with the rhetoric and poetic of their creative activity, the manuscript context of their poems, and their writings' reception. In addition to inviting readers to consider their poems not just as individual pieces but also as they have ordered them, in particular contexts, both Petrarch and Machaut simultaneously build on classical and medieval traditions and break from those traditions in important and radical ways.

Significant differences between Machaut's and Petrarch's styles also stand out, especially since the Petrarchan style has had so much influence on subsequent developments in lyric poetry. In particular the seriousness with which lover-poets, modelled after the persona in Petrarch's *Rime Sparse*, present themselves contrasts sharply with the comic irony, rhetorical self-consciousness, and undermining of a unified, harmonious worldview characteristic of Machaut's poetic oeuvre.[18] Certainly the two poets negotiated their relationship to tradition in very different ways. Perhaps most obviously, Petrarch was emphatic about the newness of what he was doing and, at the same time, its links to classical lyric poetry. Machaut was also powerfully influenced by Latin poetry, especially Ovid's witty treatments of love and Boethius's *Consolation of Philosophy*, but the influence of earlier French vernacular writing is also significant. Even more important, though, are the differences in the ways the two authors presented themselves to the intellectual world they were part of and to posterity. One of the reasons for the twentieth-century renewal of interest in Machaut's rhetorical poetics may be its relationship to metafiction and to what Linda Hutcheon calls 'narcissistic narrative', which appears 'to turn in on the reader, forcing him to face his responsibility for the text he is reading, the dynamic "heterocosm" he is creating through the fictive referents of literary language'.[19]

## *Ethos and Literary Curses*

Literary curses have a long textual history with relevance to metafiction and 'narcissistic narrative', to Casanova's observations about literary competition, and

[18] Richard Lanham explores in *The Motives of Eloquence: Literary Rhetoric in the Renaissance* (New Haven: Yale University Press, 1976), pp. 1–35, the extent to which a 'sincere', 'serious', and transparent style has been valued more highly than a 'rhetorical style', one that draws attention to style and the games writers play with language.

[19] Linda Hutcheon, 'Composite Identity: The Reader, the Writer, the Critic', *Narcissistic Narrative: The Metafictional Paradox* (Waterloo, ON: Wilfrid Laurier University Press, 1980), p. 138.

to new awareness in the fourteenth century that literature not only expresses truth but also participates in the construction of truth.[20] Two examples of early literary curses Machaut is likely to have known, Psalm 109 (108 in the Vulgate numbering) and Ovid's 'Ibis', in which all the linguistic and rhetorical skills of the writers serve to amplify, complicate, and intensify the power of the curse, provide a background to the complexity of literary curses in the Middle Ages and an understanding of how Machaut and his readers may have responded to the verb *maudire*.

Psalm 109 includes an extended curse that was frequently cited and quoted throughout the early Christian period and the Middle Ages. In the Douay translation of the Latin Vulgate, after opening with 'O God, be not thou silent in my praise: for the mouth of the wicked and the mouth of the deceitful man is opened against me', the curse follows a few verses later:

> May his days be few: and his bishopric let another take.
>
> May his children be fatherless, and his wife a widow.
>
> Let his children be carried about vagabonds, and beg; and let them be cast out of their dwellings.
>
> May the usurer search all his substance: and let strangers plunder his labours.
>
> May there be none to help him: nor none to pity his fatherless offspring.
>
> May his posterity be cut off; in one generation may his name be blotted out.
>
> May the iniquity of his fathers be remembered in the sight of the Lord: and let not the sin of his mother be blotted out.[21]

As the Psalm concludes, the speaker enumerates the ways he has suffered, and then says,

> Help me, O Lord my God; save me according to thy mercy.
>
> And let them know that this is thy hand: and that thou, O Lord, hast done it.
>
> They will curse and thou wilt bless: let them that rise up against me be confounded: but thy servant shall rejoice.
>
> Let them that detract me be clothed with shame: and let them be covered with their confusion as with a double cloak.[22]

[20] See Laurence de Looze, *Pseudo-Autobiography in the Fourteenth Century: Juan Ruiz, Guillaume de Machaut, Jean Froissart, and Geoffrey Chaucer* (Gainesville: University Press of Florida, 1997), pp. 11–16, for a discussion of 'the poet's new role as a shaper of truth' in the fourteenth century.

[21] *The Holy Bible: Douay-Rheims Version*, trans. from the Latin Vulgate (Baltimore, MD: Murphy, 1899; repr. Rockford, Illinois: Tan Books, 1971), ll. 8–14.

[22] *The Holy Bible: Douay-Rheims Version*, ll. 26–29.

Interpretation of this Psalm has varied over time, but there is general agreement that the speaker's situation justifies his calling God's wrath down upon his enemy.[23] The Old Testament context — for example, passages such as Deuteronomy 27 and 28, where Moses and the Levitical priests inform the people of Israel about the curses that will result from disobedience to God's will — encourages fear of and admiration for curses, especially those associated with disobedience to God's will. The presence of a curse in the 'Song of Deborah' in Judges 5. 23, the oldest text in the Bible, suggests a respect for and a fear of curses — and the people articulating them — that is deep and culturally significant. However, Christian understanding of Old Testament curses had to take into account Christ's instructions to his disciples: 'Bless them that curse you and pray for them that calumniate you.'[24] Many examples of texts urging Christians not to curse survive. Yet the number of religious writers, such as Gregory the Great (sixth century), the Venerable Bede (seventh-eighth centuries), and Smaragdus of Saint-Mihiel (eighth-ninth centuries), who justify prohibitions against cursing, and the many texts including curses that survive, indicate cursing continued to be a common speech act.

By the sixth century, some Church authorities, grappling with Old Testament evidence that God himself cursed and acknowledging the power of curses, had distinguished between two kinds of curses in the Bible and had laid the foundation for the idea that some cursing was acceptable, even that curses could be incorporated into liturgies, either as part of a mass or as a free-standing service. Lester Little notes in *Benedictine Maledictions* that in the thirteenth century Thomas Aquinas resolved difficulties understanding biblical curses by arguing that 'scriptural curses were of the sort that are not really curses in substance, but only accidentally so, because the chief intentions of the speakers are directed not to evil but to good'.[25] Geoffrey Chaucer's *Friar's Tale* provides a particularly vivid,

[23] *The New Oxford Annotated Bible* specifies that the speaker is articulating a counter-curse and asking God to deliver him from the effects of his enemy's curse; *The Anchor Bible* specifies that the speaker is an unjustly accused man calling down God's wrath against an evil judge and his associates.

[24] *The Holy Bible: Douay-Rheims Version*, Luke 6. 28.

[25] Lester K. Little, *Benedictine Maledictions: Liturgical Cursing in Romanesque France* (Ithaca: Cornell University Press, 1993), p. 99. The book presents many examples of liturgical curses surviving from the ninth to the twelfth centuries and their sources, justifications, and uses. Little gives as one example that 'an excommunication formula pronounced against assassins in the year 900 at Reims [where Machaut was later a canon] specifies that there should fall upon the assassins' heads "all the maledictions by which the Lord through Moses threatened transgressors of the divine law"' (p. 106).

slightly later example of another distinction, between a 'real' curse empowering the devil to carry off the Summoner with the widow's pan and language using the formula of a curse without the impact of a curse.[26] Similarly in Machaut's 'Je maudi', the ethos of the curse and its meaning depend on the situation and motivation of the speaker. The speaker in Machaut's ballade probably does not want harm to come to his lady any more than the carter in Chaucer's tale wants harm to come to his horse.

Ovid's 'Ibis', a 644-line tour de force written during the poet's exile at Tomi on the Black Sea (probably 8 or 9 CE), provides a second example of the complexity of literary curses as a context in which to understand Machaut's 'Je maudi'. Ovid's poem especially foregrounds the idea that the curse can draw attention to the artistry of the writer as much as or even more than to the potential supernatural linguistic power of the curse. In 'Ibis', Ovid draws on a wide range of literary examples to call down upon his unnamed enemy the worst miseries and violent deaths imaginable. One editor of the poem remarks, 'The greater part of the work consists of a long series of imprecations, in the course of which the whole of mythology is ransacked for instances of violent deaths, which the poet prays will be his enemy's lot.'[27]

In addition to alluding to earlier accounts of violent deaths, Ovid also aligns himself with two earlier Greek writers especially famous for their curses. Near the beginning, the speaker says,

> I will suffer thee [the unnamed enemy he attacks in the poem] a short while to dissemble who thou art. Afterwards, if thou dost continue, my satire unrestrained shall hurl at thee missiles tinged by Lycambean blood. Now, in such wise as Battiades calls curses down on his enemy Ibis, so do I call curses down on thee and thine.[28]

[26] The devil, riding with the Summoner in *The Friar's Tale*, distinguishes between the curse of a carter, when his horse and cart are stuck in the mud ('"The feend", quod he, "yow fecche, body and bones, | As ferforthly as evere were ye foled, | So muche wo as I have with you tholed! | The devel have al, bothe hors and cart and hey!"'; ll. 1544–47) and the curse of the old widow ('"Unto the devel blak and rough of hewe | Yeve I thy body and my panne also!"'; ll. 1622–23) and then when asked by the devil whether she really means what she says, says of the Summoner, to the devil, '"so fecche hym er he deye, | And panne and al, but he wol him repente!"' (ll. 1628–29). The devil demonstrates to the carter that he pays attention to intention and situation before responding to the words of a curse.

[27] J. H. Mozley, 'Introduction', *The Art of Love and Other Poems*, ed. and trans. by J. H. Mozley (Cambridge, MA: Harvard University Press, 1962), p. x.

[28] Ovid, 'Ibis', in *The Art of Love and Other Poems*, ed. and trans. by Mozley, p. 257.

In these lines, Ovid specifies that his curse intensifies its power by drawing on Archilochus's verbal attack on Lycambes and his daughters (around 700 BCE), which was notorious for resulting in their deaths, and the famous attack by the Alexandrain poet Callimachus (referred to above as Battiades) on his enemy, in a poem also called 'Ibis'.[29] Ovid then proceeds to call on the gods of land and sea; on earth, sea, air, constellations, the sun, the moon, night, fauns, satyrs, streams, nymphs; the race of demigods; and gods 'old and new from ancient chaos down to our own time' to witness 'the dreadful spells' to be 'chanted against that faithless head, and grief and anger play their parts', giving assent to the speaker's desires and letting no part of his supplication fail. The curse proper begins,

> May the earth refuse thee her fruits and the river his waters, may wind and breeze deny their breath. May the sun not be warm for thee, nor Phoebe bright, may the clear stars fail thy vision. May neither Vulcan nor the air lend thee their aid, nor earth nor sea afford thee any path. Mayst thou wander an exile and destitute, and haunt the doors of others, and beg a little food with trembling mouth.

The speaker goes on to specify that the torment will continue long after death: 'Twisted thongs shall crack and twined serpents hiss, and torches smoke before thy guilty face. By these furies shalt thou be driven while living and by these when dead, and thy punishment shall outlast thy life.'[30] Part of the wonder of the poem is Ovid's ability to sustain the ferocity of his attack for so many lines, with so much variety, drawing on so many literary and mythical sources.

However, a paradoxical result of Ovid's references to and amplification of earlier curses is to undermine the seriousness of the curse. Although the speaker could be that angry with the unnamed detractor, the poem comes across as being more about Ovid's power as a writer than about the power of his curse. Information about where and how Ovid's poetry was read during the Middle Ages provides evidence that Ovid was valued more for his skill as a writer than for what he had to say. In *Ovid and Medieval Schooling*, Ralph Hexter examines medieval

[29] Greek literature was known in the Western Middle Ages largely through Latin translations and citations in Latin texts. Ovid's works, in contrast, were widely known and cited throughout the Middle Ages. See Ralph J. Hexter, *Ovid and Medieval Schooling: Studies in Medieval School Commentaries on Ovid's 'Ars amatoria', 'Epistulae ex Ponto', and 'Epistulae Heroidum'* (Munich: Arbeo-Gesellschaft, 1986), and James H. McGregor, 'Ovid at School: From the Ninth to the Fifteenth Century', *Classical Folia*, 32 (1978), 29–51. Concluding a review of Lindsay Watson's study of Greek curses, Marco Fantuzzi expresses admiration that 'one of the commonest speech acts of everyday life could give rise to a variety of the most intellectually refined poetry of Greece' (*Journal of Roman Studies*, 85 (1995), 270–71 (p. 271)).

[30] Ovid, 'Ibis', pp. 259–63.

school commentaries on Ovid's *Ars amatoria*, *Epistulae ex Ponto*, and *Epistulae Heroidum* for evidence of how widely Ovid was read and how his texts were interpreted. Hexter's study concludes that school commentaries on Ovid's texts served multiple purposes in the curriculum, especially providing examples for grammatical instruction, 'examples of rhetoric, of argumentation in verse', and 'a compendium of classical mythology, for some [students] an introduction to the more basic stories, for others information about the truly recherché'.[31] Edwin Quain surveys readings of classical authors, including Ovid, reflected in medieval commentaries on classical texts and concludes, 'The writers of antiquity, both pagan and Christian, were in the medieval schools known as *auctores*, writers who possessed an *auctoritas* to which respect and admiration were due[...]. The *auctor* was cited but his words were interpreted to suit the purpose of the writer.' He goes on to say, 'In view of the many condemnations of pagan immorality of which we have evidence, it is impossible to suppose that the medieval writer really believed that Ovid, for instance, had a high moral purpose in writing the *Ars amatoria*. Ovid, as an *auctor*, was the possession of the teacher of the Middle Ages and he could be used for whatever purpose the teacher wished.'[32]

In the Middle Ages students often began reading Ovid's *Remedia amoris* as part of their grammar lessons shortly after learning the alphabet, the Lord's Prayer, and the Psalter. Anthologies of readings for students include Ovid's works as grammatical and, for more advanced students, rhetorical models. In his study 'Ovid at School: From the Ninth to the Fifteenth Century', James H. McGregor examines 'five major sources of information on medieval grammar curricula', which specify Ovid's writings played significant roles in the curriculum, 'while each suggests some care in exposing students to all that Ovid wrote'.[33] Although it seems unlikely that 'Ibis' was a school text, Mozley reports that twelfth- and thirteenth-century manuscripts of 'Ibis' survive in Frankfurt, Berlin, Tours, Vienna, Cambridge, and Paris, and McGregor lists one instance of 'Ibis' in a twelfth/thirteenth-century educational anthology and a surprisingly large number of occurrences of 'Ibis' in medieval library catalogues: five in the twelfth century, six in the thirteenth century, one in the fourteenth century, and three in the fifteenth century.[34]

[31] Hexter, *Ovid and Medieval Schooling*, p. 214.

[32] Edwin Quain, 'The Medieval Accessus ad Auctores', *Traditio: Studies in Ancient and Medieval History, Thought and Religion*, 3 (1945), 215–64 (p. 225).

[33] McGregor, 'Ovid at School', p. 39.

[34] Mozley, 'Introduction', p. xiii; McGregor, 'Ovid at School', pp. 50–51.

Machaut's poem clearly shares a 'horizon of expectation' with the Psalm curses and Ovid's 'Ibis', especially in connection with the power of language and the complexity of ethos. A curse can empower for good or for ill, with the outcome dependent on the circumstances, motivation, and skill of the speaker. Machaut's 'Je maudi' especially shares with Ovid's 'Ibis' the idea that the poem is more about the author's power as an author than about the curses or the objects of the curses.[35]

The following fourteenth-century Italian sonnet, probably written by Cino da Pistoia, suggests Machaut's poem (and its ethos) should be read as one piece of a larger fourteenth-century intellectual pattern:

> I curse the day when I first saw the light from your treacherous eyes and the point where/when you came into the top of the heart to draw the spirit outside; And I curse the beloved rasp that has scoured my words and the beautiful colors which I have found through you and have put into rhyme to do such that the world will ever honor you; And I curse my hard mind which is firm in holding that which kills me, namely your beautiful and guilty figure, for which Love often perjures himself, so that everyone ridicules him and me, because I trust to take the wheel from fortune/for the future.[36]

This Italian sonnet raises questions in much the same way Machaut's ballade does, but much less is known about its rhetorical situation and context since even the sonnet's authorship can only be hypothesized by internal evidence, while Machaut's authorship of 'Je maudi' is absolutely certain, its position in the complete-works manuscripts is stable, and a poetic prologue to one complete-work manuscript including 'Je maudi' articulates his poetic purposes. Consider-

[35] There are some notable differences among these curse poems. For example, Machaut repeats the verb *maudire* in the first person singular indicative, while the Psalm text and Ovid's 'Ibis' more often use the second person optative. Moreover, the speaker in Machaut's poem never specifies what will happen as a result of the curses, leaving open an interpretative gap for readers to fill in. While neither the Psalm curse nor 'Ibis' specifies the object of the curses, leaving a different kind of interpretative gap — one that opens up the applicability of the curses to multiple recipients — both are directed at human enemies and go into very great detail about what the results of the curses will be. Machaut's curse in contrast, consistently strikes around the lady without any direct hit. The closest Machaut comes to cursing a human being is to curse his own heart and thoughts. Although the complexity of ethos and tone in Machaut's curse seems closer to that of Ovid's 'Ibis' than to the Psalm curse, fourteenth-century readers encountering Machaut's curse would likely recall the ethical complexity of Old Testament and liturgical curses — and the New Testament injunctions against cursing as substance for the gap — and at the same time would be aware of intellectual concerns about pagan classical texts' being used as grammatical and rhetorical models in the schools.

[36] Translated by George H. Brown. This sonnet has also been attributed to Dante Alighieri.

able evidence survives about themes and ideas related to the ideology of Machaut's work as a whole, resulting in understanding of the literary reflexivity of Machaut's poetry, such as the 'subtle game' Machaut played when he introduced writing, literature, and books as a 'third term' in the traditional subject matter of literary works, warfare and love.[37]

Awareness of a second, quite similar curse poem posing as a love poem provides an impetus to consider that political and religious instability and philosophical developments in this literary-historical period are relevant to meaning in both poems. Confidence in absolute truths was severely undermined in fourteenth-century Europe by the Papal schism, the Hundred Years' War, plague, and increases in socioeconomic mobility. Thirteenth-century scholarly debates about the nature of Truth, the impact of which had been limited to the intelligentsia, in the fourteenth century devolved into uncertainties affecting a wider spectrum of thinkers. For example, William of Ockham's writing about how little philosophical truth natural reason is capable of without the aid of divine revelation, though not radically different from what his predecessors such as Thomas Aquinas had taught, contributed to a scepticism that was new to Christian thinkers. Ockham argued that experience — knowledge of individual things — was key to an understanding of truth and because 'universals are nothing but constructs in the mind (*concepts*), created by substituting one set of terms for those derived intuitively from experience[...]; most of what had been supposedly "proven" as true was a product of fallacious reasoning'.[38] A major implication of this philosophical shift is that the first-person subjectivity of poetry can take on new importance as a possible authority in truth seeking. However, many fourteenth-century poets were also conscious of the power of art to deceive, to be, in Dante's words, 'bella menzogna', a beautiful lie.[39] Writers like Machaut evince the power of poetry to explore the complexity of truth and celebrate human achievement in the context of profound doubt.

## *Ambiguities*

Similarities in the central images in these three poems highlight the different relationships between ambiguity and the complexity of truth. For example, eyes

[37] Cerquiglini-Toulet, *Color of Melancholy*, p. 88.

[38] De Looze, *Pseudo-Autobiography*, p. 13.

[39] Dante Alighieri, *Convivio*, II. 1. 3.

serve as central images in the opening quatrains of both Italian sonnets and in the first stanza of Machaut's ballade. All three poets build on the poetic convention that eye contact makes a person vulnerable to love, especially in the form of Cupid's arrow, which enters a person's body through the eyes and travels from there to the heart. The Italian curse sonnet spells out the conceit most explicitly: the light from the lady's treacherous eyes entered the speaker's heart and drew out his spirit. In Petrarch's sonnet the eyes explicitly have bound the speaker but also implicitly are the entry point for the arrows that pierced and wounded the speaker's heart. In both poems the named eyes clearly are the lady's while the speakers' eyes are implicated.

In Machaut's ballade, however, the two eyes cursed are explicitly the speaker's eyes, 'the eyes by which I saw the sweetness of my lady'. The second stanza includes a curse on the 'glance by which love was begotten in my heart', suggesting that the lady's eyes may also have participated in the engendering, or begetting, of love, in what could potentially have been a reciprocal relationship.[40] Significantly, although it seems most likely that the 'greeting, charm, and attire' cursed in the series that concludes with the glance are the lady's, they could also be the speaker's. If he had dressed and behaved differently, his 'doleful heart' might not have ended up in the 'strange country' reiterated in the refrain. And when the curse turns to 'the hour when she was born', it is possible that 'elle' refers to 'l'amour', a feminine noun, rather than — or in addition to — the lady. A curse on Love's false seeming, proven falseness, immense pride, and harshness devoid of tenderness or pity suggests a very different emotional and intellectual stance from a curse on the lady's false seeming and so on. While the Italian curse sonnet presents the conventional misogynist situation of the innocent man brought down by the woman's treachery and presents her in a role like the enemies in the Psalm curse and 'Ibis' (albeit in a comic register), Machaut's poem (also working in a comic register) at least suggests the possibility that the speaker should take some personal responsibility for being in the condition in which he finds himself. Machaut's lady has ended his joy and slain him with sorrow, but she escapes being presented as the certain enemy deserving to be cursed. The speaker's subjectivity and presentation of the lady in 'Je maudi' are surprisingly complex.

This reading of what the eyes in the poem reveal about the speaker's subjectivity and involvement in the love relationship may be more convincing in light

[40] The word I translate as 'glance', *le regart*, has a broad semantic range, including a sustained look as well as a glance and the more abstract senses of esteem and consideration. See A. J. Greimas, *Dictionnaire de l'ancien français: Le Moyen Âge* (Paris: Larousse, 1994).

of thematic development in narrative poems for which Machaut is better known. Shirley Lukitsch writes that the 'Prologue' introducing the most authoritative complete-work manuscript of Machaut's work suggests that Machaut

> saw in love poetry a means of restoring in man a lost state of psychic and spiritual integrity. Poetry, for him, is not recreative, but re-creative; it is consolatory not in Deschamps', but in Boethius' sense of the word — a means of restoring the soul to a state of rational love and thus making a man at one with himself and with the natural order.[41]

But Machaut never presents the re-creative power of love poetry as a simple matter. William Calin points out that in the *Remede de Fortune* and *Voir Dit*, 'while seemingly proclaiming communication, community, success, and the process of writing, Machaut also makes a place for non-communication, solitude, failure, and the process of reading'.[42] A number of critics see in Machaut's explorations of poetic practices the powerful influence of writers such as Boethius, Alain de Lille, and Jean de Meun. Sylvia Huot, for example, analyses the increasing degrees of irony in Machaut's appropriations of the 'comedy and the audacity of Jean de Meun's erotic allegory, his brilliant distortions of such authors as Boethius and Alain de Lille, his merciless lampooning of the pretensions of courtly diction' but also concludes that 'the very success of such an enterprise [as Machaut's use of the *Roman de la Rose*], the real force of the satire, is bound up in the fact that, in a different sense, poetry *can* transform the erotic into the sacred, through the power of allegory' . Machaut affirms the potency of writing and interpretation, of poetic discourse, to create a literary space for the interplay and mutual glossing of the many registers — sacred and erotic, chivalric and clerkly, mythic and historic — of language and experience.[43] I add to this list the interplay and mutual glossing of curse and blessing.

In this context, the uncanniness and ambiguity of Machaut's curse poem indicate new possibilities and responsibilities in courtly love relationships, poems, and human existence more generally. The traditional stance of the lover-poet as a helpless victim is complicated by the possibility that he brought the situation on himself. Contributing to the uncanniness, the ambiguity draws attention to ways

[41] Lukitsch, 'The Poetics of the *Prologue*: Machaut's Conception of the Purpose of his Art', *Medium Ævum*, 52 (1983), 258–71 (p. 268).

[42] Calin, 'Medieval Intertextuality: Lyrical Inserts and Narrative in Guillaume de Machaut', *French Review*, 62 (1988), 1–10 (p. 8).

[43] Sylvia Huot, *The 'Romance of the Rose' and its Medieval Readers: Interpretation, Reception, Manuscript Transmission* (Cambridge: Cambridge University Press, 1993), p. 272. Also see Wimsatt for a discussion of other evidence about influences on Machaut's thinking about poetry.

the poem transgresses the horizon of expectation established by the medieval poetic conventions for love poetry. The trope of the person who becomes a poet (or writer) as a direct result of some inspiring life experience — especially love — continues to be powerful in the twenty-first century. Less familiar, but very important to an understanding of Machaut's lyric poetry and its roles in literary-critical history, is the idea of literary reflexivity often associated with Petrarch but equally applicable to Machaut: that the poet-author who struggles like an ordinary human being in his love relationships is the subject of his literary work. Kevin Brownlee notes in *Poetic Identity in Guillaume de Machaut*:

> Perhaps the single most important result of Machaut's concept of poetic identity involves a widening of the range of contexts in which the poet could portray himself qua poet, an increase in the range and number of poetic stances open to him — all under the general rubric of serving love through poetry.[44]

Laurence de Looze writes in *Pseudo-Autobiography in the Fourteenth Century*:

> The confluence of the life as a book, the poet as the writer (or creator) of the book, and the casting of the poet as protagonist enabled the poet to grant himself a kind of secular afterlife — to control, that is, the terms in which he would be remembered. The literary work came to depict the poet's life as a process of creating literary works about that life. The various aspects of the book all fold back in on the poet.[45]

Just as the success of writing within a particular genre may depend on the extent to which the writer pushes the boundaries of that genre, expands the 'horizon of expectation', Machaut's success in presenting himself as a distinguished poet-musician serving Love by depicting lover-poets struggling to understand the very issues the poems are about may depend on the extent to which he challenges his readers' understanding of what it means to be a poet and a musician praising women and writing about love. The truths he seeks are closely related to the truths Petrarch seeks but explored with rhetorical self-consciousness in place of a serious style.

The three poems' treatments of the idea of fame or reputation and Fortune provide another example of complexity. Petrarch's sonnet specifies that the poet gains fame because of his writing in response to the love situation: '[B]lessed be

[44] Kevin Brownlee, *Poetic Identity in Guillaume de Machaut* (Madison: University of Wisconsin Press, 1984), p. 20.

[45] De Looze, *Pseudo-Autobiography*, p. 9. Daniel Poirion, William Calin, Jacqueline Cerquiglini, Sylvia Huot, Leonard W. Johnson, R. Barton Palmer, and others have also explored aspects of poetic identity that relate to de Looze's discussion of pseudo-autobiography in Machaut's writings.

all the pages where I gain fame.'[46] The Italian curse sonnet specifies that the world will 'honour' the lady because of the poet's refined words, figurative language, and rhyme while the poet, in contrast, will be an object of ridicule. The irony is immediately evident: even though the identity of the author is uncertain, the lady honoured by the curse poem has no existence other than her 'treacherous eyes' and 'beautiful and guilty figure', which may be every bit as figurative as the rasp and beautiful colours that are objects of the curse in the second quatrain. The poem itself is a testament to the poet's reputation, to his deserving fame, despite our not being sure who he is. Thus the curse sonnet achieves an end similar to that of Petrarch's sonnet though through irony rather than through a serious tone.

Machaut's poem includes elements similar to both Italian sonnets but achieves a different effect. The turn from curse to blessing in the final stanza foregrounds similarities to Petrarch's sonnet. For a few lines the poem adopts the serious tone that is sustained throughout Petrarch's sonnet. This parallel draws attention to a feature of Petrarch's poem that might otherwise not be noticed: the lady herself is never blessed. Petrarch blesses the 'sweet trouble' he felt, the 'bow and arrows that pierced' him, and even the wounds that resulted, but Petrarch's sestet emphasizes that the blessing is directed at the poet's own words and pages, which have brought him fame.

The lady also is never actually cursed in either Machaut's ballade or the Italian curse sonnet — though Machaut comes close, cursing 'greeting, charm, attire and the glance by which love was begotten'. The curses, like the blessings in Petrarch's sonnet, are directed at time and place, but, unlike Petrarch's blessings, also at the curser's heart, thought, loyalty, desire, and love in Machaut's poem and at the curser's 'hard mind' (*mente* can also mean 'intellect', 'intelligence', 'understanding') in the Italian sonnet. Like the Italian curse sonnet, Machaut's 'Je maudi' addresses the fame or renown of the lady by concluding with a prayer for God's blessings on the lady: 'But I beseech God that he defend her fame, her well-being, her peace, bestow honour on her and forgive her having slain with sorrow *my doleful heart in a strange country*.' However, also like the Italian curse poem, the attention to the lady's fame is ironic, since her main fame will be that she has brought about the death of the speaker. But the effect of the irony seems quite different from the effect of the Italian curse poem, partly because the meaning of

[46] Durling, *Petrarch's Lyric Poems*, p. 138, translates the passage as 'where I gain fame for her', but the Italian, 'ov'io fama l'acquisto', is not that specific. The final tercet of the sonnet reads, 'et benedette sian tutte le carte | ov'io fama l'acquisto, e'l pensier mio, | ch'è sol di lei sì ch' altra non v'à parte'.

the lines immediately before the curse becomes a prayer for the well-being of the lady is less clear than any other statement in the poem. That lack of clarity is relevant to the transformation from curse to prayer and to the larger themes in the poem.

As in the first two stanzas, in the third stanza the verb *curse* has a series of objects, here 'Fortune and her false turns, | the planet, the hour, the fate'. However, the nested relative clauses that follow, 'Qui mon fol cuer mirent en tel errour | Qu'onques de moy fu servie n'amée', seem to mirror the condition of error more than clarify the relationship between the speaker's foolish heart, the lady, love, and fortune. The sentence may be translated as follows:

> And also I curse Fortune and her false turns,
> the planet, the hour, the fate
> which might view my foolish heart in such error
> that I never served nor loved.[47]

The third person plural, present subjunctive *mirent*, 'might view', is in a grammatically straightforward relative clause but is a very odd verb to be associated with Fortune, the planet, hour and fate. Translating the next clause as an active expression rather than duplicating the passive voice of the French, as is often necessary in order to achieve idiomatic English, doesn't really resolve the uncertainty about who or what was 'never served nor loved' by the speaker. More important, if he had never served nor loved the lady, then presumably there would be no need for the curse, and his heart would not be in a strange country, slain with sorrow. However, the convoluted quality of the syntax and the uncertainty of meaning do seem appropriate for the idea about the effects of love expressed by the poem as a whole: love results in confusion that is related to fame and Fortune.

The closing lines of the Italian curse sonnet are also about fame and fortune and also not entirely clear. Presumably it is 'the lady's beautiful and guilty figure' for which Love perjures himself, but that puts Love in direct contrast to the speaker, whose 'hard mind is firm in holding' that which killed him. Thus the speaker and Love seem to become the object of everyone's ridicule for contrasting reasons — the speaker for being firm and Love for lying. Adding to the complexity, the final word of the Italian curse sonnet, *ventura*, can mean either 'future' or 'fortune'. While editors usually capitalize *Amor*, indicating personification of

[47] Jacques Leclercq translates, 'which led my foolish heart so far astray | That, loving her, I held her service dear' (*An Anthology of Medieval Lyrics*, ed. by Angel Flores (New York: Modern Library, 1962), p. 154).

Love as Cupid, *ventura* is not capitalized in any edition I have seen. However, the wheel image of the final line strongly suggests the wheel of Fortune, one of the most common visual images of the Middle Ages, with the association that good luck will be followed by bad (and less emphatically, bad luck followed by good) in a turning of events out of human control. Yet the poem presents the final action, taking the wheel, in a structure aligning it with the certainty of *io maledico*, 'I curse', controlled by the verb *credo*, 'I trust/believe'. The speaker trusts to take the wheel for or from Fortune with the same certainty that he curses the series of objects earlier in the poem. Thus both curse poems seem to be playing with stances of control versus vulnerability, with the speaker in the poem perceiving himself as a pathetic, helpless victim. In Machaut's ballade, however, the authorial stance and the combination of ambiguity and linguistic control suggests humans are capable of a different relation to love and fortune.

As with the discussion of the eyes in the poem, it is useful to turn to discussion of Machaut's narrative poetry for fuller understanding of the theme of fortune. When the speaker in 'Je maudi' curses 'Fortune and her false turns' in the last stanza, his situation is similar to that of the lover in *Remede de Fortune* before he has been instructed by Hope. Douglas Kelly explains,

> Desire is subject to Fortune because desire may be satisfied or denied by someone or something not subject to the will of the person who desires. The possibility of denial of the object of desire causes fear, suffering, despair, death. All this is exemplified in the first part of the *Remede*, where the lover, afraid to speak and convinced he has lost the esteem of his lady, retires in solitude to die a lover's death.[48]

In *Remede de Fortune* the lover ultimately learns, in Douglas Kelly's words, that 'love, rightly understood, is not a manifestation of desire'. Rather it is

> founded on virtue because of the fidelity of the lover. The constant heart is not subject to Fortune (vv. 2804–10).This does not exclude hope for love, at least love of a Platonic sort. All good men and women admire virtue, as Boethius taught. Thus the lady whose foremost quality is *bonté* (v. 177) cannot fail to recognize the faithful aspirant to her love (vv. 1796–1808, 1827–58). The lover himself may rest content in the awareness of the *bonté* he gains from love for his lady; he too becomes virtuous, and virtue, as Boethius said, is its own reward. What more could he 'desire' — or rather, hope for?[49]

'Je maudi' only suggests some of the possibilities spelled out in *Remede de Fortune*. However, until the final stanza the speaker's situation is very similar to the situation of the lover in *Remede de Fortune*. One of the characteristics of *Remede de*

[48] Kelly, *Medieval Imagination*, p. 132.

[49] Kelly, *Medieval Imagination*, p. 133.

*Fortune* is that readers are likely to grasp the message of the poem much more quickly than the lover-poet does. The reference to Fortune at the beginning of the final stanza of 'Je maudi' combines with the grammatical ambiguity and the shift to a prayer for the well-being of the lady to suggest a reader might profitably read the poem from the vantage point the lover-poet achieves by the end of *Remede de Fortune*. Confusion and unhappiness are as likely to result from a love relationship as the fame Petrarch has achieved from his pages of poetry. Machaut's 'Je maudi' draws readers' attention to human ridiculousness as well as potential for greatness — and suggests everyone will finally be responsible for the choices made in love and life.

I hope I have demonstrated that Machaut's artistry in 'Je maudi' is as complex and interesting as is his narrative poetry. All three fourteenth-century poems examined here affirm the power of love, even (or especially) when painful. However, the curse poems surface complexities and draw attention to human ridiculousness as well as the potential for human greatness, while Petrarch's sonnet emphasizes the power of love to enhance a love-poet's greatness and fame, to bless a man who can give 'scattered rhymes' an appearance of unity and coherence even when awareness of potential meaninglessness and a 'tangle of ambiguity' lurk below the surface.[50] Petrarch has scattered his words, but he has also brought them back together in the poem and in the lyric collection. One reason for the extraordinary influence of Petrarch's vernacular lyrics is that the seemingly transparent sincerity and simplicity of many of the poems (perhaps the ones most often anthologized) has allowed so many subsequent writers to appropriate that sincerity in their own attempts to make sense of the complexities of truth.[51] The two curse poems, when read with Petrarch's sonnet, tend to deflate the seriousness Petrarch has so craftily established and in doing so suggest a version of human relation to truth with a different tonality. One more example from Machaut's narrative verse may support my conclusion. In a session sponsored by the International Machaut Society at the Forty-second International Congress on Medieval Studies in Kalamazoo, Michigan, 10 May 2007, Burt Kimmelman suggested that Machaut may have written *The Judgement of the King of Navarre* in direct response to the international celebrity surrounding Petrarch's having been crowned Poet Laureate in Rome in 1341. Setting himself up in a new poem as a poet brought to court for slandering women and then having the judge declare

[50] William J. Kennedy, *Authorizing Petrarch*, pp. 19–21.

[51] See the first two chapters in Kennedy, *Authorizing Petrach*, for a discussion of the complexities not only of Petrarch's lyrics but also of critical responses to the lyric sequence.

him guilty provides for Machaut a very different kind of public relations effort from Petrarch's crowning in Rome, one layered with ironies.

Read together, Petrarch's 'Blessed be the day' and Machaut's 'Je maudi' provide evidence that international literary competition pre-dates the sixteenth century. The two poems may also invite readers to resist the temptation to see in differences between the poems evidence that one should be valued more highly than the other. By drawing attention to the illogic of love and its tendency to contribute to human error and irrational and/or less-than-admirable behaviour, Machaut's 'Je maudi' deflates confidence in human greatness. However, read in the larger context I suggest here, Machaut's poem at the same time raises awareness of the importance of striving for greatness despite being aware of all the difficulties and opportunities for foolishness. No less important, with other works in Machaut's oeuvre, the poem also illustrates the fun readers can have collaborating with writers in the process of bringing to life imaginative worlds.

*Santa Clara University*

# 'MAKEN MELODYE': THE QUALITY OF SONG IN CHAUCER'S *CANTERBURY TALES*

Christina Francis

Throughout *The Canterbury Tales*, Chaucer presents several of his pilgrims and characters as possessing singing voices. For example, he describes the Prioress: 'Ful weel she soong the service dyvyne, | Entuned in hir nose ful semely'.[1] As any study of his work will show, Chaucer chooses the specific details of his descriptions very carefully. D. W. Robertson has remarked, 'Chaucer's references to melody or harmony are significant and should not be neglected as being merely decorative.'[2] In answer to Robertson's call for attention, three articles have illuminated the representation of music in Chaucer's work quite extensively. First, David Chamberlain's 'Musical Signs and Symbols in Chaucer: Convention and Originality' examines Chaucer's familiarity with music theory, particularly from the philosophical and scriptural traditions.[3] Second, David Higdon more specifically focuses on references to music found in Chaucer's

[1] Geoffrey Chaucer, *The Canterbury Tales*, in *The Riverside Chaucer*, ed. by Larry D. Benson (Boston: Houghton Mifflin Company, 1987), II. 122–23. Further references to this work are given after quotations in the text. I would also like to acknowledge the helpfulness of Larry Benson's *A Glossarial Concordance to the Riverside Chaucer* (New York: Garland, 1993).

[2] D. W. Robertson, *A Preface to Chaucer: Studies in Medieval Perspectives* (Princeton: Princeton University Press, 1962), p. 133.

[3] David Chamberlain meticulously surveys Chaucer's philosophical and spiritual understanding of music, providing examples from the canon of Chaucer's work. He aims to demonstrate both Chaucer's familiarity with conventional representations of music, as well as Chaucer's originality in transforming convention into interesting symbolism, in 'Musical Signs and Symbols in Chaucer: Convention and Originality', in *Signs and Symbols in Chaucer's Poetry*, ed. by John P. Hermann and John J. Burke, Jr (Tuscaloosa: University of Alabama Press, 1981), pp. 43–80.

*General Prologue*.[4] Third, Nicolette Zeeman's 'The Gender of Song in Chaucer' analyses how song, particularly that of male singers, creates a 'means of staging the unstable differentiations of sexual identity', resulting in 'brutal repudiation'.[5] For the purposes of this essay, I would like to carve out a smaller section of the discussion on music, namely the quality of human singing and its comparison to birds, birdsong, and the bird figure of the siren. To that end, in a consideration of the passage above, the description of the Prioress reveals two things. First, it identifies the type of music the Prioress is making, that is, music directed to religious devotion. Second, it characterizes the quality of her voice: she sings in tune through her nose. These details emphasize perspectives about medieval music, namely the importance of method to performance and of the rationale behind singing.

Elizabeth Eva Leach, in her book *Sung Birds: Music, Nature, and Poetry in the Later Middle Ages*, defines a spectrum of song in the Middle Ages: 'The peculiar properties of human music making, like those of the human soul, could be situated between the songs of birds and the choirs of angels.'[6] In *The Canterbury Tales*, Chaucer treats his readers to a range of singing voices, many of which demonstrate the worst qualities of song. In particular, Chaucer showcases two types of inappropriate singers. First, he presents singers through comparisons to birdsong, and second, he describes music makers that use their song as a means of seduction. Through these portrayals, Chaucer creates a rhetorical trope: human song, its quality and purpose, can identify the rationality or irrationality of the

[4] David Leon Higdon, in his article 'Diverse Melodies in Chaucer's "General Prologue"', *Criticism*, 14 (1972), 97–108, reads the music in the prologue as a means for Chaucer to comment upon the moral standing of the pilgrims. Specifically, he classifies the pilgrims into three categories: 1) those who make music, 2) those who make noise, and 3) those who resist music or remain silent, and he examines how these three groups establish images of concord and discord within the text. Higdon develops his discussion about all types of musical reference by analysing the 'General Prologue'.

[5] Nicolette Zeeman, 'The Gender of Song in Chaucer', in *Studies in the Age of Chaucer*, ed. by Frank Grady (St Louis: New Chaucer Society, Washington University, 2007), pp. 145, 181, particularly addresses gender and sexuality in her review of the male singers in Chaucer's *Canterbury Tales* and points to their inherent narcissism. Her observations about singing mirror some of my own discussion; while I recognize the significance of gender and its connections to the portrayal of singers, I have chosen to focus instead on the quality of song produced by these singers, regardless of gender.

[6] Elizabeth Eva Leach, *Sung Birds: Music, Nature, and Poetry in the Later Middle Ages* (Ithaca: Cornell University Press, 2007), p. 24.

performer. Most of the time, Chaucer's pilgrims and their characters get it wrong; they fail to understand the implications of their song, focusing on its pleasure, rather than its devotional power. While singing and music permeate *The Canterbury Tales*, this essay will examine the more specific references to singing voices as they appear in *The Nun's Priest's Tale*, *General Prologue*, *The Miller's Tale*, and *The Prioress's Tale*.

As most scholars agree, Chaucerian animals can act as a source for commenting upon the behaviour of humans. According to Beryl Rowland, 'Fables, the Bible, hermeneutical writings, natural histories, encyclopedias, manuscript illustrations, sculpture and carving, all saw animals as exhibiting human traits, as having conscious motives or even moral standards.'[7] Like many other medieval authors, Chaucer uses animal imagery to highlight the less attractive characteristics of human nature.[8] Thomas P. Harrison agrees with that assessment and summarizes Chaucer's unique use of birds even more specifically:

> Chaucer's birds remain symbolic in their traditional character as patterns comparable with the infinite variety of human nature. His originality in this regard lies [...] in transforming the world of encyclopedia and employing its lore for graphic sketches of humankind.[9]

The range of Chaucer's use of birds in his texts demonstrates the range of birds in various types of literature of the medieval period. What interests me here are the instances of birds and birdsong and their connections to human behaviour, and more specifically human singing. The fable of *The Nun's Priest's Tale* offers just one such example in which the story of a rooster and his incomparable voice comments upon human failings such as vanity and pride. Within the story, Chauntecleer's voice is described as 'murier than the murie orgon | On

[7] Beryl Rowland, *Blind Beasts: Chaucer's Animal World* (Kent, OH: Kent State University Press, 1971), p. 10. The usage of animals in such ways owes much to the *Physiologus* tradition. This tradition presents a host of subjects, including animals, stones, and plants, with their allegorical interpretations. Originally derived from a Latin source, the *Physiologus* was rewritten and revised over the course of the Middle Ages influencing writers throughout the period, and might well have been the 'most popular book of all, after the Bible' (Thomas Honegger, *From Phoenix to Chauntecleer: Medieval English Animal Poetry* (Tubingen: Francke, 1996), pp. 17–18). See also Joyce Salisbury, 'Human Animals of Medieval Fables', in *Animals in the Middle Ages*, ed. by Nona C. Flores (New York: Garland, 1996), p. 62, for an accounting of the usage of birds in literature.

[8] Rowland, *Blind Beasts*, p. 18.

[9] Thomas P. Harrison, *They Tell of Birds: Chaucer, Spenser, Milton, Drayton* (Austin: University of Texas Press, 1956), p. 47.

messe-dayes that in the chirche gon' (ll. 2851–52), as well as 'as myrie a stevene | As any aungel hath that is in hevene' (ll. 3291–92). These comments offer high praise for Chauntecleer's music. However, Chauntecleer's 'human' failings suggest that he may not be a musical example worth following.

In the Middle Ages, distinct philosophies governed music learning and its performance. Albert Seay's study of music in the Middle Ages summarizes fundamental views on music found in the philosophy of Boethius. Namely, music allows for the expression of the 'beauty and perfection of God and his creations, the world and man'.[10] Additionally, Boethius believed that 'music is a number made audible'.[11] Thus, during the Middle Ages, music was considered one of the important areas of study in a liberal arts education and was examined hand in hand with mathematics. It was also linked to grammar and rhetoric studies in that focus on pitch, tone, and note corresponded to concerns with the composition and delivery of sentences. Music, therefore, formed a 'fundamental part of literate education'.[12] Philosophically, medieval music fulfilled two criteria: it must be both rational and natural. Boethius divided music into three types: *musica mundana*, *musica humana*, and *musica instrumentalis*. Of *musica humana*, or human singing, he made the specific association between the body and the 'bodiless life-force of reason'.[13] An understanding of how these elements, body and soul, blend in harmony could lead to an understanding of music.

[10] Albert Seay, *Music in the Medieval World*, 2nd edn (Englewood Cliffs, NJ: Prentice-Hall, 1975), p. 20.

[11] Seay, *Music*, p. 19.

[12] Leach, *Sung Birds*, p. 15. One very successful music teacher of the Middle Ages, Guido d'Arezzo, constructed a system for helping students learn notes and scales that came to be known as the Guidonian Hand (Nan Cooke Carpenter, *Music in the Medieval and Renaissance Universities* (New York: Da Capo, 1972), p. 22). Despite this device, emphasis remained on deep learning and not just rote memorization (Bruce W. Holsinger, *Music, Body, and Desire in Medieval Culture: Hildegard of Bingen to Chaucer* (Stanford: Stanford University Press, 2001), p. 269). For more information on the Guidonian Hand, see Stefano Mengozzi, 'Virtual Segments: The Hexacord System in the Late Middle Ages', *Journal of Musicology*, 23 (2006), 426–67.

[13] Boethius, *De institutione musica*, excerpted in Guilio Cattin, *Music of the Middle Ages*, trans. by Steven Botterill, 2 vols (Cambridge: Cambridge University Press, 1984), II, 164–65. David Chamberlain's article 'Musical Signs and Symbols in Chaucer' also provides a nice survey of the connections between music and the body and soul, from a variety of philosophical sources, reinforcing the effects of reason on music and virtue (p. 53). Holsinger's *Music, Body, and Desire* further explores the musicality of the body, pushing the understanding of Boethius *musica humana* and the body's relationship to making music.

Furthermore, Boethius elevated the quality of reason above the skill of the musician: 'Unless the hand performs in accordance with that which reason ordains, it is in vain. [...] The musician is he who has the ability to make judgements in accordance with speculation and reason, set forth and adapted to music.'[14] Bruce Holsinger, in his book *Music, Body, and Desire in Medieval Culture*, has challenged the notion that medieval music lacked a strong interest in musical aesthetic, proposing instead that 'patristic writers on music and musical phenomena were motivated not by an overweening desire to escape the flesh, but rather by the challenge of reconciling the pleasures of musical embodiment with the incarnational religiosity they practiced'.[15] Holsinger's examination of the patristic writers reveals the material body as a stringed instrument, so that the 'history of the body and the history of music become indistinguishable'.[16] This 'resonance of the flesh' as Holsinger calls it conflicts somewhat with the intellectual quality of music to which Boethius subscribes. Despite the emphasis on the body in Holsinger's discussion of music, the emphasis on its purpose remains the same, as an expression of God's perfection and his beauty. Holsinger examines the music of Hildegard of Bingen to illustrate how 'the musical body can achieve a kind of visionary clarity'.[17] The body Holsinger emphasizes is one inspired by the soul and God, not by appetites of the flesh or animals.

With irony, Chaucer acknowledges this connection between music and rationality, between performance and performer, in *The Nun's Priest's Tale*: 'Therwith ye han in musyk moore feelynge | Than hadde Boece, or any that kan synge' (ll. 4483–84). In this scene, the fox flatters Chauntecleer excessively and successfully. Interestingly, 'feelynge' would be the last thing Boethius would endorse.[18] Earlier in the tale, Chauntecleer and Pertelote perform a duet, and as Chamberlain points out, 'The sweetness of their erotic harmony is what really deceives Chauntecleer, of course, into forgetting the warning of his dream.'[19] Thus Chaucer drives home the point of the need for reason. Those affected by music on a sensual level, or those producing music purely for sensual purpose, were likened

[14] Boethius, *De institutione musica*, XXXII. 165–66.

[15] Holsinger, *Music, Body, and Desire*, p. 30.

[16] Holsinger, *Music, Body, and Desire*, p. 39.

[17] Holsinger, *Music, Body, and Desire*, p. 94.

[18] Chamberlain, 'Musical Signs and Symbols', p. 47.

[19] Chamberlain, 'Musical Signs and Symbols', p. 61. Zeeman elaborates on Chauntecleer's sexuality, classifying his 'voracious chicken heterosexuality' as 'sexual polymorphousness' ('Gender of Song', p. 178).

to beasts. Music held the power to 'rob humans of their humanity'.[20] To avoid this consequence, humans, differentiated from beasts by reason according to the Great Chain of Being, should listen to music in order to appreciate its technical elements. Active listening to music, regardless of the performer, human or animal (like birdsong), could prevent the medieval hearer from associations with beasts or beastly behaviour.[21] The performance and reception of music was a matter of training, something which beasts did not possess. Additionally, music might be seen as an 'instrument of discipline', a way to curtail the sensual appetites of the body.[22] In the case of Chauntecleer, his music is vain, made in response to flattery or desire, not through reasoned judgement.[23]

As the human voice often echoes the voice of birds, medieval music theorists distinguish between them. They identify birds as having one quality of music — nature. Birdsong is the product of a natural instrument.[24] Even so, the distinctions between birdsong and human music-making focus upon rationality. The bird cannot identify the qualities of its own song; therefore, even though the bird produces a pleasing melody, its song cannot be categorized as music. When a bird sings, it does not consciously attempt to present meaning. For Leach, these associations suggest a potentially unfavourable view of human performance.[25]

[20] Leach, *Sung Birds*, p. 21.

[21] Leach, *Sung Birds*, p. 3. Another example in *Troilus and Criseyde* also demonstrates this point. As Troilus languishes from lovesickness, Pandarus repeatedly attempts to rouse him from his stupor. At one point, Pandarus remarks: 'Or artow lik an asse to the harpe, | That hereth sown whan men the strynges plye, | But in his mynde of that no melodie | May sinken hym to gladden, for that he | So dul ys of his bestialite?' (I. 730–35). Pandarus draws a correlation between the bestial behaviour of an ass responding to harp playing and Troilus's inability to hear the 'melodie' of the music. Animals cannot perceive the technical qualities of music; their response is completely sensual. Thus, Troilus is behaving no better than a beast; he is irrational. For a more in-depth discussion of Boethian music in *Troilus and Criseyde*, see Julia Bolton Holloway, 'The Asse to the Harpe: Boethian Music in Chaucer', in *Tales within Tales: Apuleius through Time*, ed. by Constance S. Wright and Julia Bolton Holloway (New York: AMS, 2000).

[22] Holsinger, *Music, Body, and Desire*, pp. 95–97.

[23] Zeeman makes the further point that 'Chauntecleer's narcissistic artistic self-imagining' is ultimately responsible for him almost 'entering the entrails of the beast'. His singing has made 'him oblivious to the predators around him' ('Gender of Song', pp. 179–81).

[24] Matthew Head explores the origins of music and their connections to birdsong, displaying a range of perspectives about birdsong from the Bible to the eighteenth century ('Birdsong and the Origins of Music', *Journal of the Royal Musical Association*, 122 (1997), 1–23).

[25] Leach, *Sung Birds*, p. 41.

Humans frequently sing without intention or meaning. Leach's remarks reinforce Boethius: 'The quality of a song — its sounding performance — does not differentiate the bird-brained imitator from the rational, thinking artist. [...] Ultimately the practioner [must] *understand* the measure and numbers of music', reaffirming reason as a defining factor in music.[26] First, unreflective listeners could be affected by methods of production, and second, the performer should claim responsibility for the quality and purpose of his or her music-making. A singer would not want to be compared to a bird or its song. Such a comparison would move the performed music away from what elevates it, rational thought. Other condemned elements of music include: 'excessive volume, theatrical gestures, melodic over-elaboration, and effeminate high-pitched tones'.[27] Each of these qualities could cast the song in a negative light, potentially even leading to criticism of the performer. Chaucer incorporates many of these negative qualities of medieval music-making into his descriptions of characters and their singing voices, effectively introducing them to censure.

Though Chaucer compares various characters' singing voices to birds, he does not necessarily condemn birdsong entirely. In the right setting and context, birdsong highlights things being in their natural order. In *The Parliament of Fowls*, the dreamer enters a garden to hear birds singing 'with voys of aungel in here armonye' (l. 191); however, this birdsong soon turns to 'so huge a noyse' (l. 312), the contrast between the harmony of angels and the subsequent noise placing the birdsong on the spectrum of music. The birds in this poem are gathered to choose their mates for the year, but the process has been stalled by the posturing of the eagles. As each of the competing suitors makes his case, the reader experiences an interesting portrayal of human courtship. Once the mating of the eagles has been resolved — the female eagle decides to delay her mating decision for one year, then the birdsong returns:

> But first were chosen foules for to synge,
> [...]
> To synge a roundel at here departynge,
> To don Nature honour and pleasaunce.
> (ll. 673–76)

In this poem, birdsong clearly accompanies the proper order of things — reproduction.

[26] Leach, *Sung Birds*, p. 43.

[27] Leach, *Sung Birds*, p. 239.

Chaucer also opens *The Canterbury Tales* with birdsong: 'When smale foweles maken melodye, | That slepen al the nyght with open eye' (ll. 9–10). This image accompanies other colourful depictions of spring, such as 'shoures soote' (l. 1), 'Zephires [...] sweete breeth' (l. 5), and 'tendre croppes' (l. 7), all celebrating the reverdie tradition. Not only does the birdsong of these small fowls announce springtime, but the phrase 'maken melodye' also becomes a metaphor for sexual reproduction. Life must regenerate. Additionally, the time references of 'when' (l. 1) and 'thanne' (l. 12) establish the cycle of these yearly events that take their cue from birdsong.[28] It strikes an interesting chord that Chaucer's pilgrims also begin their journey to the tune of birds singing and nature's reproduction. Presumably, the journey that the pilgrims undertake is a rational response to nature's music, a product of God's beauty and perfection. However, it is the human interpretation and application of 'maken melodye' throughout the rest of *The Canterbury Tales* that complicates this image.[29]

Chaucer begins to develop the singing voices of his pilgrims within the portraits of the *General Prologue*. One of the first characters given a clear singing voice is the Squire:

> He koude songes make and wel endite,
> Juste and eek daunce, and weel purtreye and write.
> So hoote he lovede that by nyghtergale
> He sleep namoore than dooth a nyghtyngale.
> (ll. 95–98)

Here Chaucer makes a direct correlation between the singing voice of the Squire and his sexual ability. His passionate encounters during the 'nyghtergale' (night-time) are then connected to the nightingale, a bird known for singing at night. The nightingale has a long tradition of literary use.[30] Elizabeth Eva Leach

[28] Higdon points out that Chaucer creates a tension between the concordant sound of small fowls singing in the *General Prologue* and the discordant sound of the Miller's bagpipe playing, leading the pilgrims out of town ('Diverse Melodies', p. 97).

[29] Chamberlain explores Chaucer's continued use of the symbol 'melodye', arguing for its status as a highly original way to make meaning and frame *The Canterbury Tales* from beginning to end. His article surveys all uses of 'melodye', tracking its progression from erotic sign to spiritually divine and virtuous symbol. He pays particular attention to the significant placement of *The Manciple's Tale* with its story of the crow's revelations right before *The Parson's Tale* ('Musical Signs and Symbols', pp. 71–80).

[30] One very prominent tradition is the story of Philomela within Ovid's *Metamorphoses*, in which Ovid relates how she was transformed into a nightingale, singing her mournful tune.

examines portrayals of the nightingale in great depth, concluding that in a 'positive secular context, the nightingale is the bird of love, spring, the poet, his messenger, and so on, and birdsong signals beauty, poetry, natural inspiration, and the desire that precedes and generates poetic language'.[31] One common association with the nightingale was as a herald of the spring. Early Christians read this behaviour allegorically, seeing the nightingale as a Christian soul awaiting Christ, and the nighttime song of the bird as the 'vigilance of monastic virtue'.[32] Even so, according to Wendy Pfeffer, the 'incorporation of the nightingale in pious works was a delicate operation'.[33] A negative tradition of portrayal also exists in which the nightingale represented the realm of courtly love and its 'song may be considered inappropriately self-preening singing that is elaborate or stagy in performance'.[34] Considering the other elements of the Squire's portrait — the curly locks, the associations with flowers and springtime, and performing for the favours of ladies — readers would associate the Squire with the courtly lover

According to John M. Fyler, 'It is hard to overestimate Ovid's importance to later writers as a source of material' (*Chaucer and Ovid* (New Haven: Yale University Press, 1979), p. 1). Fyler's book details the tremendous influence Ovid has on Chaucer's work.

[31] Leach, *Sung Birds*, p. 91. According to Wendy Pfeffer, the Occitan troubadours associated the nightingale 'as parallel to the poet, inciting the troubadour to sing or reminding the poet of his unhappiness in love and his inability to compose' ('Spring, Love, Birdsong: The Nightingale in Two Cultures', in *Beasts and Birds of the Middle Ages: The Bestiary and its Legacy*, ed. by Willene B. Clark and Meradith T. McMunn (Philadelphia: University of Pennsylvania Press, 1989), p. 90).

[32] Wendy Pfeffer, *The Change in Philomel: The Nightingale in Medieval Literature* (New York: Lang, 1985), p. 30.

[33] Pfeffer, *Change in Philomel*, p. 41. Furthermore, when incorporated into religious works, the bird often died. In this way, the focus on the temporal sexuality of the bird might be shifted to spiritual matters (pp. 49–50).

[34] Leach, *Sung Birds*, p. 101. In the twelfth-century *Romance of the Rose*, translated by Chaucer, birdsong fills the air upon entry into the garden, or *locus amoenus*. The female figure Idleness describes Mirth's visits: 'And eke with hym cometh his meynee | That liven in lust and jolite. | And now is Myrthe therynne to here | The briddis how they syngen clere | The mavys and the nyghtyngale' (ll. 615–19). The garden's beautiful setting offers Mirth and his companions a 'swetter place | to pleyen inne' (ll. 622–23). Chaucer presents similar birdsong imagery in several garden settings, such as those appearing in the dream visions *The Book of the Duchess*, *The Legend of Good Women*, and *The Parliament of Fowls*. In the dream vision *Book of the Duchess*, the narrator awakens in a chamber surrounded by birds: 'With smale foules a gret hep | That had affrayed me out of me slep | Thorgh noyse and swetnesse of her song (ll. 295–97). Similarly, in *The Parliament of the Fowls*, Chaucer introduces a sensual garden at the beginning of the narrator's dream vision.

tradition.[35] Higdon classifies the Squire as 'nature animated' in a way that 'underline[s] the sexuality and danger' of his character.[36] Thus his singing takes on the 'self-preening' quality referred to by Leach. The emphasis on nighttime and singing pushes the Squire's song into the sensual category, rather than song dedicated to poetic creation or God. Chamberlain agrees that the Squire's singing illustrates his 'frivolity and eroticism'.[37] The unorganized and fractured quality of the Squire's later storytelling supports these conclusions.[38] Chaucer then celebrates the beauty of the voice, through its association with the nightingale, but also condemns the sensual and irrational purpose of the voice.

The next example of the nightingale's sexualized birdsong occurs in *The Miller's Tale*. Upon spying the married Alison, Absolon, accompanied by his gitern, decides to serenade her outside her bedroom window: 'He syngeth in his voys gentil and smal' (l. 3360). Using the words *gentil* and *small* to characterize Absolon's voice provides the first avenue for criticizing his character. Those qualities seem more appropriate for a female than a voice.[39] Earlier in the tale, the narrator relates other details about Absolon's musical skill, such as that he plays 'songes on a small rubible [rebeck]' (l. 3331). Robert Boenig explains how the rebec, an instrument used for 'faster, lighter, and higher pitched' music, complements Absolon's voice and reinforces Absolon's effeminate qualities.[40] Interestingly, Absolon ignores the offerings of other married ladies. He is irrationally intent on conquering Alison, so much so that Chaucer compares his

[35] Throughout *The Canterbury Tales*, Chaucer includes other courtly lovers who enjoy singing. In *The Knight's Tale*, 'Whan that Arcite hadde romed al his fille, | And songen al the roundel lustily, | Into a studie he fil sodeynly, | As doon thise lovers in hir queynte geres' (ll. 1528–31). And Aurelius from *The Franklin's Tale* 'syngeth, daunceth, passynge any man' (ll. 929–30). However, the singing in these cases occurs as conventional elements of romance and courtly love, rather than as a developed character trait. In Chaucer's own *Tale of Sir Thopas*, the character Sir Thopas 'fil in love-longynge' upon hearing birdsong (ll. 771–72). None of these characters voices are compared to birds or birdsong.

[36] Higdon, 'Diverse Melodies', p. 102.

[37] Chamberlain, 'Musical Signs and Symbols', p. 55.

[38] Derek Pearsall cautions against the temptation to read the modesty topos or use of *occupatio* in *The Squire's Tale* as a sign of inadequacy in the Squire (*The Canterbury Tales* (London: Routledge, 1985), p. 140).

[39] Zeeman reads all of the qualities associated with Absolon as diminutive, infantilizing, feminizing, and sentimental ('Gender of Song', p. 155).

[40] Boenig also argues that the gittern and the rebec were often, but not always, associated with disreputable players ('Absolon's Musical Instruments', *English Language Notes*, 28 (1990), 7–15 (pp. 9–10)).

pursuit to that of a cat chasing a mouse (ll. 3346–47), and correspondingly, his song acquires a predatory quality. Examining the serenade scene from another perspective, Peter Beidler demonstrates the similarities between the lyric that Absolon sings under Alison's window and Marian lyrics, calling attention to its blasphemous misuse of prayer for the purposes of seduction.[41] Zeeman closely marks how Absolon's behaviour in the portrayal of his singing at Alison's window parallels *Song of Songs*.[42] Even though Alison rebuffs him, he continues to sing to her on other occasions. The Miller then compares Absolon's singing to birdsong: 'He syngeth, brokkynge as a nyghtyngale' (l. 3377). In many medieval texts, a nightingale's song is often characterized as high-pitched. Leach identifies how high-pitched singing, an unnatural trait for adult men, suggests feminization.[43] This description follows an accounting of how much attention Absolon, preening like a bird, pays to his looks. In some ways, the Squire and Absolon share many similar qualities, such as their long locks, singing voices, and ineffectual rhetoric. Absolon fancies himself a poet, yet his effeminate voice suggests inadequacy not only with his poetry but also in his ability to perform sexually. Clearly, Absolon is not the student of music that he should be.

Another character connected to the nightingale is the Wife of Bath. In the prologue to her tale, the Wife of Bath claims: 'Well koude I daunce to an harpe smale, | And synge, ywis, as any nyghtyngale' (ll. 457–58). This self description occurs within the section of her prologue when she discusses husband number four. Several lines later she confesses how drinking wine makes her wanton, thereby reinforcing her sexual appetites. The Wife of Bath sings as part of her revelry. John F. Plummer examines the nature of female song, commenting that it tends to focus 'largely on love and sex'.[44] In particular, he connects women's song with its 'headstrong carnality [and ...] hapless sexual carelessness' in the *fabliau* as a 'counterpoint to the male-voiced love song'.[45] It would be very easy to categorize the Wife of Bath as this type of singer. However, Chaucer never gives us the content of her songs; we can only guess.

[41] Peter G. Beidler, '"Now, Deere Lady": Absolon's Marian Couplet in the *Miller's Tale*', *Chaucer Review*, 39 (2004), 219–22.

[42] Zeeman's examination of *Song of Songs* provides yet another way for her to categorize Absolon's unstable sexuality ('Gender of Song', pp. 160–61).

[43] Leach, *Sung Birds*, p. 252.

[44] John F. Plummer, 'The Woman's Song in Middle English and its European Backgrounds', in *Vox Feminae: Studies in Medieval Woman's Songs*, ed. by John F. Plummer (Kalamazoo: Medieval Institute Publications, 1981), p. 135.

[45] Plummer, 'Woman's Song', p. 151.

Other examples of revelry and song, not necessarily by female singers, occur at the beginning of *The Cook's Tale*, in which the character is described as follows: 'At every bridale wolde he synge and hoppe; | He loved bet the tavern than the shoppe' (ll. 4375–76); and at the beginning of *The Pardoner's Tale* where

> Syngeres with harpes, baudes, wafereres,
> Which been the verray develes officeres
> To kindle and blowe the fyr of lecherye,
> That is annexed unto glotonye.
> (ll. 479–82)

In this final example, the singers are explicitly connected to the devil, as if to say that song without reason leads down this path.[46] At the very least, by associating herself with the nightingale's birdsong, the Wife of Bath makes an explicit claim to sexual expression. Certainly, no one would argue that she preens more than any other character. The Wife of Bath is also compared to a magpie, a bird that imitates.[47]

[46] Robert Boenig reveals an interesting connection between the types of instruments played together at the beginning of *The Pardoner's Tale* and the discordant nature of the music made as indicative of the need for harmony, or teamwork, the ultimate lesson of the tale ('Musical Irony in *The Pardoner's Tale*', *Chaucer Review*, 24 (1990), 253–58 (p. 257)).

[47] In medieval discourse, magpies were considered mischievous chatterers, capable of mimicry, and often identified with women (Dorothy Yamamoto, *The Boundaries of the Human in Medieval English Literature* (Oxford: Oxford University Press, 2000), p. 50). Even more interesting, 'Chaucer's "magpies" are typically those self-assured, sexually assertive women who walk abroad in their finery, deliberately challenging men's gaze' (p. 51). Because the magpie is not known particularly for its birdsong, its two primary associations are the noise it makes and its mischievousness. Comparisons to bird imitators such as the magpie also represent another way in which the human voice is criticized. Leach calls this 'birdspeak' (*Sung Birds*, pp. 40–43). When being judged according to its rationality, birdspeak represents the worst type of song — noise. This can be seen in no less than four of Chaucer's tales, where the magpie appears as a comparative image. In *The Reeve's Tale*, the narrator describes the Miller's wife: 'She was proud, and peert as is a pye' (l. 3950). The wife figure of this tale continuously expounds on her social status, taking on airs she does not truly possess, and ultimately ends up guilty of marital infidelity. Next, in the prologue to her tale, the Wife of Bath claims, 'I was yong and ful of ragerye [passion], | Stibourne and strong, and joly as a pye' (ll. 455–56). The verbosity of her tale's prologue argues for her enjoyment in hearing herself speak. The narrator of *The Shipman's Tale* characterizes the wife figure in the tale: 'Forth she gooth as jolif as a pye' (l. 209). And finally, although not a woman, the character January in *The Merchant's Tale* receives a similar description: 'He was al coltissh, ful of ragerye, | And ful of jargon as a flekked pye' (ll. 1847–48). The Shipman's wife becomes the dupe for exchanging her favours for sex, and January is cuckolded within his own garden. Within each of these tales, the character associated with the magpie is made to appear ridiculous in some way.

Thus, her song and her speech link her to the songs of beasts, not the choir of angels.

Alison from *The Miller's Tale* also sings; however, Chaucer does not compare her voice to the more complicated nightingale. The narrator remarks, 'But of hir song, it was as loude and yerne | As any swalwe sittyng on a berne' (ll. 3257–58). The adjectives used to characterize her voice, *loude* and *yerne*, suggest that her voice is not the product of serious study, learning, or inspired soul. The comparison also emphasizes the position of the bird, sitting on its branch. Alison's singing, like the swallow's, emerges as a call to nature. Her song lacks rational purpose, and the image reduces her to a beast incapable of reason and thus incapable of producing true music. Notably, Emily in *The Knight's Tale*, which *The Miller's Tale* parodies, possesses a singing voice described as 'an aungel hevenysshy' (l. 1055). These two women represent the polar opposites of the human voice in song. Furthermore, in the lines following the description of Alison's song, the narrator compares her to a 'kyde or calf' (l. 3260) and a 'joly colt' (l. 3263). Both these animal associations reinforce the interpretation of her song. An attentive audience would be in tune with her character — her irrational bestiality — through her singing.

The final example of a songster whose voice echoes birds is the Summoner from the *General Prologue*. The description of the Summoner blatantly identifies him as lecherous: 'As hoot he was and lecherous as a sparwe' (l. 626).[48] Chaucer uses a simile to connect the Summoner to a sparrow, but he does not elaborate on the Summoner's singing voice until the Pardoner's portrait: 'This Somonour bar to hym a stif burdoun; | Was nevere trompe of half so greet a soun' (ll. 673–74). The meaning of the word *burdoun* (to hum or to drone) provides readers with a notion of the quality of the Summoner's singing voice.[49] In other words, the Summoner accompanies the Pardoner with a 'monotonous and repetitious ground melody'.[50] Despite the quality of his voice, its direction is ambiguous. Is he singing directly to the Pardoner, or merely accompanying him? Chamberlain

[48] Chaucer also compares the Summoner's speaking to the behaviour of a jay: 'And eek ye knowen wel how that a jay | Kan clepen "Watte" as well as kan the pope' (ll. 642–43). Like the magpie characters discussed earlier, the voice of the Summoner lacks distinction; it is indistinguishable from any other because of its ability to imitate. Chaucer's next lines reinforce his ignorance: 'But whoso koude in oother thyng hym grope, | Thane hadde he spent al his philosophie' (ll. 644–45). The Summoner lacks rational control over his voice. Even more problematically, the Summoner imitates the Pope.

[49] Emma Pope M. Dieckmann, 'The Meaning of "Burdoun" in Chaucer', *Modern Philology*, 26 (1929), 279–82 (p. 280).

[50] Quoted in Dieckman, 'Meaning of "Burdoun"', p. 281.

identifies the 'burdoun' as one of Chaucer's more original musical signs that signals a 'fleshly rather than spiritual orientation', an erotic rather than a rational quality.[51] Considering his ecclesiastical position, the Summoner should be one figure with a properly trained and directed voice. Like the Summoner, each of the characters whose singing voices receives comparison to birdsong follows a path to *cupiditas*. They sing for the wrong reasons, for pleasure, not for a rational purpose. However, not just the performers of music should turn a reasoning ear to song. Often the inattentive or irresponsible listener can be seduced into inappropriate behaviour. In *The Legend of Good Women*, Chaucer describes the problem with irresponsible listening. The birdsong in the garden setting entices the narrator away from his books: 'Whan that I here the smale foules synge, | And that the floures gynne for to sprynge. | Farewel my stodye' (G, ll. 37–39). Birdsong can disrupt the hearer, or take him away from rational behaviour. The narrator of the poem falls victim to the sensual pleasure of the music, an action that might lead to moral peril.[52] By contrast, the Clerk in the *General Prologue* seems to prefer books to instruments of music:

> Twenty bookes, clad in blak or reed,
> Of Aristotle and his philosophie
> Than robes riche, or fithele, or gay sautrie.
> (ll. 294–96)

Chaucer's clerk would rather keep his nose in a book than express himself with fiddle or harp. He values erudition over decadence. Yet other clerks, such as those found in *The Miller's Tale* and *The Reeve's Tale*, value music differently. In the case of *The Reeve's Tale*, the clerks respond to the 'melodye' of the Miller's snoring: 'Herdestow evere slyk a sang er now?' (ll. 4168, 4170). They then proceed to violate both the Miller's daughter and wife. These clerks do not understand true music. They respond to the worst type of song, if snoring can be called such. It is up to the listeners to discern appropriate musical styles and react rationally and morally. According to Leach, 'Medieval writers often marked beautiful but immoral music as feminine. [...] The metaphorical heritage of the monstrous figure of the siren, a hybrid bird-woman with a beautiful but deadly song, [...] is used to encapsulate the related moral perils of the bestial, the feminine, and the sexual.'[53] With the siren, music acts as the lure into carnality. Leach examines

[51] Chamberlain, 'Musical Signs and Symbols', pp. 44, 55.

[52] Leach, *Sung Birds*, p. 259.

[53] Leach, *Sung Birds*, p. 239.

music as enticement, concluding that regardless of its performer — 'fowler, a siren, the devil, or a courtier, the unreflective animal is led into danger by its senses'.[54] The two most commonly associated sins are lust and greed.[55] In *The Canterbury Tales*, Chaucer offers several singers that use song as a means of enticement.

One of Chaucer's sirens appears in *The Miller's Tale*, where Chaucer presents the clerk Nicholas as an adept music student. First, the narrator describes Nicholas:

> He made a-nyghtes melodie
> So swetely that al the chambre rong,
> And *Angelus ad virginem* he song,
> [...]
> Ful often blessed was his myrie throte.
> (ll. 3214–18)

Nicholas does not sing courtly love songs. Instead, his blessed throat, like that of the Prioress, brings forth a melody that celebrates religious devotion. Even so, his use of the Marian lyric, 'The Angel to the Virgin', reminds readers of the courtly love lyric in which a lover pays tribute to a beautiful lady. This association perverts any devotional intention of the song, particularly considering Nicholas's other behaviours. Through his singing, Nicholas lays the groundwork for his seduction of Alison, like a siren. At the same time, Nicholas also possesses enough rhetorical skill — he 'spak so faire' (l. 3288) — to seduce Alison, resulting in their liaison: 'He kiste hire sweete and taketh his sawtrie, | pleyeth faste, and maketh melodie' (ll. 3305–06).[56] Jesse Gellrich has outlined how *The Miller's Tale* parodies medieval forms of music, creating in music a 'metaphor of love', because Nicholas plays upon Alison as he plays upon instruments.[57] However, I see the distinctions made about music and the singing voices of the characters as more complex than a simple parody.

More specifically, Chaucer describes the song styles of each character within *The Miller's Tale*, saying something different about each one. Additionally,

[54] Leach, *Sung Birds*, p. 256.

[55] Leach, *Sung Birds*, p. 260.

[56] Zeeman agrees that the narrator of *The Miller's Tale* 'uses the imagery of music for sex [...] and perhaps even for masturbation' ('Gender of Song', p. 159).

[57] Jesse M. Gellrich, 'The Parody of Medieval Music in *The Miller's Tale*', *Journal of English and Germanic Philology*, 73 (1974), 176–88 (pp. 177–79).

'maketh melodie' in this context is not the natural reproduction of the *General Prologue;* rather it represents illicit sex. The latter point is reinforced by a second use of 'melodie' in the story: when Alison and Nicholas dupe John to be alone, the narrator refers to them as participating in 'revel and melodye' (l. 3652). Chamberlain regards this usage of 'melodye' as a 'mutation of a seemingly virtuous literal sign [...] to a wholly erotic figurative sign'.[58] It is interesting to note that Alison's husband, John, does not sing at all. This could suggest impotence on his part, as all the other characters of the tale possess singing voices. Katherine Zieman explores the relationship between Nicholas's rhetoric and John's hearing and subsequent action, pointing out that John does not possess the ability to interpret what he hears or understand the significance of his actions.[59] This argument reinforces my points about active listening, of rhetoric or song, both methods of discourse studied together. Thus, Chaucer classifies Nicholas as a character that makes music with a beautiful voice for nefarious purposes. Both he and Alison thus pursue an immoral path, the irrational choice of any beast.

The portrait of the Friar in the *General Prologue* offers another siren. Identified as 'wantowne and a merye' (l. 208), the Friar brags about his many conquests that result in shotgun weddings, and his manipulation of wives in the parish. Not surprisingly, Chaucer points out his exceptional singing voice:

> And certainly he hadde a murye note:
> Wel koude he synge and pleyen on a rote;
> Of yeddynges he baar outrely the pris.
> (ll. 235–37)

The Friar literally takes the prize for his singing of ballads.[60] His music pleases the ear and achieves a response from its audience. These lines follow the description of the Friar giving knives and pins to the fair wives (ll. 233–34), easily interpreted as a distribution of love tokens or favours. While Chaucer does not connect the Friar's song to birds, he does connect the singing to lascivious behaviour:

[58] Chamberlain, 'Musical Signs and Symbols', p. 54. In *The Merchant's Tale*, Chaucer also uses the phrase 'maken melodye' in a way contrary to its appearance in the *General Prologue*. In this narrative, January creates a pleasure garden for his wife, May: 'He made a gardyn walled al with stoon | [...] | [in which to] Disporten hem and maken melodye' (ll. 2029–40). This garden is built to keep his wife exclusively available for his sexual desires.

[59] Katherine Zieman, 'Chaucer's Voys', *Representations*, 60 (1997), 70–91 (pp. 77–78).

[60] Higdon pays particular attention to the fact that the Friar sings ballads and not hymns ('Diverse Melodies', p. 103).

> Somwhat he lipsed, for his wantownesse,
> To make his Englissh sweete upon his tonge;
> And in his harping, whan that he hadde songe.
> (ll. 264–66)

His singing possesses qualities not generally connected to rational music-making. He purposefully affects a lisp in order to emphasize the softer sounding *s*. The sound evokes the image of the serpent whispering in Eve's ear. Like a siren, the Friar uses his song to lure the wives of his parish into carnal behaviour. His singing emphasizes sensuality not reason, and therefore condemns him as performer, as well as leads his audience into sin. Of course, as a Friar, his music-making should be much more devotional.

Finally, the dangers of an inappropriate singing voice are embodied in the Pardoner, the essence of the siren figure. The portrait begins with the Pardoner singing in duet with the Summoner: 'Ful loude he soong "Com hider, love, to me!"' (l. 672).[61] This reference to the Summoner represents the only occasion in the *General Prologue* in which Chaucer substantially overlaps character portraits.[62] Interestingly, Michael A. Calabrese notes how this phrase echoes the Song of Songs, 'parodying or blaspheming a book interpreted as a love song between Christ and the church'.[63] Chaucer, however, also characterizes the Pardoner's voice as 'small as hath a goot' (l. 688). This could designate the quality of the Pardoner's voice as unpleasant, or the word *small* could be glossed as 'high', indicating a feminized voice, such as those compared to a nightingale.[64] Higdon points to the 'loude' quality of the Pardoner's song, emphasizing that the Pardoner's purpose is focused on gaining attention.[65] Holsinger highlights the Pardoner's 'polyphonically perverse' ability to alter his voice, through timbre, volume, and pitch, in order to suit his purposes, a skill useful for a siren figure.[66]

[61] The Summoner could be considered a type of siren as well; however, his portrait does not directly connect his singing with his temptation of others through false summons.

[62] Holsinger, *Music, Body, and Desire*, p. 177. Furthermore, Holsinger examines the polyphonic nature of the Pardoner and Summoner's song that produces anxiety over same sex singing (pp. 177–80).

[63] Michael A. Calabrese, '"Make a Mark That Shows": Orphean Song, Orphean Sexuality, and the Exile of Chaucer's Pardoner', *Viator: Medieval and Renaissance Studies*, 24 (1993), 269–86 (p. 276).

[64] Similar associations of smallness were made with Absolon's voice.

[65] Higdon, 'Diverse Melodies', p. 106.

[66] Holsinger, *Music, Body, and Desire*, p. 182.

All of these qualities in the Pardoner's singing voice condemn the Pardoner to moral censure. Other physical details reinforce the feminization of the Pardoner and thereby reinforce an interpretation of his singing voice.[67]

In total, the quality of the Pardoner's voice problematizes the way he uses song:

> Wel koude he rede a lessoun or a storie,
> But aldebest he song an offertorie;
> For wel he wiste, whan that song was songe,
> He moste preche and wel affile his tonge
> To wynne silver, as he ful wel koude;
> Therefore he song the murierly and loude.
> (ll. 709–14)

In this passage, the Pardoner uses song like a siren, enchanting his parishioners to buy his relics.[68] In this context, his skill is unparalleled, almost comparable to the devil's silver tongue. Leach summarizes: 'If a man allowed inappropriate, especially effeminate, music to act upon him without engaging rational judgment, the passive nature of listening would feminize him; the behaviour or character alteration that such music could effect in him might have serious consequences for him as much as it has for animals, thereby also bestializing him.'[69] His performance condemns him as well as the inattentive listeners, those untrained in the understanding of true music. Each of the siren figures — Nicholas, the Friar, and the Pardoner — achieve significant success through their song. However, they sing for immoral and thus irrational purposes.

The only songs that do not receive criticism are those raised for spiritual purposes. Few of the pilgrims, or the characters in their tales, sing with such devotion or demonstrate such studied skill as the Prioress and the young boy. The

[67] For a more developed review of the sexuality of the Pardoner, see Zeeman's discussion which pays attention to the exchange between the Host and the Pardoner, in which 'Chaucer brings the imaginary of the masculine singer, with his sublimating arts of love, rhetoric, and song, face to face with "lower" places and body parts' ('Gender of Song', p. 171). See also Calabrese's essay, '"Make a Mark That Shows"', mentioned above, Carolyn Dinshaw's chapter on the Pardoner in her book *Chaucer's Sexual Poetics* (Madison: University of Wisconsin Press, 1990), or Richard Firth Green's essay 'The Pardoner's Pants and Why They Matter', *Studies in the Age of Chaucer*, 15 (1993), 131–45.

[68] Calabrese draws parallels between Orpheus, with his ability to manipulate and audience, to 'soften the heart of hell', and the Pardoner ('"Make a Mark That Shows"', p. 274). This comparison reinforces the interpretation of the Pardoner as a siren figure.

[69] Leach, *Sung Birds*, p. 254.

Prioress ends her tale with a miracle of song produced by a schoolboy, demonstrating perfection in his performance, and perhaps achieving a song closer in quality to the choir of angels than the songs of beasts. When the Prioress finally tells her tale during the pilgrimage to Canterbury, she relates the story of a child and his song. The narrator reveals:

> This litel child, his litel book lernynge,
> As he sat in the scole at his prymer,
> He *Alma redemptoris* herde synge,
> As children lerned hire antiphoner;
> [...]
> And herkned ay the wordes and the noote,
> Til he the firste vers koude al by rote.
> (ll. 516–22)

With this description, the narrator draws a correlation between study and the singing voice. The more appropriate singing voice is gained through vigorous study and directed to a worthy purpose. However, as Holsinger argues, Chaucer's mention of the child learning 'by rote' complicates this idea: 'The clergeon's musical learning is ostensibly anything but a product of schoolroom *disciplina*.'[70] Even so, Chaucer also makes explicit connections between the child's learning and corporal punishment, revealing a 'long tradition of imagining violence as an integral part of the pedagogical transmission of the medieval Latin liturgy'.[71] The child has made a point of ignoring his 'prymer' for which he will be 'beten thries in an houre' (ll. 541–42) in favour of 'diligence | To konne it al er Cristmasse be went' (ll. 539–40). While the child does not follow an approved method of study and the narrator reveals his lack of understanding of what the Latin verses say (l. 523), the child does demonstrate a curiosity about the nature and purpose of the song — service to Christ's mother. Regardless of the method of educational delivery, technique remains important. Chaucer certainly never compares the child's singing to birds or animals. The passage reveals that the child pays attention to words and notes, the mechanical elements that comprise music. Zeeman also reinforces the positive image inherent in the child's insistence on learning

[70] Holsinger, *Music, Body, and Desire*, p. 271. Holsinger discusses the location and method of the boy's learning in greater detail. His larger argument reveals interesting connections between music, violence, and the body, elements all represented prominently in *The Prioress's Tale.*

[71] Holsinger, *Music, Body, and Desire*, p. 272. Holsinger also connects the teaching device, the Guidonian Hand, as an image 'embodying the constant threat of musical violence' (p. 279).

music.[72] In subsequent lines, when describing the child's song, the narrator comments, 'And thane he song it wel and boldely, | Fro word to word, acordynge with the note' (ll. 546–47). The craft and technique of making music are important.

Holsinger makes one final point that reinforces the medieval views about *musica humana* and demonstrates the importance of balance of nature and reason, of Boethius's body and soul, as seen in the final words of the child in *The Prioress's Tale*:

> Wherfore I synge, and synge moot certeyn,
> In honour of that blisful Mayden free
> Til fro my tonge of taken is the greyn;
> And after that thus seyde she to me:
> 'My litel child, now wol I fecche thee,
> What that the greyn is fro thy tonge ytake.
> Be nat agast; I wol thee nat forsake'.
> (ll. 656–69)

Holsinger reads the image of the grain as a literal connection between the musical body and the soul, a connection performed by a 'thoroughly indoctrinated Christian actor'.[73] Despite this compelling observation of the child as a passive vessel, listening to the child's song does not produce a bestial result.[74] His is not a siren's song. Instead, the music intends to elevate its listeners. His music possesses 'swetnesse' (l. 555) and 'swich sentence' (l. 563). Interestingly, these are two qualities also needed to produce a good tale. Ultimately, the child's singing brings the community together with a single, if disturbing, purpose.[75] With this tale, Chaucer comes closest to portraying the perfect type of music.

As this essay has been suggesting, it is entirely possible to read human music-making within Chaucer's poetic works. By understanding the ways that Chaucer presents music, most specifically the human voice raised in song, readers can

[72] Zeeman further concludes that the child's preoccupation with his art is narcissistic like many of the other clerical singers she discusses ('Gender of Song', p. 173).

[73] Holsinger, *Music, Body, and Desire*, pp. 290–91.

[74] Some might argue that the child's singing through the Jewish quarter lends itself to the violence visited upon him (Zeeman, 'Gender of Song', p. 174). According to the narrator, however, the fault in this episode lies with the listeners, not the song.

[75] It is worth mentioning that *The Second Nun's Tale* includes a similarly disturbing singer, Cecilia, who 'to God alone in herte thus sang she' (l. 134). Like the Prioress's schoolboy, her life ends violently. Holsinger discusses this connection (*Music, Body, and Desire*, pp. 284–85).

identify new ways to understand the characters of Chaucer's work, particularly *The Canterbury Tales*. Just like the physiognomy that Chaucer relies upon so heavily throughout his work, the human voice is also a trope, an indicator of how Chaucer's characters misuse their voices to celebrate or pursue pleasure. The connections of these voices to birds, birdsong, and the siren, further emphasize the bestiality and irrationality of the inappropriate music makers. At the end of *The Canterbury Tales* in the Retraction, Chaucer famously apologizes for a good portion of the material in his book. Several lines in particular are relevant to this current discussion: 'And many another book, if they were in my remembrance, and many a song and many a leccherous lay, that Crist for his grete mercy foryeve me the synne' (1086). These lines follow his denouncement of specific works like *Troilus and Criseyde* and *The Canterbury Tales*. Whether or not he truly felt repentant for writing such works, by including songs as part of his 'sinful' work, Chaucer acknowledges the inherent dangers of inappropriate music-making. For most of the characters of *The Canterbury Tales*, music does not possess the appropriate rational quotient. Many of the songsters exhibit the worst qualities of the preening nightingale. Other characters use music-making as a means of seduction and manipulation.[76] In the end, the only character that produces music that exhibits both reason and nature is the little schoolboy from *The Prioresse's Tale*, and that was a miracle.

*Bloomsburg University*

[76] Many of these singers occupy the focus of Zeeman's exploration of the connections between song and unstable sexuality ('Gender of Song'). She concludes this survey with the point that these singers suffer serious repudiation in the text.

# Enacting Liturgy: *Estote fortes* in the Croxton *Play of the Sacrament*

John Damon

Late medieval romance, lyric, and hagiography have often been studied as literatures in and of themselves, rather than as portions of the widespread literary discourses of the period. The same can be said of both drama and liturgy. This narrowing of reference provides modern readers and researchers an artificially narrow, and therefore distorted, view of the culture that produced them. When viewed in isolation, each genre lacks the rounded cultural context necessary for understanding the texts, despite the fact that crucial issues interpenetrate the literate discourses of the era, which include both prose and verse romance, chronicle, lyric, drama, hagiography, liturgy, and sermon studies, as well as studies of other legal, artistic, and historical discourses. It is instructive to see how a single element within one literate discourse also appears and plays a crucial role in other, seemingly unrelated genres and forms. An operative example of this phenomenon can be observed by examining a wide range of texts, representing various medieval genres, that incorporate the antiphon *Estote fortes in bello*.

This short, anonymous lyric differs from the vast majority of medieval antiphons in that it has no identifiable source within the Old or New Testaments of the Latin Bible. Through its use in a variety of medieval genres, the antiphon becomes a thread within the varied tapestry of medieval literature. It was incorporated into various modes and, most interestingly, on various sides of a medieval cultural schism concerning the legitimacy of violence within the Christian tradition. A close examination of the antiphon's use in a late medieval dramatic text known as the Croxton *Play of the Sacrament* also serves to clarify a major point of scholarly debate about that work: the question of whether the play's Jews represent themselves only or, in addition, serve as a counter for the English heretical sect known as the Lollards, a possibility that has been a point of considerable debate among scholars of late medieval English drama.[1] The association of the antiphon in other contexts with the struggle between Lollards and adherents of the traditional church reinforces the frequently made claim that the Croxton play conflates Jews and Lollards by means of the label 'heretics'.[2] The argument that *The Play of the Sacrament* intimately connects the roles of Jews and unorthodox Christians within a thoroughly hegemonic worldview is strengthened, and at the same time modified, by the appearance of the antiphon at a crucial point in the play. A close examination of its use within the Croxton *Play of the Sacrament* demonstrates that, by the fifteenth century, the antiphon functioned as a site of contentious dispute between adherents of the orthodox religion of the period and the Lollards, deployed on both sides of this late medieval English religious conflict to justify opposing positions on crucial questions of doctrine and practice. The centrality of the antiphon in the play's resolution demonstrates how the short religious lyric functioned as a two-edged sword in a widespread cultural conflict concerning the legitimacy of violence for adherents of the Christian faith.

Throughout the medieval period, the antiphon's primary use lay within the liturgy itself, its typical liturgical setting being, and still remaining today in Roman Catholic worship, the Common of an Apostle[3] (that is, the special service used on the holy day of one of the Twelve Apostles for whom an individual service has not been provided in a church's service books); however, even earlier, it was used instead in services honouring the archangel Michael. These liturgical uses deserve particular attention since the antiphon's origins remain unidentified, being a direct quotation of no known biblical passage, whether canonical or non-canonical. It does resemble, in some of its wording, the battle between Michael and the dragon in the Book of Revelation, portions of the Nag Hammadi or Dead

[1] *The Play of the Sacrament*, in *Non-cycle Plays and Fragments*, ed. by Norman Davis, Early English Text Society (EETS), series 2, 1 (London: Oxford University Press, 1970), pp. 58–89.

[2] See, for example, Robert L. A. Clark and Claire Sponsler, 'Othered Bodies: Racial Cross-Dressing in the Mistere de la Sainte Hostie and the Croxton *Play of the Sacrament*', *Journal of Medieval and Early Modern Studies*, 29 (1999), 61–87; Steven F. Kruger, 'The Bodies of Jews in the Late Middle Ages', in *Early English Drama: An Anthology*, ed. by John C. Coldewey (New York: Garland, 1993).

[3] For the contextualization of the antiphon within the Common of an Apostle, see John Edward Damon, 'An Early Middle English Homily for the Common of an Apostle', *Notes & Queries*, 238 (1993), 10–11.

Sea Scroll text *The Battle of the Sons of Light against the Sons of Darkness*,[4] and similarly, it is echoed in a short Anglo-Saxon religious homily or lyric called 'In Praise of St Michael', the original context of which can only be inferred.[5] The existence of a limited group of extant homilies on the antiphon *Estote fortes* provides a point for comparison. Research has uncovered ten or more Latin homilies, from England and the Continent, that explicate the antiphon, but only two, slightly divergent Middle English versions have been found, one located in the Lambeth Palace Library in London and the other at Corpus Christi College Cambridge.[6] The translations of the antiphon used in the play text and those employed in the two earlier vernacular texts show a significant pattern of difference that rules out direct reliance on either of them for the play's paraphrase. The play's pseudo-sermon thus clearly identifies the context as a struggle over doctrine, a clash over interpretation, not the core belief itself. The existence during the same period of a number of Latin sermons on this antiphon, one of them by a known English author, Ailred of Rievaulx[7] indicates a broader pattern of which the vernacular sermons are merely a part. That pattern involves the extension of crusade preaching into the daily liturgical practice of the church.

[4] See *The Complete Dead Sea Scrolls in English*, trans. by Geza Vermes, rev. edn (New York: Penguin, 1997); *The Scroll of the War of the Sons of Light against the Sons of Darkness*, ed. by Yigael Yadin, trans. by Batya Rabin and Chaim Rabin (Oxford: Oxford University Press, 1962); and Florentino García Martínez, *The Dead Sea Scrolls Translated: The Qumran Texts in English*, trans. by Wilfred G. E. Watson, 2nd edn (Grand Rapids: Eerdmans, 1996).

[5] See Raymond J. S. Grant, *Three Homilies from Cambridge, Corpus Christi College 41: The Assumption, St. Michael, and the Passion* (Ottawa: Tecumseh, 1982); and Richard F. Johnson, 'Archangel in the Margins: St. Michael in the Homilies of Cambridge, Corpus Christi College 41', *Traditio*, 53 (1998), 63–91.

[6] Use of this antiphon as a sermon's lection is exceedingly rare. Only one other vernacular homily, appearing in two different versions, explicates this text. See *Old English Homilies and Homiletic Treatises of the Twelfth and Thirteenth Centuries*, ed. by Richard Morris, EETS, o.s., 29, 34 (London: Trübner, 1868), pp. 184–93; and *Old English Homilies of the Twelfth Century: Second Series*, ed. by Richard Morris, EETS, o.s., 53, repr. edn (Woodbridge: Boydell and Brewer, 1998). These give slightly different readings: the antiphon in London, Lambeth Palace, MS 487 reads: 'Estote fortes in bello & pugnate cum antiquo serpente. et accipietis regnum eternum dicit dominus'; that in Trinity College Cambridge B. 14.52 gives an abbreviated form: 'Esto[te] fortes in bello. et pugnate cum antiquo serpente'. All future references to these homilies are to *First Series* or *Second Series* and page numbers.

[7] Ailred of Rievaulx, 'Sermo XVII: In Natali Sanctorum Apostolorum Petri et Pauli', *Aelredi Rievallensis sermones I–XLVI: Collectio Claraevallensis prima et secunda*, ed. by Gaetano Raciti, Corpus Christianorum Continuatio Mediaevalis, 2A (Turnhout: Brepols, 1989), pp. 134–39.

The Croxton play concerns a band of non-Christians bent on desecrating a stolen communion wafer (the *Sacrament* of the title) in a series of acts of sacrilege. A pattern of repeated verbal signals, relatively unremarked in previous analyses of the play, conflates Jews and Muslims, producing an undifferentiated category of nonbelievers, a pattern that prepares the audience attuned to contemporary religious conflicts to link these two groups to the Lollards. Shortly after the play opens, Jonathas, the leader of a band of Jewish merchants, introduces the pattern of mixed Jewish and Islamic references. In his opening line, he swears:

> Now almyghty Machomet, marke in þi mageste,
> Whose lawes tendrely I have to fulfyll,
> After my dethe bryng me to thy hyhe see,
> My sowle for to save yff yt be thy wyll;
> For myn entent ys for to fulfyll,
> As my gloryus God the to honor.[8]

Jonathas portrays the prophet Mohammed as his 'gloryus God'; however, only a few lines later within the same speech, he identifies himself not as a Muslim but as a Jew: 'Jew Jonathas ys my name | [...] For I am chefe merchaunte of Jewes, I tell yow be ryght'.[9] Rather than presenting Jonathas as either Jew or Muslim, the play treats him as a representative of both groups.

This pattern of bivalent religious identification contrasts orthodox English Christianity with Judaism and Islam as a single counter within a composite religious other, figured merely as those who do not follow Christian orthodoxy. Jasdon, servant to Jonathas, also swears 'be Machomete so myghty' and declares 'almyghty Machomyght be with yow!'[10] In addition, within the corpus of late medieval English play cycles, the name *Mohammed* functions as an operative counter for a broad range of religious faiths regarded as irreligious, nonconformist, or heretical.[11] Prayers to or invocations of Mohammed identify the

[8] *Play of the Sacrament*, ed. by Davis, pp. 62–63.

[9] *Play of the Sacrament*, ed. by Davis, p. 64.

[10] *Play of the Sacrament*, ed. by Davis, pp. 64, 68. See also p. 72: 'Now, by Machomyth so myghty, þat meuyth in my mode!'

[11] For the use of the name of Mohammed as a counter for other religious figures, see the following, all within *Medieval Drama*, ed. by David Bevington (Boston: Houghton Mifflin, 1975): 'The Ten Commandments, Balaam and Balak, and the Prophets (Chester)', p. 349; 'The Offering of the Magi (Wakefield)', pp. 410–12, 417, 419–20, 423; 'Herod the Great (Wakefield)', pp. 438, 441, 450–52; 'The Death of Herod (N Town)', p. 457; 'The Passion Play II (N Town)', pp. 522,

speakers as outside the bounds of Christian orthodoxy, whether those so identified would have historically been Muslims, Jews, or worshippers of various pantheistic deities. At the core of the play lies this crucial link between two types of unbelievers, those from outside the body of Christendom — Jews/Muslims/pagans — and those within the body of nominal Christians who become part of the body of unbelievers through their faithlessness. A Christian actually carries out the plot to steal the host, the literal body of Jesus in orthodox Christian dogma. The prominence of his role in the play, from beginning to end, marks wayward Christians as a major focus, despite the importance of the band of Jews in most critical commentary.

After briefly introducing the pious purpose of the play and its setting in 'Aragon [...] | In Eraclea, that famous cyté', Primus and Secondus Vexillator give a preview of the plot:[12]

Secundus [Vexillator]. Therin wonneth a merchaunte off mekyll might,
Syr Arystorye was called hys name,
Kend full fere with mani a wyght,
Full ⌜fer⌝ in þe worlde sprung hys fame.
Primus. Anon to hym ther cam a Jewe,
With grete rychesse for the nonys,
And wonneth in þe cyté of Surrey — þis full trewe —
Þe wyche hade gret plenté off precyous stonys.
Off þis Cristen merchaunte he freyned sore,
Wane he wolde haue had hys entente.
Twenti pownd, and merchaundyse mor
He proferyd for þe Holy Sacrament.[13]

532; 'The Scourging (Wakefield)', pp. 554–55, 561, 567–68; 'The Crucifixion of Christ (York)', pp. 571, 573; 'The Resurrection of the Lord (Wakefield)', pp. 615, 623, 625; and 'Mary Magdalene (Digby)', pp. 694, and 724–27. See also the following: 'Caesar Augustus', in *The Wakefield Mystery Plays*, ed. and trans. by Martial Rose (New York: Norton, 1961), pp. 145, 148–49, 151; 'The Conspiracy', in *The Wakefield Mystery Plays*, ed. and trans. by Rose, pp. 331, 335, 336, 349–50. See also, all within *The N-Town Play: Cotton MS Vespasian D.8*, ed. by Stephen Spector, EETS, s.s., 11–12, 2 vols (Oxford: Oxford University Press, 1991), vol. I: 'The Magi', p. 172; 'Slaughter of the Innocents', pp. 189, 195; 'Herod', pp. 296–98; 'The Trial Before Herod', p. 311; 'The Guarding of the Sepulchre', pp. 348–49. The ubiquity of such references is demonstrated by the appearance within a fragmentary, twelve-line manuscript text of the following phrase, 'O Mahound, þou grete god and tru' ('The Ashmole Fragment', in *Non-cycle Plays*, ed. by Davis, p. 120).

[12] *Play of the Sacrament*, ed. by Davis, p. 58.

[13] *Play of the Sacrament*, ed. by Davis, p. 58.

Following the brief Banns, and with audience already primed for what will take place, the play opens on the merchant's company: Aristorius himself, his priest Isoder, and Peter Paul, his clerk. Aristorius immediately identifies himself by his religion:

> Aristorius Mercator. Now Cryst, þat ys our Creatour, from shame he cure vs;
> He maynteyn vs with myrth þat meve vpon þe mold;
> Vnto his en[d]elesse joye myghtly he restore vs,
> All tho that in his name in peas well them hold.[14]

However, the themes Aristorius introduces — freedom from shame, mirth, endless joy, and peace — signal a particular focus to his Christianity, one more consistent with Lollards than with the institutional Church. Following, as it does, the Banns' summary of the plot, this speech would link such views with the role Aristorius will play: a venal and irreligious figure who places the love of money above the dictates of his faith.

Aristorius's role in the play is sinister, but despite his eventual willingness to sell out his religion for monetary gain, he at first refuses to aid Jonathas. His vacillating responses to the host-desecraters reveal moral fidelity and religious zeal. When Jonathas requests his help in obtaining the host, Aristorius rejects the overture in what appears at first to be a seem firm and unequivocal manner:

> Aristorius. Sir Jonathas, sey me for my sake,
> What man[er] of marchandis ys þat ⌜ye⌝ mene?
> Jonathas. Yowr God, þat ys full mytheti, in a cake,
> And thys good anoon shall yow seen.
> [Aristorius] Nay, in feyth, þat shall not bene.
> I will not for an hundder pownd
> To stond in fere my Lord to tene;[15]
> And for so lytell a walew in conscyen[c]e to stond bownd.[16]

Rather than absolute and categorical, his refusal is in fact based on questionable reasoning which highlights his mercantile approach to moral decision-making: fear of God ('stond in fere my Lord to tene')[17] and, more significantly, an un-

[14] *Play of the Sacrament*, ed. by Davis, pp. 58–89.

[15] *Medieval Drama*, ed. by Bevington, p. 766 n. 289, glosses: 'To live in fear (for my soul) as a result of having injured my Lord'.

[16] *Play of the Sacrament*, ed. by Davis, p. 67.

[17] Davis, 'Glossary', pp. 134–64, 'ten(e)', p. 159, defines *ten[e]* as to 'anger or annoy'; Francis H. Stratmann, *A Middle English Dictionary, containing words used by English writers from the*

willingness 'in conscyen[c]e to stond bownd' for such a small amount of money ('for so lytell a walew'). The emotions of fear and greed determine his actions rather than moral reasoning based on religious belief. Within the play, these character traits mark him out as a villain. Of the two characters, Jonathas plays the less treacherous role, lacking belief in Christian doctrine rather than betraying his stated beliefs as Aristorius does.

The dialogue between the two men establishes the positions each holds on the idea of host desecration. Aristorius is reluctant for fear of temporal or divine retribution and insufficient remuneration, but Jonathas expresses an underlying willingness to convert to Christianity should his testing of the host warrant it:

> Sir, þe entent ys, if I myght knowe or vndertake
> Yf þat he were God allmyght,
> Off all my mys I woll amende make,[18]
> And doon hym wourshepe bothe day and nyght.[19]

Compared to the venality of Aristorius, the Jew's desire reflects moral reasoning, showing him to be, within the play's implied moral compass, less venal and more principled than the Christian merchant. Jonathas's explanation seems to mollify Aristorius somewhat, but for his own part, he now expresses what appear to be his main concerns: desire for gain and fear of the religious authorities. He rejects the idea of undertaking such a dangerous task without sufficient remuneration, shifting from outright refusal to a transactional mode contingent upon determining his reward and allaying his fear of retribution:

> Jonathas, trowth I shall þe tell;
> I stond in gret dowght to do þat dede,
> To yow þat dere all for to sell[20]
> I fere me þat I shuld stond in drede;
> For and I vnto þe chyrche yede,
> And prelate or clerke myght me aspye,

*twelfth to the fifteenth century*, rearranged, rev., and enl. by Henry Bradley (Oxford: Clarendon Press, 1981), defines it as 'harm or irritate'.

[18] *Medieval Drama*, ed. by Bevington, p. 766 n. 293, glosses, 'i.e., If in fact he is God almighty, I will atone for all my sins'.

[19] *Play of the Sacrament*, ed. by Davis, p. 67.

[20] *Medieval Drama*, ed. by Bevington, p. 766 n. 297, glosses, 'To sell that loved one (i.e., Christ) to you'.

> To þe bysshope þei wolde go tell þat dede
> And apache me of eresye.[21]

Aristorius identifies his core fear: that he will be seen and either the 'prelate or clerke' would inform 'þe bysshope' of his act 'of eresye', revealing the shallowness of his beliefs. Jonathas is able to quickly overcome the merchant's fears, and, after brief negotiations, they reach agreement on a relatively safe plan for the theft and a payment of 'an hundder pownd, neythr mor nor lasse, | of dokettys good'.[22] United now in a common purpose, they carry out the plot.

Aristorius has thus shown himself to lack reverence for the host and appropriate religious scruples; on the other hand, Jonathas has shown his willingness to convert should the miracle of the host be found genuine. The interchange ends with a reinforcement of the melding of Muslim and Jew in the role of Jonathas:

> Jonathas. Syr, almighty Machomyght be with yow!
> And I shall cum again right sone.
> Aristorius. Jonathas, ye wott what I haue seyd, and how
> I shall walke for that we haue to doun.[23]

That Aristorius does not react to the invocation of Mohammed's protection shows a lack of religious sectarianism on his part, despite the high value evidently placed on it by those around him, and from this point onward he expresses no hesitation about carrying out his bargain. After having successfully stolen the communion wafer, he meets Jonathas as arranged, greeting him with kindly words:

> Aristorius. Welcom, Jonathas, gentyll and trew,
> For well and trwly þou kepyst thyn howre;
> Here ys þe Host, sacred newe,
> Now wyll I home to halle and bowre.[24]

The description of Jonathas as 'gentyll and trew' is echoed a few lines later by Jonathas himself, who says to his companions upon returning with the host: 'Now, Jason and Jasdon, ye be Jewys jentyll'.[25] Davis glosses the word *gentyll* as

[21] *Play of the Sacrament*, ed. by Davis, p. 67.

[22] *Play of the Sacrament*, ed. by Davis, p. 68.

[23] *Play of the Sacrament*, ed. by Davis, p. 68 (*Medieval Drama*, ed. by Bevington, p. 766 n. 335, glosses the final speech as, 'i.e., I shall go about doing what has to be done'.)

[24] *Play of the Sacrament*, ed. by Davis, p. 70.

[25] *Play of the Sacrament*, ed. by Davis, p. 70.

'noble, courteous', or sometimes 'dear',[26] an adjective that presents a marked contrast to the ethos of the play in regard to these characters. The play's intended or imagined audience would hardly have considered the stealing of the host and its subsequent mistreatment as noble, courteous, or gentle. The play further stigmatizes the Jews and their Christian accomplices by a careful process that identifies the present-day Jews within the play with the historical Jews considered the guilty party in the Crucifixion. This broadening of focus can also be seen in other plays within the Corpus Christi cycles.

In the various cycle plays, the identification of Islam with Judaism further conflates Jews and Lollards with worshippers of the Devil. In the Twenty-second play of the Wakefield cycle, 'The Last Judgement', the 3rd Evil Soul declares:

> Alas, carefull catifys may we rise,
> Sore may we wring oure handys and wepe!
> For cursid and sore covitise
> Dampnyd be we in hell full depe.
> Roght we never of Godys service;
> His commaundementys wold we not kepe;
> Bot oft times made we sacrifice
> To Sathanas when othere can slepe.[27]

The admitted role as Satan worshipper clearly identifies this character and his companions as members of one of the most extreme groups among the damned. Similarly, in Wakefield's 'The Judgement', when Tutivillus, the only named sinner, appears, he represents the vilest of the vile, as his name implies. Who holds this cameo role of the most damned of the damned?

> Tutivillus I am oone of youre ordir and oone of youre sons;
> I stande at my tristur when othere men shones.
> 1st Demon Now, thou art min[e] awne querestur! I wote where thou wonnes.
> Do tell me.
> Tutivillus I was your chefe tollare,
> And sithen courte rollar;
> *Now am I master Lollar,*
> And of sich men I mell me.[28]

[26] Davis, 'Glossary', p. 144; Stratmann, *A Middle English Dictionary*, p. 263, defines it as 'gentle, noble, generous'.

[27] *Medieval Drama*, ed. by Bevington, p. 638.

[28] *Medieval Drama*, ed. by Bevington, pp. 644–45, emphasis added.

Tutivillus's self-identification as a 'master Lollar' adds a new element to the group of the despised unbelievers, a group that now conflates a wide range of characters — Jews, Muslims, Roman pagans, devil worshippers, and Lollards.

Jonathas the Muslim-Jew and his followers perform a series of actions that reenact the torment of Jesus leading up to his death. David Bevington argues that the 'central action of the play' involves 'a series of tortures and indignities designed to prove that it is merely a wafer of bread', which he terms 'an extended symbolic reenactment of Christ's Passion':[29]

> When, for example, [Aristorius] agrees to steal the host out of the church in return for money, we are reminded of Judas' bargaining with the chief priest to betray Christ in return for thirty pieces of silver. When the Jews desecrate the host, they assume roles as the torturers of Christ. They are five in number since they must inflict five wounds on the host. Jonathas administers the fifth and final wound, thereby reenacting the role of the blind soldier[30] who pierced Christ's side at the Crucifixion (l. 468). The number five also signifies the five words with which Christ blessed the host at the Last Supper: 'Eat, this is my body' (l. 404). The host bleeds, in token of Christ's blood which was shed for man.[31]

Here Bevington presents a point-by-point analysis of the ritual elements in the 'torments' inflicted on the host, highlighting the imagined audience's perception of 'an essential symbolic relationship between dramatic presentation and ritual reenactment'.[32] The interplay between the rites of the Christian church and performance of the play anticipates the crucial role of ritual in the work's final scene, when the antiphon *Estote fortes* is enacted and explicated in a pseudo-sermon, about which Bevington says, 'The long concluding action [...] is heavily liturgical [...]. Adding to the impressiveness of the occasion is the illusion of an actual ecclesiastical service.'[33] The play thus involves its audience in the very rituals created by the Church to reenact the central mysteries of the faith: Jesus's suffering, death, burial, and resurrection.

Central to the play's catechetical function is the representation of Jesus rising from the dead. As Bevington dryly comments:

[29] David Bevington, 'Introduction: *The Play of the Sacrament* From Croxton', in *Medieval Drama*, ed. by Bevington, pp. 754–56 (p. 754).

[30] Longinus or Longeus Latus, whose role and legend are discussed in David Bevington, 'Introduction: Christ's Death and Burial (York)', in *Medieval Drama*, ed. by Bevington, p. 580.

[31] Bevington, 'Introduction: *The Play of the Sacrament* From Croxton', p. 754.

[32] Bevington, 'Introduction: *The Play of the Sacrament* From Croxton', p. 755.

[33] Bevington, 'Introduction: *The Play of the Sacrament* From Croxton', p. 755.

> Today we can scarcely imagine how this play could have moved its audience to faith in the miracle of Christ's real presence in the mass. The theatrical devices seem obvious and even comic, involving as they do the sudden removal of Jonathas' hand from his arm and the appearance of Christ's image in a boiling oven.[34]

Yet the play subordinates these essentially unbelievable elements to the core idea that attempts to torture the host are destined to end in defeat through the direct intervention of the divine, confirmed when the Jews encounter the ever-living Christ who, appearing out of the fire, says to them:

> Oh ye merveylows Jewys,
> Why ar ye to yowr kyng onkynd,
> And [I] so bitterly bowt yow to my blysse?
> Why fare ye thus fule with yowre frende?
> Why peyne yow me and straytly me pynde,
> And I yowr loue so derely houe bowght?
> Why are ye so vnstedfast in yowr mynde?
> Why wrath ye me? I greve you nowght.
> Why wyll ye nott beleue that I haue tawght,
> And forsake yowr fowle neclygence,
> And kepe my commandementys in yowr thowght,
> And vnto my godhed to take credence?
> Why blaspheme yow me? Why do ye thus?
> Why put yow me to a newe tormentry,
> And I dyed for yow on the crosse?[35]

The Jews also aver that the basic tenets of Christianity, rather than being a wholly different and distinct faith, represent heresy against the tenets of Judaism. Jason, another one of the servants of Jonathas, states that Christian belief in Jesus's virgin birth represents a heretical perspective: 'Ageyns owr law this is false heresy'.[36] Jasdon concurs, saying:

> They saye þat Jhesu to be owr kyng,
> But I wene he bowght þat full dere.
> But they make a royall aray of hys vprysyng;
> And that in euery place ys prechyd farre and nere.
> And how he to hys dyscyples agayn dyd appere,

[34] Bevington, 'Introduction: *The Play of the Sacrament* From Croxton', p. 755.

[35] *Play of the Sacrament*, ed. by Davis, pp. 80–81.

[36] *Play of the Sacrament*, ed. by Davis, p. 71.

> To Thomas and to Mary Mawdelen,
> And syth how he styed by hys own power;
> And thys, ye know well, ys heresy full playn.[37]

The use of the language of orthodoxy, especially in the final line ('heresy full playn'), represents a crucial inversion employed in the play, in which Jews reflect Christian attitudes about many religious issues, but always through the lens of their own orthodoxy.

The Jews in the play mirror many of the beliefs and concerns of orthodox Christians, yet within the English Corpus Christi play cycles, they undergo a radical realignment, going from being God's chosen people into functioning as emblematic of infidelity and deceit. This inversion will itself be reversed in the Croxton play's conclusion. Ruth Nissé describes the radical and sudden transformation that occurs at the centre of the N-Town enactment of the Passion, which she skilfully connects to 'the typological, apologetic understanding of history and the vision of sacramental wholeness that ideally structured urban Corpus Christi drama':

> In this annual vision, Old Testament Jews seamlessly become 'figures' of New Testament truth, Jesus' Jewish disciples become Christians, and the Jewish judges and torturers who star in the following sequence of Passion plays are already doomed to destruction with Jerusalem.[38]

The play negotiates between contrasting conceptualizations of Jewish-Christian difference. The two groups emerge from a shared heritage as God's divinely anointed followers to become opposites and yet replicates, mirror images of each other.

Previous studies of *The Play of the Sacrament* have tended to ignore — one is tempted to say, to elide — the content of the Bishop's short sermon that ends the play. Most analyses mention the staged service only in very generic terms. One exception is Sister Nicholas Maltman, who notes that following the bishop's placing of the host on the altar, he then delivers what she terms 'a short homily' explicating the antiphon *Estote fortes*, which she identifies as the antiphon for Matins on the Feast of All Saints in the Sarum Use.[39] She is certainly correct when

[37] *Play of the Sacrament*, ed. by Davis, p. 71.

[38] Ruth Nissé, *Defining Acts: Drama and the Politics of Interpretation in Late Medieval England* (Notre Dame: University of Notre Dame Press, 2005), p. 107.

[39] Sister Nicholas Maltman, 'Meaning and Art in the Croxton *Play of the Sacrament*', *English Literary History*, 41 (1974), 149–64.

she asserts that the choice of text is not 'haphazard'.[40] However, rather than merely functioning as a 'warning to the Jews that they repent and confess their sins' and a reminder to Christians that they are 'part of a larger struggle between God and evil, between Christ and Satan' which can only be won 'through the passion of Christ' and that victory in this struggle 'has an eternal reward',[41] the sermon's enactment here reprises the central themes of the play, explaining not only or even primarily to Jonathas and his followers but all unbelievers, in particular wayward Christians and Lollards represented by Aristorius, have only one path to redemption: the espousing of the dominant Christian ideology of the official church of Western Christendom.

The 'sermon' begins with the quotation and explication of the antiphon *Estote fortes*, a choice that, far from being haphazard, has serious implications for an accurate understanding of the sermon's role in the play and the meaning of the work as a whole.

*Here shall þe merchant and hys prest go to þe chyrche, and þe bysshop shall entre þe chyrche and lay the Ost* on *the auter, saying thus*:

Episcopus *Estote forte⸢s⸣ in bello et pugnate cum antico serpente,*
*Et accipite regnum eternum, et cetera.*

My chyldern, ye be strong in batayll gostly[42]
For to fyght agayn the fell serpent
That nyght and day ys ever besy;
To dystroy owr sollys ys hys intent.
Look ye be not slow nor neclygent
To arme yow in the vertues seuyn.
Of synnys fo[r]gotyn take good avysement,
And knowlege them to yowr confessor full euyn.

For that serpent, the deuyll, ys full strong,
Meruelows myschevos for man to mene;
But that the Passyon of Cryst ys meynt vs among,
And that ys in dyspyte of hys infernall tene.[43]

[40] Maltman, 'Meaning and Art', p. 159.

[41] Maltman, 'Meaning and Art', p. 159.

[42] Davis, 'Glossary', p. 144, and Stratmann, *A Middle English Dictionary*, p. 263, define 'gostly'/'gāst-lîc' as 'spiritual'.

[43] *Medieval Drama*, ed. by Bevington, p. 784 nn. 878–79, glosses this clause, 'Were it not that the Passion of Christ is proclaimed among us, in defiance of the devil's hellish harms'.

Beseche owr Lord and Sauyowr so kene
To put doun that serpent, cumberer of man,
To withdraw hys furyous froward doctryn bydene,
Fulfyllyd of þe fend callyd Leuyathan.[44]
Gyff lawrell to that Lord of myght
That he may bryng vs to the joyows fruycion,
From vs to put the fend to flight,
That neuer he dystroy vs by hys temptacion.[45]

Despite a relative dearth of commentary on this pseudo-sermon, its anomalous nature and its relationship to its two Middle English affiliates require careful consideration. Although no direct translation of the antiphon is supplied, the explication pointedly refers to a spiritual rather than physical struggle: 'in batayll gostly', a sense only implied in the Lambeth/Trinity homily. This spiritual emphasis also appears in the clause 'To dystroy owr sollys ys hys intent'. Even more significant in this regard is the call not for the individual to defeat the serpent but rather for the Christian warrior to 'beseche owr Lord and Sauyowr so kene | To put doun that serpent'. Most significant of all is the focus on doctrine: 'To withdraw hys furyous forward *doctryn* bydene' (emphasis added). The sermon signals that the play's primary context is late medieval religious conflicts within Christianity.

The antiphon's appearance in *The Play of the Sacrament* has no liturgical function except as a call to conversion and repentance. The emphasis on repentance as a prerequisite for following Christ into battle is entirely consistent both with the pseudo-sermon on the Croxton play and also with Christopher Tyerman's recent observation, based on earlier work by Maier and Cole, that 'preachers under Innocent III [...] employed the crusade in their efforts to put pastoral theology into practice'.[46] Thus just as crusading advocates used pastoral opportunities to aid in recruitment, preachers could employ the ethos of the

[44] *Medieval Drama*, ed. by Bevington, p. 784 nn. 878–79, glosses, 'To revoke completely the menacing, perverse claims of authority disseminated by the fiend, called Leviathan (after Isaiah 27:1)'.

[45] *Play of the Sacrament*, ed. by Davis, p. 85.

[46] Christopher Tyerman, *The Invention of the Crusades* (Toronto: University of Toronto Press, 1998), p. 67; Christoph T. Maier, *Preaching the Crusades: Mendicant Friars and the Cross in the Thirteenth Century* (Cambridge: Cambridge University Press, 1994); Penny J. Cole, *The Preaching of the Crusades to the Holy Land, 1095–1270* (Cambridge, MA: Medieval Academy of America, 1991), pp. 111–14. Innocent III's pontificate extended from 1198 to 1216.

crusades to reinforce key theological principles. Cole devotes an entire chapter of her book on preaching the crusades to the topic of crusading itself as penance. Why, then, might the anonymous author or authors of the Croxton *Play of the Sacrament* have chosen to present such a sermon as the final major action of the work?

One answer is that Lollards did not ignore liturgy in their attacks on the abuses of the Church. As Amnon Linder argues in *Raising Arms*:

> Liturgy inspired Christianity to raise armies and to furnish them with the sinews of war; it exhorted crusaders to enter battle, sang their victories, and lamented their defeats. Rites were also effective channels of information and propaganda, for the knowledge they imparted was perceived by the faithful as authoritative, as sharing the authority of the divinely ordained rite in which it was comprised. Rites, furthermore, addressed the entire community as well as each individual, their appeal simultaneously collective and personal. Liturgy is interwoven, therefore, into the very fabric of the crusade. It can be observed in two complementary circles: an outer circle — of a predominately collective character — generating commitment and support among the non-combatants, and an inner circle — focused mainly on the individual crusader and the actual crusade i.e., the crusading action on the field.[47]

Thus the enactment of a homily based on a crusading-related antiphon in the conclusion of the Croxton *Play* links the entire drama to the earthly battles of Christians against 'heretical' Muslims in the Holy Land and, more centrally, to Christian heretics at home.

The essence of the antiphon's tripartite structure is captured in the structuring of the play's embedded sermon, each stanza serving to summarize one of its sections, thereby transforming the play's resolution into a call for orthodoxy's triumph over heresy. The antiphon is not merely incidental but rather intrinsic and essential to the entire pseudo-sermon performed at this crucial point in the text, which functions as an unusual climax to the play's events. The emphasis in the Lambeth/Trinity homilies on repentance as a prerequisite for following Christ into battle is entirely consistent with Tyerman's recent observation, based on earlier work by Maier and Cole, that 'preachers under Innocent III [...] employed the crusade in their efforts to put pastoral theology into practice'.[48] Thus just as crusading advocates used pastoral opportunities to aid in recruitment,

[47] Amnon Linder, *Raising Arms: Liturgy and the Struggle to Liberate Jerusalem in the Late Middle Ages*, CELAMA, 2 (Turnhout: Brepols, 2003), p. xv.

[48] Tyerman, *The Invention of the Crusades*; Christoph T. Maier, *Crusade Propaganda and Ideology: Model Sermons for the Preaching of the Cross* (Cambridge: Cambridge University Press, 2000); Cole, *Preaching of the Crusades*, pp. 111–14.

preachers could employ the ethos of the crusades to reinforce key theological principles. Cole devotes an entire chapter of her book on preaching the crusades to the topic of crusading itself as penance, but the Croxton play shows no direct relationship to crusading, except for its crucial melding of Muslim and Jew into a composite other. Despite common concerns about Christian relations with persons of other faiths, the Croxton sermon contains no evident call to crusade but appears instead to be a call to repentance and unity.

The Croxton *Play of the Sacrament* presents a most unusual and enigmatic use of the antiphon *Estote fortes in bello*. The enactment of the antiphon within the confines of a theatrical production during the late medieval period calls attention to the attitudes about theatre and theatrical representations held by the Lollards and the orthodox churchmen who actively opposed them. Like later dissenters who rejected the dramatic arts during the early modern period, Lollards in their religious philosophy tended against the enactment of theatrical performances, especially when performing religious drama, and it would therefore be particularly appropriate that they would have been subjected to abuse in theatrical productions. In a seminal study that first raised the issue of a connection between the Croxton *Play of the Sacrament* and the Lollards, Cecilia Cutts argued that 'the play was a deliberate piece of anti-Lollard propaganda composed and presented for the purpose of strengthening the faith of the people in the face of heretic teachings and influence'.[49] She points out that, unlike close French, Italian, and Dutch analogues, the Croxton play emphasizes a broad range of religious beliefs:

> Where the continental tales emphasize only the doctrine of transubstantiation, and subordinate even that to the anti-Jewish and relic aspects, the English play gives all its attention to pure doctrine and expands its teaching to include not only transubstantiation but also baptism, confession, penance, pilgrimage, respect for images, reverence for the Blessed Virgin, the spiritual power and authority of a Bishop, which is notably greater than that of a priest.[50]

In contrast to prior assumptions, she presents a strong case for a continuing struggle between Catholic orthodoxy and Lollard heterodox beliefs through the end of the fifteenth century, arguing that 'throughout the century the Church used every conceivable means of combating the heresy'.[51] Cutts supplies detailed evidence for continuing anti-Lollard activity throughout the fifteenth century.

[49] Cecilia Cutts, 'The Croxton Play: An Anti-Lollard Piece', *Modern Language Quarterly*, 5 (1944), 45–60 (p. 45).

[50] Cutts, 'Croxton Play', p. 47.

[51] Cutts, 'Croxton Play', p. 52.

Lollard views have also been identified as underlying certain late medieval dramatic cycles by scholars such as Greg Walker, editor of *Medieval Drama: An Anthology*, who says: 'the unbelievers against whom (the play) was directed may well have been the Lollards and others influenced by the opinions of the fourteenth-century heretic John Wyclif, who denied the real presence' of Christ in the consecrated host.[52] The probable date of its original creation, identified by Greg Walker as 1461, places it significantly later than other Lollard and anti-Lollard uses of the antiphon, yet Walker's association of the play with that cultural conflict seems in keeping with the evidence provided by a close examination of the uses of the antiphon in various literary and social discourses.

Scholars, however, do not agree about whether *The Play of the Sacrament* actually expresses views on Lollardy. Connecting the play to anti-Lollard ideas has been subjected to scathing critique by scholars, including David Lawton, who says:

> Cecilia Cutts, a graduate student at the University of Washington in the 1930s, wrote a fine dissertation on the play that made a fateful surmise. Since, Cutts reasoned, the Jews were expelled from England in 1290, there can have been no actual Jews at the time of the play's composition (which she took to be close to the date mentioned in the manuscript for the alleged events of the play, 1460). Therefore the Jews of the play were likely to be figures for something more familiar and local to the play's audience: Christian heretics, namely Lollards.[53]

Lawton presents a concise recapitulation of the conceptual linkage between Jews and Lollards as intimately connected aspects of heretical attacks on the one true, orthodox faith. What Lawton terms the 'fateful surmise' remains a viable alternate to the position of literalists who see Jews as Jews alone, and not as symbols of those in opposition to the one true Faith. Lawton also discusses Cutts's response

[52] Greg Walker, Introduction, 'Croxton, *The Play of the Sacrament*', in *Medieval Drama: An Anthology*, ed. by Greg Walker (Oxford: Houghton Mifflin, 2000), pp. 209–12.

[53] David Lawton, 'Sacrilege and Theatricality: The Croxton *Play of the Sacrament*', *Journal of Medieval and Early Modern Studies*, 3 (2003) 281–309 (pp. 288–89). For an alternative perspective on the functions of Lollards and Jews in the play, one which does not focus on the binary opposition between them but instead sees them as alternative aspects of the play's exploration of religious conflict see Donnalee Dox, 'Theatrical Space, Mutable Space, and the Space of Imagination: Three Readings of *The Croxton Play of the Sacrament*', in *Medieval Practices of Space*, ed. by Barbara Hanawalt and Michal Kobalka, Material Cultures, 23 (Minneapolis: University of Minnesota Press, 2000) pp. 167–98. See also Donnalee Dox, 'Medieval Drama as Documentation: "Real Presence" in the Croxton Conversion of Ser Jonathas the Jew by the Myracle of the Blessed Sacrament', *Theatre Survey*, 38 (1997), 97–115.

to attacks on her position, describing how she provided 'an account of the play as ideological drama — written, in her view, to defend the Host, the orthodox Body of Christ, against Lollard challenge and critique of the doctrine of transubstantiation', conceding that transubstantiation is indeed 'at stake within the play':[54]

> [I]t is first expounded by the doubting Jews themselves, again by them on their conversion, and repeated, with added material on penance and baptism, by the Bishop at the play's end. The repentant Jews are told by Jesus '*Ite et ostendite vos sacerdotibus meis*' [...] — a tag, grounded in Luke 17:14, which was prominent in orthodox attacks on heresy.[55]

Lawton goes on to undercut the validity of the Lollard hypothesis, not by attacking it directly, but by pointing out reductionist views that have stemmed from Cutts's initial critique, admitting, however, that 'there seems to be some evidence in anti-Lollard culture as it develops for an occasional, general, and forensic connection between Lollards and Jews'.[56] The links between the final sermon in the play and Orthodox critiques of Lollardy thus add weight to the likelihood that the play concerns the Lollard positions on vital religious issues.

The depth of discussion and the interplay of arguments for and against the identification of the sacrament-defiling Jews in the play and Lollard heretics continues unabated. Ruth Nissé is among those who discount the possibility that the play represents the Lollards through the highly charged figures of the Jews, yet, as she herself notes in her article on the *Tretise of Miraclis Pleyinge*, 'In this Lollard assessment, miracle plays can indeed turn Christians into [...] phantasmatic "Jews" by enacting what must necessarily be interpreted, by representing allegory carnally or literally, in signs removed from the things they signify.'[57] Lacking a significant body of Jews within England, why would a dramatist stage a play condemning these absent presences? Far more likely is that the play would represent the Lollards as 'phantasmatic "Jews"', forcing the audience to recognize the representation of their local, homegrown heretics 'in signs removed from the things they signify': figural Jews identifying in sharply marked terms the less easily caricatured Lollards whose visual and even linguistic presences would not reflect in a significantly evident fashion the homegrown heretics. However, what this analysis has revealed is that the Jews are not the primary targets of the play's

[54] Lawton, 'Sacrilege and Theatricality', p. 289.

[55] Lawton, 'Sacrilege and Theatricality', p. 289.

[56] Lawton, 'Sacrilege and Theatricality', pp. 288–89.

[57] Ruth Nissé, 'Reversing Discipline: The *Tretise of Miraclis Pleyinge*, Lollard Exegesis, and the Failure of Representation', *Yearbook of Langland Studies*, 11 (1997), 163–94 (p. 180).

invective. Like Aristorius, Lollards onstage would appear as and speak like Christians and yet would carry the hidden disease of heresy.

In the context of late medieval England, a connection between Jews and Christian heretics would reflect the state-promulgated position that only the official religion presented a true means of salvation. Unorthodox Christians and their Jewish accomplices in the Croxton *Play of the Sacrament* would thus represent all those who would question current religious orthodoxy, whether Jews or Muslims, pagans or devil worshippers, unbelievers or radical Christian Lollards.

*University of Nebraska, Kearney*

# Arthurian Literature:
# Composition and Production

# The Rhetoric of Symbolism: The Grail of Fertility and Sterility

Anita Obermeier

In her witty modern novel *To the Chapel Perilous*, Naomi Mitchison mirrors the medieval variety of Grail questers and stories by featuring a plurality of Grail winners — various Grails performing different feats for their successful questers.[1] Her novel splinters the perceived metanarrative of the Grail into a number of competing mininarratives. The indeterminacy of the Grail shape and meaning, now as then, turns the Grail into a symbol that allows authors to imbue it with divergent rhetoric and meaning, as Dhira B. Mahoney writes: 'The Holy Grail is a standard symbol in the English language for an object of search far-off, mysterious, out of reach.'[2] In Chrétien's *Perceval* — where 'a grail' is first mentioned — it is a serving dish holding a mass wafer.[3] Of course, the fact that Chrétien's piece was unfinished encouraged a slew of continuators, versions, and the dethroning of Perceval as the original Grail quester, as well as the narrowing of 'a grail' to 'the Holy Grail'. This essay enters the scholarly discussion on the symbolism of the Grail in regards to its status as a symbol of fertility and sterility.

Theories abound as to the origin of the Grail from ancient fertility cults, Christian ritual, and Celtic mythology. While theories of origin are valuable —

[1] See Anita Obermeier, 'Postmodernism and the Press in Naomi Mitchison's *To the Chapel Perilous*', *Studies in Medievalism*, 13 (2004), 237–58.

[2] Dhira B. Mahoney, 'Introduction', in *The Grail: A Casebook*, ed. by Dhira B. Mahoney (New York: Garland, 2000), pp. 1–101 (p. 1).

[3] See the helpful chart on the differences between literary versions of the Grail and its questers in Mahoney, 'Introduction', p. 101. For a general overview on French Arthurian scholarship, see Keith Busby and Karen A. Grossweiner, 'France', in *Medieval Arthurian Literature: A Guide to Recent Research*, ed. by Norris J. Lacy (New York: Garland, 1996), pp. 121–209.

and they have been discussed at length[4] — I am more interested in the literary and rhetorical treatments of human reproduction vis-à-vis the Grail in the medieval texts.[5] Even if one posits that the wound of the Fisher King represents emasculation and infertile lands — as Jessie L. Weston does — and interprets the Grail as an element of the great feminine force, which can restore the son's fractured power — as Jean Markale theorizes[6] — with the Vulgate *Quest for the Holy Grail* and its Middle English reincarnation, Malory's *Morte Darthur*, the feminine

[4] For excellent discussions of Grail origins, see Glenys Witchard Goetnick, 'The Quest for Origins', in *The Grail: A Casebook*, ed. by Mahoney, pp. 117–47; Richard Barber, 'The Search for Sources: The Case of the Grail', in *A History of Arthurian Scholarship*, ed. by Norris J. Lacy (Cambridge: Brewer, 2006), pp. 19–36; John Cary, *Ireland and the Grail* (Aberystwyth: Celtic Studies Publications, 2007); and John B. Marino's extensive overview of the three modern scholarly strains trying to link the Grail to Celtic, Christian, or esoteric mystical origins (*The Grail Legend in Modern Literature* (Cambridge: Brewer, 2004), especially pp. 28–47, 117–48, and the bibliography on pp. 151–65). For an extensive older bibliography, see *Arthurian Legend and Literature: An Annotated Bibliography*, ed. by Edmund Reiss, Louise Horner Reiss, and Beverly Taylor (New York: Garland, 1984), pp. 177–250. For the theory that the grail stories emanated from fairy tales, see Fritz Peter Knapp, 'Der Gral zwischen Märchen und Legende', in *Beiträge zur Geschichte der Deutschen Sprache und Literatur*, 118 (1996), 49–68, and Willy Krogmann, 'Der Heilige Graal und seine Herkunft aus dem Märchen', in *Deutsch-französisches Gespräch im Lichte der Märchen* (Münster: Aschendorff, 1964), pp. 72–93. For a psychological, especially Jungian, approach, consult Emma Jung and Marie-Louise von Franz, *The Grail Legend*, trans. by Andrea Dykes, 2nd edn (London: Sigo, 1986). See also *The Grail, the Quest and the World of Arthur*, ed. by Norris J. Lacy (Woodbridge: Brewer, 2008).

[5] Richard Barber theorizes on the dangers of giving too much credence to source studies: 'each stage in the development must be susceptible to documentation; there must be sources and analogues: nothing can be created *ex nihilo*. But this, in my view, is the arch-heresy of literary criticism, and its greatest danger: to deny the imagination. It is this that scholars need to remember that as they try to interpret and illuminate. We are dealing with imaginative literature, and we must allow imagination pride of place. Poets and writers are creators; the Grail is the creation, not of mysticism, not of pagan religion, not even of Christian tradition, nor of the scholars themselves, but of the poetic imagination working on and with all these materials' ('Search for Sources', p. 36).

[6] Jessie L. Weston, *From Ritual to Romance* (New York: Peter Smith, 1920; repr. 1983); Jean Markale, *Women of the Celts*, trans. by A. Mygind, C. Hauch, and P. Henry (Rochester, VT: Inner Traditions International, 1986), p. 200. Adam McLean posits that Celtic 'cauldrons, Grails and alchemical vessels are all feminine mystery symbols', ultimately corresponding to the 'Triple Goddess: The Old Woman — Virgin — Mother aspects' ('Alchemical Transmutation in History and Symbol', in *At the Table of the Grail: Magic and the Use of Imagination*, ed. by John Matthews (London: Routledge & Kegan Paul, 1984), pp. 49–65 (p. 60)). See also Sherlyn Abdoo, 'Woman as Grail in T. S. Eliot's *The Waste Land*', in *Centennial Review*, 28 (1984), 48–60.

principle has been severely diminished in the Grail quest;[7] it is now restricted to celibate males and results in the individualized face-to-face meeting of two virginal men: Galahad and Jesus. The Grail, along with human fertility and sterility, furnishes a rather different trajectory in one of its greatest manifestations, Wolfram von Eschenbach's *Parzival*, where the eponymous hero gets married and has children. Mahoney has grouped medieval Grail narratives into three strains: 'the Perceval strain, the Joseph of Arimathea strain, and the *Queste* strain'.[8] For the purpose of this essay on fertility and sterility, I offer instead three slightly different strains: the French Perceval strain (Chrétien's *Perceval* and its continuations, Robert de Boron's *Joseph of Arimathea*, and *Perlesvaus*), the German Perceval strain (Wolfram's *Parzival*), and the Vulgate Cycle strain (including Malory). The works contained in those strains elucidate this shift in Grail symbolism, suggesting that the Grail can occupy symbolic literary spaces of healing infertility to requiring voluntary sterility based on the authors' clerical or knightly status and ideological worldview.

For many modern minds, the Grail is an object to be attained, but it is also a symbol with shifting meanings. To this effect, Richard Barber argues that the 'Grail is not a single concept whose meaning has been lost, but a literary symbol that has developed over the years'.[9] Umberto Eco has wrestled with the history of symbol and allegory, supplying a definition by German Romantic poet Johann Wolfgang von Goethe that echoes medieval ideas and very much also sounds like a description of the Grail:

> [S]ymbolism transforms the experience into an idea and an idea into an image, so that the idea expressed through the image remains always active and unattainable and, even though expressed in all languages, remains inexpressible. Allegory transforms experience into a concept and a concept into an image, but that concept remains always defined and expressible by the image.[10]

[7] For the one exception to exclusion of women, see Janina P. Traxler, 'Dying to Get to Sarras: Perceval's Sister and the Grail Quest', in *The Grail: A Casebook*, ed. by Mahoney, pp. 261–78; Ben Ramm, '"Por coi la pucele pleure": The Feminine Enigma of the Grail Quest', in *Neophilologus*, 87 (2003), 517–27; and Ginger Thornton and Krista May, 'Malory a Feminist? The Role of Percival's Sister in the Grail Quest', in *Sir Thomas Malory: Views and Re-views*, ed. by D. Thomas Hanks, Jr (New York: AMS, 1992), pp. 43–53.

[8] Mahoney, 'Introduction', p. 2.

[9] Barber, 'Search for Sources', p. 36.

[10] Umberto Eco, *The Limits of Interpretation* (Bloomington: Indiana University Press, 1990), p. 8. He furthermore provides the very interesting definition of the origin of a symbol: 'Originally a symbol was a token, the present half of a broken table or a coin or a medal, that performed its

Furthermore, 'Neoplatonism views symbols as signs that point to something unknowable.'[11] The Grail seems to fall into that category; I posit that Chrétien's Grail functions as a symbol, as its vague description and purpose provide the polyvalent latitude that a symbol needs. Robert de Boron and the Vulgate Cycle authors attempt to allegorize it, thus narrowing its meaning to a monovalent entity. E. Jane Burns theorizes that specifically in the Vulgate Cycle, we can see 'signs per se where the "arrows" curve around and point to themselves'.[12]

Modern readers expecting one authoritative metanarrative of the Grail story will be disappointed. This narrative plurality, however, is a particular trait of medieval rhetoric and literary theory where rewriting an existing story into something new was considered more authoritative than completely inventing a new one. So not just in the fortuitous cases of the unfinished *Romance of the Rose*, Chaucer's *Canterbury Tales*, or Chrétien's *Perceval* is the vernacular text 'regularly viewed as an open-ended document, always capable of being "continued"'.[13] Because of the central position of *auctoritas* in medieval rhetoric, these rewritings feature intertextuality, announced and unannounced, as well as interauctoriality because many medieval authors provide references in their works to one or more of their previous works and other authors. Intertextuality takes us 'beyond the traditional notion of the text as an autonomous, privileged, or originary object' and demonstrates how texts are related to each other in an *imitatio veterum*.[14] An intertextual approach facilitates the examination of the 'relationships among medieval literary works and other philosophical, historical, and religious texts'.[15] As Burns explains further:

social and semiotic function [i.e., its function as a sign] by recalling the absent half to which it potentially could be reconnected' (p. 9).

[11] Simon Brittan, *Poetry, Symbol, and Allegory: Interpreting Metaphorical Language from Plato to the Present* (Charlottesville: University of Virginia Press, 2003), p. 53.

[12] E. Jane Burns, *Arthurian Fictions: Rereading the Vulgate Cycle* (Columbus: Ohio State University Press, 1985), p. 20.

[13] Burns, *Arthurian Fictions*, p. 30.

[14] Laurie A. Finke and Martin B. Shichtman, 'Introduction: Critical Theory and the Study of the Middle Ages', in *Medieval Texts & Contemporary Readers*, ed. by Laurie A. Finke and Martin B. Shichtman (Ithaca: Cornell University Press, 1987), pp. 1–11 (p. 5); Manfred Pfister, 'Konzepte der Intertextualität', in *Intertextualität: Formen, Funktionen, anglistische Fallstudien*, ed. by Ulrich Broich and Martin Pfister (Tübingen: Niemeyer, 1985), pp. 1–30 (p. 1).

[15] Finke and Shichtman, 'Introduction', p. 5.

> Whereas the theological tradition stresses the importance of copying the sacred Word exactly, rhetoricians valorize individual invention, explaining how to take source material (generally in Latin) and transform it through expansion, abbreviation, and ornamentation. Invention is thus based on the rewriting and reworking of previous texts. The task of the author is not to respect the autonomy of his source but to tamper actively with its contents.[16]

And tamper they did in the epigonal romances after *Perceval.*

The intertextuality of the Grail story and the French Perceval strain begin with Chrétien's bildungsroman, *Perceval*,[17] the baseline story to illustrate a trajectory for the fertility and sterility concerns, inventions, and deviations of the continuators and later authors. Fertility and sterility concerns are encapsulated in Perceval's encounter with Blancheflor, his visit to the Grail Castle, and the three personages who illuminate one part each of his struggle with the failed visit to the Grail Castle. The sexually unsophisticated Perceval spends three nights with Blancheflor, who first visits him scantily clad to enlist his help against her enemies, throwing herself at his mercy. During the first night, they kiss and spend the night together in his bed, 'boche a boche' (mouth to mouth; l. 2045).[18] Critics have argued heatedly whether they sexually consummated their brief relationship.[19] Arthur Groos describes the pair as 'randy' and interprets Perceval's request of Blancheflor's 'druërie' (love; l. 2084) before he fights the seneschal as 'concubinage'.[20] Klenke opposes this claim that 'druërie' generally means 'affection of

[16] Burns, *Arthurian Fictions*, p. 26.

[17] For major criticism on Chrétien and the story of the Grail, see Jean Frappier, *Chrétien de Troyes: The Man and his Work*, trans. by Raymond J. Cormier (Athens: Ohio University Press, 1982), pp. 127–55; *Chrétien, Troyes, and the Grail*, ed. by Urban T. Holmes, Jr, and Sister M. Amelia Klenke (Chapel Hill: University of North Carolina Press, 1959); *Perceval/Parzival: A Casebook*, ed. by Arthur Groos and Norris J. Lacy (New York: Routledge, 2002); Douglas Kelly, *Chrétien de Troyes: An Analytic Bibliography* (London: Grant & Cutler, 1976); *A Companion to Chrétien de Troyes*, ed. by Norris J. Lacy and Joan Tasker Grimbert (Cambridge: Brewer, 2005), especially Rupert T. Pickens, '*Le Conte du Graal*: Chrétien's Unfinished Last Romance' (pp. 169–87); Harry F. Williams, 'Interpretations of the *Conte del Graal* and their Critical Reactions', in *The Sower and his Seed: Essays on Chrétien de Troyes*, ed. by Rupert T. Pickens (Lexington: French Forum, 1983), pp. 146–54.

[18] All references to Chrétien's *Perceval* are taken from Chrétien de Troyes, *The Story of the Grail (Li Contes del Graal), or Perceval*, ed. by Rupert T. Pickens, trans. by William W. Kibler (New York: Garland, 1990).

[19] M. Amelia Klenke, 'The Spiritual Ascent of Perceval', *Studies in Philology*, 53 (1956), 1–21. See especially pp. 12–18 for her rebuttal of adherents to a less chaste interpretation.

[20] Arthur Groos, *Romancing the Grail: Genre, Science and Quest in Wolfram's 'Parzival'* (Ithaca: Cornell University Press, 1995), pp. 108, 100.

any kind'.[21] The couple spends a third night together with a lot of kissing and heavy petting, but the major argument against sexual consummation and possible fertility consists in the fact that the author keeps referring to Blancheflor as 'la pucele' (the maiden; ll. 2051, 2566, 2877) before and after the nights spent with Perceval. Perceval leaves to find his mother and in Chrétien's version never returns to Blancheflor as the Grail adventure diverts his path.

His second adventure consists of the enigmatic visit to the Grail Castle with its parade of bleeding lance, candelabra, and bejewelled golden Grail[22] that necessitates *post-facto* explanations by three different personages. Perceval's angry cousin reveals to him, in no uncertain terms, his failure at the Grail Castle. She discloses the condition of the Fisher King:

> but he was wounded and maimed
> in the course of a battle
> so that he can no longer manage alone,
> for he was struck by a javelin
> through both thighs,
> and is still in so much pain
> that he cannot ride a horse.[23]

This revelation echoes a scene from the beginning when Perceval's mother gives her son some family history about how Perceval's father 'was wounded through his thighs | so that he was maimed in the body'.[24] Wounds in the thigh are often identified as sexual, referring to infertility.[25]

[21] Klenke, 'Spiritual Ascent of Perceval', p. 15.

[22] Some argue for the lance as a phallic and the cup as yonic symbol, although here the Grail is not a cup, but a dish (Edmund Reiss, 'The Birth of the Grail Quest', in *Innovation in Medieval Literature: Essays to the Memory of Alan Markman*, ed. by Douglas Radcliff-Umstead (Pittsburgh: Medieval Studies Committee, University of Pittsburgh, 1971), pp. 20–34 (p. 24)). For a discussion of the Grail in connection to the legend of Longinus, see Konrad Burdach, *Der Gral: Forschungen über seinen Ursprung und seinen Zusammenhang mit der Longinuslegende* (Darmstadt: Wissenschaftliche Buchgesellschaft, 1974), especially pp. 416–541.

[23] 'Mes il fu an une bataille | Navrez et mahaigniez sans faille, | Si que puis aidier ne se pot, | Qu'il fu navrez d'un javelot | Par mi les hanches am[b]edos | S'an est ancor si angoissos | Qu'il ne puet sor cheval monter': Chrétien de Troyes, *Perceval*, ed. by Pickens, trans. by Kibler, ll. 3475–81.

[24] 'Fu par mi les hanches navrez, | Si que il mahaigna del cors': Chrétien de Troyes, *Perceval*, ed. Pickens, trans. Kibler, ll. 418–19.

[25] In the Welsh *Peredur*, the Grail is not a vessel of sorts, but a severed head. Claude Sterckx 'shows that, since the Celts considered the head to be the source of sperm, which was held to reach

Both the thigh wounds of Perceval's father and the Fisher King were obtained in chivalric combat.[26] Additionally, Perceval's father had sent his two older sons to serve with two different kings, but both of them died in combat; the grief over their deaths killed Perceval's father (ll. 441–66), pointing starkly to the sterilizing aspects imminent in chivalry. The existing secular chivalric system leads to maiming and death, not only cutting life short, but also wiping out of family and dynastic lines. 'Even Arthur's lineage has no diachronic significance — it perishes with him', Groos points out.[27] Brigitte Cazelles, in her book *The Unholy Grail*, highlights the idea that 'both Arthurian chivalry and Grail chivalry in the *Conte du Graal* are to be understood as promoting violence and aggression'.[28] While Perceval's father dies of a broken heart because of his two elder sons's premature demise, and his mother dies of the same because of Perceval, the Fisher King can be healed by Perceval's asking the fated question: 'He would have totally regained use | of his limbs and ruled his lands, | and much good would have come of it!'[29] Although it is not explained how this question would have effected all of this — maybe to show compassion on Perceval's part[30] — the implication is both personal and communal: the healing of the Fisher King would not only

the genitals via the spinal column, decapitation and castration were one and the same thing. In that case, transferring the emphasis from the severed head to the Fisher King and his wound would not alter the thrust of the episode' (Goetnick, 'Quest for Origins', p. 130). These ideas are also present in the ancient Persian triad of seed/brain/marrow, in which one faction prefers the theory that semen originates from the brain — the other that semen springs from spinal marrow (Erna Lesky, *Die Zeugungs- und Vererbungslehren der Antike und ihr Nachwirken* (Wiesbaden: Steiner, 1950), pp. 10–11).

[26] For an overview of maimed kings, see William A. Nitze, 'The Fisher King in the Grail Romances', *PMLA*, 24 (1909), 365–418, and Eithne M. O'Sharkey, 'The Maimed Kings in the Arthurian Romances', *Études Celtique*, 8 (1959), 420–28.

[27] Groos, *Romancing the Grail*, pp. 11–12.

[28] Brigitte Cazelles, *The Unholy Grail: A Social Reading of Chrétien de Troyes' 'Conte du Graal'* (Stanford: Stanford University Press, 1996), p. 8. For a full study of *Peredur*, see Glenys Goetnick, *Peredur: A Study of Welsh Tradition in the Grail Legends* (Cardiff: University of Wales Press, 1975).

[29] 'Que toz eüst regaaigniez, | Ses manbres et terre tenist, | Et si granz biens en avenist': Chrétien de Troyes, *Perceval*, ed. by Pickens, trans. by Kibler, ll. 3554–56. Matilda Tomaryn Bruckner postulates that Chrétien 'problems the irrelevance of mothers, alive or dead' ('Rewriting Chrétien's *Conte du graal* — Mothers and Sons: Questions, Contradictions, and Connections', in *The Medieval Opus: Imitation, Rewriting, and Transmission in the French Tradition*, ed. by Douglas Kelly (Amsterdam: Rodopi, 1996), pp. 213–44 (p. 214)).

[30] L. P. Johnson, 'The Grail Question in Wolfram and Elsewhere', in *Perceval/Parzival: A Casebook*, ed. by Groos and Lacy, pp. 199–218.

restore him personally but also be beneficial communally to the land and its people, possibly in a sense of defence against intruders, as both the Fisher King and Perceval's father had to withdraw from their feudal social positions into isolated locales.[31]Furthermore, it proves that the Grail itself as an object is ancillary in this process because the human agency of Perceval is necessary to redeem the Fisher King. If that were not the case, the Grail could heal the Fisher King on its own.

The second interpreter of Perceval's experience, the Ugly Maiden at Arthur's court, asserts more strongly the detrimental and infertile consequences of Perceval's failed question to the community. This messenger reinforces the sterilizing outcroppings of disturbed feudal and social order: aside from the rich king not being healed from his wound, he cannot lead his lands, which means that

> Ladies will lose their husbands,
> lands will be laid waste
> and maidens, helpless,
> will remain orphans;
> many a knight will die;
> all these troubles will occur because of you.[32]

These predictions clearly indicate disruptions in human relationships. Dead husbands cannot father children; devastated lands do not grow crops; and helpless maidens could be raped — possibly producing forced fertility — or impoverished and married below their station, or not married at all, suffering forced sterility. Without venturing too far into theories of origins, one could say that in Chrétien's *Perceval* the Grail may still symbolize part of atavistic and pagan rites that conferred fertility and youth. The healing of the Fisher King is also tied to the revivication of the land and the people, carrying with it a communal benefit.

The last hermeneutician Perceval encounters, his maternal hermit uncle, divulges that Perceval's other maternal uncle is served by the Grail and that this king's son is the Rich Fisherman (ll. 6381–99).[33] The hermit's explanations delineate Perceval's failing, but unlike in later versions, these are not related to

[31] Both Edward Whitmont and Jean Markale see this mechanism as reversals of patriarchal domination and reinstatements of the great Feminine (Goetnick, 'Quest for Origins', p. 124).

[32] 'Dames an perdront lor mariz, | Terres an seront essilliees | Et puceles desconseilliees | Qui orfelines remandront, | Et maint chevalier an morront: | Tuit cist mal avandtront par toi': Chrétien de Troyes, *Perceval*, ed. by Pickens, trans. by Kibler, ll. 4644–49.

[33] On the importance of maternal uncles and nephews, see William A. Nitze, 'The Sister's Son and the *Conte del Graal*', *Modern Philology*, 9 (1912), 291–322.

sexuality. Perceval's dual sin encapsulates his thoughtless departure that killed his mother through grief and that, because of this sin, he could not ask the essential question that would have healed his uncle. Thus, Perceval's dilemmas stay entirely on familial but non-sexual planes. After the hermit episode, Perceval disappears from the story, which now segues again to the adventures of Gawain and breaks off without returning to the Grail story, prompting the slew of continuators. In the patron panegyric to Philippe of Flanders with which Chrétien opens the Grail story, he utilizes the agricultural/biblical metaphor of the sower and the seed: 'Chrétien sows and cast the seed of a romance that he begins, and sows it in such a good place that is cannot fail to be bountiful.'[34] Ironically, Chrétien probably never suspected that he indeed turned into the sower of a very powerful seed, the idea of the Grail that has captivated so many medieval and modern writers.[35]

In the forty-year span between 1185 and 1225, four continuators added 60,000 octosyllabic lines to Chrétien's *c.* 9200 original lines.[36] Rupert T. Pickens, Keith Busby, and Andrea M. L. Williams characterize the *Perceval* and all its continuations as follows: 'Chrétien, spiritual and mystical; the First Continuation, wildly supernatural, exuberant and archaic; the Second Continuation, secular and conventional; Manessier, rational and reassuring; Gerbert de Montreuil, solemn and sermonizing'.[37] These brief encapsulations of the continuations also

[34] 'Crestïens seme et fet semance | D'un romans que il ancomance, | Et si le seme an si bon leu | Qu'il ne puet estre sanz grant preu': Chrétien de Troyes, *Perceval*, ed. by Pickens, trans. by Kibler, ll. 7–10.

[35] See also Kevin J. Harty's essay in the present volume: 'Arnold Fanck's 1926 Film *Der Heilige Berg* and the Nazi Quest for the Holy Grail'.

[36] These continuations are extant in fifteen manuscripts, but only one provides them in their entirety (Nigel Bryant, 'Introduction', in *Perceval: The Story of the Grail*, trans. by Nigel Bryant (Cambridge: Brewer, 1982), pp. xix–xvi (p. xi)). For a summary of the continuations and discussion of their complicated dating, transmissions, redactions, and interpolations, consult Rupert T. Pickens, Keith Busby, and Andrea M. L. Williams, 'Perceval and the Grail: The Continuations, Robert de Boron and *Perlesvaus*', in *The Arthur of the French: The Arthurian Legend in Medieval French and Occitan Literature*, ed. by Glyn S. Burgess and Karen Pratt (Cardiff: University of Wales Press, 2006), pp. 215–73 (pp. 222–47); Richard Barber, *The Holy Grail: Imagination and Belief* (Cambridge, MA: Harvard University Press, 2004), pp. 9–38; Annie Combes, '*The Continuations of the 'Conte du Graal'*', trans. by Alexia Gino-Saliba, in *A Companion to Chrétien de Troyes*, ed. by Lacy and Grimbert, pp. 191–201; and William Roach, 'Transformations of the Grail Theme in the First Two Continuations of the Old French "Perceval"', in *Proceedings of the American Philosophical Society*, 110 (1966), 160–64. Also see Matilda T. Bruckner, *Chrétien Continued: A Study of the 'Conte du Graal' and its Verse Continuations* (Oxford: Oxford University Press, 2009).

[37] Pickens, Busby, and Williams, 'Perceval and the Grail', p. 229.

match those stories' outlook on fertility and sterility. Relevant rhetorical and intertextual episodes appear especially in the second and third continuation, mostly focusing on the nature of the relationship between Perceval and Blancheflor.[38]

The secular Second Continuation (*Continuation-Perceval* or Wauchier de Denain), dating closer to 1200 than 1225, depicts more secular fertility agendas, specifically when Perceval returns to Blancheflor's country, Beaurepaire. In juxtaposition to Perceval's failed attempt to revive the Fisher King's wasteland, the fruits of his liberation of place and 'pucele' from their enemies in Chrétien are immediately manifest in rich fields, towns, and people; Wauchier highlights that a society without the disruptions and destruction of war will prosper.[39] Perceval's reunion with Blancheflor both advances and frustrates their relationship. Wauchier reports the outcome of another night spent together in ambiguous terms: 'I don't want to tell you about the rest of what happened; but if Perceval did not fail to do more, Blancheflor did not object, for she was so full of courtesy that on no account would she refuse anything he wished to do'.[40] Therefore, Blancheflor informs Perceval that 'in the morning, without delay, you will marry me and the land will be yours; and you'll keep it in peace: there will be no war'.[41] Perceval, however, claiming another urgent adventure, refuses to marry her, arousing her ire. One can speculate if her anger stems from having given up her virginity to him that night and risked pregnancy out of wedlock or from feeling spurned.

[38] Dating to around 1200, the First Continuation (*Continuation-Gauvain* or Pseudo-Wauchier) is a pure Gawain romance, as it features only Gawain and some other unrelated stories. Perceval is not a character in this part, and Gawain ends up in the Grail Castle. Even though he sees the same progression of lance and Grail and is furthermore told about their significance, he fails to assemble the pieces of a sword, falls asleep, and is deemed unworthy. For the full Old French text, see *The Continuations of the Old French Perceval of Chrétien de Troyes*, ed. by William Roach, II: *The First Continuation*, ed. by William Roach and Robert H. Ivy (Philadelphia: University of Pennsylvania Press, 1950). This continuation contains two episodes that are interesting about fertility and sterility, but they are unrelated to the Grail, and I will deal with them in my forthcoming monograph, *Seed, Sex, Superiority: Fertility and Sterility in Medieval Literature*.

[39] The passages for all continuations are taken from the translations of Nigel Bryant, who includes parts and summaries of the continuations, and refer to page numbers: Chrétien de Troyes, *Perceval: The Story of the Grail*, pp. 142–43.

[40] *Perceval*, trans. by Bryant, p. 145; 'Je ne vos voil mie conter | Dou seurplus conmant il ala, | Mes s'am Perceval ne pecha, | Am Blancheflor ne remest mie, | Qui est plainne de cortoisie | Que chose qui bien li seïst, Por [r]iens ne li contredeïst': *The Continuations of the Old French Perceval of Chrétien de Troyes*, ed. by William Roach, IV: *The Second Continuation* (Philadelphia: American Philosophical Society, 1971), ll. 22834–40.

[41] *Perceval*, trans. by Bryant, p. 146; 'Et le matin sanz nul respit | M'esposeroiz, vostre iert la terre, | Bien la tanroiz am pes sans guerre': *The Second Continuation*, ed. by Roach, ll. 22888–90.

Unlike, the second continuator who alluded to sexual consummation between Perceval and Blancheflor, Gerbert de Montreuil emphasizes Perceval's virginity and chastity throughout, as evident in the encounters with Escolasse, Perceval's temptation by a demon, the lady on the mule, and his chaste marriage to Blancheflor.[42] The girl named Escolasse raves about his having been at the Grail Castle and having asked about the Grail because his action has revived the wasteland. Her gratitude goes so far as to offer her body to him, which he rejects with the statement, 'I refuse you only because it would be a very great sin if I ruined your virginity or mine' (p. 200).[43] Perceval is also unsuccessfully tempted by a demon in the guise of the beautiful Fisher King's daughter. Gerbert answers his own metatextual and rhetorical question about the motifs of the demon: 'to make him sin, because he wanted to break his chastity and prevent him knowing about the Grail' (p. 211).[44]

Gerbert presents an intriguing intertextual echo to the Second Continuation in Perceval's encounter with a lady on mule who faces the following quandary: she slept with her lover the night before their intended wedding, but then he reneged on his promise to marry her. Ironically, she is now on a quest to find her cousin Perceval, with the hope that he would take revenge on the faithless lover who has moved on to marry another woman. Gerbert provides this episode to chastise Wauchier, who alluded to the same kind of situation with Perceval and Blancheflor discussed above. Gerbert ensures that he can further steer the story toward chastity by holding up this kind of rhetorical mirror to Perceval. In Gerbert, who had possibly been influenced by the Vulgate *Quest*,[45] chastity and the Grail quest have now become linked.

[42] The Third and Fourth Continuations are written by two named poets, independently of each other, and probably overlapping in time. Gerbert de Montreuil picks up in the midsentence of the Second Continuation, and Manessier writes the Third Continuation. It is believed, however, that Manessier's version dates from between 1214 and 1227 and Gerbert's to 1225–30, and that Gerbert's is an interpolation between the Second Continuation and Manessier's (Pickens, Busby, and Williams, 'Perceval and the Grail', pp. 222–47). I will, however, refer to Gerbert's as the Third Continuation and Manessier's as the Fourth to stay in sequence.

[43] 'Ne je voir ne vous refus mie | Se por che non, ma dolce amie, | Que trop feroiegrant pechié | Se je avoie despechié | Vo pucelage ne le mien': Gerbert de Montreuil, *La Continuation Perceval*, ed. by Mary Williams, 3 vols (Paris: Librairie Ancienne, 1922), I. 649–53.

[44] 'Savez por coi l'a tant hasté | L'anemis? Por faire pechier, | Por che qu'il voloit despechier | Sa chaasté et metre en point | Que du Graal ne seüst point': Gerbert de Montreuil, *La Continuation Perceval*, ed. by Williams, I. 2558–62.

[45] Pickens, Busby, and Williams, 'Perceval and the Grail', pp. 240, 243.

Gerbert's chastity agenda cumulates in Perceval's return and marriage to Blancheflor. Unlike the previous times, Perceval takes charge and proposes that they be 'joined in the sacrament of marriage' (p. 231).[46] This phrasing seems to be inspired by Pope Innocent III's pronouncement of marriage as a sacrament in the early thirteenth century. Perceval and Blancheflor still spend the night before their wedding together, oozing desire, but it is Blancheflor who initiates this encounter. Gerbert categorically states[47] that they do not go beyond kissing and embracing, thus rhetorically rewriting and refusing the sexual ambiguity of Wauchier. The wedding night stands in stark contrast to their previous carnal fervour, as both decide that *caritas* is preferable to *cupiditas*, that not only chastity but also virginity passed carnal love (p. 235). Given the fertility and sterility concerns embedded in the Perceval stories from the maimed fathers to the wasted land, a chaste marriage is a nonsensical strategy, as the continued benefit to the land and people comes from a stable dynastic line. Gerbert's choice thus illustrates the competing agendas of the aristocracy and church.[48]

These competing agendas culminate the morning after the chaste wedding night, as Perceval sees a bright light and hears a voice giving him the promise of the future fertility of his line versus the current self-imposed sterility: 'from your line will come a girl [...]. She will be married to the rich king [...]. But she will bear a son [...]. And other sons will be born from her who will conquer several lands' (p. 236).[49] Paradoxically, it is not explained how these descendants emanate from his non-defined and celibate line. Is it a promise to him or to someone related to him? Perceval, takes off again leaving behind his wife, sent along with Gerbert's blessing, who proudly pronounces that he 'has contributed his part according to the true sources' (p. 236)[50] because he has finally resolved the contested story of Perceval's and Blancheflor's physical relationship with a chaste marriage. A celibate aristocracy serves no apparent rational feudal function in the chivalric

[46] '[E]nsamble | Par sacrement de mariage': Gerbert de Montreuil, *La Continuation Perceval*, ed. by Williams, I. 6472–73.

[47] 'De l'acoler et du baisier': Gerbert de Montreuil, *La Continuation Perceval*, ed. by Williams, I. 6559.

[48] For the concept of chaste marriages, see Dyan Elliott, *Spiritual Marriage: Sexual Abstinence in Medieval Wedlock* (Princeton: Princeton University Press, 1993).

[49] 'Et de ta lignie venra, | Ce saches tu, une pucele | [...] Mariee ert au riche roi [...] Mais un fius de li naistera [...] Autre enfant de li naisteront | Qui pluisors terres conquerront': Gerbert de Montreuil, *La Continuation Perceval*, ed. by Williams, I. 6906–07, 6909, 6913, 6915–16.

[50] 'Mais or en a faite sa laisse | Gerbers, selonc de vraie estoire': Gerbert de Montreuil, *La Continuation Perceval*, ed. by Williams, I. 7000–01.

world of the Middle Ages, but rather, 'Gerbert's formulations' of chivalry, 'written in the vernacular for lay audiences', John W. Baldwin maintains, 'represent the internalization of ecclesiastical principles by aristocratic society'.[51]

Author of the Fourth Continuation, the rational and reassuring Manessier eliminates Perceval's and Blancheflor's nightly interactions entirely, but Perceval is still tempted by a demon in the form of Blancheflor; he resists and finally returns to her to rid her of another overzealous suitor. Manessier, however, emphasizes other elements related to fertility and sterility. He is the first to confirm the identity of the Grail maiden as the Fisher King's daughter and makes explicit her status as highborn virgin, without which 'she would never have held it [the Grail] in her hands'.[52] Furthermore, in a fascinating revision and re-invention of the story of the Dolorous Stroke, the Fisher King maims himself with the broken pieces of the sword that killed his brother, King Gon of Sert. He can only be healed if he is avenged on the killer of his brother, which Perceval does. This scene marries the quest to the vengeance motif. Long gone are the compassion and the simple question that would have healed. Now physical healing bizarrely requires the killing of another. Perceval's reward is the privilege of looking into the Grail as it is carried through the Grail Castle hall, but the immediate society benefits from the end of the Grail adventures as well, a boon for which the original Grail story in Chrétien had hoped. Retaining some of its pagan symbolism, in a visit to Arthur's court, the Grail still functions as a cauldron of plenty and serves the court for as long as Perceval is there.[53] The unmarried Perceval becomes the new king for seven years of peace. Then, Perceval hands over his kingship, withdraws to a hermitage along with the Grail, becomes a priest, and eventually dies with the promise of his soul going to heaven accompanied by the Grail, which was then not seen on earth again — even that final exit of the Grail was public, as others witnessed it. The adventures of the Grail and the continuators have come to an end, but other authors expand and reshape the Perceval story further, adding new types of symbolism.

[51] John W. Baldwin, *Aristocratic Life in Medieval France: The Romances of Jean Renart and Gerbert de Montreuil, 1190–1230* (Baltimore: Johns Hopkins University Press, 2000), p. 95.

[52] *Perceval*, trans. by Bryant, p. 273; 'Pucelle virge, n'autremant [...] Ja antre ses mains nou tenist': *The Continuations of the Old French Perceval of Chrétien de Troyes*, ed. by William Roach, v: Manessier, *The Third Continuation* (Philadelphia: American Philosophical Society, 1983), ll. 32795, 32798.

[53] For a discussion of the Grail's nourishing functions, see Anne Berthelot, 'Le Graal nourricier', in *Banquets et manières de table au moyen âge* (Aix-en-Provence: Université de Provence, 1996), pp. 451–66.

In Robert de Boron's surprisingly tidy, albeit more Christianized, prose version of the Grail story — his trilogy on *Joseph of Arimathea, Merlin,* and *Perceval* — fertility and sterility are pitted against each other in prophecies about Bron's children.[54] Given the lack of prehistory on the Grail in Chrétien, Robert supplies a genesis of the Grail and is the first to identify it with the chalice of the Last Supper, which had been entrusted to the care of Joseph of Arimathea. In the *Joseph* section, the Holy Spirit reveals to Joseph that only 'the third man of Bron's line will fill' the seat vacated by Judas.[55] Later designated as the rich Fisher King, Bron is the brother-in-law to Joseph and married to Enigeus; they have twelve sons, reminiscent of the Twelve Apostles, and seek out Joseph's advice about the future of their offspring. Through an angel, the Grail relays Jesus's mission for Bron's children: they should marry, 'but the one who does not take a wife shall have the others as his disciples'.[56] The youngest son, Alain li Gros, who refuses to marry, is exalted for his filial disobedience and put in charge of his brothers because Jesus has chosen him as his servant. In the circuitous kinship and destiny routes common in romance, from the marriage-shy Alain li Gros, 'will be born a male child', for whom the Grail is meant (p. 41). Thus, self-professed chastity will paradoxically lead to fertility after all — fertility directly ordered by the Grail. Perceval is this male child, and he will achieve the Grail, as intended, in the eponymously titled third part of Robert de Boron's work and become the Grail lord. Henry and Rénee Kahane argue that Robert de Boron wrote a Christian

[54] Robert de Boron's trilogy features Merlin as the all-seeing mage of past and future events and that ends with the betrayal and defeat of Arthur and the Round Table, firmly tying the Arthurian world to the Grail. Chronologically, we are stepping backward again. Dating of these competing and intertextual versions has been vexingly difficult, and while some scholars argue that Boron wrote before Chrétien, most feel that he had been influenced by Chrétien and that at least his *Perceval* is datable to 1200 (Nigel Bryant, 'Introduction', in *Merlin and the Grail: Joseph of Arimathea, Merlin, Perceval: The Trilogy of Prose Romances Attributed to Robert de Boron*, trans. by Nigel Bryant (Woodbridge: Brewer, 2001), p. 7 n. 15). All quotations are from this translation.

[55] Robert de Boron, *Joseph d'Arimathie*, trans. by Bryant, p. 38; 'Et ainsin te dis que cist leus ne pooit estre raenpliz devant que li tiers hon de ton lignage le raenplira, et ce iert del fil Bron et de Ennigeus dont isir doit': Robert de Boron, *Joseph d'Arimathie: A Critical Edition of the Verse and Prose Versions*, ed. by Richard O'Gorman (Toronto: Pontifical Institute of Mediaeval Studies, 1995), p. 283.

[56] Robert de Boron, *Joseph d'Arimathie*, trans. by Bryant, p. 39; '[E]t qu'il aient fames, cil qui avoir les voudront. Et cil qui n'en vodra nule avoir, si seront li autre ci deciple, et il sera maitres': ed. by O'Gorman, pp. 291–93.

story against Chrétien's still more secular one.[57] With the emphasis on Christian content comes the emphasis on chastity that was absent from Chrétien. Just as Chrétien had his poetic continuators, so does Robert de Boron's romance of the Grail get 'recast in three successive prose versions: the *Didot Perceval*, the *Perlesvaus* and the Vulgate's *Queste del Saint Graal*'.[58]

The *Perlesvaus* or *High Book of the Grail* immediately asserts its Christology opening with the Grail as the vessel of the crucified Christ and presents almost entirely a romance of human sterility.[59] The Arthurian realm is sterile — as 'weakness suddenly beset [Arthur's] resolve' (p. 20) — 'characterized by depopulation, the infertility of nature, and crisis of social order'.[60] This crisis is exemplified by an unusual illustration of fertility and sterility. In this Arthur-centred romance, he and Guinevere — she traditionally depicted as sterile — have a son together by the name of Loholt, who in another bizarre turn of events, is murdered by Arthur's seneschal, Kay. In typical Kay fashion, he often claims others' spoils and deeds. Kay kills a sleeping Loholt, nonetheless, decapitates him, puts head and body in a tomb, and claims the head of the giant Loholt had killed, sporting it as his trophy back at the Arthurian court. Decapitation has been interpreted as a form of castration, and it is in a way also Arthur's castration. Kay's murderous and treasonous act not only deprives Arthur of a son but the kingdom of an heir and

[57] Henry and Rénee Kahane, 'Robert de Boron's Joseph of Arimathea: Byzantine Echoes in the Grail Myth', *Jahrbuch der Österreichischen Byzantinistik*, 38 (1988), 327–38.

[58] Burns, *Arthurian Fictions*, p. 9. For the *Didot-Perceval*, see Ernst Brugger, 'Der sog. Didot-Perceval', *Zeitschrift für französische Sprache und Literatur*, 53 (1930), 389–459, and Pickens, Busby, and Williams, 'Perceval and the Grail', pp. 253–59.

[59] Not surprisingly, dating is also contentious, especially vis-à-vis the *Quest for the Holy Grail*. Lucien Foulet dates the *Perlesvaus* closer to 1250 and thus clearly after the *Quest*, while Raphael Levy, Nitze, and J. Neale Carman date it before the *Quest* into the 'first decade of the thirteenth century and the *Queste* between 1213 and 1223' (Nigel Bryant, 'Introduction', in *The High Book of the Grail: A Translation of the Thirteenth-Century Romance of Perlesvaus*, trans. by Nigel Bryant (Woodbridge: Brewer, 1978), pp. 1–17 (p. 1)). All translations are from this edition. For a discussion of the intertextuality of the *Perlesvaus*, see Norris J. Lacy, '*Perlesvaus* and the *Perceval* Palimpsest', in *Perceval/Parzival: A Casebook*, ed. by Groos and Lacy, pp. 97–103.

[60] '[T]ant que une volentez delaianz li vint': *Le Haut Livre du Graal: Perlesvaus*, ed. by William A. Nitze, and T. Atkinson Jenkins, 2 vols (Chicago: University of Chicago Press, 1932), I, 26. R. Howard Bloch, *Etymologies and Genealogies: A Literary Anthropology of the French Middle Ages* (Chicago: University of Chicago Press, 1983), p. 20. See also Angus J. Kennedy, 'Punishment in the Perlesvaus: The Theme of the Waste Land', in *Rewards and Punishments in the Arthurian Romances and Lyric Poetry of Mediaeval France*, ed. by Peter V. Davies, and Angus J. Kennedy (Woodbridge: Brewer, 1987), pp. 61–75.

successor. Death is the ultimate form of denied fertility. Later, when Kay unwittingly reveals himself as the killer, he flees to Arthur's enemy, Brien of the Isles, only to return to devastate his realm during Arthur's Grail pilgrimage.[61] At that time, Guinevere dies out of grief for Loholt. Keith Busby argues that:

> Loholt is necessary in the *Perlesvaus* in order to preserve the relationship between Arthur and Gauvain, but it also enables the author to remove Guenièvre from the story, a remarkably original touch. His motivation for doing this is evident enough, for one of his central concerns is to re-establish the nobility of the figures of Gauvain and Lancelot and to eradicate, partially at least, the memory of their sinful pasts.[62]

Thus, the Perlesvaus author's rhetorical revision and reinvention hinge on the utilization of sterility.

Several further incidents reinforce the sterility of nature and humanity. The King of the Castle Mortal conquers the Grail Castle; the Fisher King is dead, and the Grail withdraws. The Grail disappears with the cryptic message that Perceval might find out where it went. Even though the Grail chapel stays intact, the work ends with the ruined Grail Castle, another form of human sterility in contrast to spiritual fecundity. All who look for the Grail either do not come back or join the religious life, trading earthly fertility for heavenly one. There is not even a Blancheflor here — only heavy Christian allegory. We can now compare this French clerical allegory to a more knightly German perspective.[63]

In a competing rhetorical reinvention, the second strain in this discussion of the Grail as a symbol of fertility and sterility is Wolfram von Eschenbach's *Parzival*, or the German Perceval strain,[64] which introduces an entirely different Grail trajectory with a new and positive picture of procreation. Despite the fact that Wolfram claims he bases his story on a Provençal author named Kyot,[65]

[61] For a discussion of the Celtic elements and sources of Kay, see M. Antonia Cor, 'The Role of Kay in the Perlesvaus', *Medieval Perspectives*, 2 (1987), 177–83.

[62] Keith Busby, 'The Enigma of Loholt', in *An Arthurian Tapestry: Essays in Memory of Lewis Thorpe*, ed. by Kenneth Varty (Glasgow: University of Glasgow, for the International Arthurian Society, 1981), pp. 28–36 (p. 34).

[63] Groos, *Romancing the Grail*, p. 95.

[64] For Parzival scholarship, see Joachim Bumke, *Die Wolfram von Eschenbach Forschung seit 1945: Bericht und Bibliographie* (Munich: Fink, 1970); Bodo Mergell, 'Wolfram und der Gral in neuem Licht', *Euphorion*, 47 (1953), 431–51; and *A Companion to Wolfram's 'Parzival'*, ed. by Will Hasty (Columbia, SC: Camden House, 1999).

[65] Some scholars take the Kyot theory at face value; others think of it as an elaborate construct. See Sidney Johnson, 'Doing his Own Thing: Wolfram's Grail', in *A Companion to Wolfram's 'Parzival'*, ed. by Hasty, pp. 77–95 (pp. 79, 84–86), and Timothy McFarland, 'The

he relies on Chrétien's main story in Chapters 3–11, although he augments Chrétien's 9334 lines to 16,000. Wolfram adds another new 9000 lines in Books I–II and XV–XVI.[66] Even though it has been argued that Wolfram's *Parzival* Grail utopia features a society without love,[67] Wolfram is clearly more marriage positive and thus fertility friendly. Even on a superficial linguistic level, Wolfram's language conveys a positive sense about conception, birth, and maternity. Repeatedly, persons are identified matronymically rather than patronymically, or with the phrases, born from 'a woman's womb', or as 'a woman's child'.[68] Fertility dominates Books I and II — which Wolfram added — where Wolfram elucidates the prehistory of Gahmuret, Parzival's father, in order to relate the conception and birth stories of both Parzival and his half-brother Feirefiz.[69]

Wolfram delineates the procreational interactions of Gahmuret, the second-born son of the Angevin king, with queens Belacane and Herzeloyde. Subject to the feudal constraints of French primogeniture, Gahmuret fights for Belacane, a Moorish queen in the Arabic East, impregnates her with the interracial child, Feirefiz, but leaves her based on their different religions and his love for adventure.[70] In Book II, Wolfram portrays Parzival's conception and birth in an

Emergence of the German Grail Romance: Wolfram von Eschenbach, *Parzival*', in *The Arthur of the Germans: The Arthurian Legend in Medieval German and Dutch Literature*, ed. by W. H. Jackson and S. A. Ranawake (Cardiff: University of Wales Press, 2000), pp. 54–68 (p. 57).

[66] He may have also known Robert de Boron's work. For opinions on the genesis of the *Parzival*, see Joachim Heinzle, 'Gralkonzeption und Quellenmischung: Forschungskritische Anmerkungen zur Entstehungsgeschichte von Wolframs "Parzival" und "Titurel"', in *Wolfram-Studien*, III (Berlin: Schmidt, 1975), pp. 28–39, and Henry Kratz, *Wolfram von Eschenbach's 'Parzival': An Attempt at a Total Evaluation* (Berne: Francke, 1973), pp. 144–71.

[67] Joachim Bumke, 'Die Utopie des Grals: Eine Gesellschaft ohne Liebe?', in *Literarische Utopie-Entwürfe*, ed. by Hiltrud Gnüg (Frankfurt: Suhrkamp, 1982), pp. 70–79. See also Walter Blank, 'Die positive Utopie des Grals: zu Wolframs Graldarstellung und ihrer Nachwirkung im Mittelalter', in *Sprache-Literatur-Kultur: Studien zu ihrer Geschichte im deutschen Süden und Westen*, ed. by Albrecht Greule and Uwe Ruberg (Stuttgart: Steiner, 1989), pp. 337–53.

[68] See examples in ll. 109. 1–18, 187. 24–25, 328. 27, 333. 27–28, 441. 7–9, 454. 27, 463. 23, 467.28–30, 471.3. All quotations from Wolfram's *Parzival* are taken from Wolfram von Eschenbach, *Parzival*, Studienausgabe, 2nd edn (Berlin: de Gruyter, 2003); translations are my own.

[69] The *Bliocadran*, a possible prologue to Chrétien's *Perceval*, contains some history of Perceval's father and scholars have theorized whether Wolfram had known the *Bliocadran*. See Lenora D. Wolfgang, 'Prologues to the Perceval and Perceval's Father: the First Literary Critics of Chrétien were the Grail Authors Themselves', *Oeuvres & Critiques*, 5 (1980–81), 81–90.

[70] '[D]ô phlac diu küneginne | einer werden süezer minne | und Gahmuret ir herzen trût [...] diu ê hiez magt, diu was nu wîp [...] dô hete si in ir lîbe | zwelf wochen lebendic ein kint': Wolfram, *Parzival*, I. 44. 27–29, 45. 24, 54. 17–20, 55. 14–15.

intertwined display of male martiality and female sexuality. Both Ampflise, Queen of France, and Herzeloyde,[71] Queen of Walois, compete for Gahmuret. Gahmuret tries to rebuff Herzeloyde with the claim that he still loves his wife, Belacane,[72] explaining that he had left because she had restricted him too much from knightly 'aventiure', the antagonist to 'minne'. Gahmuret's ambivalence about the proposed marriage manifests itself in the continued negotiations with Herzeloyde to keep going to tournaments, illustrating his unwillingness to trade entirely his homosocial adventure for heterosexual love.[73] Gahmuret threatens that he may leave her, too, should she curtail him severely. Despite a blissful wedding night and sexual union, Herzeloyde never gets a chance to curtail him, as he is killed in combat shortly thereafter, leaving another pregnant woman behind.

Gahmuret's death prompts a crisis of fertility with the pregnant and grieving Herzeloyde. In danger of losing the baby, whom Wolfram calls 'the one who will blossom above all knights',[74] Herzeloyde is force-fed and exclaims:

> I am much younger than he was, yet am his mother and his wife. I carry here his body and his live seed in me, given and conceived by our mutual love. When God is of loyal mind, then he will let him bear fruit by me, for I have been damaged by the actions of my proud, noble husband.[75]

Invoking the typical medieval conception theory notion that men have seed to implant in women, in whom seed grows into fruit, Herzeloyde considers herself in the incestuous-sounding dual role of Gahmuret's wife and mother; in gestating

[71] For a discussion of the significance of Herzeloyde, see Sidney M. Johnson, 'Herzloyde and the Grail', *Neophilologus*, 52 (1968), 148–56.

[72] The problem of bigamy is not even raised, presumably because a union between a Christian and a non-Christian was not binding under medieval canon law. See Kratz, *Wolfram von Eschenbach's Parzival*, p. 193.

[73] The tensions between these homosocial and heterosexual realms are not uncommon in chivalric literature. For instance, Lancelot explains in Malory's *Morte Darthur* that he does not want to get married because he would have to stay home with his wife and avoid his knightly predilections. See *The Works of Sir Thomas Malory*, ed. by Eugène Vinaver, rev. by P. J .C. Field, 3rd edn, 3 vols (Oxford: Clarendon Press, 1990), I, 270–71. This tension is also at the heart of Chrétien's *Yvain*, whose hero is persuaded to go in search of adventures by Gawain, right after having married the Damsel Savage.

[74] '[W]an si truoc in ir lîbe | der aller ritter bluome wirt': Wolfram, *Parzival*, II. 109. 10–11.

[75] '[I]ch was vil junger danne er,| und bin sîn muoter and sîn wîp, | ich trage alhie doch sînen lîp | und sînes verhes sâmen. | den gâben unde nâmen | unser zweier minne. | hât got getriwe sinne, | sô lâzer mirn ze frühte komn. | ich hân doch schaden ze vil genomn | An mînem stolzen werden man': Wolfram, *Parzival*, II. 109. 24–110. 30.

his seed, she is growing another Gahmuret, which gives motive to her later over-protectiveness of her son. This is reinforced when she clutches her 'child and womb', talking herself out of suicide: 'God should send me the noble fruit of Gahmuret. [...] May God avert me from foolish anguish. It would be Gahmuret's second death, if I were to slay myself, while I still carry in me what I received from his love.'[76]

Furthermore, in a scene absolutely unique to Wolfram and maybe to medieval literature, Herzeloyde rips her shift and nurses from her own breast to assure that the deprived child has sustenance, saying: 'You are the container of a child's nourishment, sent out ahead by the child itself, since I first found it alive in my body.'[77] While some critics have interpreted this passage as imitative of the Virgin Mary,[78] I contend that it carries a deeper fertility concern. The ancient conception theories expounded by Aristotle, Hippocrates, and Galen that were utilized by medieval scholastics and physicians are based on the hematological theory of conception. In a man, blood is transformed into sperm while in a woman blood is transformed into breast milk.[79] Therefore, those fluids necessary for the baby both come from blood. Since Herzeloyde drinks her own breast milk while the baby is *in utero*, I argue, she is charging the potentially failing fertility of Gahmuret's seed with her own blood-derived milk to ensure the fetus's survival and provides her own imprint of fertility on the baby. The treatment works so well that at his birth two weeks later Perceval nearly killed his mother because of his size. Additionally, Wolfram emphasizes that Herzeloyde, instead of having a customary wet nurse, nursed her son herself because 'she thought that she had called Gahmuret back into her arms'.[80]

[76] '[K]int und bûch': Wolfram, *Parzival*, II. 110. 12; 'mir sol got senden | die werden fruht von Gahmurete [...] got wende mich sô tumber nôt; | daz waer Gahmurets ander tôt. | ob ich mich selben slüege; | die wîle ich bî mir trüege | daz ich von sîner minne enphienc': Wolfram, *Parzival*, II. 110. 14–15, 16–21.

[77] '[D]u bist kaste eins kindes spîse: | die hât ez vor im her gesant, | sît ichz lebende im lîbe vant': Wolfram, *Parzival*, II. 110. 30–111. 2.

[78] For this and other Arthurian parallels for Herzeloyde, see Will Hasty, 'At the Limits of Chivalry in Wolfram's *Parzival*', in *A Companion to Wolfram's Parzival*, ed. by Groos and Norris, pp. 223–41 (pp. 233–34).

[79] See Francoise Héritier-Augé, 'Semen and Blood: Some Ancient Theories Concerning their Genesis and Relationship', in *Fragments for a History of the Human Body*, ed. by M. Feher (New York: Zone, 1989), pp. 159–75 (p. 168).

[80] '[S]i dûht, si hete Gahmureten | wider an ir arm erbeten': Wolfram, *Parzival*, II. 113. 13–14.

In Books III and IV, fertility concerns comprise Parzival's dealings with Gurnemanz and Condwiramurs. Parzival's lessons from Gurnemanz appear self-serving as he tries to incite Parzival's interest in his daughter, Liaze, so that Gurnemanz's lineage carries on, for he had previously lost three sons. Gurnemanz instructs Parzival that men and women 'are one body' that they 'blossom forth from a single seed'.[81] In Book IV, like Perceval, Parzival rescues a maiden, Condwiramurs, and spends three nights with her. Wolfram, however, is more decisive in his poetry than Chrétien: nothing happens on the first night because of Parzival's ignorance and her strong sense of chastity. It is a delicate situation in which a maiden has to woo a knight so that he takes up her military defence with enough reward promised but nothing offered yet. On the second night, after he had defeated Kingrun and been offered her love and lands, nothing happened either because of his restraint. Wolfram phrases it oxymoronically: the Red Knight 'left the queen a maiden, but she believed she was his wife', even putting on the headdress of married women in the morning.[82] The third night's consummation — Wolfram alludes to it such, 'If I have to tell you, he found sweet closeness'[83] — also engenders twin sons for Parzival, who only emerge at the end of Wolfram's story when Parzival and Condwiramurs reunite as the Grail couple.

Wolfram's motto of extramarital chastity and marital fidelity, not virginity, is reflected in the story of Anfortas, Parzival, and the Grail as a symbol of fertility. In Book IX, Parzival's hermit uncle, Trevrizent, explains the Grail and its society: Grail servants are picked in heaven on Good Friday and their names appear as inscriptions on the Grail, here a stone called *lapsit exillis*,[84] to be summoned to

[81] '[M]man und wîp diu sint al ein; [...] si blüent ûz einme kerne gar': Wolfram, *Parzival*, III. 173. 1, 5.

[82] '[D]ie künegin er maget liez | si wânde iedoch, si waer sîn wîp': Wolfram, *Parzival*, IV. 202. 22–23.

[83] '[O]b ichz iu sagen müeze | er vant daz nâhe süeze': Wolfram, *Parzival*, IV. 203. 7–8.

[84] This Grail stone has the power to burn the phoenix to ashes, from which it then rises again. The stone also functions as a life preserver, as people who look at it once a week, will not age or die. On Good Friday, a dove brings a white wafer from heaven and lays it on the stone. The Grail then becomes a horn of plenty and feeds the Grail society members with any food they wish. Friedrich Ranke suggests a gemstone ('Zur Symbolik des Grals bei Wolfram von Eschenbach', *Wege der Forschung*, 57 (1966), 38–48 (p. 38)). Claus Riessner argues against a jewel ('Überliefertes und Erfundenes in Wolframs von Eschenbach Vorstellung vom Gral', *Studi Germanici*, 21–22 (1983–84), 13–30 (p. 22)). Accepting Wolfram's Hispano-Arabic source for Kyot, the Arabic/Jewish astronomer Flegantis, Hans-Wilhelm Schäfer proposes that Wolfram's Grail is a stone chalice, specifically the chalice of San Juan de la Peña, now in the Cathedral of

Munsalvaesche, the Grail Castle. As grown Grail servants, only the women tend and can carry the Grail while the men guard it and Munsalvaesche. These Grail servants also have a fertility related purpose: 'If a land somewhere becomes lordless [...] wishing for a lord from the Grail company, they shall be granted one. [...] Thus maidens are given away openly from the Grail, the men secretly, for their progeny returns to serve there, in case their children are called back to add to and serve the Grail company.'[85] Parzival's mother, Herzeloyde, had originally been sent to King Castis from the Grail. The catch, however, is that knights serving the Grail must stay celibate, except those knights sent out to be lords of lordless lands, whereas the 'king alone can lawfully take a pure spouse'.[86] Trevrizent himself ran afoul of that restriction on love of women, but more importantly, these passages illustrate that the Grail fosters fertility. Sending a Grail knight or maiden to an ailing land stabilizes the society politically, but as importantly, these emissaries are responsible to help perpetuate that royal or princely line.

Trevrizent's continuing explanation of the Grail society reveals Parzival's ancestry and destiny vis-à-vis the Grail family: his mother was sister to the Grail king, Anfortas.[87] The Grail also looks for humility in its servants; a lack thereof is the reason for the ailing Grail king. Titurel was once the Grail king, succeeded by his son Frimutel, who in turn passes the Grail kingship to his oldest son, Anfortas, brother to Trevrizent. Thus, Grail kingship perpetuates itself along regular human procreational lines. The current Grail king, Anfortas, was given too much to the service of love: '"Amor!" was his battle-cry'.[88] Anfortas is punished and humiliated

Valencia ('Wolframs "calix lapideus"', *Zeitschrift für deutsche Philologie*, 103 (1984), 370–77 (pp. 370, 377)). James F. Poag discusses Wolfram's Grail as a symbol of Christ, 'Wolfram von Eschenbach's Grail-Stone: A Christological Symbol', *Christianity and Literature*, 28 (1979), 31–39. See also Johnson, 'Doing his Own Thing', pp. 77–93.

[85] '[W]irt iender hêrrenlôs ein lant, [...] sô daz diu diet eins hêrren gert | vons grâles schar, die sint gewert. [...] Sus gît man vome grâle dan | offenlîch meide, verholn die man, | durch fruht ze dienste wider dar, | ob ir kint des grâles schar | mit dienste suln mêren': Wolfram, *Parzival*, IX. 494. 7, 9–10; 495. 1–5.

[86] '[G]ein wîben minne er muoz verpflegn. | wan der künec sol habe eine | ze rehte ein konen reine': Wolfram, *Parzival*, IX. 495. 8–10.

[87] For a detailed comparison of the Chrétien's Fisher King and Wolfram's Anfortas, see Louise Gnädinger, 'Rois Peschiere/Anfortas: Der Fischerkönig in Chrestiens and Wolframs Graldichtung', in *Orbis medievalis: mélanges de langue et de littérature médiévales offerts à Reto Radulf Bezzola à l'occasion de son quatre-vingtième anniversaire*, ed. by Georges Guntert and others (Berne: Francke, 1978), pp. 127–48.

[88] 'Amor was sîn krîe': Wolfram, *Parzival*, IX. 478. 30.

for his hubris in a joust when a poisoned spear pierces 'his testicles'[89] — no euphemism here — a wound that cannot be healed despite immense efforts, except by the compassionate question. This genital wound also precludes Anfortas from fathering the next Grail king, thus the need for a new Grail king in the form of the sister's son, Parzival. Wolfram does not allude to repercussions on the land or the people suffering, keeping the sterility issue to the level of the Grail family. This sterility is remedied in Books XV and XVI when the Grail messenger, Cundrie, reports that Parzival's name had appeared on the Grail, an equivalent to the Perilous Seat in other Grail versions. Parzival's question restores Anfortas, he is reunited with his wife Condwiramurs and their twin sons, and spends a night of passionate sexual love with her. Wolfram clearly pursues an agenda very different from Gerbert's chaste marriage solution.

Why does Wolfram present such a radically different Grail story? We should keep in mind that he was writing concurrently to many of the French continuators and thus has every right to provide his own Grail ideology. Henry Kratz states that Wolfram 'had no intention of describing anything except a symbol that has no existence in the real world'.[90] Furthermore, Kratz expounds on the politics and history of the Holy Roman Empire of Wolfram's time; the political chaos that surrounded the succession of Henry VI († 1197) and resulted in the rivalries between the Guelphs and the Ghibellines, lasting for almost two decades, provided the backdrop for Wolfram's version of the Grail story: 'Hereditary succession must have seemed to Wolfram the only answer for an orderly transfer of power — the confusion and turmoil caused by the electoral system of determining the emperor must have made the hereditary succession of the crown seem a vast improvement.'[91] Based on the concerns of imperial succession and the fact that Wolfram was not a cleric and did not subscribe to an overly ambitious agenda of virginity, Parzival 'wins the grail without renouncing his very worldly, courtly/chivalric orientation',[92] and human fertility plays a pivotal role in Wolfram's *Parzival.*

[89] '[H]eidruose sîn': Wolfram, *Parzival*, IX. 479. 12.

[90] Kratz, *Wolfram von Eschenbach's Parzival*, p. 429.

[91] Kratz, *Wolfram von Eschenbach's Parzival*, pp. 433–34. Wolfram may have modelled his utopian state on Frederick II's kingdom of Sicily (Andreé Lefevere, 'Introduction', in *Wolfram von Eschenbach: Parzival*, ed. by Lefevere (New York: Continuum, 1991), pp. vii–xxv (pp. x–xi)).

[92] Hasty, 'At the Limits of Chivalry', p. 240. A. D. Horgan claims that Parzival only ascends to the second level of Grail interaction, both in Wolfram and in the Quest, and that the third level is reserved for Galahad ('The Grail in Wolfram's *Parzival*', *Medieval Studies*, 36 (1974), 354–81 (p. 367)).

Fertility, however, faces a much tougher celibacy agenda in the third Grail strain, the *Quest* thread, which returns us to the realm of French romances. J. Neale Carman has proposed that the author of the *Quest*, one of the five romances of the Vulgate Cycle, composed after 1215, had been purposefully imitating the *Perlesvaus* in some of its allegorical zeal.[93] The Vulgate *Lancelot* author 'intended to dispose' of the Perceval tradition, as Annie Combes asserts.[94] Cistercian influence[95] privileged chastity and virginity as virtues of the successful Grail quester, effectively disqualifying Lancelot, and giving the later Grail stories their main trajectory in the virginal Galahad. Perceval's decline happens to the benefit of Lancelot's and Galahad's ascent in the now newly oriented Grail narrative, something that Combes calls 'a bold move'.[96] Perceval does not get dropped entirely from the narrative, as he still is a member of the trio of finalists in the Grail quest; the other two are of Lancelot's clan: his son Galahad and his cousin Bors. That Perceval remains one of the final three signals that the Vulgate Cycle authors were not audacious enough to expunge Perceval entirely and break with the existing story. Instead, they rewrite, reinvent, and refocus that story.[97]

Already in the Vulgate *Lancelot* is the emphasis of the *Quest for the Holy Grail* on virginity and non-procreation heightened: in the prophecy that Galehaut receives about the Grail winner, 'that man must be, from birth to death, so utterly virginal and chaste as never to feel love for a woman, married

[93] J. Neale Carman, 'The Symbolism of the *Perlesvaus*', *PMLA*, 61 (1946), 42–83 (p. 83 n. 85). For other scholarly interpretations, see Fanni Bogdanow, 'An Interpretation of the Meaning and Purpose of the Vulgate *Queste del Saint Graal* in the Light of the Mystical Theology of St. Bernard', in *The Changing Face of Arthurian Romance: Essays on Arthurian Prose Romances in Memory of Cedric E. Pickford*, ed. by Alison Adams and others (Woodbridge: Brewer, 1986), pp. 23–46; *A Companion to the Lancelot-Grail Cycle*, ed. by Carol Dover (Woodbridge: Brewer, 2003); Miranda Griffin, *The Object and the Cause in the Vulgate Cycle* (London: Legenda/Modern Humanities Research Association, 2005), especially Chapter 2.

[94] Annie Combes, 'From Quest to Quest: Perceval and Galahad in the Prose *Lancelot*', *Arthuriana*, 12 (2002), 7–30 (p. 7). See also Dolores Warwick Frese, 'Augustinian Intrusions in the *Queste del Saint Graal*: Converting "Pagan Gold" to Christian Currency', *Arthuriana*, 18 (2008), 3–21, and Arthur Edward Waite, *The Holy Grail: The Galahad Quest in the Arthurian Literature* (New Hyde Park, NY: University Books, 1961).

[95] Richard Barber, 'Chivalry, Cistercianism and the Grail', in *A Companion to the Lancelot-Grail Cycle*, ed. by Dover, pp. 3–12.

[96] Combes, 'From Quest to Quest', p. 17.

[97] See also Dhira B. Mahoney, 'Malory's Percivale: A Case of Competing Genealogies?', in *Perceval/Parzival: A Casebook*, ed. by Groos and Lacy, pp. 253–65 (p. 256).

or not'.[98] The Grail finalists are ranked by their sexual non-engagement. Lancelot sees another knight healed by the Grail, but is paralyzed and cannot act because of his sinful love for Guinevere; Bors is denied the final vision of the Grail because he had lost his virginity in a scenario of trickery; Perceval is virginal but tempted; and Galahad is a virgin, who is not even confronted by female temptation. When the authors of the *Quest* decided to privilege Lancelot's kin group, they also needed to invent a new Grail winner. Combes argues that with 'the invention' of Lancelot's son Galahad 'the text cuts free from tradition'.[99] Two main events in the *Lancelot* are key to my argument about the Grail as a symbol of fertility and sterility: Bors's fathering of Helain le Blanc and Lancelot's engendering of Galahad.

The circumstances of the trickery that ensnared Bors, who had vowed to stay virginal all his life, seem worse than that of Lancelot; the Bors episode may have been written specifically as a typological episode to Lancelot's later sexual exploitation and to create a hierarchy of sexual behaviour and chastity with which to rank the final Grail questers. Bors, who spurns King Brandegorre's daughter, is tricked by the princess's governess go-between with a magical ring that changes his virginal heart. The Vulgate author editorializes on the sex act and conception, saying: 'They joined together in carnal union so that the flowers of virginity were scattered between them. The grace and divine will of God worked in such a way during their union that the lady conceived Helain the White who later became Emperor of Constantinople.'[100] The author mitigates and diffuses this technical act of fornication for its supposed good, claiming that God tries to compensate for the 'couple's sin and ignorance' with 'a noble fruit'.[101] This

[98] *Lancelot, Part III*, trans. by Samuel N. Rosenberg, in *Lancelot-Grail: The Old French Arthurian Vulgate and Post-Vulgate in Translation*, ed. by Norris J. Lacy, II: *Lancelot* (New York: Garland, 1993), pp. 252–53; 'et par les rains du nombril poes vous sauoir quil sera uirges et castes en toutes coses. De quoi il resemblera pucele uirgene.' All Old French quotations are taken from *The Vulgate Version of the Arthurian Romances*, ed. by H. Oskar Sommer, 8 vols (Washington, DC: Carnegie Institution of Washington, 1908–16), IV, 27.

[99] Combes, 'From Quest to Quest', p. 21.

[100] *Lancelot, Part IV*, trans. by Robert L. Krueger, in *Lancelot-Grail: The Old French Arthurian Vulgate and Post-Vulgate in Translation*, ed. by Norris J. Lacy, III: *Lancelot* (New York: Garland, 1995), pp. 55–56; 'si sentraprochent si carnelment ensamble que lez flors de uirginite sont espandues. Et si ouura tant a cele assamblee la grace de dieu et sa volente deuine que la damoisele conchut helain le blanc qui puis fu empereres de constantinoble': Sommer, *Vulgate Version*, IV, 269–70.

[101] *Lancelot, Part IV*, trans. by Krueger, p. 56; 'en pechie & par ignorance denfans [...]. Ains y mist fruit si haut': Sommer, *Vulgate Version*, IV, 270.

downplaying of the fornication aspect makes the conception of Helain le Blanc divinely guided and almost asexual.

In this foil to the Bors episode, Lancelot the flower of earthly chivalry, who will be rejected in the Grail quest, nevertheless fathers Galahad, the epitome of celestial chivalry. Simeon, nephew of Joseph of Arimathea, prophesied to Lancelot in Part IV that his lineage will issue forth the Grail knight. Robert de Boron's Alain li Gros and Gerbert's Perceval have likewise been told this, but with Lancelot we see it executed. Since Lancelot plays a pivotal role, he actually sees the Grail in a procession at Corbenic Castle, the castle of King Pelles of the Land Beyond. Here the Grail still functions as a horn of plenty as the reverence paid to it by the court results in tables covered in the finest food. Subsequently, Lancelot is drugged by Brisane, the tutor to King Pelles's daughter and Grail maiden, so that he would sleep with her thinking it was Guinevere, for no one believed he would intentionally betray his longstanding love for the Queen. As with Bors, the ruse works and the author editorializes the mechanics of conception and the theological hurdles behind it:

> [S]o the best and most handsome knight who ever lived and the most beautiful and highest-born maiden of that day were joined together. Their desires stemmed from different motives: she did it not so much for his beauty or from lust or bodily desire, but so as to receive the fruit that would restore that entire land to its original beauty, that land which had been laid waste and destitute by the dolorous blow from the Sword with the Strange Straps. [...] But he desired her in a very different way, because he did not covet her for her beauty, but believed she was his lady the queen [...]. Lancelot knew her in sin and adultery and in opposition to God and Holy Church. Yet nonetheless the Lord [...] looked at this coupling in light of its value to the land, for He did not wish it to remain a wasteland forever; so He permitted them to engender and conceive a fruit, by virtue of which the flower of virginity that was corrupted and violated there blossomed forth in another flower whose goodness and tenderness would replenish and console many a land.[102]

[102] '*Lancelot, Part V*', ed. by William W. Kibler, in *Lancelot-Grail*, ed. by Lacy, III, p. 164; 'Ensi sont mis ensamble li mil[e]dres cheualiers & li plus loiaus qui a ce tamps fust, et la plus bele pucele & del plus haut lingnage, qui fust au tamps de lors, si sentredesirent par diuerses ententions. Car elle ne le fist mie tant pour la biaute de lui ne pour escauffement de char comme elle fist por le fruit recheuoir dont tous li pais deuoit reuenir en sa premiere biaute qui par le dolerous cop de lespee auoit este desertes & escillies [...] Et cil la desiroit tout en autre maniere, quar por sa biaute de la conuoitoit il pas, mais il quidoit que ce fust sa dame. [...] Et il connut ceste en pechie & en auoltire. [...] li sires [...] regarda cele assamblee selonc le preu a ceuls del pais comme cil qui ne voloit mie quil fussent tous iors en escil, si lor donna tel fruit a engendrer et a conceuoir, que pour la flor de uirginite, qui illuec fu corrompue, fu restoree vne autre fleur, dont grans biens vint al pais': Sommer, *Vulgate Version*, IV, 110–11.

Whereas in the two previous Grail strains the question would heal the land, here the proper knight has to be conceived first. God effectively genetically engineers a person that would otherwise not exist and only serves this one purpose. In both cases of semen theft from Bors and Lancelot, God is presented as a pragmatist who guides and justifies these acts of fornication and adultery, along with these products of gifted bastardy, because of their beneficial outcome.

In the Middle Ages, the competing conception theories of Aristotle and Galen postulated that women either did not (according to Aristotle) or did (according to Galen) have to experience pleasure in order for conception to occur.[103] The daughter of King Brandegorre certainly did, as she greatly desired Bors. The author explains that King Pelles's daughter did not have the same sexual desires as Bors's partner, but she must have experienced some pleasure for conception to occur in the Galenic theory. In the confines of a heavy virginity agenda, possibly influenced by the rising veneration of the Virgin Mary and her 'holy motherhood' — as Peggy McCracken asserts[104] — an Aristotelian adherence would be expected. It cannot be established entirely whether the Vulgate Cycle authors were followers of Aristotle's or Galen's theory, but according to McCracken, 'the ideal mother [is] a virgin who desires a child, conceives in her first sexual encounter, and never has sex again'.[105] While the women, who stay unmarried after their illegitimate births, are absolved of their sin based on the sons they bear, the men's sexuality ranks them in the Grail quest. Bors's progeny is not central to the story of the Grail, except to signal Bors's blemished status as a virginal man. Lancelot's progeny is absolutely central, superseding the father. It is puzzling, however, why the prophesied Grail winner could not be born from a legitimate union, as he was in *Parzival*.[106] Traditionally, Perceval had been related to the Grail family, so these kinship patterns are preserved by the Vulgate Cycle authors inside the Lancelot kin group. Because of the centrality of Lancelot, the desirability of his paternity, and his love for Guinevere, the conception of Galahad would have to happen outside of wedlock. Lancelot's involvement is nonetheless

[103] See Sophia M. Connell, 'Aristotle and Galen on Sex Difference and Reproduction: A New Approach to an Ancient Rivalry', *Studies in History and Philosophy of Science*, 31 (2000), 405–27.

[104] Peggy McCracken, 'Mothers in the Grail Quest: Desire, Pleasure, and Conception', *Arthuriana*, 8 (1998), 35–48 (p. 42).

[105] McCracken, 'Mothers in the Grail Quest', p. 42.

[106] Lancelot is married to Elaine in the English *Chronicle of John Harding* and begets Galahad in wedlock.

paradoxically unfair: he is vilified and excluded from the achievement of the Grail for his love of Guinevere, a love that is exploited and manipulated to trick him into sleeping with King Pelles's daughter and fathering Galahad, the 'holy bastard'.[107] Despite their programme of celibacy in the Vulgate Cycle, the authors are still stuck with the limitations of human procreation.

Previous Grail authors as well as the Vulgate Cycle writers greatly emphasize the healing of the land. The Grail Maiden's virginity is corrupted in an act that would otherwise be hugely damaging to a virginal princess in the framework of medieval romance in order to heal the land, or so the Vulgate authors assert. When Galahad achieves the Grail at the end of the *Quest* and is asked to heal the Maimed King with the lance and the blood, no further healing of the land is mentioned. Actually, the healed thigh wound of the King serves no future human fertility either, as he immediately joins the celibate Cistercians. Galahad himself is charged to take the Grail away from Logres to Sarras because the people of Logres do not transcend their earthliness and are undeserving of it.[108] This Grail quest in the Vulgate Cycle culminates and dead-ends in several levels of human sterility: there is no regenerating benefit to the land; Perceval becomes a hermit and then dies; Galahad, after his face-to-face encounter with another virginal man, Jesus, and his final private beatific vision in Sarras, dies as well. This result may be attributable to the purported Cistercian authorship of the Vulgate Cycle; celibate authors may more easily privilege virginity and spiritual fertility over human procreation, even if they need to make use of it on the path to that beatific vision.

Helen Cooper, in her essay on the influence of the Lancelot-Grail Cycle, posits that 'English interest in Lancelot [...] is barely traceable in English before 1400'.[109] It falls to Sir Thomas Malory to be the premier importer and redactor of the Lancelot-Grail Cycle into English literature. Specifically the Grail section is one of the most faithfully utilized ones. Mahoney argues that Malory does 'not so

[107] See Karen Cherewatuk, 'Born-Again Virgins and Holy Bastards: Bors and Elyne, and Lancelot and Galahad', *Arthuriana*, 11 (2001), 52–64. For a broader context, see Karen Cherewatuk, *Marriage, Adultery and Inheritance in Malory's Morte Darthur* (Cambridge: Brewer, 2006).

[108] Kathryn Karczewska, *Prophecy and the Quest for the Holy Grail: Critiquing Knowledge in the Vulgate Cycle* (New York: Lang, 1998), pp. 155–68.

[109] Helen Cooper, '*The Lancelot-Grail Cycle* in England: Malory and his Predecessors', *A Companion to the Lancelot-Grail Cycle*, ed. by Carol Dover (Woodbridge: Brewer, 2003), pp. 147–62 (p. 151).

much secularize' his source 'as anglicize it'.[110] While the main trajectory of the French *Quest* is retained and chivalric standards measured against spiritual values, Malory cuts 'much of the doctrinal exegesis of the French' to arrive at a value system more in accordance to his fifteenth-century world where 'spiritual pursuits could be considered complementary rather than competitive elements of a knightly life'.[111] This holds true of the conception trickeries Lancelot and Bors undergo in Malory's *Book of Sir Tristram of Lyoness*. While Malory relates Lancelot's adventure fairly closely, he saves us the lengthy moralizing and mitigating explanation the Vulgate Cycle writer proffers. In his redaction, Malory, however, changes the order of things. Lancelot exclaims that 'for there was never knight disceyved as I am this nyght'.[112] In the Vulgate Cycle, Bors has already been deceived and Lancelot follows, but Malory only cursorily mentions this episode two pages after Lancelot's mishap when Bors is being tested in the Grail Castle. It is literally a parenthetical reference giving the reason for his blemished sexual state and his downgrade in the Grail quest. For Malory, Bors's typological adventure to Lancelot's matters little and Bors's progeny, while named, no longer aspires to exceptionalism — no Emperor of Constantinople here. Despite the fact that 'God does not steal the show', as Cooper asserts,[113] the final meeting of Galahad and Jesus parallels the Vulgate Quest closely and results in the same human sterility, the same singularized celestial salvation without communal terrestrial benefit.

Brigitte Cazelles, in her social reading of Chrétien's Grail, argues that it is 'an empty container bereft of intrinsic value. There, [is] a vacuity that discloses the function of the symbol as a receptacle whose meaning resides entirely with its holders and beholders' and that 'the Grail is both a discourse and a vision'.[114] Sometimes the Grail writes, and otherwise it is written about. Cazelles's assessment also applies to post-Chrétien Grail stories and in the context of the

[110] See Dhira B. Mahoney, 'The Truest and Holiest Tale: Malory's Transformation of *La Queste del Saint Graal*', in *Studies in Malory*, ed. by James W. Spisak (Kalamazoo: Medieval Institute Publications, 1985), pp. 109–28 (p. 110) (repr. in *The Grail: A Casebook*, ed. by Dhira B. Mahoney, pp. 379–96). See also Sandra Ness Ihle, *Malory's Grail Quest: Invention and Adaptation in Medieval Prose Romance* (Madison: University of Wisconsin Press, 1983).

[111] Mahoney, 'Truest and Holiest Tale', p. 110.

[112] *The Works of Sir Thomas Malory*, ed. by Vinaver (II, 796).

[113] Cooper, 'Malory and his Predecessors', p. 158.

[114] Cazelles, *Unholy Grail*, p. 227.

Grail's position vis-à-vis human procreation. In the fertility or sterility context, Chrétien's Grail appears neutral, if anything, highlighting the consequences of a violence-driven chivalric culture. The more limiting chastity and virginity agenda is initially foisted upon Perceval in the rhetoric of Gerbert's continuation, Robert de Boron, as well as the authors of *Perlesvaus* and the Vulgate Cycle, in an ecclesiastical push to insert church values into aristocratic realms and to charge the Grail with their own sterility symbolism. Wolfram's *Parzival* stands in stark contrast to these values based on the historical situation in Germany and his knightly rather than clerical status. Since the Vulgate Cycle version of the Grail is the one that Malory anglicizes and popularizes in his *Morte Darthur*, this Grail requesting human sterility of his followers and privileged knight, Galahad — this version of the two virginal men meeting at the end of the Grail quest — becomes the de facto metanarrative of the Grail, at least in the Anglo-American world. Unless one goes back and unpacks the intertextual connections and competing rhetorical agendas of the Grail symbol in its medieval ramifications, the Galahad story with its sex-negative, anti-procreational, and anti-communal outlook stands monolithically alone. Mitchison recognized that, too, and admirably captured the competing Grails and their winners in *To the Chapel Perilous*.[115]

*University of New Mexico*

[115] I would like to express my gratitude to the Research Allocation Committee at the University of New Mexico for funding part of this research project, and to Cynthia Fillmore for providing that research support.

# Arnold Fanck's 1926 Film *Der Heilige Berg* and the Nazi Quest for the Holy Grail

Kevin J. Harty

In 2000, Dhira B. Mahoney edited the Grail volume for Garland's series on Arthurian characters and themes.[1] This collection of twenty original and reprinted essays by diverse hands examines the Grail legend in its many forms from medieval to postmodern times. And just like a latter-day reincarnation of Chrétien's Grail maiden who carried a platter abundantly laden and decorated, so too Professor Mahoney offers us in her Grail volume a seminal collection that offers much to any reader (Grail quester or not) who takes it in hand. Individual essays in the volume discuss the origins of the Grail; its ever-changing symbolism; the role Chrétien, his multiple continuators, and Robert de Boron played in disseminating a much expanded version of the legend of the Grail, transforming it from a simple cornucopia into the vessel associated with the Last Supper; the linking of the literary theme of the wasteland with the healing powers of the Grail; the adoption of the Grail as a true measure of knightly honour and prowess in literary treatments of the Arthurian legend on both sides of the English Channel; Wolfram's further expansion of the legend in German and Hardyng's in late Middle English; Malory's embrace of the centrality of the quest for the Grail in his great synthesis of the many medieval versions of the Arthuriad; the continuing post-Malorian fascination with the Grail by writers as diverse as Tennyson,

I am grateful to, and happy once again to acknowledge the help I received in researching this essay from, Olwen Terris at the British Universities Film and Video Council and David Sharp at the Library of the British Film Institute, who also made it possible for me to obtain a copy of the still from *Der Heilige Berg* that accompanies the text of this essay.

[1] *The Grail: A Casebook*, ed. by Dhira B. Mahoney, Arthurian Characters and Themes, 5 (New York: Garland, 2000).

Charles Williams, T. S. Eliot, and Walker Percy; the Grail in art — most notably Victorian art — and the contemporary Grail of cinema, especially in films by Coppola, Boorman, and Rohmer.

In her introduction to the volume,[2] Professor Mahoney emphasizes the positive associations that the Grail has usually had, and the essays that follow reinforce that view of the Grail, a view generally found in cinematic treatments of the Grail. Such cinematic treatments date from at least 1904 when Thomas Edison attempted unsuccessfully to present a film version of a staging of Wagner's opera that opened in New York on Christmas Eve. Other films about the Grail indebted to a number of literary and musical traditions would soon follow, and Edison himself returned to the Grail as the subject for a film that he produced in conjunction with the Boy Scouts of America in 1917. After the Second World War, the Grail continued to be a popular theme in films from directors and producers as different as Richard Thorpe, the Monty Python Troupe, Robert Bresson, Eric Rohmer, Hans-Jürgen Syberberg, Richard Blank, Bruce Baillie, Steven Spielberg, and Terry Gilliam.[3] And even when filmmakers have looked to Wagner as a source, the resulting films have generally been free of the ideological baggage that Wagner's opera carries with it thanks to the subsequent links between the composer (and especially his descendants) and National Socialism in Germany.

[2] Dhira B. Mahoney, 'Introduction', in *The Grail: A Casebook*, ed. by Mahoney, pp. 1–100.

[3] For a complete Grail filmography, see Kevin J. Harty, 'The Grail on Film', in *The Grail, the Quest, and the World of King Arthur*, ed. by Norris J. Lacy (Woodbridge: Brewer, 2008), pp. 185–206. For discussions of the cinematic traditions of the Grail in general or of individual Grail films, see the essays by Martin B. Shichtman (pp. 561–73) and Linda Williams (pp. 575–90) in Mahoney's *The Grail: A Casebook*; Robert J. Blanch, 'The Fisher King in Gotham: New Age Spiritualism Meets the Grail Legend', in *King Arthur on Film: New Essays on Arthurian Cinema*, ed. by Kevin J. Harty (Jefferson, NC: McFarland, 1999), pp. 123–39; *Cinema Arthuriana, Twenty Essays*, ed. by Kevin J. Harty (Jefferson, NC: McFarland, 2002), especially the essays by Harty (pp. 7–33), Norris J. Lacy (pp. 34–43), David D. Day (pp. 127–35), Donald L. Hoffman (pp. 136–48), Jeff Rider — and his students — (pp. 149–62), and Ulrich Müller (pp. 177–84); Kevin J. Harty, '*The Knights of the Square Table*: The Boy Scouts and Thomas Edison Make an Arthurian Film', *Arthuriana*, 4 (1994), 313–23; Kevin J. Harty, 'Parsifal and Perceval on Film: The Reel Life of a Grail Knight', in *Perceval/Parsifal: A Casebook*, ed. by Arthur Groos and Norris J. Lacy (New York: Routledge, 2002), pp. 301–12; and Brian Levy, 'Subversion of Medievalism in *Lancelot du Lac* and *Monty Python and the Holy Grail*', in *Postmodern Medievalisms*, ed. by Richard Utz and Jesse G. Swan, Studies in Medievalism, 13 (Cambridge: Brewer, 2004), pp. 99–126.

Undeniably, however, the history of the legends associated with the Grail has had some darker chapters thanks to the Nazi appropriation of the legend of the Grail. This essay examines a little-noted cinematic link between the Grail legend and Nazi ideology contemporary with the rise of the National Socialists to power in the late 1920s. That film, Arnold Fanck's 1926 *Der Heilige Berg*, clearly an embodiment of Nazi ideology, serves as yet another example of the Nazi appropriation of the sacred to support an ideology that was anything but sacred.

The online catalogue of the British Film Institute offers the following synopsis of Arnold Fanck's 1926 film *Der Heilige Berg*: 'a mountain story of Diotima, the dancer and her lover [...] wandering through smoky halls in search of the Holy Grail'.[4] While that synopsis is succinct enough, it does not accurately reflect the plot of the film, but it is at least one of the few references to Fanck's *Der Heilige Berg* to comment on the film's relationship to the legend of the Holy Grail, the supposed cup from which Christ drank at the Last Supper and the source of endless fascination down through the ages as a religious and cultural icon.[5]

*Der Heilige Berg* was in its time well known thanks to a wide release throughout Germany, England, and the United States — though under various titles.[6]

[4] See *Film Index International*, <http://fii.chadwyck.co.uk>.

[5] See also Anita Obermeier's essay, 'The Rhetoric of Symbolism: The Grail of Fertility and Sterility', in the present volume.

[6] In England, the film was released in 1927 under the title *The Wrath of the Gods*. In the United States, the film was also released in 1927, but under the title *Peaks of Destiny*. The film is also variously referred to as *The Holy Mountain* and *The Sacred Mountain* in a number of discussions. For representative reviews, none of which mention the Grail scene, and some of which suggest variations in (or misunderstandings of) the film's scenario as it was released more widely, see: for the German release, *Berliner Morgenpost*, 16 December 1927, n.p., and *Die Weltbühne*, 11 January 1927, pp. 64–65; for the British release, *Bioscope*, 8 June 1927, p. 28, *Sunday Times* [London], 29 May 1927, p. 6, and *Westminster Gazette*, 28 May 1927, p. 7; for the American release, *Chicago Daily Tribune*, 21 December 1927, p. 33, *Harrison's Reports*, 10 (1928), p. 34, *Motion Picture News*, 21 January 1928, p. 213, *New York Times*, 29 November 1927, p. 31, *Pathéscope Monthly*, June-July 1933, pp. 8–9, and *Variety*, 30 November 1927, p. 19. Universum Film AG (UFA) also released a two-page press sheet to accompany the American release of the film; a copy of that press sheet can be found in the Film Library at the Museum of Modern Art in New York. In his autobiography, *Er führte Regie mit Gletschern, Stürmen und Lawinen: ein Filmpionier erzählt* (Passau: Nymphenburger Verlagshandlung, 1973), Fanck includes excerpts — all glowing — from British, German, Austrian, Swiss, French, Swedish, and Flemish reviews of the film: see pp. 162–65. When the film was released on DVD by Kino Video in 2003, there was a fresh spate of reviews, which again made virtually no mention of the Grail scene. See, for

Truth to tell, *Der Heilige Berg* is not by any objective standard a good film, but it is nonetheless notable for a number of reasons, not the least of which being its association with the Nazi version of the legend of the Holy Grail, which will be the main focus of this essay. Generically, *Der Heilige Berg* is a mountain film (*Bergfilm*), a new cinematic form Fanck (1889–1974) introduced, that remained popular in Germany from the days of the Weimar Republic until well into the 1950s, but which found special favour under the Nazis because it so clearly and early reflected National Socialist ideology and mythology. Typically, such films are set in an idealized mountain setting in which the natural is glorified, if not deified, and against which a battle plays out that tests the character of the main protagonists, who are usually personifications of the ideals of German masculinity.[7]

*Der Heilige Berg*, Fanck's second mountain film, grafts a documentary onto a melodrama about a love triangle involving a dancer and two mountain climbers, one younger and one older. The film opens with a prelude in which the dancer Diotima, 'whose life is dance', performs a free-form (almost comical) hymn to the sea, whose waves her very movements seem to control. As much as Diotima is associated with the sea, she is at the same time drawn to the mountains, where she hopes 'to satiate all her desires' with a man atop a holy mountain, whom she has only seen in her dreams.

The end of the prelude finds Diotima performing onstage at the Grand Hotel situated at the foot of a range of mountains capped by the most unscalable of peaks known simply as the Santo. As Diotima performs her dance of desire to a packed hotel ballroom crowd, she catches the attention of two mountaineers, Vigo, a young medical student, and his older companion, simply referred to throughout the film as 'the Friend'. Both fall in love with Diotima at first sight,

instance, *Classic Images*, 340 (2003), 44; 344 (2004), 37; 352 (2004), 42; *Sight and Sound*, 14 (2004), 78; *Sunday Telegraph* [London], 18 August 2002, p. 21; and *Washington Times*, 23 August 2003, p. D04. The score for the film composed by Edmund Meisel had previously been released on a double CD — along with that of *The Battleship Potemkin* — by Edel in 1995, arranged and conducted by Helmut Imig, and performed by the Orchestra della Svizzera Italiana. The liner notes for the CD again make no mention of the Grail sequence.

[7] For a quick overview of the mountain film as genre, see *The Encyclopedia of European Cinema*, ed. by Ginette Vincendau (New York: Facts on File, 1995), pp. 202–03. Interestingly, the genre was revived in the 1970s and the 1980s by the Austrian film and television industries to criticize the country's Nazi past. For a fuller discussion of the mountain film and Arnold Fanck's contribution to this film genre, see *Berge, Licht und Traum: Dr. Arnold Fanck und der deutsche Bergfilm*, ed. by Jan-Christopher Horak (Munich: Bruckmann, 1997).

with Vigo following her around like some Alpine 'stage-door Johnny' and the Friend retreating to the mountains to savour alone what he has seen.

Diotima's preference is clearly for the Friend, but Vigo misinterprets her many acts of kindness as something more than they are intended to be. When Vigo wins several Alpine skiing competitions, inspired by Diotima, her innocent embrace of the victor is witnessed and misinterpreted by the Friend, who had thought that he and Diotima were to marry, thus uniting sea and mountain. Furious, the Friend challenges Vigo to join him in a suicidal attempt to climb the north face of the Santo.

The two set off in the most horrific weather conditions, and halfway through their nighttime climb, Vigo slips and is left dangling by a rope off a cliff. So steep is the precipice that the Friend cannot anchor the rope to pull Vigo up to the ledge on which the Friend is standing and instead somehow musters the strength to hold on to the rope so that Vigo does not plunge to his death, the mountaineer code of loyalty and friendship trumping his earlier jealousy. The Friend's efforts are in vain, however, as both freeze to death before a rescue party that Diotima helps to organize can reach them the next morning.

As the night passes, the Friend slips into a dreamlike trance, in which he envisions Diotima and himself entering a cathedral of ice. The film's final frames return to the sea, above which the intertitles indicate looms 'the holy mountain, a symbol of the greatest values that humanity can embrace — fidelity — truth — loyalty — faith'.

Fanck indicated that the film's scenario, which he called 'a drama poem with scenes from nature', was based on events that had occurred in the Alps over a period of several years. More importantly, Fanck wrote the screenplay with one person in mind for the role of Diotima, Leni Riefenstahl, who made her screen-acting debut in the film and performed her 'Dance of the Sea' live at the film's opening on 17 December 1926 and 'an improvisation to Schubert's Unfinished Symphony' before each evening performance for several nights thereafter, generally to enthusiastic audience response and critical acclaim in the press.[8]

Given Riefenstahl's penchant for constantly reinventing her life to suit multiple purposes and political agendas, the details of her early association with Fanck are the matter of some debate. It is clear that her role as Diotima in *Der Heilige Berg* launched her career in the film industry; she previously had been a little-noticed dancer. Her original sponsor was the Jewish Austrian banker Harry Sokal, who took her to a screening of Fanck's 1924 film *Der Berg des Schicksals*

[8] Audrey Salkeld, *A Portait of Leni Riefenstahl* (London: Pimlico, 1997), p. 37.

and introduced her to the film's star, Luis Trenker, who would play the role of the Friend in *Der Heilige Berg*. Sokal subsequently arranged a meeting between Fanck and Riefenstahl, after which the director described the then still little known dancer as 'the most beautiful woman in Europe', who would 'soon' become 'the most famous woman in Germany'.[9]

Soon enough Riefenstahl was cast as Diotima, perhaps only coincidently after Sokal bought Fanck's nearly bankrupt film company and print laboratory in the process of merging them with what had already proven to be the most important and successful German film company, UFA, which financed, produced, and released *Der Heilige Berg*[10] and went on to become essential to the Nazi propaganda effort. Indeed, while it would soon become less advantageous to Riefenstahl to court the Jewish Sokal's favour to advance her career, Sokal personally financed a quarter of the production costs for *Der Heilige Berg*.[11] Sokal subsequently fled Nazi Germany in 1933, having been forced to relinquish his interests in UFA, and became one of Riefenstahl's most vocal post-war detractors.[12]

Riefenstahl would soon enough, of course, find a more powerful patron, Adolph Hitler, who in 1932 during one of their meetings declared that the 'most beautiful thing I have ever seen in a film was Riefenstahl's dance on the sea in *The Holy Mountain*'.[13] Again, Riefenstahl's penchant for continued self-reinvention produces an often-frustrating biographical muddle, but she clearly was early on an admirer of Hitler and a Nazi fellow traveller. According to Jürgen Trimborn, when she first heard Hitler speak, she left the rally almost in a trance and virtually devoured every page of *Mein Kampf*, a copy of which she immediately bought.[14]

The relationship of the *Bergfilm* genre to Nazi ideology was all but cemented by *Der Heilige Berg* and by Riefenstahl's role in the film. Two of the film's harshest critics have made this point from different perspectives. Siegfried Kracauer, writing first as a contemporary reviewer of the film and then subsequently with

[9] See Luis Trenker, *Alles gut gegangen: Geschichten aus meinem Leben* (Hamburg: Mosaik, 1956), p. 209.

[10] See Jürgen Trimborn, *Leni Riefenstahl: A Life*, trans. by Edna McCown (New York: Faber and Faber, 2007), pp. 28–37.

[11] See Horak, *Berge, Licht und Traum*, p. 39.

[12] Salkeld, *A Portait of Leni Riefenstahl*, p. 36. For further comments on the ups and downs of Sokal and Riefenstahl's relationship, see Salkeld, *A Portait of Leni Riefenstahl*, pp. 34–38.

[13] Quoted by Steven Bach in *Leni: The Life and Work of Leni Riefenstahl* (New York: Knopf, 2007), p. 91.

[14] Trimborn, *Leni Riefenstahl*, pp. 56–57.

hindsight in his book-length study of Nazi film, initially was one of the lone dissenting critics of the film when it opened. In his review for the *Frankfurter Zeitung*, Kracauer complained that *Der Heilige Berg* was a 'masterpiece for small youth groups that attempt to counter everything that they call mechanization by means of an overrun nature worship [and] panic-stricken flight into the foggy brew of vague sentimentality'.[15]

Subsequently, Kracauer linked *Der Heilige Berg* and other Fanck mountain films directly to Riefenstahl's 1935 unapologetically Nazi film vehicle *The Triumph of the Will*.[16] According to Kracauer, the kind of heroism displayed in *Der Heilige Berg* 'was rooted in a mentality kindred to the Nazi spirit. Immaturity and mountain enthusiasm were one. [...] [T]he idolatry of glaciers and rocks was symptomatic of an antirationalism on which the Nazis would capitalize.'[17] Susan Sontag later expanded upon Kracauer's criticism:

> Fanck's pop-Wagnerian vehicles for Riefenstahl were not just 'intensely romantic'. No doubt thought of as apolitical when they were made, these films now seem in retrospect, as Siegfried Kracauer has pointed out, to be an anthology of proto-Nazi sentiments. Mountain climbing in Fanck's films was a visually irresistible metaphor for unlimited aspiration toward the high mystic goal, both beautiful and terrifying, which was later to become concrete in Führer worship.[18]

Fanck and Riefenstahl went on to make several additional films together, and Fanck remained a loyal party stalwart throughout the Nazi period, though not as famously so as Riefenstahl.[19]

[15] *Frankfurter Zeitung*, 4 March 1927, p. 1. English translation as found in Bach, *Leni*, p. 47.

[16] Siegfried Kracauer, *From Caligari to Hitler: A Psychological History of the German Film* (Princeton: Princeton University Press, 1947), pp. 257–58. When I presented a shorter version of this essay as a paper on 9 May 2008 at the Forty-third International Congress on Medieval Studies held at Western Michigan University in Kalamazoo, Professor Laurie Finke of Kenyon College was kind enough to point out that the Grail in *Der Heilige Berg*, once it begins to give off smoke or steam, clearly resembles the Olympic torch and thereby foreshadows *The Triumph of the Will* in a way not noted by Kracauer.

[17] Kracauer, *From Caligari to Hitler*, p. 112.

[18] Susan Sontag, *Under the Sign of Saturn* (New York: Farrar, Straus & Giroux, 1980), p. 76.

[19] Fanck also directed Riefenstahl in *Der Große Sprung* (1927), *Die Weiße Hölle vom Piz Palü* (1929), *Stürme über dem Mont Blanc* (1930), *Der Weiße Rausch* (1931), and *SOS Eisberg* (1933). For a complete filmography of Fanck's films, see Fanck, *Er führte Regie*, pp. 387–95, and *Filmhefte*, 2 (1976), 37–45.

Nowhere does the Nazi link to *Der Heilige Berg* become clearer than in the Friend's dream vision of Diotima and himself in a cathedral made of ice whose centre point is clearly a Grail bearing altar. An intertitle labels the scene 'His World'. When the Friend — a proto-Nazi Everyman figure — concentrates on holding on to the rope bearing the now dead body of Vigo as the frozen corpse dangles over the side of the mountain, the camera zooms in for a close-up of his face, and that image quickly dissolves into a scene of Diotima and the Friend walking hand in hand in a more hospitable world of ice, a gigantic Gothic cathedral formed from glaciers. As they enter this clearly holy place, they are drawn to the central altar, which bears a Grail. As the couple mounts the altar steps, the Grail, which first starts to give off smoke or steam, begins to shatter, as does the Friend's reverie. The now-ruined cathedral with its shattered Grail becomes a symbol for the also now-dead Friend as the scene in the cathedral of ice dissolves into a second close-up of what is now the face of a man who has also frozen to death. The Nazi ideal has been realized by the Friend, but only briefly.

As I indicated earlier, little has been made of this Grail scene, and *Der Heilige Berg* does not merit mention in any serious studies of the myth of the Holy Grail, as perverted by the Nazis or otherwise. The most thorough study of the film remains a 1999 doctoral thesis by Thomas Bogner, but, while Bogner does comment briefly on the scene in the cathedral of ice, he does so in terms of German romantic pantheism rather than of the more traditional Grail associations the film evokes.[20]

Nazi ideology and mythology are nothing if not bizarre, and as Kevin Sim's 1999 documentary for British television, *Hitler's Search for the Holy Grail*, makes abundantly (and embarrassingly) clear the number of academics and holders of PhDs who rushed to join the Nazi Party and even the ranks of the SS for personal advancement only gave a patina of pseudo-credibility to that ideology and mythology when it came to the Holy Grail. Officially, the cult of the Holy Grail — and that of the associated Holy Spear or Lance — was seen as having Aryan pre-Christian origins until it was appropriated by the Jews.[21]

[20] Thomas Bogner, 'Zur Rekonstruktion filmischer Naturdarstellung am Beispiel einer Fallstudie: Natur in Film "Der heilige Berg" von Dr. Arnold Fanck' (unpublished doctoral thesis, University of Hamburg, 1999), especially pp. 92–93.

[21] On the academic pedigrees of the upper echelons of the SS and their willingness to help Nazis pervert the sacred into the profane, see Michael H. Kater, *Das 'Ahnenerbe' der SS 1935–1945: Ein Beitrag zur Kulturpolitik des Dritten Reiches* (Stuttgart: Deutsche Verlags-Anstalt, 1974), passim.

Fig. 1. The cathedral of ice and its Grail-laden altar in *Der Heilige Berg*. Still courtesy of the British Film Institute.

The mystical origins of Nazism were, moreover, older than any theories advanced by, or based on, Wagner[22] and Nietzsche. They were based on a view of spiritualism that privileged the soul over the body, and that saw the Aryan past as the first and most 'genuine manifestation' of the soul's inner force — which in turn alone could 'penetrate [life's true] secret mysteries'.[23] The key icon for those

[22] The complicated relationship between Nazi ideology and several generations of the Wagner family is beyond the scope of this essay, but the topic has been the subject of two very interesting (and damning) recent studies. See Jonathan Carr, *The Wagner Clan* (New York: Atlantic Monthly, 2007), especially pp. 172–91, and Brigitte Hamann, *Winifred Wagner: A Life at the Heart of Hitler's Bayreuth*, trans. by Alan Bance (Orlando: Harcourt, 2005), especially pp. 89– 121, which details the pro-Nazi spirit readily apparent at Bayreuth at a time coincidental with the production and release of Fanck's *Der Heilige Berg*.

[23] For a fuller explanation of the myths underlying the rise of Nazism, see G. L. Morse, 'The Mythical Origins of National Socialism', *Journal of the History of Ideas*, 22 (1961), 81–96, from which I have gleaned these admittedly very general comments.

mysteries was the Holy Grail, hence the Nazi fascination with finding it — a search so well known even long after the end of World War II that it could without any explanation form the basis of Steven Spielberg's 1989 film *Indiana Jones and the Last Crusade*.

And the new keepers of the Grail were none other than the brotherhood of the SS and the *Ahnenerbe*,[24] whom Heinrich Himmler dubbed a new society of Grail knights modelled on the Knights of Arthur's Round Table and who met for Grail-associated rituals at his triangular castle of Wewelsburg in Westphalia.[25] Nazi theories of and myths about the Grail ultimately looked to the Cathars, a heretical cult known for their secret rituals, that was suppressed — more properly exterminated — in the thirteenth century.[26] The Cathar strongholds had been in the Pyrenees, and it was to there that the earliest Nazi Grail questers turned to find the object of their desire.

The key figure in the Nazi quest was Otto Rahn, who was repeatedly dispatched by his superiors to various locales formerly associated in medieval times with the Cathars. Rahn authored two books,[27] produced endless maps using mystical triangulations, explored numerous grottos and caves, but seems to have uncovered nothing. Rahn eventually ended up in Dachau, first as a guard and then as a prisoner, where he was executed under circumstances that remain unclear, perhaps because he turned out to be Jewish or was a homosexual.[28] Another Nazi

[24] For a detailed account of Himmler's attempts to cast the members of the SS as latter-day Grail knights and of his further appropriation of the legends usually associated with Knights of the Round Table, again see Kater, *Das 'Ahnenerbe' der SS 1935–1945*, passim.

[25] For two very different views of the Nazi quest for the Grail, see Andrew Sinclair, *The Discovery of the Grail* (New York: Carol and Graf, 1998), pp. 246–53, and Nigel Pennick, *Hitler's Secret Sciences* (Sudbury, Suffolk: Spearmann, 1981), pp. 162–67.

[26] Since history is always written by the victors, what little we know about the Cathars and their rituals comes from sources hostile to them. For an unbiased, full discussion of Catharism, see Jean-Louis Biget, 'Mythographie de catharisme', *Cahiers de Fanjeaux*, 14 (1979), 271–342.

[27] *Crusade Against the Grail*, trans. by Christopher Jones (1933; Rochester, VT: Inner Traditions, 2006) and *Luzifers Hofgesind: eine Reise zu Europas guten Geistern* (Leipzig: Schwarzhäupter, 1937). See Also Jean-Michel Angebert, *The Occult and the Third Reich: The Mystical Origins of Nazism and the Search for the Holy Grail*, trans. by Lewis A. M. Sumberg (New York: Macmillan, 1971), pp. 3–56.

[28] Christian Bernadac advances the theory that Rahn was executed in Dachau because he could not produce certificates attesting to his racial purity, his mother's family having at some point in the past perhaps having been Jewish. See *Le Mystère Otto Rahn* (Paris: Éditions France-Empire, 1978), pp. 391–97. Hans-Jürgen Lange speculates that Rahn was executed because he was homosexual. See *Otto Rahn und die Suche nach dem Gral* (Engerda: Arun, 1999), pp. 205–13.

Grail quester, Rudolf Hess, was convinced that the sacred vessel was in or near Scotland, which may explain in part his strange flight or defection to England in 1941.[29]

Fanck's *Der Heilige Berg* anticipates and is one with Rahn's efforts. Early responses to the film at home and abroad, while ignoring the Grail sequence, nonetheless saw *Der Heilige Berg* as surpassing in 'point of sheer visual beauty' anything that the Germans have yet done in the cinema,[30] and as giving expression to a 'blend of sport, sensation and mysticism' that spoke to the German notion of 'ennoblement'[31] — all Nazi code words.

While Fanck's film certainly reflects the Nazi fascination with and quest for the Grail, it had in turn its own influence on later Nazi aesthetics. Carsten Strathausen quotes a comment made by Britain's pre-war ambassador to Nazi Germany to Albert Speer, Hitler's chief architect, that the Lichtdom (Cathedral of Light) that Speer had constructed in Nuremberg was 'solemn and beautiful at the same time, as if one stood in an overwhelming cathedral of pure ice'.[32] The cinematic prototype of Speer's work was, of course, the ice cathedral in Fanck's *Der Heilige Berg,* an earlier and largely uncommented upon reliquary for the Nazi image of the Holy Grail.

The Nazi imprint on German film from 1933 until the end of the Second World War is well documented.[33] But Fanck's *Der Heilige Berg* clearly shows that German cinema had, through the genre of the mountain film, readily embraced Nazi ideology before Hitler totally solidified his position by becoming chancellor, and that part of that embrace was the appropriation of what many would argue was among Christianity's most sacred icons and relics, the Holy Grail from which Christ supposedly drank at the Last Supper, which may have subsequently, according to yet other legends, caught the blood flowing from his side when it was pierced during the final moments of the Crucifixion.

*La Salle University*

[29] Sinclair, *Discovery of the Grail*, p. 253.

[30] Evelyn Gerstein, 'Four Films of New Types', *Theatre Arts Monthly*, 11 (1927), 295–98 (p. 297).

[31] Huntly Carter, *The New Spirit in the Cinema* (London: Shaylor, 1930), p. 269.

[32] Carsten Strathausen, 'The Image as Abyss: The Mountain Film and the Cinematic Sublime', in *Peripheral Visions: The Hidden Stages of Weimar Cinema*, ed. by Kenneth S. Calhoon (Detroit: Wayne State University Press, 2001), pp. 171–89 (p. 182).

[33] All subsequent studies of Nazi cinema are indebted to Siegfried Kracauer's 1947 groundbreaking study, *From Caligari to Hitler*, cited above in note 16.

# Folklore Motifs and Diminishing Narrative Time as a Method of Coherence in Malory's *Morte Darthur*

Judith Lanzendorfer

How many books did Malory write?[1] Was it eight, or one? This question of unity is, arguably, one of the most intriguing and hotly debated issues in Malory studies. Volumes have been written on both sides of this issue, but perhaps the most useful for the purposes of this study is D. S. Brewer's 'Orality and Literacy in Chaucer'.[2] Brewer notes that 'unity here [in the *Morte*] cannot mean structural unity of a kind we expect from a modern novel, or that we find in an ancient epic; and the term unity [...] should be abandoned [...] perhaps

[1] All references to Malory are from *The Works of Sir Thomas Malory*, ed. by Eugene Vinaver (Oxford: Oxford University Press, 1990).

[2] Some articles that deal with the structure of Malory's text include, Robert Ackerman, '"The Tale of Gareth" and the Unity of *Le Morte Darthur*', in *Philological Essays: Studies in Old and Middle English Language and Literature, in Honour of Herbert D. Merritt,* ed. by James L. Rosier (The Hague: Mouton, 1970), pp. 196–203; Judson Boyce Allen, 'The Medieval Unity of Malory's *Morte Darthur*', *Mediaevalia*, 6 (1980), 279–309; Karen Cherewatuk, 'Sir Thomas Malory's "Grete Booke"', in *The Social and Literary Contexts of Malory's 'Morte Darthur'*, ed. by D. Thomas Hanks (New York: Brewer, 2000), pp. 42–67; Andrea Clough, 'Malory's *Morte Darthur*: The "Hoole Book"', *Medievalia et Humanistica*, 14 (1986), 139–56; Elizabeth Edwards, *The Genesis of Narrative in Malory's 'Morte Darthur'* (New York: Brewer, 2001); Charles Moorman, *The Book of Kyng Arthur: The Unity of Malory's 'Morte Darthur'* (Lexington: University of Kentucky Press, 1965); K. J. Saycell, 'Organic Unity and Interlace: Some Aspects of Malory's *Morte Darthur*', *Unisa English Studies*, 17 (1979), 1–7; and Fiona Tolhurst, 'Why Every Knight Needs his Lady: Re-viewing Questions of Genre and "Cohesion" in Malory's *Le Morte Darthur*', in *Re-viewing 'Le Morte Darthur'*, ed. by K. S. Whetter and Raluca L. Radulescu (New York: Brewer, 2005), pp. 133–47.

the best term, of a useful elasticity, is cohesion'.[3] Focusing on the *Morte*'s cohesion can help to expand analysis of Malory's stories beyond the confines of modern structure and narrative technique; it allows a reader to shift focus away from the need to make all parts of a text fit together seamlessly. This essay then highlights folkloric elements embedded within the *Morte*, one useful way to underscore the coherence of the text. Subtle folklore motif references, particularly related to Malory's rite of passage tales, indicate that the text does have coherence and should be considered one whole book.

The emphasis that I place on folklore and rite of passage tales is not entirely new. Several previous studies have emphasized the inclusion of folklore and folk motifs in Malory's work. For instance, Robert Wilson's landmark 'The Fair Unknown in Malory' demonstrates how the Fair Unknown group of folk texts is closely aligned with Malory's *Morte*. Also, Jeffery Jerome Cohen's more recent 'Decapitation and Coming of Age: Constructing Masculinity and the Monstrous' deals with beheading contests as a form of rite of passage in folklore.[4] In Malory, however, beheading contests also include a female companion, who often barters for defeated knights' lives. This is the case in *La Cote Mal Tayle*, where the protagonist must show his prowess in battle and also satisfy his lady by granting mercy to defeated knights. In this tale, it is mercy rather than brute force that indicates adulthood. Although studies like Wilson's and Cohen's have done much to further the integration of folklore and literary studies, they have mainly been limited to the use of folklore within individual books. Such analysis, although not intentionally, may reinforce the idea that Malory's text should be read as eight separate works with each text analysed as a separate and distinct unit. On the contrary, this essay underscores the prevalence of folklore throughout Malory's work. The reflectivity of folklore motifs creates a sense of cohesion in the text and binds Malory's *Morte Darthur* into one book.

As a master adaptor and re-worker of texts, it is not surprising that Malory integrates various folkloric elements in the *Morte*. Perhaps the most common and

[3] Derek Brewer, 'Orality and Literacy in Chaucer', in *Mündlichkeit und Schriftlichkeit im englischen Mittelalter*, ed. by Sabine Volk (Tubingen: Narr, 1988), pp. 85–119.

[4] For articles that deal with folklore and rites of passage, see Robert Wilson, 'The Fair Unknown in Malory', *PMLA*, 58 (1943), 1–21; Kathleen Ashley, 'Victor Turner and the Forest of Folklore', *Medieval Folklore*, 2 (1992), 1–20; Mary Douglas, *Purity and Danger: An Analysis of Concepts of Pollution and Taboo* (Boston: Routledge & Kegan Paul, 1980); *Oral-Formulaic Theory*, ed. by John Miles Foley (New York: Garland, 1990); Jeffrey Jerome Cohen, 'Decapitation and Coming of Age: Constructing Masculinity and the Monstrous', *Arthurian Yearbook*, 3 (1993), 171–90.

well-known genre of folklore that Malory uses is the maturation rite of passage tale. Certainly, the most obvious rite of passage progresses from birth, to maturation, to death. Within this overarching cycle, however, there are several smaller rites of passage; the process of maturing from childhood to adulthood is just one of these transformations. In real life, a maturation rite of passage will contain both a physical and a mental component.[5] Although the physical component is important, it is dealt with less in Arthurian works than the mental process of maturation. For this reason, I have focused my attention only on the mental process of change from childhood to adulthood — along with the fears, anxieties, and triumphs that accompany it. Further, I concentrate on the tales in the *Morte* that most clearly fit into this subtype of the rite of passage tale: *Balin*, *Gareth of Orkney*, *La Cote Mal Tayle*, and *Alexander the Orphan*. A companion tale that reflects on the core four is *Torre and Pellinor*.

I have included two tables as a visual reference for points discussed at length later in this article. The tables highlight two folk motifs related to the rite of passage maturation process and identify the texts, noted earlier, in which they appear. Table 1 deals with motifs that Stith Thompson in his *Motif-Index* would categorize as 'Reversal of Fortune'.[6] These motifs all relate to the character of the initiate, specifically his orphaned status. Table 2 focuses on the 'Tests', particularly the actions of the initiate in his final battle before achieving adulthood.[7] It should be noted that I stress only the most common form of folklore in the *Morte*.[8] The text is rich with folk motifs and elements that can underscore how cohesive the *Morte* is overall.

The tables that I have created are best understood when the information is viewed vertically, by reading down each column. This shows how many of the motifs span from Book I to Book VIII and may be found in as many as four of the eight tales in Malory's work. I have also added page numbers in the tables. These

[5] By physical here I mean the actual biological process of maturation, not the physical actions that an initiate might take to progress in a rite of passage.

[6] Stith Thompson, *Motif-Index to Folk Literature* (Bloomington: Indiana University Press, 1989), pp. 1–6.

[7] The initiate is the main character who engages in the rite of passage, or rather, the protagonist of each tale.

[8] One may, for instance, look to the page numbers listed for the other motifs included in the table, such as H335.44 *Suitor Task: Kill (Defeat) Unwelcome Suitor*, as an example of a motif that goes beyond the specific tales included in this study. One need only consider the many times Guenevere, for instance, is saved by Lancelot as a variation on this motif. There are countless other ladies whose liberty is secured by Knights of the Round Table through this motif.

numbers reflect the amount of narrative that is spent detailing the initiate's actions in association with a given motif. The information on the chart shows how the amount of narrative time devoted to each motif diminishes as one advances through the text. Both of these issues will be dealt with in more detail later in this article.

**Table 1. Reversal of Fortune in Malory's *Morte Darthur***

| **Reversal of Fortune** | **L 111** Hero of Unpromising Origins | **L 111.4** Orphan Hero | **L 111.44** Mistreated Orphan Hero | **L142.3** Son Surpasses Father in Skill |
|---|---|---|---|---|
| Book I, *Torre and Pellinor* | | 1 p. (102) | | |
| Book I, *Balin* | 6 pp. (61–66) | 6 pp. (61–66) | 4 pp. (61–64) | 5 pp. (74–78) |
| Book IV, *Gareth* | 4 pp. (293–97) | 4 pp. (293–97) | 4 pp. (293–97) | 7 pp. (319–26) |
| Book V, *La Cote* | 4 pp. (459–62) | 4 pp. (459–62) | 4 pp. (459–62) | 3 pp. (471–73) |
| Book V, *Alexander* | 3 pp. (635–37) | 3 pp. (635–37) | 3 pp. (635–37) | 2 pp. (640–41) |
| Book VIII, *Slander* | | 2 pp. (1177–78) | | |

**Table 2. Tests in Malory's *Morte Darthur***

| **Tests** | **H 125.1** Identity by Sword | **H 335.44** Suitor Task: Kill (Defeat) Unwelcome Suitor | **H 1216** Mother Sends Son to Find Father | **H 1242.1** Unpromising Hero Succeeds in Combat | **H 1561.2** Single Combat, Proves Honour |
|---|---|---|---|---|---|
| Book I, *Torre and Pellinor* | | | | | |
| Book I, *Balin* | 3 pp. (88–90) | | | 6 pp. (73–78) | 6 pp. (73–78) |
| Book IV, *Gareth* | | 7 pp. (319–26) | 15 pp. (297–313) | 6 pp. (319–25) | 6 pp. (319–25) |
| Book V, *La Cote* | | 3 pp. (471–73) | 9 pp. (462–71) | 3 pp. (471–73) | 3 pp. (471–73) |
| Book V, *Alexander* | | 2 pp. (640–41) | 1 and 3 pp. (636, 641–43) | 2 pp. (640–41) | 2 pp. (640–41) |
| Book VIII, *Slander* | 2 pp. (1177–78) | | | | |
| Book VIII, *Vengeance* | 1 p. (1183) | | | | |

Each motif noted in the table behaves within the text in a similar way. Because of this, I will only discuss two motifs at length. Motif L 111.4 (*Orphan Hero*) represents the social status of the protagonist. Motif H 1561.2 (*Single Combat, Proves Honour*) focuses on the protagonist's actions in his rite of passage. These, and the rest of the motifs, are important on two levels. First, they function as repeated narrative elements that create intratextual echoes, or places in the text where the story reflects back on itself. These echoes usually refer to previous tales, though they may also anticipate future action. The motifs are also important because of their cumulative effect. Their inclusion gains significance when one recognizes them as part of a continuum that builds in meaning, with one motif referring to subsequent ones. The repetition and the cumulative nature of the motifs serve to bind the *Morte* together into a cohesive whole. (For another exploration of Malorian intratexuality, see Alan Lupack's essay, 'Malory's Intratexts', in the present volume.)

Examining the repetition of motifs L 111.4 (*Orphan Hero*) and H 1561.2 (*Single Combat, Proves Honour*) may be considered a preliminary way to establish the coherence of Malory's text. For instance, the motif L 111.4 (*Orphan Hero*) is found in the beginning (Book I), middle (Books IV and V), and end of the text (Book VIII).[9] Indeed, the whole of the *Morte* is rife with orphans. One need only think of the title character, Arthur, as an example of a man whose father is deceased before his son reaches maturity. The three young men under consideration here — La Cote, Alexander, and Gareth — also are linked together through their status in society as literal orphans. We learn of La Cote Mal Tayle's and Alexander the Orphan's social status in the *enface*.[10] La Cote 'had a fadir, a noble knight, and as he rode an-huntyng upon a day hit happed hym to ley hym downe to slepe, and there cam a knight that had been longe his enemy. And whan he saw that he was faste on slepe he all to-hew hym' (66). We also learn that the torn and tattered coat that La Cote wears is the one that his father wore when he was being murdered. A similar murder initiates the *enfance* of Alexander the

[9] I work with the medieval definition of orphan here. It refers to the characters being fatherless. For a discussion on class issues in Malory, see Karen Cherewatuk, *Marriage, Adultery, and Inheritance in Malory's 'Morte Darthur'* (New York: Brewer, 2006), and Dhira B. Mahoney, 'Malory's *Tale of Gareth* and the Comedy of Class', *Arthurian Yearbook*, 1 (1991), 165–93.

[10] An *enfance* is a portion of text that recounts the parents and activities of the protagonist as he matures. Although this portion of text is often dismissed as simply background information, it is actually very important from the perspective of rite of passage. It sets up for the reader the social status and worldview of the initiate as he embarks on his rite of passage.

Orphan. As his name so plainly suggests, he has been made an orphan, but this time his father, King Bodwyne, was killed by his own brother, King Mark.

Malory also presents Gareth to the reader as an orphan, but his introduction is a bit different from the other two protagonists previously discussed. Instead of having an *enface* that sets up his orphaned status, Gareth's low station seems to be self-imposed. He could come to court with the riches and entourage that his mother has sent with him, but Gareth chooses to distance himself from his family relations by coming to court with no wealth and accompanied only by two men, who actually serve to carry him in on their arms. This display presents Gareth as a poor weakling, and gives no indication of the wealth and family name to which he rightly belongs.[11] Because of this, he is immediately labelled by Sir Kay a 'vylayne borne' (294) and sent to the kitchen where he becomes a 'tourner of brochis, an a ladyll-washer' (300). This is just the beginning of how name and identity are interconnected in this tale. As Dhira B. Mahoney's 'Narrative Treatment of Name in Malory's *Morte Darthur*' indicates, the giving, receiving, and use of name is integral to the self-worth of characters and serve as motivations to action in the text.[12] When Gareth does not give his name and humbly accepts his renaming, he accepts a low social position. From this point he works to prove his worth, rather than simply having it handed to him because of his family name.

If one reads the *Morte* as eight separate works, the orphaned status of Gareth at the beginning of his tale seems to be metaphorical. We have not been told in an *enfance* that Gareth's father has died. If a reader is observant, though, Gareth's orphaned status will be remembered from Book I, *Torre and Pellinor*. Here Gawain comments, 'yonder knight [Sir Pellinor] ys putte to grete worship, which grevith me soure, for he slewe oure fadir kynge Lott' (102). If we read the *Morte* as one self-reflective book, then we should realize that by the time Gareth arrives at court he is an orphan, though only by medieval standards. It is true that his mother is still alive, and indeed later in the tale she comes to court to shame Arthur verbally because he has not recognized and treated his nephew in a proper manner. Still, Gareth's father is dead, and it is this that constitutes him as an orphan in medieval society. The father provides a lineage for his child, bequeaths titles and riches, and establishes the child's place within the social order. If the

[11] It may be argued that Gareth distances himself because of the ignoble reputations of some members of his family. Two of Gareth's brothers help expose the affair between Lancelot and Guenevere. I do not believe, however, that it is shame which prompts Gareth to hide his identity. Instead he takes a difficult route to respectability because he wants to prove his worth.

[12] See Dhira B. Mahoney, 'Narrative Treatment of Name in Malory's *Morte Darthur*', *English Literary History*, 47 (1980), 646–56.

father is absent, then the child has no one to give him wealth and establish his social worth. He is, in essence, alone in a world that relies on name and family ties to mark one as a member of a group.[13] As such we should read Gareth at the beginning of his book as an orphan, which connects him to the other orphans introduced after his tale.

If a reader does not remember that Gareth is a literal orphan, he still can fit into the schema of the *Morte* because it also includes many metaphorical orphans. For instance, after he has established his adult identity, name, and place in society, Gareth chooses to discard all of this and again become like an initiate. This occurs during his final, fateful battle. When he enters this battle, he does so without armour because he is not willing to choose sides between his brothers and the man who knighted him, Lancelot. Gareth's situation in his final battle is a difficult one. On one side, Aggravain and Mordred, two of Gareth's brothers, undermine social stability by making Lancelot and Guenevere's affair public. This leads to the attempted burning of Guenevere and the first great battle of the war. Although this is the case, a reader must not forget that Lancelot is having an affair with a woman who is above his station and his king's wife, actions that are contrary to rules of proper behaviour. With which side should Gareth align himself? He chooses to side with neither and both at the same time. Although Arthur orders Gareth to be present at the battle, it is Gareth who chooses how he is present at the battle. Gareth chooses to go into battle unarmed, without any identification for one side or the other. He tries to use his unarmed body to build a bridge between the two opposing factions, but unfortunately what Gareth's neutrality actually accomplishes is to distance the two sides even further. He goes into the battle as an unknown, and the results are tragic — 'hit mysfortuned [Lancelot] to sle sir Gaherys and sir Gareth, the noble knight' (1177) because Gareth wore no shield to indicate his identity. In the end, Gareth's self-imposed status as a metaphorical orphan from his fractioned society (the break between Lancelot and his kin) end in the death of this most beloved son.

Perhaps the most significant metaphorical orphan one encounters in the *Morte* is Balin. As with *The Tale of Gareth*, there is no *enface* to Balin's story that would confirm that he is a literal orphan, so a reader must view his status as metaphorical. When we are introduced to the character Balin le Sauvage,[14] we are

[13] See Ruth Morse, 'Sterile Queens and Questing Orphans', *Quondam et Futurus*, 2 (1992), 41–53.

[14] Balin, like many of the initiates goes through several name changes. When we first meet him he is 'le Sauvage', the prisoner, but later becomes 'The Knight with Two Swords'. This is

presented with a character who is separated from society because he is a prisoner: 'there was a poore knight with kynge Arthure that had bene presonere with hym half a yere for sleyng of a knight which was cousine unto kynge Arthure' (62). Balin's physical location of being in prison is a clear example of social separation because his body is removed from rest of the court. Because of the gravity of his crime Balin has been labelled le Sauvage, which seems to indicate that he is a 'wild, barbarous uncivilized person',[15] a dangerous character who must be removed from the rest of society because of his dishonourable deeds.

Balin's presentation in the text has most often been analysed from the perspective of psychology or providence.[16] Perhaps most notable is Kenneth Tucker's 'The Sword and the Shadow: A Jungian Reading of Malory's "Tale of Balin"', which analyses the purpose and function of Balin's character as part of the psychological state of society.[17] Studies focusing on underlying forces that drive character motivation and action lead nicely into a discussion of folklore. In both, the orphan may be seen as the 'other' marginalized by society. Whether through the lens of psychology or folklore, through a father murdered or imprisonment, the characters in the tales connect because society marks them as outsiders. From this low social standing they must work to prove that they deserve to be reintegrated into society as worthy adult males.

In addition to repetition of the social status of the protagonists, their actions also repeat; motif H 1561.2 (*Single Combat, Proves Honour*) appears in the representative tales in the beginning (Book I) and middle (Books IV and V) of the *Morte*. This motif represents the final battle that the initiate needs to accomplish to prove his adult status to his society. For instance, in *Balin* Malory actually describes the two brothers together in their final battles. Balin and his brother are so skilled that they warrant the description: as 'sente from hevyn as angels other deviles from helle. *And kynge Arthur seyde himself* they were the doughtyeste

similar to Sir Kay's naming Gareth as 'Beaumains' — 'beautiful hands' — another derisive name, when he arrives at court.

15 See the entry for 'sauvage' in the *Middle English Dictionary*, ed. by Hans Kurath (Ann Arbor: University of Michigan Press, 1997).

16 See Deborah Ellis, 'Balin, Mordred and Malory's Idea of Treachery', *English Studies*, 68 (1987), 66–74; Robert Kelly, 'Malory's "Tale of Balin" Reconsidered', *Speculum*, 54 (1979), 85–99; and K. S. Whetter, 'On Misunderstanding Malory's Balyn', in *Re-viewing 'Le Morte Darthur'*, ed. by Whetter and Radulescu, pp. 149–62, among others.

17 Kenneth Tucker, 'The Sword and the Shadow: A Jungian Reading of Malory's "Tale of Balin"', *Journal of Evolutionary Psychology*, 12 (1991), 2–17.

knyghtes that every [*sic*] he sawe, for they gaff such strokes that all men had wondir of hem' (76, emphasis mine). One might remember that at the beginning of his story Balin is a prisoner and labelled 'savage' because he has killed King Arthur's cousin. Balin begins at a very low point, as one of the outcasts of society, but during the course of his tale he reverses this status. His reputation is improved so much that he is actually complimented by the King, who initially imprisoned him. King Arthur's statement is a clear indication of how much Balin has learned and progressed during his rite of passage and how, at the end of his tale, he is considered to be a valued and well-respected member of the society.

Similarly, in *The Tale of Gareth*, the lead character also greatly increases his social status. To do this, Gareth battles several knights (the Black, Green, Red, and Indigo Knights) before he encounters his most difficult foe, the Red Knight of the Red Lands.[18] The Red Knight forces knights into battle and when they are defeated beheads them and hangs them and their shields on a tree (196). Not only does he murder knights and mutilate their corpses, but he also exposes the defeated knights to public postmortem shaming. By hanging the knights' shields on the tree, the Red Knight of the Red Lands is 'naming' the dead knight and showing how, in the end, the knight was not worthy to win in battle. The Red Knight of the Red Lands commits horrible and unknightly deeds, so when Gareth engages him in battle he risks much in fighting this foe. If Gareth loses, then certainly he will die, but more importantly he will lose any honour that he has gained in his rite of passage. During the public battle, though, Gareth proves victorious and skilled enough as an adult male and worthy knight.[19] Although Gareth does much to progress toward adulthood with his defeat of the Red Knight of the Red Lands, his rite of passage is not complete. He next engages in a very public tournament, during which he defeats several more knights in battle.

[18] Although there has not been specific discussion on the symbolism of colours in *La Cote*, for a general overview see Alfred L. Kellogg, 'Malory and Color Symbolism: Two Notes on his Translation on the *Queste del Saint Graal*', in *Chaucer, Langland, Arthur: Essays in Middle English Literature* (New Brunswick, NJ: Rutgers University Press, 1972), pp. 11–28.

[19] Public displays of prowess were very important in Arthurian society. To recognize this importance, one must remember that Gareth's earlier method of advertising his wins in more private battles. He required a defeated knight to go to Arthur's court with a 50-to-100-knight entourage and announce that Gareth had overcome him in battle and pledge himself and his accompanying knights to Arthur's service. This was the only way in which victories in private battles would become known to the public at large. See Victor Turner, 'Betwixt and Between: The Liminal Period in Rites of Passage', in *The Forest of Symbols: Aspects of Ndembu Ritual* (Ithaca: Cornell University Press, 1967), pp. 98–99.

It is only after his name is announced to the crowd and he has publicly displayed his prowess that the narrator ends the tale by renaming him a 'noble knight', and his rite of passage is complete (363).

In *La Cote* and in *Alexander* final battles also establish honour and maturity. In *La Cote*, for instance, Maledysaunt notes that 'hit may be no younge knyghtes dede that shall enchyve this adventure to the ende' (471), and indeed it is not. It is only after a great deal of trial and error that La Cote learns from his mistakes and progresses on his rite of passage toward adulthood. When he encounters his final battle, with Sir Plenourys, he actually loses the fight, but in doing so wins his name as an adult. Plenourys says 'fayre knight, dysmay you not, for had ye bene freysshe whan ye mette with me as I was, I wote well that I coude nat have endured you' (473). These are important words because they come from a well-established knight who is described as 'full noble' (473). As La Cote finishes his adventure he is shown to be well-respected by his peers; this reinforces the idea that La Cote has made significant advances in his rite of passage and that he now is accepted as an adult by his society.

Likewise, in *Alexander*, he learns from his final battle and through it establishes himself as worthy adult male. Like Gareth's final battle with the Red Knight of the Red Lands, Alexander's final battle with Sir Sagramour is public. When he overcomes Sir Sagramour in combat, Alexander immediately stands out as a potential love interest to Alys le Beale Pylgrym. She enquires if she might see Alexander's face and then asks for his name. She later marries Alexander, thus furthering his role as an adult male by establishing his status as a husband and father. These two roles serve to reinforce expected behaviours and stabilize society.

These folklore motifs, such as those discussed earlier, function as intratextual echoes, in which Malorian passages are narratologically self-reflective. These echoes can be identified if even one reads only selected tales from *Morte*, but they can be recognized more easily if one reads from Book I through Book VIII in the order in which the tales appear in the Winchester Manuscript. The reason for this is somewhat obvious. A reader will be able to identify the repetition of motifs by remembering previously read tales. It is simply easier for a reader to make the connection between the orphaned status of La Cote and Gareth, for instance, if the one tale is read after the other. Understanding the importance of the repeated motifs would be much more difficult if Book V were read before Book I or Book IV.

To illustrate this, by the time Alexander the Orphan makes his appearance in Book V, the reader has already encountered motif L 111.4 (*Orphan Hero*) in the tales about Balin, Gareth, and La Cote. With the characterization of each protagonist as an orphan, the reader is reminded of orphans that had been introduced in earlier tales and may anticipate the inclusion of more orphans in later sections of the text. Likewise, the repetition of battles in connection to motif H 1561.2 (*Single Combat, Proves Honour*) reminds the reader of the connections among the different combat situations. Although the details of the battles change among the four tales, the idea that an unpromising orphan meets his opponents in combat and overcomes them stays consistent. The valiant way in which Balin encounters his foes repeats as one reads about Gareth's battles, then La Cote's, and then Alexander's.

The repeated inclusion of motifs like L 111.4 (*Orphan Hero*) and H 1561.2 (*Single Combat, Proves Honour*), therefore, works against Vinaver's thesis that Malory's text should be viewed as eight separate works. The motifs do not make the tales distinct from each other; instead, the motifs remind a reader of the repetitions within Malory's work. Early portions of the book are implicitly present in the narrative each time he reintroduces motif in the text. The inclusion of these motifs, thus, creates a similarity among the tales and points toward the *Morte* as a cohesive text.

A reader might counter the former statement with the argument that Malory included orphans or combat scenes in his stories simply because he was interested in them, and that their reappearance and repetition does not prove coherence. If the repetition of motifs were the only evidence for coherence, then this argument would certainly have a great deal of weight. It is undermined, however, because of a second way with which Malory establishes coherence in his text — the diminishing amount of narrative time spent with each motif when he (re)introduced it in the *Morte*.

Book I then lays the foundation for the rest of the text; this includes information about the social status of Malory's characters. When Balin and motif L111.4 (*Orphan Hero*) appear, the reader learns important information about the way society views orphans. One of the main hallmarks of the initiate, exacerbated by his status as an orphan, is that he has nothing and therefore is nothing in the eyes of society. As Victor Turner notes, the initiate has 'no status, no property, insignia, secular clothing, rank, kinship position, nothing to demarcate him structurally from his fellows. His condition is indeed the very prototype of sacred poverty'.[20] When we are introduced to Balin we learn that he is a prisoner, a man who is figuratively *and* literally set apart from society. Information about his lowly

[20] Turner, 'Betwixt and Between', pp. 98–99.

status spans six pages (61–66) of the story. When the same motif is introduced in *Gareth*, the description of his orphaned status encompasses five pages (293–97), mainly with references to his low status as a kitchen knave (300). In *La Cote* the information is given in four pages (459–62), including Kay's rude renaming of him as 'La Cote Male Tayle' or the 'knyght wyth the evyll-shapyn coote' (459). In *Alexander*, whose tale properly titled includes the word 'orphan', this is dealt with in three pages (635–37). In *Slander in Strife*, it is dealt with in two pages (1177–78), during which we learn of how Gareth reinstates his position as an initiate by discarding his armour in his final battle.

The same sort of pattern occurs in relation to the characters' actions. There are six pages of text concerning motif H1561.2 (*Single Combat, Proves Honour*) in *Balin* (74–78). In this tale, we read of his final battle that re-establishes him as a member of society, with Arthur even praising him and his brother by saying that they were 'the doughtyeste knyghtes that every he sawe, for they gaff such strokes that all men had wonder of hem' (76). Malory deals with it in six pages in *Gareth* (319–25), during which he defeats his most impressive opponent, the Red Knight of the Red Lands. La Cote (471–73) encounters the knight Plenourys, whom he does not defeat but who praises him highly. Finally, *Alexander* (640–41) has his final battle with Sagramour. In each instance, the amount of time that is spent in discussing single combat between the initiate and his opponent diminishes as one reads through the *Morte*. The same sort of shrinking narrative also marks the other motifs noted in the tables, indicating that an important pattern in the text is emerging. A reader, though, might question what this pattern means.

Certainly one argument that may explain the diminishing amount of information given as one moves through the *Morte* is that the stories themselves are progressively shorter. The number of pages in which a motif is discussed might be proportional to the length of the tale; shorter tales will have less information about each of the motifs than longer tales. This argument, initially, seems to be valid: *Balin* is 32 pages, *La Cote* is 16 pages, and *Alexander* is 15 pages. Therefore, the fact that the texts are shorter seems to explain the smaller amount of time spent on each motif in the narratives.

However, the length of *Gareth* and the manner in which the motifs behave in this text cause problems with the argument. *Gareth* is seventy pages, which is longer than any other rite of passage tale in the *Morte*. If the number of pages in which a motif is discussed is proportional to the length of the tale, then one should expect that the motifs in *Gareth* would be discussed in greater depth than they are in *Balin*, which is thirty-eight pages shorter than *Gareth*. This, however, does not occur. Even though *Gareth* is longer than *Balin*, seven of the eight motifs that appear in *Gareth* are dealt with in less or the same number of pages as in *Balin*. Because of this, the diminished amount of time spent on each motif cannot be explained by the progressively shorter length of the tales.

If the diminishing amount of information does not correspond to the length of the tale, then what is the reason for it? The explanation is related to the text's reflection on itself. Simple repetition of motifs provides one way that the text presents itself as self-referential and reflective. This process, however, is complicated when a reader considers that each time a motif is reintroduced, less time is spent in the narrative developing it. Instead of repeating basic information — and orphan's social status or combat situations — that has already been established in earlier tales, Malory gives only the information that the reader needs to identify the narrative situation.

For instance, if readers, medieval or modern, have been perceptive when reading through Malory's *Morte*, then they likely have recognized the repetitiveness of the text.[21] Readers may not necessarily recognize that the repetitions are folkloric motifs, but they will likely remember reading about Balin as an orphan and the difficulties that he encountered because of his social status. When a reader comes to the tale of *Gareth* and recognizes that he has the same status as Balin, then details about Gareth's status can be 'filled in by the reader. Since the information about this motif builds upon itself, it is possible to give less information about a character's orphaned status in each tale. So, by the time one reads *Slander and Strife*, the information about motif L111.4 (*Orphan Hero*) has diminished from six to only two pages.

Likewise, information about motif H 1561.2 (*Single Combat, Proves Honour*) shrinks as one reads through the tales. Like motif L111.4 (*Orphan Hero*) the information about this final battle occupies six pages in *Balin*. The battle is also dealt with in *Gareth* and *La Cote*, so by the time that readers encounter the final battle in *Alexander*, they should be able to fill in information about the battle. For this reason, the final battle scene in *Alexander* may be presented in two pages, as opposed to the six in *Balin*.

The notion that it is not necessary to repeat basic information about the protagonists' social status or actions in each tale acts against Vinaver's theory that the *Morte* should be viewed as eight separate works. If Vinaver's theory were correct, then the amount of information given about each orphan and each

[21] Joyce Coleman, *Public Reading and the Reading Public in Late Medieval England and France* (Cambridge: Cambridge University Press, 1996), underscores the attitudes toward the written word in medieval England and France.

character's final battle would need to be fully explored. They, however, are not. The diminished amount of information given in each of the tales points toward a structure in the *Morte* that is, although not unified by modern standards, nevertheless coherent. The reflectivity of the tales through the repetition of motifs and the diminishing amount of information connected with them create an important pattern in Malory's text; this pattern is a subtle method for recognizing coherence in the *Morte*.

By analysing how Malory's tales incorporate folkloric elements, a reader can gain a new understanding and appreciation of Malory's text. Perhaps most important in this analysis are questions about meaning, structure, and unity for the *Morte* — topics that have been debated since the Winchester Manuscript was found. These and other questions can be answered when a reader recognizes that the folk motifs often occur in tales that have didactic purposes, such as the maturation rite of passage tale. The maturation rite of passage tale has been a formula with which to teach young people all over the world and through the ages about the difficulties and trials on their path toward adulthood. In this way, folk motifs that derive from realistic circumstances (how does one establish oneself as an adult in society, how does one find a mate? etc.) are included in tales with similarly realistic narratives. As such, it is not important that Alexander beats Sir Sagramour in battle, just to beat him. It is important that he proves his prowess in battle, a hallmark of adulthood in Arthurian society. It is additionally significant that immediately after he has proven himself as an adult, he is approached by a potential mate, whom he later marries. The process of growing up and establishing oneself as an adult in society is learned behaviour, and the tales noted here highlight the process through which one becomes an adult.

The controversy among critics concerning the way in which the *Morte* should be viewed — as one or eight texts, as an organic entity or one that was planned out by its author, etc. — will continue into the future. As part of this discussion, a reader might consider how the time of transition from oral/manuscript to print culture has an effect on Malory's text. Consciously or unconsciously, Malory wove many elements of folklore into his *Morte*. The motifs noted in this article are only a few of the many that may be identified and studied in the whole of the text. They, and others, recur and create patterns that link the tales to one another, creating a web of intratextual echoes in the text. When readers understand and recognize these connections, they will find an answer to the question: How many books did Malory write? By identifying and analysing the folk elements in the text, a critic can answer that Malory wrote one cohesive book.

*University of Findlay*

# Malory's Intratexts

Alan Lupack

The intertextuality of Malory's *Morte Darthur* is well documented. There is a long tradition in Malory scholarship of ferreting out the sources of Malory's romance, even at times conjecturing that a source must have existed when none is to be found, and analysing his work in terms of his changes to his sources. Malory's use of parts of the Vulgate and Post-Vulgate cycles, of the Prose *Tristan*, of the *Alliterative Morte Arthure* and the *Stanzaic Morte Arthur*, of a section of the *Perlesvaus*, and of Hardyng's *Chronicle* has been established. It is also obvious that he drew on basic story types and motifs such as the Nine Worthies, the chastity test, and the Fair Unknown tale. Critics have examined Malory's sources and analogues and discussed at length how Malory adapted them, sometimes quoted directly from them, or changed them to suit his aesthetic or thematic purposes.[1]

[1] H. Oskar Sommer's edition of the Caxton version of Malory's *Le Morte d'Arthur*, 3 vols (London: Nutt, 1889–91), includes a long study of Malory's use of his sources. In the third volume of his edition of the Winchester Manuscript, Eugène Vinaver provides 'Commentary', which frequently refers to Malory's sources, sometimes quoting passages from those sources and comparing them to Malory's text. In *Le Morte Darthur of Sir Thomas Malory and its Sources* (New York: Dutton, 1917), Vida D. Scudder examines Malory's sources and concludes that the 'original genius of the author of the *Morte* is primarily evident in his broad principle of selection and arrangement' (p. 368). When Vinaver published the Winchester Manuscript as the *Works* of Malory, the study of Malory's sources became important to those arguing for the unity of the *Morte*. To counter Vinaver's theory of multiple tales, R. M. Lumiansky, in *Malory's Originality* (Baltimore: Johns Hopkins University Press, 1964), led a group of scholars, each of whom examined one of the tales in relation to its sources and commented on changes made to enhance the unity of the whole book. In *Malory's Morte Darthur* (Cambridge, MA: Harvard University Press, 1976), Larry D. Benson looked at the *Morte* in relation to the French prose cycles of the thirteenth to fifteenth centuries and the English romance tradition. Malory's sources are

Textuality suggests authority in many medieval works, and Malory's *Morte Darthur* is no exception. But the significance of textuality in the *Morte* is not limited to intertextual references to texts, real or imagined, outside the romance or to traditions that may have shaped Malory's understanding of romance and of the stories he reworked. There is also a pattern of intratextuality, by which I mean that there are texts within the larger structure of the *Morte* that not only have a dialogic connection to other texts and traditions outside the work but that also represent discrete genres within the text which take their full meaning both from their intertextual relationships and from their connections to other material, and sometimes other texts, within the *Morte* itself.[2] Malory's intratexts might be read to include the eight books that Vinaver saw as separate romances or, narrowing the focus, the tales within those books such as the story of *La Cote Male Tayle*, *Alexander the Orphan*, etc., in *The Book of Sir Tristram*.

But I would like to narrow the focus even further to consider specific forms of texts that are embedded within these tales. Malory uses these texts within the text for a variety of purposes, including structural linking, revelation of theme, and definition of character.[3] Quite a few of these intratexts support Malory's concern

summarized and his use of them discussed in 'Malory and his Sources' by Terence McCarthy (in *A Companion to Malory*, ed. by Elizabeth Archibald and A. S. G. Edwards (Cambridge: Brewer, 1996), pp. 75–95). Others have focused on the sources of individual tales. To cite all such articles is beyond the scope of the present essay; thus I refer only to a few representative examples. Vinaver's *Le Roman de Tristan et Iseut dans l'œuvre de Thomas Malory* (Paris: Champion, 1925) identifies three manuscripts of the French Prose *Tristan* that represent the version that Malory would have known. In *Aspects of Malory*, ed. by Toshiyuki Takamiya and Derek Brewer (Cambridge: Brewer, 1981)), two essays focus on sources: Edward D. Kennedy's 'Malory and his English Sources' (pp. 27–55) and P. J. C. Field's 'The Source of Malory's *Tale of Gareth*' (pp. 57–70). Field has also written on 'Malory's Minor Sources' (*Notes & Queries*, 26 (1979), 107–10) and on 'Malory and Perlesvaus' (*Medium Aevum*, 62 (1993), 259–69). And Dhira Mahoney has looked at the relationship between Malory's version of the Grail quest and that found in his French source in 'The Truest and Holiest Tale: Malory's Transformation of *La Queste del Saint Graal*', in *Studies in Malory*, ed. by James W. Spisak (Kalamazoo: Medieval Institute Publications, 1985), pp. 109–28.

[2] In her essay in the present volume, Judith Lanzendorfer speaks of another kind of intratextuality used by Malory. She refers to recurring folk motifs that 'function as repeated narrative elements that create intratextual echoes, or places in the text where the story reflects back on itself' (p. 237).

[3] With Jill Mann's warning — that we should banish from the vocabulary of Malory criticism 'the word "character" as inappropriate to his representation of human figures' — in mind, I speak of 'definition of character' rather than 'development of character' ('Malory: Knightly

to define the codes that govern the action of the *Morte* and to present Launcelot as the epitome of chivalry. Malory's internal texts include both oral forms such as prophecies, interpretations, and proverbs, and written forms such as letters and inscriptions (on tombs, swords, etc.). In a couple of cases, even visual texts are used to convey or comment on the larger action and themes.[4] These intratexts may have an intertextual dimension and some of their meaning may be derived from their response to or changes in sources or analogues; but they also work, sometimes on several levels, as a response to or comment on a theme or idea elsewhere in the *Morte*. Malory uses oral forms in a manner different from dialogue, even though they generally occur in dialogue. When characters speak, they may be deliberately deceptive, as Mark sometimes is, or evasive, as even Launcelot can be. But more formal texts take on the weight of authority, even when their authoritative pronouncements are ignored by those for whom they are intended or who would benefit most from them.

## *Prophecies and Interpretations*

One form of intratext used by Malory is the prophecy. These texts gain their authority intertextually from a long tradition. But they have an intratextual dimension and authority as well because of the characters, such as Merlin and holy men and women who utter them, and because they are generally proven true

Combat in *Le Morte D'Arthur*', in *Medieval Literature: Chaucer and the Alliterative Tradition*, ed. by Boris Ford (Harmondsworth: Penguin, 1983), pp. 331–39 (pp. 331–32)).

[4] Though I will not treat such visual texts in the body of this essay, it is worth noticing how such texts might work in a manner similar to verbal intratexts. For example, early in his reign when Arthur puts down the uprising against his rule, he has images made of twelve rebellious kings 'and eche one of hem helde a tapir of wexe in hir honde that brente nyght and day. And kynge Arthure was made in the sygne of a fygure stondynge aboven them with a swerde drawyn in hys honde, and all the twelve fygures had countenaunce lyke unto men that were overcom' (I, 78, ll. 3–8). The sepulchral images of the Kings serve as a sign of honour to their nobility, with perpetual flames as reminders of their passing, as a sign of Arthur's dominance, and as a warning to others who might consider opposing his rule. Similarly, when Morgan elicits from Tristram a promise to bear a shield that depicts a knight with one foot on a king's head and one on a queen's, it is meant as a 'rebuke' to Launcelot and a means of sending to Arthur a message about the love between Launcelot and Guinevere (cf. II, 554–55). But it also reveals Tristram's character, since his nobility does not allow him to see in the blatant message a criticism of Launcelot and Guinevere. In addition, one might read the text of the image as suggesting that Launcelot gains his chivalric superiority from the code and order established by Arthur coupled with his ennobling love for Guinevere.

within the text itself. Coupled with prophecy is the interpretation or explanation, either of prophecies or of dreams or visions. Elizabeth Edwards notes the connections between prophecies and what she calls explanations: 'If prophecy is one method of acquiring knowledge about the text, there are also explanations which account for or describe the significance of what *has* happened. The real difference between prophecy and explanation in the *Morte Darthur* is only positional; prophecy is an anterior form of explanation.'[5] Prophecies are authoritative, but those who should be warned by them often ignore or disbelieve them. This is part of a pattern of human blindness exhibited by characters in Malory's romance to such a degree that it becomes thematic. Merlin is, as Catherine La Farge has observed, 'the character who evokes the greatest willed deafness in others'. Whereas in Malory's French source some of his predictions are too obscure to be understood, a common feature of the prophetic tradition generally, in Malory, the characters tend to ignore a perfectly clear prediction. Such is the case when Arthur ignores Merlin's warning 'that Launcelot scholde love hir [Guinevere], and sche hym agayne' (I, 97, l. 31).[6] Balin displays a similar blindness when he is warned by the lady who wore the sword that he alone was able to draw of the consequences of keeping the weapon (I, 64). In addition, 'prophecy is also a thematic device by which Malory shows human free will in conflict with divine will and with fate or destiny'.[7] Or, one might say, sometimes free will accords with fate, as seems to be the case with Balin, whose adherence to the chivalric virtue of taking the adventure causes him to keep the sword and consequently slay the man he loves most in the world.

At other times, characters may try to circumvent the prophecy, as Arthur does when he slays the babies born on May Day because of Merlin's prediction that one of those children will destroy Arthur and all his land (I, 55). But the predicted event comes about anyway because the ship founders and Mordred survives. Prophecy also 'provides structure in the *Morte Darthur* in that several key prophecies link together events, at the beginning and end of the book, in a way that frames and double-frames the whole'.[8] Such is the case with Merlin's pre-

[5] Elizabeth Edwards, *The Genesis of Narrative in Malory's 'Morte Darthur'* (Cambridge: Brewer, 2001), p. 31.

[6] Catherine La Farge, 'Conversations in Malory's *Morte Darthur*', *Medium Ævum*, 56 (1987), 225–38 (pp. 228–29). All citations of Malory's *Morte Darthur* are from *The Works of Sir Thomas Malory*, ed. by Eugène Vinaver, revised by P. J. C. Field, 3rd edn, 3 vols (Oxford: Clarendon Press, 1990), cited by volume, page, and, where appropriate, line numbers in the text.

[7] Jane Bliss, 'Prophecy in the *Morte Darthur*', *Arthuriana*, 13 (2003), 1–16 (p. 1).

[8] Bliss, 'Prophecy', p. 1.

diction that no one will be able to handle Balin's sword 'but the beste knyght of the worlde, and that shall be sir Launcelot othir ellis Galahad, hys sonne' (I, 91, ll. 21–23), a prediction that later proves true when Galahad draws the sword from the stone in which Merlin placed it (cf. Malory, II, 862).

*The Tale of the Sankgreal* is rife with visions and prophecies, often explained by hermits. In her excellent study of hermits in the *Morte*, Dhira Mahoney notes that these recluses display, among other qualities, 'powers of prophecy', an 'ability to interpret dreams and visions', and an 'intimate acquaintance with marvels'.[9] Especially in the story of the Grail, these hermits and recluses frequently provide the authoritative voices needed to explain to the knights on the quest (and to the reader of the text) the sometimes cryptic symbolism of their visions. The hermit Nascien, for example, interprets Gawain's and Ector's dreams and vision. Gawain dreams of one hundred and fifty bulls, all black except for three white bulls, one of which has a black spot. Ector dreams that he and Launcelot get up from two chairs and mount horses; in time, a man beats Launcelot, clothes him in penitential clothes, and places him on a donkey. Reaching a well, Launcelot tries to drink but the water recedes from him. In his dream, Ector rides to the house of a rich man where a wedding is being celebrated, but a king tells him this place is not for him. When they awake, both have a vision of a bridled hand carrying a burning candle that enters a chapel and vanishes. After being directed to the hermit Nascien, they tell him their dreams and vision. Nascien explains that the bulls were the knights of the Round Table, only three of whom were spiritually fit for the quest. He then interprets Ector's dream as referring to Launcelot's attempt to purify himself on the quest by wearing a hair shirt; the 'asse betokenyth mekenes'; and the water in the well 'betokenyth the hyghe grace of God'. Nascien even goes beyond the details of the vision, as interpretation becomes prediction, and mentions the twenty-four days of 'vengeaunce' that Launcelot will experience because of his twenty-four years of sin. Nascien then reveals that the bridle 'signifieth abstinens' and the candle 'signyfieth the ryght way of Jesu Cryste' (II, 945–48). As the voice accompanying the vision declared, Gawain and Ector lack these qualities, and so they will not achieve the Grail.

Nascien's explanations do not only interpret; they also foretell the results of the Grail quest with only the white bulls — Galahad, Percival, and Bors — achieving the quest. In addition, his understanding of the presumably divinely inspired visions lends the weight of authority to his assessment of Launcelot's

[9] Dhira B. Mahoney, 'Hermits in Malory's *Morte Darthur*: The Fiction and the Reality', *Arthurian Interpretations*, 2.1 (1987), 1–26 (p. 1).

character: 'ne were that he ys nat stable, but by hys thoughte he ys lyckly to turne agayne, he sholde be nexte to enchev[e] hit sauff sir Galahad, hys sonne; but God knowith hys thought and hys unstablenesse' (II, 948, ll. 24–27). This assessment is remarkably like Launcelot's own when he visits Guinevere in the convent and declares that on the quest for the Grail he would have 'forsakyn the vanytees of the worlde, had nat youre love bene' and that were it not for that love, he would have 'passed all the knyghtes that ever were in the Sankgreall except syr Galahad, my sone' (III, 1253, ll. 14–17). Nascien also adds to his judgement of Launcelot a final prediction: 'And yett shall he dye ryght an holy man, and no doute he hath no felow of none erthly synfull man lyvying' (II, 948, ll. 27–29). Once again Malory uses an authoritative text to bolster the reputation of his protagonist. Not only is Launcelot the greatest of sinful knights, which includes all men since all (except Galahad) are sinners, but — despite his love for Guinevere, which paradoxically makes him unstable in a spiritual sense because he is so stable in his commitment to his beloved — whatever sin is found in his love will be overshadowed by the virtues that will allow him to die a holy man.

This discussion of instability is surely meant to be read in conjunction with another authoritative comment on stability, that of the narrator when talking about the nature of love in the often cited May passage. The narrator observes that 'lyke as wynter rasure dothe allway arace and deface grene summer, so faryth hit by unstable love in man and woman, for in many persones there ys no stabylité' (III, 1119, ll. 14–16). He goes on to assert that 'love nowadayes' is 'sone hote sone colde' and declares that this 'ys no stabylyté' (III, 1120, ll .1–2). He concludes his long and atypical intrusion into the narrative by noting that while Guinevere lived, 'she was a trew lover, and therefor she had a good ende' (III, 1120, ll. 12–13). The references to *stability* in love recall the talk of Launcelot's spiritual instability, which is due to that very stability in love. The two authoritative passages, Nascien's and the narrator's, confirm that both Launcelot and Guinevere will have good ends, which is a comment on their characters and on their love.

While there are quite a few other prophecies and interpretations that function as authoritative intratexts in the *Morte*, these should suffice to demonstrate how Malory uses these texts both as a plot device and as a means of revealing character and underscoring theme.

## *Proverbs*

Like other intratexts in Malory, proverbs speak with the weight of authority. They are not used merely to give a colloquial flavour to speech — Malory is not interested in speech as a means of achieving realism or characterization[10] — but rather as general truths which suggest ways that characters should act, comment on the ways they do act, or define a fate they cannot resist. Malory prefaces a few of his proverbs with a reference to their being old saws or old-said saws; but even without this marker, the nature of certain expressions as conventional wisdom is obvious.[11] As P. J. C. Field notes, generally 'the proverbs in Malory's book impress in conveying not an individual personality but a common humanity and shared attitudes'.[12] Malory's proverbs take on added interest in light of the fact that they are often not borrowed by Malory from his sources. In her study of *The Book of Sir Tristram*, Helen Cooper has observed that it 'is especially rich in concise antitheses with a proverbial resonance' and that many of these expressions 'are without parallel in the French'.[13]

Proverbs are sometimes used to define honourable and shameful action and to comment on character, which for Malory is generally predetermined and revealed rather than developed. Launcelot speaks specifically of Mark when he says 'Harde hit ys to take oute off the fleysshe that ys bredde in the boone' (II, 550, ll. 14–15), but it is a maxim that applies to knights both good and bad. Mark epitomizes dishonourable conduct. When the narrator comments that 'he was a fayre speker, and false thereundir' (II,595, l. 2), he not only portrays Mark as a duplicitous character — an assessment that is confirmed when Launcelot, in a letter to Tristram, calls Mark 'Kynge Foxe' and says he always works with wiles and treason (II, 615, ll. 30–31) — but also, by contrast, suggests the nobility of Launcelot and Arthur, who are always true to their word.

[10] This point is made nicely by Mark Twain in his *A Connecticut Yankee in King Arthur's Court* (New York: Signet, [n.d.]) when he has Hank Morgan respond to Sandy's tale of the battle between Gawain and Marhaus, a passage taken from Malory, by saying, 'Sir Marhaus the king's son of Ireland talks like all the rest; you ought to give him a brogue, or at least a characteristic expletive.' Sandy accepts Hank's suggestion that she have Marhaus use the expression 'be jabers', and she inserts that into Marhaus's speech when she resumes her story (p. 96).

[11] Quite a few of Malory's proverbs are listed in Bartlett Jere Whiting's *Proverbs, Sentences, and Proverbial Phrases from English Writings Mainly before 1500* (Cambridge, MA: Belknap Press of Harvard University Press, 1968).

[12] P. J. C. Field, *Romance and Chronicle: A Study of Malory's Style* (London: Barrie & Jenkins, 1971), p. 127.

[13] Helen Cooper, 'The Book of Sir Tristram de Lyones', in *A Companion to Malory*, ed. by Elizabeth Archibald and A. S. G. Edwards (Cambridge: Brewer, 1996), pp. 183–201 (p. 197).

Quite a few, though certainly not all, of Malory's proverbial expressions relate to chivalry[14] and love. Since these are important themes and two of the major codes that impose conflicting demands on Malory's characters, it is not surprising that received wisdom about the obligations and consequences of these pursuits should figure prominently. During the Roman wars, Clegis and Bors agree with Launcelot that his bold action was better than caution because 'knyghtes ons shamed recoverys hit never' (I, 218, l. 2). This maxim applies to several figures throughout the *Morte* who are shamed, as well as to Launcelot's personal code. Arthur helps to define honourable and dishonourable conduct when, in a doubly proverbial expression, he says that 'a worshypfull man woll be lothe to se a worshypfull man shamed, and he that ys of no worshyp and medelyth with cowardise never shall he shew jantilnes nor no maner of goodnes where he seeth a man in daungere, for than woll a cowarde never shew mercy' (III, 1114, ll. 23–27). This response by Arthur to Gareth's defence of Launcelot in 'The Great Tournament' episode speaks to Gareth's character and his affection for Launcelot, but it is also a tenet of the knightly ethic that applies to other characters. One might think, for example, of Launcelot's avowal, upon hearing that his kin want to attack Tristram because 'all the noyse and brewte felle to sir Trystram, and the name ceased of sir Launcelot', that if they should 'be so hardy to wayte my lorde sir Trystram wyth ony hurte, shame, or vylany', he would slay them himself (II, 785, ll. 1–10).

Chivalric action is further proverbially defined by Guinevere. In reference to an unchivalric act by Palomides, she says that 'all men of worshyp hate an envyous man [...] and he that ys curteyse and kynde and jantil hath favoure in every place' (II, 764, ll. 27–31). Again the maxim used in a specific context has other resonances. This truth is exemplified by the support given to Launcelot in his conflict with the King and Gawain because of the courtesy and gentility he has demonstrated. This method of using an intratext that is uttered in response to a specific situation to suggest larger themes or resonate in other situations is typical of Malory. Lamorak's angry question to his brothers, who have been unhorsed in the tournament at Surluse — 'What is a knyght but whan he is on horsebacke?' (II, 667, l. 22) — not only defines the knight proverbially as a *chevalier*, but also has thematic echoes when Launcelot, on the quest for the Grail, is immobilized and cannot stop another knight from taking his helmet, sword, and horse, those things which define his knighthood. The loss, of course, symbolically implies that

[14] Elizabeth Edwards has argued that Malory's proverbs 'are about knightly conduct, and continue a book-long commentary on how the worthy knight behaves, and as such have a defining function, a function which many critics have taken to be Malory's main intention in writing' (*The Genesis of Narrative in Malory's Morte Darthur* (Cambridge: Brewer, 2001), p. 126).

in the action of the Grail quest, his knighthood is deficient. Similarly, when Sir Harry stops the wicked Sir Brewnys from striking Bleoboris as he lay on the ground with the injunction that he '[s]tryke never a knyght whan he is at the erthe!' (II, 686, ll. 7–8), this axiom of chivalric action also looks forward to the chivalric courtesy of Launcelot, who, when Bors has Arthur at his mercy and could put an end to the siege of Joyous Garde, will not allow Bors to strike the King. He will not permit such a noble man to be 'slayne nor shamed'; and knowing that one is not a knight without his horse, he 'horsed hym agayne' (III, 1192, ll. 17–21). Thus, this noble deed shows Launcelot enacting a number of the proverbs of chivalry. Launcelot himself gives voice to the most ominous of the chivalric proverbs in Malory's text: 'whan men bene hote in dedis of armys, oftyn hit ys seyne they hurte their frendis as well as their foys' (II, 537, ll. 17–18). Spoken after his wounding of Tristram in the tournament at the Castle of Maidens, it might as well have been said after his killing of Gareth as he rescues the Queen. There is in this proverb a sense of resignation to the sometimes disastrous albeit unintended consequences of knightly combat. A similar resignation is found in another proverb which also applies to the slaying of Gareth as well as to its immediate context. When Palomides knocks Arthur from his horse as he approaches Isode and Tristram accuses him of 'unknyghtly dedys done to so noble a knyght', Palomides responds, 'And a thynge [...] be done, hit can nat be undone' (II, 745, ll. 30–32). Launcelot resorts to the same conventional wisdom, with the same resonance, to console Bors who feels guilty for wounding the disguised Launcelot at the Winchester tournament: 'thys that ys done may nat be undone' (II, 1084, ll. 10–11).

Just as a number of proverbs offer insights into Malory's view of chivalric actions and their consequences, so do a number of them comment on love; and as with the chivalric proverbs, they refer to specific incidents but have wider thematic meaning. Tristram speaks to the ennobling power of love when, in response to Dynadan's cursing of love, he says that 'a knyght may never be of proues but yf he be a lovear' (II, 689, ll. 5–6). Malory generally presents true love as a virtue — it is, after all, what causes Guinevere to have a good end (III, 1120, ll. 12–13). Elaine of Astolat's observation that 'all maner of good love comyth of God' (II, 1093, l. 7) similarly implies that love is a virtue. Although one might question which of the loves in the *Morte* are 'good' loves, Malory seems to think of true love as good. And yet he recognizes love's sometimes tragic nature. In another proverbial expression, Dynadan says that 'the joy of love is to shorte, and the sorow thereof [and what cometh thereof] is duras over longe' (II, 693, ll. 33–35), a truth that is often borne out in Malory's text, as in the stories of Merlin, Tristram and Isode, Launcelot and Guinevere, and a number of more minor figures. That love is a powerful natural force is also confirmed by proverbial statements. When Gaheris kills his mother because she slept with Lamorak, whom he considers an enemy of their family, Lamorak says that Gaheris should have slain him rather than his own mother. Gaheris replies that 'a man is borne to offir his servyse' (II, 612, l. 22), suggesting that the knight's sexual activities are more natural than those of Morgause. After committing the unchivalrous act of killing Launcelot's horse, Palomides asks Launcelot to forgive him; and he does so since Palomides acted in part out of love. Launcelot recognizes that 'love is a grete maystry' (II, 740, ll. 8–9). Such a recognition that love can be an overwhelming and exculpatory force is relevant to the case of the Red Knight, Sir Ironsyde, in *The Tale of Gareth* (cf. I, 325); and it also suggests that Launcelot's affair with the Queen is less blameworthy because of his true love for her.

Malory's use of proverbs suggests that there are certain truths that underlie his sense of morality and honour, just as certain aspects of his plot and character are set by the demands of the traditions in which he is working. However, far from leading to a story in which everything is predictable, this situation leads to a romance that is quite different from Malory's sources. This is in part because the truths that are reflected in the proverbs and other intratexts are complicated by the existence of different codes. Chivalry and love impose conflicting demands on Malory's characters. It is the conflict between these and other codes, such as religion and duty to family, that prevents Malory's story from become static or predictable and that in fact make it resemble life itself.

## *Letters*

In addition to these oral forms, written texts embedded in the *Morte* also take on an authority and a meaning beyond what the usually personal and therefore subjective form suggests. Georgiana Donavin has documented the significant number of letters in Malory's text and has demonstrated the important role that letters play. She has argued for a progression from 'the self-involved epistles of the Tristram' to 'the divine letters revealing the sinfulness of such self-involvement in the Grail Quest' to 'personal messages written for the public's improvement' in the final two books.[15] Catherine Batt, building on Donavin's work, has contrasted Malory's use of letters in the *Tristram* with that of his source. Whereas

[15] Georgiana Donavin, 'Locating a Public Forum for the Personal Letter in Malory's *Morte Darthur*', *Disputatio*, 1 (1996), 19–36 (p. 19).

the French Prose *Tristan* uses letters to 'establish private spaces in counterpoint to the public social arena', Malory's 'bias is toward the reiteration of narrative coordinates, reminders of allegiances and events, at the expense of the letter as material evidence and as interiorizing mode'.[16] This is particularly true of those letters for which the full text is cited. The first of these, as Donavin reminds us,[17] is that of King Harmaunce, who was treacherously slain by two brothers whom he raised,[18] asking that a knight of Arthur's avenge his death.

Harmaunce's letter is analogous in a number of ways to Elaine of Astolat's letter; and the two, though separated by many pages of text, form a sort of epistolary diptych. Both letters are found clutched in the hand of a corpse on a barge. Elaine's barge is 'coverede with blacke samyte over and over' (II, 1095, ll. 2–3), and Harmaunce's is 'heled over with r[e]de sylke' (II, 700, ll. 25–26).[19] The two letters, as well as Gawain's letter to Launcelot in the final book, 'are deathbed pronouncements, a fact that underscores their veracity' and thus their authority.[20] Harmaunce's letter relates to chivalric obligation, the duty of a knight to avenge acts performed 'felounsly and traytourly'. The appeal for revenge is made to 'all knyghtes arraunte' (II, 701, ll. 16–20). And when Palomides undertakes the task of avenging the foul deed, he proves himself worthy of the fellowship of Arthur's knights. Elaine's letter relates to love, and so is addressed to Sir Launcelot; but she also says that 'unto all ladyes I make my mone' (II, 1096, l. 31),

[16] Catherine Batt, *Malory's Morte Darthur: Remaking Arthurian Tradition* (New York: Palgrave, 2002), p. 113.

[17] Donavin, 'Locating a Public Forum', p. 25.

[18] Interestingly, Ebell, a knight from the city that Harmaunce ruled, punctuates his oral account of the treacherous deeds with a proverb ('an olde sawe'): 'Gyeff a chorle rule and thereby he woll nat be suffysed' (II, 712, ll. 23–24). Like other proverbs, this one comments on the larger action of the *Morte* as well as on the specific incident to which it is applied. It not only speaks to the treachery of the two brothers but suggests that of Mordred as well. In a parallel between the Harmaunce and the Elaine episodes in addition to those mentioned below, Launcelot responds proverbially to Elaine's death and Guinevere's suggestion that he might have been kinder to Elaine by saying that 'love muste only aryse of the harte selff, and nat by none constraynte' (II, 1097, ll. 23–24) — and this proverb also resonates in the larger action of the romance.

[19] Malory also provides a parallel to these letters relating to chivalry and love in his account of the Grail quest. Though he does not give the full text of the letter, he says that 'sir Percivale made a lettir of all that she [his sister] had holpe them as in stronge aventures, and put hit in hir [r]yght honde. And so leyde hir in a barge, and coverde hit with blacke sylke' (II, 1004, ll. 8–11). It seems clearly intentional that the themes of chivalry, love, and religion are linked by strikingly similar depictions of letters clutched in the hands of corpses lying in fabric-covered barges.

[20] Donavin, 'Locating a Public Forum', p. 25.

thereby extending the audience and indicating that her arrival in the barge is, like that of Harmaunce, an elaborately staged performance. Elaine has designed this performance not just for Launcelot but for the ladies and presumably the knights of the court in general. The public display is important because it provides the setting for Elaine's letter, which, as Donavin has argued, 'functions on a feminist continuum, showing a woman's growing confidence in the appropriation of legal discourse' and thus helps to define Elaine's role and character. As part of this process, Elaine 'begins and ends the letter with a concession to Launcelot's superiority, but in adopting a commanding position to the last, she usurps the higher ground for herself'.[21]

I would like to expand upon Donavin's discussion of Elaine's comments on Launcelot by examining not what it says about her but rather what it says about him. Elaine begins her letter by calling him 'Moste noble knyght' and ends by asking his prayers for her soul 'as thou art pereles' (II, 1096, ll. 28 and 35). This unmitigated emphasis on Launcelot's nobility and superiority is different from what is found in Malory's sources. In the *Stanzaic Morte Arthur*, where the Maid of Ascolot's letter is addressed to Arthur and all the knights of the Round Table, she admits that Launcelot is 'the noblest knight that may go' and that there '[i]s none so doughty dintes to dele, | So real ne so fair there-to'. But she also criticizes him harshly:

> But so churlish of manners in feld ne hall,
>   Ne know I none of frend ne fo.
>
> Of fo ne frend, the sooth to say,
>   So unhende of thewes is there none;
> His gentilness was all away,
>   All churlish manners he had in wone.[22]

Similarly, in the *Mort Artu* the Maiden of Escalot addresses her complaint to all the knights of the Round Table and says that she died 'for the most valiant and yet the vilest man in the world: Lancelot of the Lake. He is the vilest man I know, for all my entreaties and laments and tears did not suffice to make him take pity on me.'[23]

[21] Georgiana Donavin, 'Elaine's Epistolarity: The Fair Maid of Astolat's Letter in Malory's *Morte Darthur*', *Arthuriana*, 13 (2003), 68–82 (p. 70).

[22] *Stanzaic Morte Arthur*, in *King Arthur's Death*, ed. by Larry D. Benson, revised by Edward E. Foster, TEAMS Middle English Texts (Kalamazoo: Medieval Institute Publications, 1994), pp. 43–44.

[23] *'The Death of Arthur' in 'Lancelot-Grail': The Old French Arthurian Vulgate and Post-Vulgate in Translation*, ed. by Norris J. Lacy (New York: Garland, 1995), IV. 114; 'Por le plus

Elaine's letter, in contrast to both the English and the French versions of this episode that Malory knew and drew upon, is an authority for Launcelot's peerless nobility, a fact so unquestionable that it is not denied even by the woman who died because he would not love her.

Like Elaine's letter, Gawain's deathbed epistle (III, 1231, l. 8–1232, l. 10) begins and ends with confirmation of Launcelot's status as a great knight — in fact, as the best knight: the 'floure of all noble knyghtes' and 'moste famous knyght of the worlde'. As with Elaine, this praise for Launcelot comes even though the great knight is in part responsible for Gawain's death: he says in the letter that he was 'smytten uppon the olde wounde that thou gaff me' and then that he was 'smytten uppon the strooke that ye gaff me'. The redundancy in affirming Launcelot's worthiness, which Gawain had questioned, and his contribution to Gawain's death, for which Launcelot bears no guilt (it was 'nat thorow thy [Launcelot's] deservynge'), confirm his nobility. Though the slaying of Gareth is not addressed directly in the letter, the recognition of Lancelot's nobility implies that Gawain now recognizes that Lancelot bears no guilt for that act either. Gawain's letter and its exoneration and praise of Launcelot seem all the more significant because the letter is not found in either the *Mort Artu* or the *Stanzaic Morte Arthur*.[24] (It is also interesting that the letter is marked in the Winchester manuscript with a marginal gloss: 'how Syr Gawayn wrote a letter to Sir Launcelot at the tyme of hys deþe'; fol. 477r.) The authority of the letter is enhanced by the chronicle-like specificity with which it records significant events: 'And so the tenth day of May last paste my lorde kynge Arthur and we all londed uppon them at Dover, and there he put that false traytoure, sir Mordred, to flyght.' In addition, the letter takes on some of the authority of prophecy as Gawain records that the letter 'wrytten with myne owne honde' was composed 'but two owrys and an halff afore my dethe'. The veracity of the letter is further confirmed by the fact that Gawain says it was 'subscrybed with parte of my harte blood'. Thus, Malory underscores the letter's authority in various ways.[25]

preudome del monde et por le plus vilain: ce est Lancelos del Lac, qui est li plus vilains que ge sache, car onques ne le soi tant prier o pleurs et o lermes que il volsist de moi avoir merci': *Le mort le roi Artu: Roman du XIIIe siècle*, ed. by Jean Frappier (Paris: Droz, 1936), p. 72.

[24] Donavin, 'Locating a Public Forum', p. 33, notes that '[t]he very length of Gawain's letter and its origination with Malory shows the author's investment in displaying an epistle of lasting value'.

[25] The authority of letters in Malory is not undermined by the fact that Mark 'countirfeted lettirs' (II, 678, ll. 15–16) claiming they are from the Pope. Tristram immediately recognizes the

## *Inscriptions*

Throughout Malory's *Morte*, inscriptions are an important type of textuality. Some inscriptions take on an added authority because they appear by supernatural or magical means. The first of these is the inscription on the stone containing the sword that will affirm Arthur's right to rule. The appearance seemingly from nowhere of such a solid object as the 'grete stone four square' (I, 12, ll. 30–31) with an anvil on it and a sword stuck through it gives a weighty authority to the text on the sword, written in gold, that proclaims that the one who draws the sword is the rightful king of all England. Similarly, when a knight's name materializes on a seat at the Round Table, it is a sign that some power is attesting to the propriety of that person's joining the order. This is true, for example, when Tristram's name is found on the seat vacated by Marhalt (II, 572, ll. 10–14), whom Tristram has slain. And the authority of the inscription seems even greater when Galahad's name appears on the Siege Perilous (II, 860, l. 11). That he is the destined Grail knight is, of course, borne out by other signs, including the inscription on the pommel of the sword in the stone that floats to Camelot, the sword originally owned by Balin, which proclaims that only the best knight in the world (meaning, in the context of the story of the Grail, the one ordained to achieve the Grail) can withdraw the sword (II, 856, ll. 13–15). In the tale of 'The Knight with the Two Swords', Malory described Merlin's inscribing of the sword, thus providing a link between the two tales as well as contributing to the pattern that establishes the authority of written inscriptions in general. Another sword, the one found on Solomon's ship, also has an inscription that indicates that only one man will be able to draw and use it (II, 986, ll. 4–6). The Grail quest is rife with intratexts, including one of the most bizarre inscriptions in the *Morte*. An old man dressed like a bishop appears to the Grail knights, and on his forehead is written: 'Se you here Joseph, the firste bysshop of Crystendom, the same which Oure Lorde succoured in the cité of Sarras in the spirituall palleys' (II, 1029, ll. 7–10). In addition to identifying the strange figure, the inscription recalls the

heavy-handed attempt at deception. Unlike the papal 'bulles undir leade' (III, 1194, ll. 16–17) that require Arthur to take back Guinevere after she has fled with Launcelot, Mark's false letters have no authority and no effect. They, like the letters Mordred had written 'as thoughe that they had com frome beyonde the see' (III, 1227, ll. 1–3) claiming that Arthur has died and denounced as false by the higher authority of the Bishop of Canterbury, are easily recognized as forgeries. It is worth noting that neither of these false letters is presented in full as a discrete text; both are merely paraphrased.

earlier history of the Grail.[26] While all of these inscriptions serve specific narrative functions, they also suggest the authority of intratexts.

Another category of written text is the sepulchral inscription. In a fascinating scene in *The Tale of Balin*, the prophecies of Merlin and a written inscription combine. Balin has slain Launceor, the son of the King of Ireland who has pursued Balin 'to revenge the despite' (I, 68, l. 30) done by the latter in slaying the Lady of the Lake in Arthur's court. When Balin slays Launceor and then fails to prevent his lady Columbe from killing herself, Mark constructs a tomb for the lovers on which is inscribed their names and the tale of their deaths: 'here lyeth Launceor, the kyngis son of Irelonde, that at hys owne rekeyste was slayne by the hondis of Balyne', and 'this lady Columbe and paramour to hym slew hirself with hys swerde for dole and sorow' (I, 71, ll. 29–72, l. 2). This inscription is noteworthy because it is a retelling in brief of the events that have just transpired. It is in effect authorized by the story just told by Malory. The burial is followed by Merlin's prediction that in this place there will be 'the grettist bateyle betwyxte two [knyghtes] that ever was or ever shall be, and the trewyst lovers; and yette none of hem shall slee other'. Then Merlin writes the names of the two knights, Launcelot and Tristram, 'uppon the tombe with lettirs of golde' (I, 72, ll. 5–10). The prophecy looks forward to a later event (cf. II, 568–69) but the inscribing of the names of the combatants also adds textual authority to the prophecy. (Malory, who is never interested in suspense, reveals well in advance that neither of these great knights will lose his life in the battle.) These texts, written and oral, interweave the events and characters from different parts of the whole book and suggest a theme of tragic love that foreshadows the fates of Tristram and Isode and Launcelot and Guinevere.

Merlin makes another prediction on this same occasion: that because Balin failed to save Columbe, he will 'stryke a stroke moste dolerous that ever man stroke, excepte the stroke of Oure Lorde Jesu Cryste'. This dolorous stroke will not only harm the truest knight living but it will also bring three kingdoms 'into

[26] Though this figure is identified by Vinaver in his 'Index of Proper Names' as Joseph of Arimathea, it is, in fact, Joseph's son, sometimes called Josephus or Josephe, and, in Middle English and Old French, sometimes Joseph. In both the *Estoire del Saint Graal* and the *Queste del Saint Graal*, Josephus is identified as the first bishop; and in the passage in the *Queste* that directly parallels this one in Malory, the figure identified as the first bishop by the inscription on his forehead is Josephus. Josephus is instrumental in bringing the servants of the Grail to Britain and in converting some of the inhabitants of Britain to Christianity. Unlike Joseph of Arimathea, who appears in both the canonical and the apocryphal gospels, Josephus is a creation of the French romancers.

grete poverté, miseri and wrecchednesse' for twelve years (I, 72, ll. 26–31). This prediction ties the Balin section to the Grail story, just as the prediction of the battle between Launcelot and Tristram ties it to *The Book of Sir Tristram de Lyones*; and all of this stems from the story of the death of Launceor and Columbe and the authorized version of that death inscribed on the tomb. At the same time, the inscription itself makes evident the tragic nature of the events. The inscription declares that Launceor was slain 'at hys owne rekeyste [...] by the hondis of Balyne' and that Columbe 'slew hirself with hys swerde for dole and sorow' (I, 71, l. 30 and I, 72, l. 2). Even though Launceor sought and initiated the combat with Balin and Columbe slew herself, Balin will suffer the consequences. Such is the tragic nature of the Arthurian world. And this tragedy is seen in the tales of Tristram and of the Grail that the adjacent prophecies allude to and in the entire *Morte*.

Another remarkable sepulchral inscription occurs later in the text, in the poisoned apple episode. Guinevere, having been accused of murdering Sir Patryse with a poisoned apple at a dinner party she hosted, is defended by Launcelot in a trial by combat against the Queen's accuser, Sir Mador, 'cosyn' (II, 1049, l. 8) of Patryse. When Launcelot defeats Mador, he sets two conditions for sparing the accuser's life. The first is a legal necessity: that he 'frely releas the quene for ever'. This guarantee that the charge will be withdrawn and never reinstated avoids the possibility of future action against the Queen. The second condition seems strange in light of the first. Launcelot insists 'that no mencion be made uppon sir Patryseys tombe that ever quene Gwenyver consented to that treson' (II, 1058, ll. 1–3). One explanation for this condition is that the Launcelot of the *Morte* is responding to something that happens in the source, the Vulgate *Mort Artu*, in which the slain knight (named Gaheris of Carahew rather than Patryse) is buried before the trial by combat, and on his tomb is inscribed: 'Ici gist Gaheriz li Blans de Karaheu, li freres Mador de la Porte, que la reine fist morir par venim' (Here lies Gaheris the White of Carahew, the brother of Mador of the Gate, poisoned by the Queen).[27]

Such an intertextual response seems a reasonable explanation only because of the authority of intratexts in Malory's romance. He forestalls the stigma that would arise from having Mador's accusation of the Queen authorized by being put into writing. Malory cites the inscription on Patryse's tomb only after Guinevere has been successfully defended by Launcelot and her innocence has been confirmed by Nyneve in a revelation of the true facts of the case: '[Nyneve] disclosed by whom hit was done, and named hym sir Pynel, and for what cause he

[27] *Le mort le roi Artu*, ed. by Frappier, p. 63; *The Death of Arthur*, ed. and trans. by Lacy, p. 111.

ded hit. There hit was opynly knowyn [...] that he enpoysynde the appyls at that feste to that entente to have destroyed sir Gawayne, bycause sir Gawayne and hys brethirne destroyed sir Lamerok de Galys which sir Pynell was cosyn unto' (II, 1059, ll. 17–25). Nyneve's revelation, another significant intratext, recounts the murder as it actually happened and links it to the feud between the families of Lot and Pellinore. Thus it confirms that Guinevere is not a destroyer of good knights; at the same time, it links the entire episode to earlier and later events.

Malory's sepulchral inscription occurs after the false accusation has been resolved. Its specificity and its truth to narrated events speak to its authority: 'Here lyeth sir Patryse of Irelonde, slayne by sir Pynell le Saveaige that enpoysynde appelis to have slayne sir Gawayne, and by myssefortune sir Patryse ete one of the applis, and than suddeynly he braste' (II, 1059, ll. 27–31). The inscription asserts its authority through its recording of specific and realistic detail. It is hardly necessary as a marker of Patryse's tomb to state that Pynell was attempting to slay Gawayne; nor is it necessary or even tasteful to record that when Patryse ate the poisoned apple, 'he braste'; but these details do make the inscription read like a credible, historical text which records the treacherous deed of Pynell and once again suggests the dangers to Arthur's court that arise from the feud that led to the slaying.

Another sepulchral inscription worthy of note is that on Arthur's tomb. After the final battle, Arthur is taken off in a barge to Avalon to have his wounds healed. Bedivere arrives at a chapel where the Bishop of Canterbury has become a hermit. The Bishop tells Bedivere that a group of ladies brought him a body and asked him to bury it. Bedivere decides to remain with the Bishop and pray for Arthur. Malory then observes that 'of Arthur I fynde no more wrytten in bokis that bene auctorysed, nothir more of the verry sertaynté of hys dethe harde I never rede', thus suggesting that authorized texts do not say for certain that Arthur is dead. He also notes that

> the ermyte knew nat in sertayne that he was veryly the body of [kyn]ge Arthur.
>
> For thys tale sir Bedwere, a knyght of the Table Ro[un]de, made hit to be wrytten; yet som men say in many p[art]ys of Inglonde that kynge Arthur ys nat dede, but h[ad] by the wyll of Oure Lorde Jesu into another place; and men say that he shall com agayne, and he shalle wynne the Holy Crosse.

Malory will not assert that this is so 'but rather I wolde sey: here in thys worlde he chaunged hys lyff'. This ambiguous statement does little to resolve the question of whether or not Malory's Arthur will come again from Avalon or is dead and buried in the hermit's chapel. Malory then adds that many men say that there ys wrytten uppon the tumbe thys:

HIC JACET ARTHURUS, REX QUONDAM REXQUE FUTURUS (III, 1242, ll. 3–29)

As the phrase 'many men' replaces the 'som men' in the previous quotation, Malory leans towards the opinion of the many. But the fate of Arthur is presented with authoritative ambiguity. The inscription has double authority — that of texts generally in Malory's book and that which comes from being written in Latin, the language of ultimate authority. In addition, the source of the inscription is not clear. It does not seem to be made by the holy hermit; rather it seems, like the inscriptions on swords or seats at the Round Table, to have appeared supernaturally and thus to have the same extraordinary authority as those inscriptions. But what is it authorizing: the fact that Arthur is lying in the grave and thus is not in Avalon having his wounds healed, which means that he will not return, or the fact that Arthur is the once and future king and will return? The two parts of the inscription and their apparent authority present a paradox that is the culmination of a pattern of paradox throughout the *Morte*, a pattern represented in its broadest form in the attitudes towards love and chivalric honour present in the work. Derek Brewer has written eloquently about 'the paradoxes of honour' in Malory.[28] And the courtly concept of love that is so essential to the plot and theme of the *Morte* is equally paradoxical. As F. X. Newman observed in the preface to a collection of essays that he edited, 'courtly love is a doctrine of paradoxes, a love at once illicit and morally elevating, passionate and disciplined, humiliating and exalting, human and transcendent. Perhaps the ultimate paradox of courtly love is that a doctrine in many ways so unmedieval should be considered the unique contribution of the Middle Ages to the lore of love'.[29]

The final inscription, in its authorized contradiction, seems of a piece with the themes and the worldview of the larger romance. It is worth noting that Malory's sources did not provide him with this ambiguity. The *Mort Artu* records as an inscription: 'Ci gist li rois Artus qui par sa valeur mist en sa subjection xii roiaumes' (Here lies King Arthur, who by his valor conquered twelve kingdoms). In the *Stanzaic Morte Arthur*, Bedivere, upon seeing a rich tomb, declares, 'Here lieth my lord that I have lorn, | Bold Arthur, the beste king', a statement that leaves little room for doubt; and there is no inscription to create doubt. In the

[28] Derek Brewer, 'The Paradoxes of Honour in Malory', in *New Directions in Arthurian Studies*, ed. by Alan Lupack (Cambridge: Brewer, 2002), pp. 33–47.

[29] *The Meaning of Courtly Love*, ed. by F. X. Newman (Albany: State University of New York Press, 1968), p. vii.

*Alliterative Morte Arthure*, the inscription, 'Hic jacet Arthurus, rex quondam rexque futurus', appears only after the effective end of the text and after the author has written 'thus passes his spirit and spekes he no more'.[30] Thus Malory seems either to have resorted to oral traditions about Arthur, to have taken the inscription from the *Alliterative Morte Arthure* and to have added an ambiguity not in that text, or to have used chronicles not usually considered among his sources to provide this ambiguous ending for Arthur.

As different as these representative intratexts within the *Morte* are — from the oral to the written, proverbs and prophecies, inscriptions and letters — they generally carry the weight of authority. Françoise Le Saux has summarized the matter nicely in a brief paragraph introductory to her article focusing on personal letters in *The Book of Sir Tristram*:

> In Malory's work, writing is predominantly the medium of public communication. Letters appear clutched in the hands of corpses, containing the last wishes of the deceased, revealing momentous secrets; charters or official missives are sent by lords or kings issuing orders or preparing military campaigns, while supernatural inscriptions announce and determine the feats of the knights of the Round Table throughout the narrative. The written word thus appears as a carrier of truth and authority.[31]

The same might be said of the spoken word when it appears in forms that bespeak authority.[32] The general truth of a proverb, the foreknowledge of a prophecy, the accuracy of an interpretation of a prediction, a dream, or a vision, the fidelity to events of an inscription, or a deathbed statement inscribed in a letter — all are used by Malory in conjunction with other sections of his romance and sometimes

[30] *Le mort le roi Artu*, ed. by Frappier, p. 250; *The Death of Arthur*, ed. and trans. by Lacy, p. 156; *Stanzaic Morte Arthur*, ed. by Benson, p. 11; the *Alliterative Morte Arthure*, ed. by Benson, p. 261.

[31] Françoise Le Saux, 'Pryvayly and Secretely: Personal Letters in Malory's "Book of Sir Tristram de Lyones"', *Études de lettres*, 3 (1993), 21–33 (p. 21).

[32] In *Orality and Literacy* (London: Methuen, 1982), Walter Ong has commented on the importance of proverbs in oral cultures for passing on accepted wisdom and even the 'law itself' which in oral cultures 'are not mere jurisprudential decoration, but themselves constitute the law' (p. 35; cf. also pp. 10 and 26 on proverbs as accepted wisdom). For Malory, proverbs seem to have some of the same effect, presenting the 'laws' of chivalry and love and thus giving authority to the sometimes conflicting demands of these codes. I am not suggesting that the *Morte* is in any way an oral production, but Malory does recognize the authority of both oral and written texts. His proverbs offer accepted societal wisdom in speech just as visions and prophecies and their interpretations often offer religious truths, and letters might be said to offer personal truths and inscriptions to offer historical truths.

in conjunction with each other, to lend authority to parts of his tale and to help him depict his characters, reveal his themes, and unite his story.

*University of Rochester*

# Index

# Tabula Gratulatoria

Felicia Nimue Ackerman, Brown University
Elizabeth Archibald, University of Bristol
Leslie Arnovick, University of British Columbia
Mary Lucille Dudy Bjork, Arizona State University West Campus
Robert E. Bjork, Arizona State University
Jean Blacker, Kenyon State University
Virginia Blanton, University of Missouri-Kansas City
Phillip C. Boardman, University of Nevada, Reno
Karen Bollermann, Arizona State University Polytechnic Campus
George Hardin Brown, Emeritus, Stanford
Phyllis Rugg Brown, Santa Clara University
Keith Busby, University of Wisconsin
Carleton Carroll, Emeritus, Oregon State University
Albrecht Classen, University of Arizona
Jeffrey J. Cohen, George Washington University
Joyce Coleman, University of Oklahoma
Raymond J. Cormier, Longwood University
Taylor Corse, Arizona State University
Michael J. Curley, University of Puget Sound
Roger Dahood, University of Arizona
Helen Damico, University of New Mexico
John Damon, University of Nebraska Kearney
Rosemarie Deist, University of San Francisco
Maria Dobozy, University of Utah
Ann Dobyns, University of Denver
Georgiana Donavin, Westminster College
Carol R. Dover, Georgetown University

Martha W. Driver, Pace University
P. J. C. Field, University of Wales
Christina Francis, Bloomsburg University
John Ganim, University of California, Davis
Alison Ganze, Western Kentucky University
William Gentrup, Arizona Center for Medieval and Renaissance Studies
Linda Georgianna, University of California, Irvine
Peter H. Goodrich, Northern Michigan University
Sarah Gordon, Utah State University
Gina Greco, Portland State University
Monica Green, Arizona State University
Joan Tasker Grimbert, The Catholic University of America
Kevin T. Grimm, Oakland University
Kathleen Cunningham Guler
Geoffrey W. Gust, Temple University
Mary Hamel, Mount Saint Mary's University
Pamela Hanford, Shasta College
Michael Hanly, Washington State University
Kevin J. Harty, LaSalle University
Don Hoffman
Elizabeth Horan, Arizona State University
Linda K. Hughes, Texas Christian University
Janet Jesmok, Emerita, University of Wisconsin-Milwaukee
Jean E. Jost, Bradley University
Henry Ansgar Kelly, Emeritus, University of California, Los Angeles
Robert L. Kelly, Emeritus, University of North Carolina, Greensboro
Don (Edward Donald) Kennedy, University of North Carolina, Chapel Hill
Sharon D. King, Associate, UCLA Center for Medieval and Renaissance Studies
Sharon Kinoshita, University of California, Santa Cruz
Christopher Kleinhenz, University of Wisconsin-Madison
Paul Knoll, University of Southern California
V.A. Kolve, University of California, Los Angeles
Norris J. Lacy, Penn State University
Judith Lanzendorfer, University of Findlay
Deborah Losse, Arizona State University
Alan Lupack, Rochester University
Andrew Lynch, University of Western Australia
Kari McBride, University of Arizona
June Hall McCash, Middle Tennessee State University

Peggy McCracken, University of Michigan
Asa Simon Mittman, California State University, Chico
Ryan Muckerheide, Arizona State University
Deborah Nelson-Campbell, Rice University
Richard Newhauser, Arizona State University
Anita Obermeier, University of New Mexico
Stephen Partridge, University of British Columbia
Sasha Ramayya, Arizona State University
Florence Ridley, Emerita, University of California, Los Angeles
Jonathan Rose, Arizona State University
Cory James Rushton, St Francis Xavier University
Jenny Rebecca Rytting, Northwest Missouri State University
Michael N. Salda, University of Southern Mississippi
Corine Schleif, Arizona State University
Elisabeth Schulze-Busacker, Università degli Studi di Pavia (Italy)
Anne Scott, Northern Arizona University
Harvey L. Sharrer, University of California, Santa Barbara
Robert S. Sturges, Arizona State University
Paul Szarmach, Medieval Academy
Paul R. Thomas, Emeritus, Brigham Young University and Co-Director, The Chaucer Studio/The Chaucer Studio Press
Ayanna Thompson, Arizona State University
Kenneth J. Tiller, University of Virginia's College at Wise
Theresa Tinkle, University of Michigan
Fiona Tolhurst, Universität Basel (Switzerland)
Janina P. Traxler, Manchester College
Richard Utz, Western Michigan University
Juliann Vitullo, Arizona State University
Rosalynn Voaden, Arizona State University
Melissa Walter, University of Oregon
Lori J. Walters, Florida State University
Retha Warnicke, Arizona State University
Donald Weinstein, Emeritus, University of Arizona
Logan E. Whalen, University of Oklahoma
Bonnie Wheeler, Southern Methodist University
K. S. Whetter, Acadia University
Tom Willard, University of Arizona
Diane Wolfthal, Arizona State University

# DISPUTATIO

All volumes in this series are evaluated by an Editorial Board, strictly on academic grounds, based on reports prepared by referees who have been commissioned by virtue of their specialism in the appropriate field. The Board ensures that the screening is done independently and without conflicts of interest. The definitive texts supplied by authors are also subject to review by the Board before being approved for publication. Further, the volumes are copyedited to conform to the publisher's stylebook and to the best international academic standards in the field.

**Titles in Series**

*Rhetoric and Renewal in the Latin West, 1100–1540: Essays in Honour of John O. Ward*, ed. by Constant J. Mews, Cary J. Nederman, and Rodney M. Thomson (2003)

*The Appearances of Medieval Rituals: The Play of Construction and Modification*, ed. by Nils Holger Petersen, Mette Birkedal Bruun, Jeremy Llewellyn, and Eyolf Østrem (2004)

*Speculum Sermonis: Interdisciplinary Reflection on the Medieval Sermon*, ed. by Georgiana Donavin, Cary J. Nederman, and Richard Utz (2004)

Ineke van 't Spijker, *Fictions of the Inner Life: Religious Literature and Formation of the Self in the Eleventh and Twelfth Centuries* (2004)

*Healing the Body Politic: The Political Thought of Christine de Pisan*, ed. by Karen Green and Constant J. Mews (2005)

Maria Dobozy, *Re-membering the Present: The Medieval German Poet-Minstrel in Cultural Context* (2005)

*The World of Marsilius of Padua*, ed. by Gerson Moreno-Riaño (2006)

Jason Taliadoros, *Law and Theology in Twelfth-Century England: The Works of Master Vacarius (c. 1115/20–c. 1200)* (2006)

*Princely Virtues in the Middle Ages, 1200–1500*, ed. by István P. Bejczy and Cary J. Nederman (2007)

*What Nature Does Not Teach: Didactic Literature in the Medieval and Early-Modern Periods*, ed. by Juanita Feros Ruys (2008)

Sabina Flanagan, *Doubt in an Age of Faith: Uncertainty in the Long Twelfth Century* (2008)

*'Sapientia et Eloquentia': Meaning and Function in Liturgical Poetry, Music, Drama, and Biblical Commentary in the Middle Ages*, ed. by Gunilla Iversen and Nicolas Bell (2009)

James M. Blythe, *The Life and Works of Tolomeo Fiadoni (Ptolemy of Lucca)* (2009)

James M. Blythe, *The Worldview and Thought of Tolomeo Fiadoni (Ptolemy of Lucca)* (2009)

*John Gower: Manuscripts, Readers, Contexts*, ed. by Malte Urban (2009)

*Mind Matters: Studies of Medieval and Early Modern Intellectual History in Honour of Marcia Colish*, ed. by Cary J. Nederman, Nancy Van Deusen, and E. Ann Matter (2009)

## In Preparation

Jeremy Tambling, *Dante in Purgatory: States of Affect*

Kenneth Rooney, *Mortality and Imagination: The Life of the Dead in Medieval English Literature*